AF324320

4/23/14
$40
FS
BG196

CHRIST AND HIS "ASSOCIATES" IN VOLTAIRIAN POLEMIC

AN ASSAULT ON THE TRINITY AND THE TWO NATURES

STANFORD FRENCH AND ITALIAN STUDIES

editor

RALPH HESTER

editorial board

JOHN AHERN
MARC BERTRAND
ROBERT GREER COHN
JOHN FRECCERO
RAYMOND D. GIRAUD
PAULINE NEWMAN-GORDON

volume XXVI

ANMA LIBRI

CHRIST AND HIS "ASSOCIATES" IN VOLTAIRIAN POLEMIC

AN ASSAULT ON THE TRINITY AND THE TWO NATURES

WILLIAM H. TRAPNELL

1982
ANMA LIBRI

Stanford French and Italian Studies is a collection of scholarly publications devoted to the study of French and Italian literature and language, culture and civilization. Occasionally it will allow itself excursions into related Romance areas.

Stanford French and Italian Studies will publish books, monographs, and collections of articles centering around a common theme, and is open also to scholars associated with academic institutions other than Stanford.

The collection is published for the Department of French and Italian, Stanford University by Anma Libri.

© 1982 by ANMA LIBRI & Co.
P.O. Box 876, Saratoga, Calif. 95071.
All rights reserved.
LC 81-70139

ISBN 0-915838-13-3

Printed in the United States of America.

CONTENTS

ABBREVIATIONS

B.	*The Complete Works of Voltaire*, ed. Theodore Besterman (Banbury, 1968-).
D.	followed by a number designates a letter in Voltaire's *Correspondence, The Complete Works of Voltaire*, ed. Theodore Besterman (Banbury, 1968-).
app. D.	followed by a number designates an appendix in Voltaire's *Correspondence* (same edition).
Denz.	Heinrich Denzinger, *The Sources of Catholic Dogma*, Roy DeFerrari, trans. (St. Louis, 1957).
Dial.	Voltaire, *Dialogues et anecdotes philosophiques*, Raymond Naves, ed. (Paris, 1966).
Dict.	Voltaire, *Dictionnaire philosophique*, Raymond Naves, ed. (Paris, 1961).
Ency.	Denis Diderot, *Encyclopédie ou Dictionnaire raisonné des sciences, des arts et des métiers* (Paris, 1751-1766).
M.	Louis Moland, ed., *Oeuvres complètes de Voltaire* (Paris, 1877-1882).
Mac.	Jean Macary, ed., *Voltaire: Facéties* (Paris, 1973).
SLNPF	*A Select Library of Nicene and Post-Nicene Fathers of the Christian Church.*
SVEC	*Studies on Voltaire and the Eighteenth Century.*

BIBLICAL ABBREVIATIONS

Ac.	Acts	Ge.	Genesis	Ml.	Malachi
Co.	Corinthians	He.	Hebrews	Mt.	Matthew
Col.	Colossians	Is.	Isaiah	Ph.	Philippians
Dt.	Deuteronomy	Jn.	John	Ps.	Psalms
Dn.	Daniel	Jr.	Jeremiah	Rm.	Romans
Ez.	Ezechiel	K.	Kings	Ws.	Wisdom
Ex.	Exodus	Lk.	Luke	Zc.	Zecharia
Ga.	Galatians	Mk.	Mark		

INTRODUCTION

How many milleniums ago did an ancestor of man discover the natural light? Certainly several at least before the ancient Stoics developed the concept and before Descartes gave it this name.[1] Ignorance of the earliest and longest portion of human existence reduces us to speculation in the manner of Rousseau. The most intelligent animal was at leisure to draw a parallel between the sun filling his eyes with light and the mysterious source of the notions in his head. Since these notions constantly reminded him that he was alive, he must have supposed that they were coming from the source of life. His senses told him that he had a body and that other bodies engaged in similar activity around him. Once he had learned to communicate with them, a lesson which intrigued the philosophes, he discovered that they had notions similar to his. Comparison of their actions and notions with his revealed the existence of a common sense identical with the natural light.

The natural light itself suggested that life resembled the source from which it flowed, hence the notion of a superman, the giver of life. But why did primitive man attribute what Voltaire calls "associates" (see p. 146) to this god? Each tribe had its own god and, seeing that the neighbors had one too, each came to believe in that one as well. Natural forces, which appeared to operate independently of each other, also acquired the status of separate deities. The coherence of the family (despite Rousseau)[2] persuaded primitive man that

[1] The phrase appears in the title of an unfinished dialogue, "La Recherche de la vérité par la lumière naturelle." He may have written it in 1641, 1647, or even later. Poliandre represents the natural light: "homme d'un médiocre esprit, mais duquel le jugement n'est perverti par aucune fausse créance, et qui possède toute la raison selon la pureté de sa nature." *Oeuvres de Descartes* (Paris, 1967), II, 1108.

[2] He speculates on the origin of language as follows: "La première [difficulté] est d'imaginer comment [les langues] purent devenir nécessaires; car, les hommes [à l'état

the gods likewise belonged to a family. Finding some more accessible than others, he appealed to them for mediation. With the trend to sophistication, he reassigned this function to hybrids conceived in an encounter between a god and a woman, usually without her consent or even knowledge. These hybrids combined human and divine traits, and passed from one state to the other. Henceforth, the basic ingredients of western theology were available.

The nature of the deity and the relationship between divinity and humanity have been developing more or less concurrently with the natural light ever since. In the eighteenth century, however, the natural light took a critical turn and threatened to disrupt the further development of theology. Voltaire's satirical assault on Christ and the Trinity was the most destructive event in this war. Now polemic must be understood in terms of both the target and the technique which, in this case, involve fields rarely embraced by a single study. One must not only explore Voltaire's career as a writer but also the development of the dogmas in question. Since the polemicist, in fact, drew some of his material from the radical Reformation, one must investigate this field too. Consequently, the following study attempts to fit three dissimilar pieces together in a coherent puzzle. The first chapter reviews the history of the three persons in the Trinity and the relations between them from Exodus to the Council of Chalcedon (a convenient terminus). It then surveys the dissidence over Christ and the Trinity in the fifteenth, sixteenth, and seventeenth centuries. An analysis of actions and writings by Voltaire, the second chapter focuses on his polemical technique and competence in exploiting the materials exposed in the preceding chapter. The conclusion offers a scrutiny of the relationship between motives and intentions, from which still another Voltairian metamorphosis emerges.

Such projects raise strategic problems whose solutions, whatever they may be, cannot satisfy all readers. I have encountered four of these: (1) the need for objectivity in an area torn by centuries of bitter conflict (first chapter), (2) the disproportion between the masses of data pertaining to the subjects under discussion (both chapters), (3) the choice between a systematic and a chronological approach (second chapter), and (4) the difficulty of discriminating between the creative and the critical treatment of irony and humor (second chapter). In an attempt to solve these problems, four major decisions have deter-

de nature] n'ayant nulle correspondance entre eux, ni aucun besoin d'en avoir, on ne conçoit ni la nécessité de cette invention, ni sa possibilité." *Discours sur l'origine et les fondements de l'inégalité parmi les hommes*, *Oeuvres complètes* (Paris, 1964), III, 146.

mined the methodology of the present study: (1) The first chapter is founded on the judgment of modern authorities. Despite religious affiliations (in most cases), these scholars have a genuine respect for scientific standards of accuracy. In following their example, I have tried to formulate the history in question as if it were any history of no particular concern to us. Faith, moreover, does not qualify here as a criterion of truth. To be sure, neither this conception of objectivity nor any other will win unanimous approval. (2) I have reduced the volume of the first chapter to half that of the second by concentrating on decisive events of permanent significance. Together with the opinion of specialists, Voltaire's curiosity has governed the selection of these events. (3) A systematic plan offers the reader a neat package appealing to the taste for logic and order with which education has probably endowed him. While this method accommodates many subjects in literary criticism, relegating the elements of Voltaire's antichristian polemic to pigeonholes would eliminate the organic vitality of the whole. A chronological plan allows the critic to preserve the integrity of each work in accordance with the author's intentions and the environment from which it emerged. The second chapter therefore develops along chronological lines, although later revisions or additions appear in the same section as the original work. (4) Voltaire's mastery of humor and irony is a formidable temptation for critics. A parasitic re-presentation of the master's art with hints and winks to the public would overstep the boundary between instruction and entertainment. Shifting the emphasis from the *utile* to the *agréable* might draw more, if not better readers! The second chapter nonetheless proceeds on the assumption that the wit in the quotations requires no support from the context, but rather commentary. Fortunately, this policy does not exclude the use of humor and irony independent of Voltaire or even at his expense.

No comprehensive study of Voltaire's antitrinitarian and antichristological polemic has appeared in print. Partial and adjacent studies are cited in the text or the notes of the appropriate sections in the second chapter, yet two must be acknowledged here. The classic thesis in this area remains *La Religion de Voltaire* (1956) by René Pomeau, an exhaustive investigation of the writer's preoccupation with religion. Since Pomeau's treatment of polemic against Christ and the Trinity conforms to this design, he rarely sees fit to pursue the kind of analysis presented below. In *Voltaire and the Socinians* (1974),[3] R. E. Florida covers largely the same ground as several sections in my sec-

[3] *SVEC*, 122. *SVEC* designates *Studies on Voltaire and the Eighteenth Century*.

ond chapter (see p. 158, n. 102), but his point of view and interpretation are different from mine. He addresses himself to the broad and, in my opinion, vague connotation of Socinianism prevalent in Trinitarian propaganda. I am concerned with the strict definition which I believe predominated in Voltaire's thinking. Needless to say, however, the work of Pomeau, Florida, and many others has facilitated the research behind the following essay.

THE TRINITY AND THE TWO NATURES

Initiated by Voltaire's contemporary Hermann Reimarus, "the quest for the historical Jesus" continues to attract more seekers than finders and cause more grinding than sharpening of the critical axe. Together with Reimarus himself, David Strauss, Albert Schweitzer, Rudolf Bultmann[1] and others have produced valuable results, but the general effort has proved redundant and inconclusive. What has been established, on the other hand, is that the man Jesus had little in common with the myth of Christ which emerged from his memory. On this crucial point, Christians like Bultmann and Schweitzer agree with freethinkers like Strauss and Reimarus. While lacking their erudition, Voltaire himself held the same opinion and greatly publicized it even before Reimarus had begun systematically to substantiate it. A proper evaluation of his polemic against the Trinity and the two natures depends on an adequate understanding of the distinction between Jesus the devout Jew and Christ not only human, but also divine and a person in the Trinity. Since knowledge of derivations begins with that of origins, however, one must first examine the other two, more anciently conceived persons before approaching their association with Christ.

YAHWEH

Biography customarily begins with an account of the subject's parents, but the biography of Jesus, insofar as it can be studied, should really begin with the origin of belief in the one he called his Father. The only comprehensive document available for this purpose is the Pen-

[1] Hermann Reimarus, "Apologie oder Schutzschrift für die vernünftigen Vereher Gottes" (fragments edited by Lessing in 1774-1778); David Strauss, *Das Leben Jesu kritisch bearbeitet* (1835-1836); Albert Schweitzer, *Von Reimarus zu Wrede; Geschichte der Leben-Jesu-Forschung* (1906); Rudolf Bultmann, *Theologie des Neuen Testaments* (1953).

tateuch, recorded no doubt only after the return from the Babylonian exile (sixth century B.C.) or far more recently than the events it relates or purports to relate. Jean Astruc, a contemporary of Voltaire, pioneered a method of inquiry back beyond the time of the original composition by dividing the text of Genesis into several independent "mémoires" which Moses, in his opinion, had used to compile this book.[2] Modern exegesis, which retains two of these sources, one designating God as Yahweh[3] and the other, as Elohim, adds a third unknown to Astruc, the Priestly tradition. As Voltaire suspected, Moses almost certainly did not compose the Pentateuch and could not have composed all of it in any case.[4] The components of the work probably originated as oral traditions transmitted from generation to generation for several centuries. The Elohist tradition reached the definitive stage of its development in the northern kingdom of Israel in the eighth century. Though plural in form, *Elohim* appears only in singular contexts, a rare phenomenon in Hebrew grammar,[5] thus one must admit the probability of what Voltaire considered a common-sense certainty, that *Elohim* once designated several gods.[6]

The Yahwist tradition attained its final form in the southern kingdom of Judea in the eighth or ninth centuries, possibly at the court of Solomon. Like *Elohim, Yahweh* has been the subject of controversy. Paradoxically, one must turn to an Elohist passage for evidence of the word's meaning because, unlike the Yahwist, who calls God Yahweh from the outset, the Elohist relates his revelation of the word to Moses:

[2] "Le livre de la Genèse est formé de deux ou trois mémoires, joints et cousus ensemble par morceaux, dont les auteurs avaient toujours donné chacun à Dieu, mais chacun un nom différent, l'un celui d'Elohim, et l'autre celui de Jehovah Elohim." Astruc, *Conjectures sur les mémoires originaux dont il paraît que Moyse s'est servi pour composer le livre de la Genèse* (Bruxelles, 1753).

[3] The consonants alone are extant, the vowels having been reconstituted. Medieval in origin, the term *Jehovah* is a less accurate reconstitution. See Roland de Vaux, "The Revelation of the Divine Name YHWH," *Proclamation and Presence: Old Testament Essays in Honor of Gwynne Henton Davies* (London, 1970), pp. 48-75.

[4] Ironically, he remarks: "En vain plusieurs savants ont cru que le *Pentateuque* ne peut avoir été écrit par Moïse." "Moïse," *Dictionnaire philosophique* (Paris, 1961), p. 320. Bertram Schwarzbach confirms "Voltaire's assumption that the current text of the Pentateuch, much less an uncorrupted version of it, was neither known nor attributed to Moses." *Voltaire's Old Testament Criticism* (Geneva, 1971), p. 79.

[5] "There are only eleven of them out of a possible 2000 or so." Ludwig Köhler, *Old Testament Theology* (London, 1957), p. 36.

[6] "Il faut renoncer au sens commun pour ne pas convenir que les Juifs admirent d'abord plusieurs dieux. Il est plus difficile de savoir ce qu'ils entendent par ce mot Dieu, *Eloïm*. Quelques commentateurs ont prétendu que ce mot *l'un de nous* signifie la Trinité; mais il n'est pas assurément question de la Trinité dans la Bible." Voltaire, "Genèse," *Dict.* (see n. 4), p. 221.

> Moses said to God, "I am to go, then, to the sons of Israel and say to them, 'the God of your fathers has sent me to you.' But if they ask me what his name is, what am I to tell them?" And God said to Moses, "I Am who I Am. This," he added, "is what you must say to the sons of Israel: 'I Am has sent me to you.'" (Ex. 3.13-14)[7]

The God of their descendants as well as their ancestors, he will answer to this name from now on. *Yahweh* is probably an archaic form of the verb *to be* meaning *he is*. Yahweh's self-identification in the passage above apparently means, "he is the one who really exists" or "lives," for the Hebrews took great pride in their "living God" (Dt. 5.26). He prohibited images of himself, while nearly all of his rivals were worshiped in the form of idols, hence the Pentateuchal scorn for these gods of stone and wood, who were not alive. A clever simplification, this idea flattered a primitive nation's pride, catered to their nomadic wanderings, and distinguished their God from rival deities. As Voltaire insists, gods are seldom identical to the idols that represent them.[8] Yahweh's rivals may have appeared as alive to their worshipers as he did to his. Only by prohibiting images of himself, a relatively superficial point, did he elevate himself above them.

However inspired, propaganda comes from man and not God. Thus men anxious to propagate belief in Yahweh must have developed the oral traditions behind the Pentateuch. These traditions probably go back to a common origin, the impact of a great leader, who alone could have accomplished what happened towards the thirteenth century southeast of the Mediterranean Sea. The emergence of henotheism and eventually monotheism from a background of polytheism poses a question to which there seems to be no other satisfactory answer. Despite Voltaire's doubts,[9] therefore, one must concede the historicity of Moses. Somehow someone like him managed to persuade or coerce several tribes of Semitic nomads, among them no doubt the one he was leading himself, to adhere to a treaty known as the covenant. For the covenant conforms to the specifications of treaties enacted by the Hittites of Anatolia in the second millennium and imposed by a powerful ruler on a subject nation.[10]

[7] *The Jerusalem Bible* (New York, 1966).

[8] "L'erreur n'était pas d'adorer un morceau de bois ou de marbre, mais d'adorer une fausse divinité représentée par ce bois et ce marbre." "Idole," *Dict.*, p. 238.

[9] *"Est-il bien vrai qu'il y ait eu un Moïse? Si un homme qui commandait à la nature eût existé chez les Egyptiens, de si prodigieux événements n'auraient-ils pas fait la partie principale de l'histoire de l'Egypte?"* "Moïse," *Dict.*, p. 320.

[10] "The parties to the treaties are the great king and his vassal... One of the parties may be an entire nation." Klaus Baltzer, *The Covenant Formulary in Old Testament, Jewish and Early Christian Writings* (Philadelphia, 1971), p. 17. Baltzer dates the treaties 2000-1200 B.C.

Yahweh replaced the Hittite king in granting his protection to the people of Israel in return for their obedience to his code of law. Adoption of the covenant meant abandonment of the old tribal religion and government as well as submission to a new theocracy under a national God represented by Moses and his successors.

Did such a change meet with no resistance, however? Exodus, which ignores the problem, claims a unanimous and spontaneous ratification of the covenant by the assembled people:

> Moses... told [them] all the commands of Yahweh and all the ordinances. In answer, all the people said with one voice, "we will observe all the commands that Yahweh has decreed." (Ex. 24.3)

Consent by public acclamation usually results from backstage threats and concessions. The myth of spontaneous unanimity does not flow from a people craving discipline, but rather a power in need of self-justification. The historical, as opposed to the Scriptural, ratification of the covenant must have been a protracted and piecemeal affair, lasting well beyond the life of Moses and recurring in different places at different times. Yet only a decisive act could have initiated such a process. Moses must have cajoled or forced each of several fellow sheikhs to rename the god or chief god of his tribe "Yahweh." Thus worship could continue as before, though in the name of the only living God, who may previously have been nothing more than the god of Moses' tribe. This was no mean feat, because the Hebrews shared the ancient belief that a name is an intimate part of the thing designated and that, in the case of a supernatural being, it can be used to invoke his power. This conviction favored further syncretism and, eventually, the development of a common theology, the theology of the Pentateuch.

According to this theology, the Lord of Israel and his vassals belong to each other exclusively. "I will live in your midst," he tells them in Leviticus; "I will be your God and you shall be my people" (26.12). He has chosen them, and not vice versa, because he "loves" (Dt. 7.8) only them among all the nations. Although we can imagine the effect of such love on those primitive and fervent men, the slightest dose of realism leaves us little choice in the search for a cause. The ingredients are: (1) the propensity of an isolated people to mistake their particularity for a kind of superiority; (2) an imaginative and intelligent individual among them bent on transforming them into a nation under his rule; and (3) a climate of belief in the supernatural that made the exercise of power dependent upon the apparent consent of the divinity. It does not follow that Yahweh chose the Hebrews as his people and appointed Moses to govern them on his behalf. It is far more likely that Moses chose Yahweh and founded his authority on Yahweh's imaginary election of Israel. But this conclusion does not impugn the sincerity of Moses, who could have succeeded in his great adventure only on faith as mighty as that ascribed to him by Exodus.

The Ten Commandments are an essential part of the covenant law. The second warns that Yahweh is "a jealous God" (Ex. 20.5) and the first that "You shall have no other gods but me" (Ex. 20.3). This very restriction nonetheless implies acknowledgment of competition with rival deities, the existence of whose cults he could hardly have denied: "Do not follow... the gods of the peoples around you" (Dt. 6.14). Whatever history may salvage from the episode of the golden calf worshiped during Moses' absence,[11] it shows that Yahweh did not easily triumph over these rivals. The weapon that assured his eventual victory was the prohibition of images and idols. The second Commandment prohibits making or worshiping likenesses of anything above, on, or below the earth. Enforced, it denied other gods the means of psychological presence upon which their followers' faith depended. Yahweh's independence of sensual aids to belief is perhaps another innovation by Moses.

To infer that the early Hebrews conceived of Yahweh as a spiritual rather than a physical being would be a mistake, for Hellenism taught them this distinction only much later. They assigned to him the uniquely material existence they assumed their own lives to be. Among the anthropomorphic allusions to Yahweh in the older books of the Bible, the sacrificial banquet in the covenant ratification ceremony is particularly revealing. Moses led Aaron, Nadab, Abihu and seventy elders up Mount Sinai:

> They saw the God of Israel beneath whose feet there was... a sapphire pavement... He laid no hand on [them]... they gazed on God. They ate and they drank. (Ex. 24.10-11)

While one could dismiss Yahweh's hand as a figure here, certainly not his feet. These many witnesses not only contemplate him, but also his appearance, far from cutting their appetite and thirst, actually whets their curiosity. Could they behave in this way if he were not human enough to put them at their ease? No, assuredly. Yahweh's mythical creation of man in his own image reverses, though unintentionally no doubt, what really happened.

A deity created by ancient man in his own image required power over nature in compensation for man's subservience to it. Yahweh's

[11] "On trouva [dans le désert] bien des ouvriers qui firent un veau d'or en une nuit, et qui réduisirent ensuite l'or en poudre, opération impossible à la chimie ordinaire, non encore inventée." Voltaire, "Moïse," *Dict.*, p. 322.

control of natural forces cannot be doubted when Moses leads the people to the foot of Sinai "to meet God":

> The mountain... was entirely wrapped in smoke, because Yahweh had descended on it in the form of fire. Like smoke from a furnace the smoke went up, and the whole mountain shook violently... Moses spoke, and God answered him with peals of thunder. (Ex. 19.17-19)

This theophany illustrates ancient man's fascination with fire, so useful to him and yet, potentially, so dangerous to him,[12] and with the smoke that rose from it towards heaven. It illustrates his fear of the unpredictable and occasionally destructive quaking of the ground under his feet and lightning followed by thunder over his head. Unable to explain these things, he resorted to the supernatural and, aware of his own superiority over the other natural beings, he attributed the inexplicable to a divine version of himself. Like other gods, Yahweh wields the forces of nature, but he has his own personality. While beings who hurl lightning and speak with the voice of thunder necessarily live in heaven, he travels in a fiery cloud of smoke called a *glory* or *shekinah*. To approach him is dangerous, unless accredited representatives arrange to meet him on a mountaintop. Several times, he warned Moses to keep the others away, a suspicious attitude, but they took Moses' word for it.

Together with the law Moses brought down with him from the sacred mountain were the threat of punishment for disobedience and the promise of a reward for compliance. The early Hebrews, unlike the Egyptians from whose slavery they had supposedly just escaped, knew nothing of an afterlife.[13] All Hebrews had so expansive a conception of this life that they may not have felt any great need for another. A deeply felt sentiment of family continuity tended to diminish the psychological barriers of birth and death which seem formidable to us. Ancestors lived on in the remembrance of descendants, who also looked forward to their posterity as if to extend life indefinitely. Genealogy brought all generations, past, present, and future, together in an unending, but cohesive unity.[14] The individual

[12] Hence the burning bush in Ex. 3.2: "The angel of Yahweh appeared to [Moses] in the shape of a flame of fire, coming from the middle of a bush."

[13] Mitchell Dahood translates several passages in Psalms by terms referring to an afterlife, such as Ps. 69.29: "Let them be erased from the scroll of life eternal." But he sets Ps. 69 in the sixth century B.C. *The Anchor Bible*, XVII (New York, 1968).

[14] "The larger or smaller group was accepted without question as a unity; legal prescription was replaced by the fact or fiction of the blood-tie, usually traced back to a common ancestor. The whole group, including its past, present, and future members, might function as a single individual through any one of those members conceived as

conscience merged with the tribal conscience to such an extent that the threat of the second Commandment to "punish the father's fault in the sons, the grandsons and the great-grandsons" (Ex. 20.5) apparently went unquestioned.

Another aspect of Yahweh's justice inaccessible to critical reason is his custom of judging an act by its effect and not the intention behind it. When Uzzah steadies the Ark with his hand to prevent it from overturning, a potential profanation, Yahweh kills him instantly for this actual profanation. To us, punishing the trivial consequence of a generous intention seems barbaric; to the Hebrews, however, death seemed appropriate for the violation of the law. The accident that happened took precedence over the one that might have happened otherwise, for Yahweh judges by results rather than hypothetical alternatives. The incident demonstrates the insignificance of an individual, even a worthy individual, involved in Yahweh's affairs.

Yahweh's foreign policy was no less ruthless than his justice. It derived from the relationship between a nation of nomads living in the desert and sedentary neighbors occupying more fertile lands. On one hand, shortages of everything from food to women drove the nomads to brigandage and raiding; on the other, retaliation and imperialism brought powerful armies against them. Since survival depended on hit-and-run warfare, Yahweh was a God who hit fearfully hard and never had to run. He drowned the entire Egyptian army in the Red Sea because they dared to pursue his people. The land of milk and honey he promised them beckoned first as a target of incursions and later as a territory exposed to conquest. Regardless of whether the massacre of Jericho actually took place,[15] it illustrates the ethic of a people who lived by war. Since those who were not with them were against them, the second Commandment states: "I punish... those who hate me; but I show kindness to... those who love me" (Ex. 20.5-6). Until after the occupation of Palestine, therefore, Yahweh was not a God of peace, but a God of war. His justice disciplined his army and his foreign policy facilitated the defeat of his enemies.

The worship of such a God helps to explain the Hebrews' success in their thirteenth-century invasion of Palestine, but it would be naïve to

representative of it. Because it was not confined to the living, but included the dead and the unborn, the group could be conceived as living forever." H. Wheeler Robinson, *Corporate Personality in Ancient Israel* (Philadelphia, 1964), p. 1.

[15] Kathleen Kenyon testifies, "the last expedition [to Jericho (led by her)] showed that almost all traces of the Late Bronze Age town of the time of Joshua had been destroyed by erosion and that the identification of one of the lines of town walls as belonging to this period was mistaken." *Archeology of the Holy Land* (London, 1970), p. 316.

credit the inspiration and efficiency of the conquest in Joshua. Like other invasions of the fertile crescent by nomads from the Arabian Desert, it probably consisted in an uncoordinated ebb and flow over several generations. First, the Hebrews apparently moved into the sparsely-settled highlands to graze their sheep and then they became involved in wars with the Canaanite city-states in the lowlands.[16] They no doubt won more battles than they lost, but, probably, the atrocities committed in Yahweh's name were exaggerated and the promise of the land under attack was invented only after it had been occupied. The transition from a nomadic to a sedentary life, which altered their religious needs, brought a change in Yahweh's mode of presence among them. From his initial abode in the heavens, he had descended to the Ark, so that they could take him with them wherever they went. Once they had settled in various parts of Palestine, he moved to the Temple in Jerusalem, a centralized location where they could come and worship him. This flexibility in keeping himself available, as if to avoid inconveniencing them, resembles priestly expediency far more than divine majesty. Their leaders, whose authority depended on Yahweh's blessing, must have made these adjustments.

The polarizing effect of a capital city favored the development of a cultural elite, whom the primitive theology of the desert could no longer satisfy. The death of witnesses, wishful remembrance of the past, and genealogical vanity encouraged speculation on Yahweh's love for Israel before the covenant. In this way, no doubt, he acquired a reputation for having guided Israel through previous ages and for having delivered her from Egypt, although the source of this legend remains elusive. Archaeologists have discovered evidence of Semitic slaves in that country before the covenant period,[17] but nothing to support the authenticity of an eastward migration like the Exodus.[18] On the contrary, the dissimilarity between Egyptian and Hebrew cultures, particularly the absence of belief in immortality among the Hebrews and the Hittite origin of the covenant protocol undermine

[16] This is the theory developed by Albrecht Alt and Martin Noth, and defended by Manfred Weippert in *The Settlement of the Israelite Tribes in Palestine* (London, 1971).

[17] "The simple linear proto-Canaanite alphabet... was freely utilized in Egyptian territory some two centuries before the time of Moses. [This] has been illustrated by the discovery of early 15th century B.C. informal notations and dedications by Semitic slaves from the Egyptian East Delta region who were being employed... in the Sinai Turquoise mines." R.K. Harrison, *Introduction to the Old Testament* (London, 1970), p. 576.

[18] "Neither the Amarna Letters [ca. 1390-1365] nor other Egyptian sources give any hint of the events recorded in Exodus" (Kenyon, p. 207).

the credibility of Yahweh's greatest exploit.[19] In ancient Palestine, however, growing confidence in the God of history inspired an accounting for all generations of ancestors back to the beginning of the world. Rivalry with other religions seems to have caused his promotion to the status of Creator and the adaptation of a Babylonian creation myth, the *Enuma elish*.[20]

During the earlier half of the first millennium, Hebrew curiosity shifted from the past to the future. Perhaps this change reflects a decline from the optimism of victorious national unity to the pessimism of divided kingdoms disintegrating under invasions by powerful neighbors. While satisfaction nurtures pride in achievement, discouragement tends to eliminate every alternative except hope. The attention of the Hebrews, in any case, was turning from history to prophecy. As the Pentateuchal traditions reached the final stage in their development, radical theologians introduced new concepts that supplemented, contradicted, or replaced the old ones.

Psalm 90, a prayer that may have originated in the ninth century, offers an example of supplement: "Before... the world came to birth, you were God from all eternity and for ever" (Ps. 90.2). The early Hebrews gave little thought to the duration of Yahweh's existence, which this passage nonetheless extends to an unending past and future. Within this eternity, creation at the beginning of the world suggested a symmetrical end to the world, last judgment. In the eighth century, Isaiah imagined the time when "Yahweh... will wield authority over the nations and adjudicate between many peoples" (Is. 2.3-4). Thus the God of Israel had jurisdiction over the other nations. Already eternal, he became universal. As a judge, he assumed an eschatological function foreign to the Pentateuchal deity, whose threats and promises imply continuity and progress, not conclusion or termination. While Isaiah describes the end as a time to hammer swords into ploughshares (2.4), Psalm 76, intended for a choir accompanied by musical instruments, celebrates the victory of Yahweh

[19] Scholars committed to traditional Judaism, Catholicism, or Protestantism, such as Samuel Yeivin, Roland de Vaux, and R.K. Harrison, naturally refuse to abandon the historicity of the Exodus. But de Vaux's position is flexible: "De même qu'il y eut plusieurs entrées en Egypte, il a pu y avoir plusieurs exodes" (I, 353). Yeivin, *The Israelite Conquest of Canaan* (Istanbul, 1971), see pp. 235-36; de Vaux, *Histoire ancienne d'Israel* (Paris, 1971); Harrison, see p. 576.

[20] E.A. Speiser compares the *Enuma elish* with Genesis 1.1-11 as follows: "There is not only a striking correspondence in various details, but—what is even more significant—the order of events is the same, which is enough to preclude any likelihood of coincidence... It would... appear that [the] opening account goes back to Babylonian prototypes." Speiser, trans., *Genesis, The Anchor Bible*, I (New York, 1964), 9-10.

over Israel's enemies, a possible allusion to the defeat of Sennacherib before the gates of Jerusalem in 701. It not only continues the warrior tradition, but also foresees the time "when God stands up to give judgment and save all the humble of the earth" (Ps. 76.9). The Mosaic deity had not sympathized with the humble, whom he expected to submit and keep their distance. He did not offer to save them or anyone else, since he considered the limits of the present life definitive. Psalm 76 therefore reveals the substitution of a paternalistic attitude for an authoritarian one and the inception of belief in the possibility of salvation and an afterlife. Composed in the seventh century, Psalm 139 credits Yahweh with faculties worthy of an eschatological redeemer, such as omniscience:

> The word is not even on my tongue,
> Yahweh, before you know about it. (Ps. 139.4)

and ubiquity: "Where could I flee from your presence" (Ps. 139.7)? The authors of the Pentateuch neither made such claims for their deity nor apparently even conceived of the ideas behind them. A decline in anthropomorphism accompanied the attribution of superhuman faculties to God during the prophetic age.

In the same century, Jeremiah ascribed to him a moral subtlety more appropriate to his universal role. Having sent the prophet to watch a potter at work, Yahweh compares himself to this craftsman and Israel to the clay: "Can I not do with you what this potter does" (Jr. 18.6)? If a sinful nation mends its ways, he will reward it. Consequently, he accepts responsibility for damping the oscillations between good and evil as he judges them. In this way, Jeremiah refined the crude combination of reward for submission and punishment for disobedience in the Pentateuch. Otherwise, his theology has little in common with the chauvinist tyranny of Moses. While trusting in the ultimate justice of God, he also worries about the success of evil in the world: "Why is it that the wicked live so prosperously" (Jr. 12.1)? Textual problems obscure his answer, but he apparently sets God's justice above human understanding. Second Isaiah (sixth century) confirms this explanation when he ascribes the following statement to Yahweh: "My ways are above your ways, my thoughts above your thoughts" (Is. 55.9). Second Isaiah likewise alters the wording of the first Commandment, perhaps inadvertently. In Exodus and Deuteronomy, Yahweh decrees, "You shall have no gods except me" (Ex. 20.3; Dt. 5.7). According to Second Isaiah, he says, "there is no other God beside me" (Is. 44.6, 45.21). The former command requires exclusive allegiance despite the competition of other gods; the latter denies the existence of rival gods in defiance of the other cults surrounding Second Isaiah in his Babylonian exile. Yahweh progressed from one of a kind to the only one of his kind and his worshipers, from henotheism to monotheism. "I... do not change" (Ml. 3.6), he nonetheless insists in the fifth-century book of Malachi. One may of course distinguish between the theological principle of immutability and the historical fact that belief in him had changed. But, in that case, one must choose between two versions of Yahweh, the ancient and the modern. Change in the deity stems from an evolution in the psychology of believers, conditioned as it always is by the life they live. The deterioration of Hebrew society was undermining confidence in the priestly and royal heirs of Pentateuchal authority. A vacuum of power bred dissent in the form of prophets challenging their corruption. That such prophets should alter the old theology by their very efforts to restore it should come as no surprise.

When Deuteronomy characterizes Yahweh's relation to his people as fatherhood, the term implies stern authority. This meaning continues in Psalms and "Third Isaiah,"[21] which nevertheless complement it by the connotation of paternal affection.[22] Rare in the Pentateuch, allusions to divine fatherhood became frequent in the later books of the Old Testament. The Hellenized Jewish author of Wisdom (first century B.C.) evokes his paternal control of nature in man's interest. Having ridiculed the futility of imploring protection from a figurehead at sea, he acknowledges, "Your providence, Father, is what steers [the vessel]" (Ws. 14.3). The personal invocation of a providential Father foreshadows a New Testament usage. In his letters to the Galatians and the Romans (57-58 A.D.), Paul combines the Greek *pater* with the Aramaic *abba* referring intimately to one's own father. In his context, the phrase "Abba, Father" (Rm. 5.8; Ga. 4.6)! is a spontaneous means of addressing oneself to God.

Mark 14.36 attributes this redundant phrase to Jesus himself in the garden of Gethsemane. The gospels report that he habitually considered God his own father and, since he spoke Aramaic, he must have used *abba* for that purpose. *Pater* was probably added later for the benefit of Hellenistic Christians. While Jesus is the first Jew known to have called God his father, the attitude if not the language already prevailed among other Galilean holy men in his day (see pp. 31,

[21] "We have identified Third Isaiah as a collection of pieces from different authors, united as a continuation of Isaiah and exhibiting a community of theme and situation." John McKenzie, ed., *Second Isaiah, The Anchor Bible*, xx (New York, 1968), lxvii.

[22] "O foolish, unwise people! Is this not your father, who gave you being, who made you, by whom you subsist" (Dt. 32.6-7)? "Father of orphans, defender of widows, such is God" (Ps. 68.5). "Do not let your compassion go unmoved, for you are our Father" (Is. 63.15-16).

37). Although he never, in the gospels, extends this intimate relationship with God to others, he encourages them to expect paternal sympathy from him. The Lord's Prayer, which he taught his followers, begins with the salutation "Father" (Lk. 11.2; Mt. 6.9). Except for the fatherly indulgence implied by this prayer, however, he remains much the same as the Yahweh of the prophets:

> What man among you with a hundred sheep, losing one, would not leave the ninety-nine in the wilderness and go after the missing one till he found it... There will be more rejoicing in heaven over one repentant sinner than over ninety-nine virtuous men who have no need of repentance. (Lk. 15.4, 7; Mt. 12-13)

By our standards, the shepherd is treating the ninety-nine sheep who do not go astray unfairly. He is obviously the traditional divine Father who treats his children with indulgent but arbitrary affection. Intentionally or otherwise, this doctrine caters to priestly favoritism.

Whenever and wherever it occurred, the Hellenization of Judaism spiritualized the Jewish deity, originally a physical being. Hellenism also fostered the development of Christology, thus diverting attention from God to Christ. When Greek curiosity about the nature of the divinity replaced the Jewish preoccupation with its function, the trend to greater intimacy with God reversed and Christian theology tended to abstraction and transcendence.

SPIRIT

Here one must turn to the second most ancient person in the Trinity. The earliest evidence occurs in the mythology of Genesis and Exodus. Once Yahweh had made heaven and earth, "his spirit hovered over the water" (Ge. 1.1) before undertaking further creative labors. This spirit, or *ruagh* in Hebrew, is Yahweh's power, the power with which he creates the world. Literally, however, *ruagh* means wind or breath, as Spinoza indicates.[23] Having made Adam, Yahweh "breathed into his nostrils a breath of life, and thus man became a living being" (Ge. 2.7). The spirit not only operates as a life-giving breath, but also as a mighty wind. Pursued by the Egyptian army, the people of Israel

[23] "Le mot *ruagh*, en son vrai sens, signifie vent" (p. 38). Spinoza notes seven other connotations: (1) "le sens d'haleine... (2) de souffle ou respiration... (3) ...courage ou force... (4) ...vertu et aptitude... (5) ...sentiment intime... pensée... volonté... (6) la pensée elle-même ou l'âme... (7) les régions du monde à cause des vents qui en soufflent, et aussi les côtés d'une chose quelconque qui regardent ces régions" (pp. 38-39). Charles Appuhn, trans., *Traité théologico-politique, Oeuvres*, II (Paris, 1965).

came to the Red Sea and "Yahweh drove [the water] back... with a strong easterly wind" (Ex. 14.21), elsewhere described as "a blast from [his] nostrils" (Ex. 15.8), so that an escape route opened up across the bottom. Thus the Hebrews thought the spirit little more than a physical attribute of Yahweh. Except for an odd passage in 1 Kings,[24] it is not a person, but a thing. In the prophetic era, the sense broadened to include the idea of inspiration, which the Hebrews nonetheless associated with physical force. When the spirit stirs Ezekiel to prophecy, for instance, it lifts or stands him up.[25] It also guarantees the authenticity of prophecy, for false prophets do not benefit from it.

The Alexandrian Jew who wrote the Book of Wisdom no longer retains the original meaning of physical power. He associates the spirit with Wisdom, an attribute of the divinity which, in accordance with a Hellenistic tendency, he personifies:

> Within [Wisdom] is a spirit intelligent, holy,
> unique, manifold, subtle,
> active, incisive, unsullied,
> lucid, invulnerable, benevolent, sharp,
> irresistible, beneficent, loving to man,
> steadfast, dependable, unperturbed,
> almighty, all-surveying,
> penetrating all intelligent, pure
> and most subtle spirits. (Ws. 7.22-23)

Several of these epithets which apply to the spirit *within* Wisdom apparently belong to a divine faculty assigned to Wisdom, for they exclude the possibility of physical energy: *intelligent, lucid, beneficent, loving to man, all-surveying, penetrating all* [*other*] *spirits*. Without actually personifying the spirit itself, they redefine it as immaterial and pervasive, qualities the author probably borrowed from Stoicism.

As a Jew, Paul inherited a version of the spirit similar to the one in Wisdom; as a Christian, he adapted it to the new religion. He also assigned a more specific purpose to it than Judaism had. In 1 Corinthians, he explains how God reveals himself to Christians by means of the spirit:

> The spirit reaches the depths of everything, even the depths of God [which] can only be known by the spirit... We have received the spirit that comes from God. (1 Co. 2.10-12)

The spirit, which continues to be a kind of inspiration, communicates

[24] During a war with Aram, Yahweh asks, "'Who will trick Ahab into marching to his death?'... The spirit came forward and stood before Yahweh... 'I will go and become a lying spirit in the mouths of all his prophets'" (1 K. 22.20-22).
[25] In Ez. 3.12, 8.3, it lifts him up and in Ez. 2.2, 3.24, it stands him up.

intimate knowledge of the divinity to Christians. A more complete understanding of Paul's conception depends on the difficult distinction between the spirit and the risen Christ in his writings, a problem that may never have occurred to him. *Lord* (Christ) and *spirit* seem interchangeable in 2 Corinthians 3.17-18:

> The Lord is the spirit, and where the spirit of the Lord is, there is freedom. And we, with our unveiled faces reflecting like mirrors the brightness of the Lord, all grow brighter and brighter as we are turned into the image that we reflect; this is the work of the Lord who is spirit.

Close analysis of the passage, however, reveals several indications of the spirit's subordination to the Lord. *The spirit of the Lord* in the first sentence and *the work of the Lord* in the second are nearly equivalent to each other and both concern the spirit. The increasingly brilliant faces of believers, a traditional element of Jewish theophanies, reflect the light, or spirit, and hence the light source, or Christ. The spirit, according to Paul, is therefore the means of revealing Christ and God. Though an attribute of both Christ and God, it has still not become a person.

Written later in the first century, the first three or synoptic gospels, which have rather little to say about the spirit, present a less advanced version of it. Luke takes the greatest interest in it and the Acts of the Apostles, which is the second volume of his gospel, treats it as a matter of some importance. The opening chapter repeats the command which the risen Christ gave the eleven disciples in the last chapter of the preceding volume: they must stay in Jerusalem for the fulfillment of a promise by the Father. Acts 1.8, which provides the substance of the promise, quotes Christ as saying:

> You will receive power when the Holy Spirit comes on you, and then you will be my witnesses not only in Jerusalem but throughout Judea and Samaria, and indeed to the ends of the earth.

Then he ascends into a cloud and disappears. The promise announces an intervention by the Holy Spirit to empower the disciples for a proselytizing mission to the entire world as it was then known ("to the ends of the earth"). According to the second chapter of Acts, such a miracle takes place ten days later at Pentecost. The twelve disciples including Matthias, Judas' newly elected successor, met with several women, Mary the mother of Jesus among them, and some of his kinfolk in a room:

> Suddenly they heard what sounded like a powerful wind from heaven, the noise of which filled the entire house... and something appeared to them that seemed like tongues of fire; these separated and came to rest

> on the head of each of them. They were all filled with the Holy Spirit, and began to speak foreign languages as the Spirit gave them the gift of speech. (Ac. 2.2-4)

The sound "like a powerful wind from heaven" shows that belief in the physical power of the spirit subsisted in Palestine, but the inverted flames are less easy to explain. Since fire removes sin in the Old Testament, it probably has that effect here too.[26] John the Baptist announces that Jesus "will baptize you with the Holy Spirit and fire" (Lk. 3.16) and Jesus, before his ascension, predicts that the disciples "will be baptized with the Holy Spirit" (Ac. 1.6). In chapter two of Acts, however, there is evidence neither of Jesus' presence nor of anything resembling baptism specifically. The inverted *tongues* of flame lick the heads of his disciples, thus eliciting discourse from each of them in a foreign *tongue*. Luke's play on the two meanings of *tongue* or *glossa* in Greek raises suspicions of amateur philology. The only foreign language the disciples could have used effectively in the next few decades of missionary work was the Greek koine spoken almost everywhere in the eastern Mediterranean basin. Perhaps some of them already spoke it. The multilingual proficiency suddenly induced by the Holy Spirit has left no trace anywhere else, either in Scripture or in any other document. Perhaps Luke misinterpreted or exaggerated an account of glossalalia in his source, for this meaningless babble under the effect of pious ecstasy occurred frequently among early Christians.[27] A strong wind may well have blown over the house the disciples were in on Pentecost, but certainly no inverted, unharmful flames licked their heads, unless hallucination or imagination produced them. It is likely that they merely underwent an intense emotional experience similar to those of modern enthusiasts. The mythical amplification of a rather ordinary event over several generations of transmission seems entirely probable in this case. The driving force behind the rapid spread of Christianity in the ancient world was proselytism and not reverence for historical accuracy.

The Pentecostal event in Acts announces the Christian missionary activity by the Spirit, which supersedes Christ in providing super-

[26] "One of the seraphs flew to me, holding in his hand a live coal which he had taken from the altar with a pair of tongs. With this he touched my mouth and said, 'See now, this has touched your lips, your sin is taken away'" (Is. 6.6-7).

[27] Voltaire describes the glossalalia of George Fox, the founder of Quakerism, as follows: "Fox thought himself inspired, and consequently was of the opinion that he must speak in a manner different from the rest of mankind. He therefore began... to hold in his breath and to exhale it in a forcible manner." *Letters Concerning the English Nation* (New York, 1974), p. 16. In the preceding letter, he recalls speaking with tongues in a Quaker meeting house as a "confused jumble of words" (p. 10).

natural support for his followers. It even enforces discipline in the primitive Jewish Christian community which, for a brief period, pooled its resources in an idealistic sort of communism. "With his wife's connivance" (Ac. 5.2), however, Ananias secretly holds some of his property back and Peter scolds him, "How can Satan have so possessed you that you should lie to the Holy Spirit" (Ac. 5.3)? Thus Ananias and, later, his wife Sapphira fall dead, liquidated by the Spirit for an anti-social crime. This episode, which irritated Voltaire,[28] betrays the fanaticism of its author. Though entirely suspect, the supernatural aspects of the story imply the novel belief that the Holy Spirit was enough of a person to demand the disclosure of such information and retaliate against anyone who failed to comply. The Pentecostal miracle makes no such impression. The episode yields a further implication of personality in the parallel between the Spirit and God, both of whom suffer the same affront: "It is not to men that you have lied, but to God" (Ac. 5.4). Yet this parallel does not prove that, according to Luke, the Spirit is either identical, equal, or inferior to God, inferiority being the most likely alternative in his day. It does show that, in his opinion, the Spirit enjoys a privileged relationship with God.

Whether or not baptism confers the Spirit raises another problem in Acts. After the Pentecost miracle, Peter preaches an inaugural sermon resembling the literary speeches ancient historians assign to major figures in their works. Among other things, he exhorts the assembled crowd to repent and submit to baptism "in the name of Jesus Christ... You will receive the gift of the Holy Spirit" (Ac. 2.38). But an incident in Chapter 8 impairs this promise. Having heard that *Samaria* (some Samaritans) had accepted the Good News, the apostles in Jerusalem delegate Peter and John to make contact with them. Though already "baptized in the name of the Lord Jesus" (Ac. 8.16), they have not yet received the Spirit. After prayer on their behalf, John and Peter "laid hands on them, and they received the Holy Spirit" (Ac. 8.17). The implication that one can obtain the Spirit only from authorized individuals contradicts what Luke had already written and suggests a church jealous of its authority. The laying on of hands, in particular, strikes one as an innovative usurpation of God's generosity as Luke originally described it. The context, which concerns a Christian convert known as Simon the Magician, further illus-

[28] "N'est-il pas horrible de faire mourir Anania parce qu'ayant vendu son fonds et en ayant donné l'argent à Pierre, il avait retenu pour lui et pour sa femme quelques écus pour subvenir à leurs nécessités, sans le dire? A peine Anania est-il mort que sa femme arrive. Pierre... lui demande si son mari a donné tout son argent aux saints. La bonne femme répond oui, et elle meurt sur-le-champ. Cela est dur." ("Pierre,"*Dict.*, p. 349).

trates this abuse. Envious of the apostles' ability to bestow the Spirit, Simon offers to buy it. Refusing indignantly, Peter curses Simon "for thinking that money could buy what God has given for nothing" (Ac. 8.20). The word *simony* comes from this very incident. Yet Peter's refusal underlines the contradiction between the generosity of God and the necessity for obtaining it from other men. These precedents in Acts reveal an early tendency to subordinate doctrine to the authority of an evolving priesthood.

The Gospel of John considers theological rather than ecclesiastical aspects of the Holy Spirit. Among the versified discourses which he, also in the manner of ancient historians, ascribes to Jesus, is one about "living water," a synonym of the Holy Spirit. Jesus allegedly delivered it in Jerusalem during the Feast of Tabernacles commemorating the spring that Moses caused to burst from a rock in the desert. This feast likewise anticipates the accomplishment of a prophecy by Zecharia that on the day of definitive national victory, a messianic expectation, "running waters will issue from Jerusalem" (Zc. 14.8). On the seventh day of the feast in Jesus' day, a procession would bring a golden pitcher of water from the fountain of Gihon, the only fresh water source in Jerusalem, up to the Temple. A priest would then pour it through a silver funnel on the altar, from which it flowed down into the ground. On this day, according to John, Jesus, who had been preaching in the Temple, "Stood there and cried out":

> If any man is thirsty, let him come to me!
> Let the man come and drink who believes in me!

"As Scripture says: From his breast shall flow fountains of living water" (Jn. 7.37-38). Yet there is no such passage in the Old Testament, nor did the quotation evidently derive from any passage to be found there. A parenthetical explanation following it in John may be a later insertion: "[Jesus] was speaking of the Spirit which those who believed in him were to receive" (Jn. 7.39). If the Spirit comes from the risen Christ, it cannot proceed from God alone, an argument used by the West against the East in a dispute that later split the Church in two. But did this distinction so much as occur to John? He appears interested merely in imposing on a tradition, whose authenticity he took for granted, the ability of Christ to bestow the spirit. Since he describes the spirit as living water, there can be little doubt that he thought it a mysterious kind of fluid and not a person, to say nothing of a person equal in any way to Christ or God. As for his source, one can only fall back on the hypothesis of a statement by Jesus in keeping with his character in the first three gospels. One can hardly imagine the synoptic Jesus presuming to substitute himself for the Gihon Fountain on the climatic day of Tabernacles in Jerusalem. John's arrangement of Jesus' life according to the feasts of the Jewish calendar escapes no careful reader of his gospel. If the tradition does go back to Jesus himself, one cannot exclude the possibility that he described the spirit as living water. But he may simply have evoked the Jewish belief in God's gift of the spirit in the form of inspiration to those of deserving faith. While John 7.39 suggests that the Spirit flows from Jesus like water, John 20.22, which is part of the resurrection appearance to convince Thomas (see p. 54), describes it as his breath blown over the disciples: "He breathed on them and said, 'Receive the Holy Spirit.'" The verse echoes Genesis 2.7 in which Yahweh breathed the breath of life into the nostrils of newly created man. This incident appears to contradict Acts 2.1-4 in which Luke set an entirely different version of the same event fifty days later at Pentecost. The discrepancy between the two texts implies that, although early Christians thought they were inspired by the Holy Spirit, they did not agree on how it came to them. They nonetheless provided western theologians in later centuries with passages which, in the absence of any critical rigor, could be taken for evidence in favor of the Holy Spirit proceeding from Christ as well as God. The bestowal of the Spirit on the disciples by breathing on them even produced the theological abstraction of spiration, the means by which the Holy Spirit supposedly proceeded. This concept would arouse Voltaire's satirical scorn (see p. 237).

Luke quotes Jesus as having said that the "Father [will] give the Holy Spirit to those who ask him" (Lk. 11.13). In the Eschatological Discourse, he also promises the disciples that the Spirit will speak through them in their defense whenever they stand accused, a decidedly personal act:

> It is not you who will be speaking: it will be the Holy Spirit. (Mk. 13.11)
>
> It is not you who will be speaking; the Spirit of your Father will be speaking in you. (Mt. 10.20)

Having removed the statement from the Eschatological Discourse, Luke broadens its meaning and makes the Spirit resemble a person even more closely: "The Holy Spirit will teach you what to say" (Lk. 12.12). Though independent of the early gospels, John continues the same trend, the probable effect of Hellenistic influences, by treating the activity of the post-ascension Spirit allegorically. Thus the spirit sent to replace Christ when he has left his followers becomes an allegorical figure called the Paraclete at times and the Spirit of Truth at others. Needless to say, this development tends to contradict the apparently impersonal conception of the Spirit as living water, but one should not expect consistency from John.

Among numerous equivalents of the difficult Greek *Paracletos* in translations of his gospel, "Counselor" and "Advocate" used together seem best to cover the range of meaning applicable to the Johannine context. But who delegates this Counselor-Advocate?

> I shall ask the Father,
> and he will give you another[29] Advocate
> to be with you for ever. (Jn. 14.16)
>
> The Advocate, the Holy Spirit,
> Whom the Father will send in my name. (Jn. 14.26)
>
> When the Advocate comes,
> whom I shall send to you from the Father,
> the Spirit of truth who issues from the Father,
> he will be my witness. (Jn. 15.26)
>
> I [Jesus] will send [the Advocate] to you. (Jn. 16.7)

John seems to be compiling successive variations in doctrine, of which, for instance, the earlier designates the Father and the later, with increasing emphasis on Christ, the Son as he who dispatches the Advocate. The two synonyms, the Advocate and the Spirit of Truth, may likewise represent different accretions of tradition accumulating in this text. Frequent incidence of such parallelism elsewhere in John supports this hypothesis. Despite his reverence for allegorical titles, he must have realized to some extent how confusing they are when taken together. One may conclude that both the Father and the Son, in his view, shared in the delegation of the Paraclete, although the distinction between the participation of each could not have been very clear in his mind. It would be difficult to argue, on the other hand, that such delegation does not imply subordination or that John intended otherwise. His allegorization of a divine attribute has the effect of creating an intermediate or separate deity.

JESUS

Paul

While the third person of the Trinity developed from an attribute of the first, the second evolved from the human life of Jesus.[30] Some of

[29] The first paraclete is apparently Christ and the "other," the Holy Spirit replacing him on earth.

[30] A few historians deny Jesus' historical existence. A recent example is George Wells, *The Jesus of the Early Christians* (London, 1971), who argues that the various traditions of Jewish messianism united to form the myth of Jesus. Paul transformed the myth into a

the earliest documentation of Christianity neglects this human life, except for the death that brought it to an end. In Paul's second letter to the Corinthians, which he wrote about twenty-five years after the crucifixion (in the mid-fifties of the first century), he dismissed this human life as irrelevant:

> We [Christians] do not judge anyone by the standards of the flesh. Even if we did once know Christ in the flesh, that is not how we know him now. (2 Co. 5.16)

He apparently did not mean to imply that he had known Jesus as a fellow man. Speaking rather for Christians in general, he meant that some of his contemporaries had been in contact with him. But he was also replying to rivals inclined like Peter to belittle his teaching because he had not known Jesus as they had. Furthermore, he was neglecting Jesus in the flesh for theological as well as polemical reasons.

In his letter to the Philippians (late fifties or early sixties), he inserted a hymn which he may have learned during his initiation to Christianity some five years after the crucifixion. The Greek text of this letter seems to have been translated from an Aramaic original, Aramaic being the language of Jesus and his disciples. Paul announces the subject of the hymn as "Christ Jesus" (Ph. 2.5). Originally an Aramaic title meaning "the annointed one," *Jesus* had become the name of the man who had born the title, while the Greek term *Christ*, which means the same thing, was apparently still a mere title in Paul's time. Jesus' true name is unknown, a fact that hinders identification of the man so entitled.[31] The hymn identifies Christ sufficiently, however, for Paul's theological purpose in writing to his fellow Christians at Corinth:

> His state was divine,
> yet he did not cling
> to his equality with God
> but emptied himself
> to assume the condition of a slave,
> and became as men are
>
> ....

theology and the evangelists provided Jesus with a biography. Well's thorough study is persuasive, but not convincing. He cites P. Alfaric, *Origines sociales du christianisme*, (Paris, 1959) and H. Cutner, *Jesus: God, Man or Myth* (New York, 1950), who also deny the historical existence of Jesus.

[31] Joseph Turmel identifies him with the Zealot leader Judas the Galilean, from Gamala near Nazareth: "Judas de Gamala est peut-être le vrai nom de celui que la tradition appelle Jésus-Christ de Nazareth." *Histoire des dogmes* (Paris, 1931), I, 320.

he was humbler yet,
even to accepting death,
death on a cross.
But God raised him on high. (Ph. 2.6-9)

Did the Aramaic original (if there was one) refer to a divine *nature* as the Greek text does in the first line, or rather a divine *function*, a more likely concept in Jewish thought free of Hellenism like that of Jesus? Perhaps Jewish Christians sang this hymn to express their belief in Jesus' divine function, but no more than that, since these earliest of Christians continued to adhere to Jewish monotheism just as Jesus had himself. The raising of Christ by God in the last line implies that he could not rise on his own, a point restricting "equality with God" in the third line to a mere equality of honor. *Condition* in the fifth line translates the same Greek word (*morphe*) as *state* in the first and, since function rather than nature characterizes slavery, the incidence of *morphe* tends to support the hypothesis of an Aramaic equivalent meaning function. The allusion to a slave implies Jesus' accomplishment of the prophecy by Second Isaiah that God would *pierce* his Suffering Servant *through* (Is. 53.5). "By his sufferings," says Yahweh, "shall my servant justify many, taking their faults on himself" (Is. 53.11). Understandably, Jewish Christians saw in this passage a prophecy of Jesus' redemptive martyrdom. They answered the scepticism of orthodox Jews by founding the concept of a suffering messiah on such Old Testament texts, but few scholars now admit any possibility of Second Isaiah having foreseen the crucifixion.[32] All attempts, in fact, to identify Christ as the object of Old Testament prophecy conflict with evidence in each case that some other figure was intended. Yet belief in the divinity of Christ must have inspired such apologetics even among early Christians, despite Voltaire's assumptions to the contrary (see p. 147). The vague terms of the sixth and seventh lines in the hymn, on the other hand, show that some of them at least took scant interest in his human life. To them it obviously meant little more than the voluntary submission of a divine figure to human death without any sacrifice of his divinity. The contradiction between divinity and mortality, which would provoke a great controversy several centuries later, scarcely seems to have occurred to them. The final lines of the hymn, which I have not quoted, heavily emphasize the supremacy over all creation of he who bears the

[32] McKenzie states: "The venerable belief... that the Servant poems... are predictions of Christ... is defended by no one today except a few fundamentalist circles" (*Second Isaiah*, p. xlix).

title of Lord, or *Kyrios* in Greek.[33] In the Septuagint, *Kyrios* translates the Hebrew *Adonai* which the Old Testament reserves for God alone, but Jewish and Christian apocalyptic writings apply it to angels.[34] Although the angelic Christ shares God's function, honor, and title, he willingly underwent the suffering of human death. Since God restored him to his previous state, he did not rise from the dead under his own power. Less than five years after the crucifixion, therefore, at least some Jewish Christians may have assigned a separate and subordinate divinity to Jesus despite accusations of polytheism by fellow Jews.

The doxology of Romans 9.5 (late fifties), which Paul may have borrowed from the Jewish Christian liturgy, distinguishes even less clearly between Christ and God. Did he intend to place God in apposition to Christ here? The answer depends on punctuation and the earliest manuscripts have little if any punctuation. Deploring the indifference of orthodox Jews to Christ, Paul argues that Christ descends from the patriarchs just as they do, according to his human ancestry, "according to the flesh." If Paul intended a pause after *flesh*, one may translate what follows as "God, who is above all, for ever blessed!" If not, "Christ, who is above all, God forever blessed!" The first alternative excludes the identification of Christ with God, while the second allows such an interpretation and scholarly opinion is divided.[35] But why not hold Paul responsible for this ambiguity? In dictating these words, he may not have wanted to express the relationship between Christ and God too clearly for fear of appearing to confirm charges of polytheism by orthodox Jews.

Likewise taken from the Jewish Christian liturgy perhaps, another passage serves as a monotheistic reminder to former pagans in the Christian community at Corinth:

[33] "[God] gave him the name which is above all other names so that *all beings* in the heavens, on earth and in the underworld, *should bend the knee* at the name of Jesus and that every tongue should acclaim Jesus Christ as Lord, to the glory of God the Father" (Ph. 2.9-11). The italicized words are quoted from Is. 45.23.

[34] "While Paul [applied] sayings of the Septuagint concerning the *Kyrios* to Christ, there is not one instance of his having done this where the saying referred to God... The ascription of the title of *Kyrios* to Christ [contributes to the evidence] that, in terms of the primitive Christian conception... Christ was a high heavenly being of angelic kind." Martin Werner, *The Formation of Christian Dogma* (New York, 1957), pp. 123-24.

[35] After a thorough examination of the oldest manuscripts, Bruce Metzger concludes: "Scribes felt that some kind of pause was appropriate... However, one cannot determine what kind of punctuation, if any, Paul in dictating the epistle, or Tertius in transcribing it, would have regarded as appropriate." "The Punctuation of Rm. 9.5," *Christ and Spirit in the New Testament* (Cambridge, 1973), p. 99.

> There is one God, the Father, from whom all things come and for whom we exist; and there is one Lord, Jesus Christ, through whom all things come and through whom we exist. (1 Co. 8.6)

This statement, which confirms the separate and subordinate implications of Philippians 2.6-9, demonstrates just how clearly Paul could distinguish between Christ and God when he wanted to. Christ according to this text is neither God, nor another God, but rather an angel second only to God. The creation comes *from* (Gk. *ex*) God, but *through* (GK. *dia*) Christ, his agent and therefore subordinate. Paul stresses this subordination in 1 Corinthians 15.28 which, in contrast with 8.6, looks forward to the end of time when Christ will return: "When everything is subject to him, the Son himself will be subject in his turn to the One who subjected all things to him." Nor does the following triadic enumeration contradict this explicit subordinationism: "The grace of the Lord Jesus Christ, the love of God and the fellowship of the Holy Spirit be with you all" (2 Co. 13.13). The attributes assigned to each person here do not suggest any metaphysical relations between them, but such triadic formulations in Paul set a precedent and this one may be still another Jewish Christian saying.

The first person named in this trinity is Christ and not God. Despite recognition of God's supremacy, Christ in Paul's letters receives most of the attention and particularly his death and resurrection. In 1 Corinthians 15.3-4, Paul reminds the former pagans of Corinth, whom he had converted to Christianity in 50-52 A.D., of the gospel he was preaching then: "I taught you what I had been taught myself, namely,"

> that Christ died for our sins,
> in accordance with the scriptures
> ....
> and that he was raised to life on the third day,
> in accordance with the scriptures.

The refrain implies a liturgical origin for this passage which, again, Paul may have learned in his own initiation to Christianity in 34-35 A.D. Though doomed to error, the application of Old Testament prophecy to Christ[36] indicates early belief in his redemptive martyr-

[36] "Those who are called Old Testament prophets were concerned with their own times and not with the distant future about which they could only speak in the vaguest way. Therefore, whether they know it or not, when the New Testament authors see prophecy fulfilled in Jesus, they are going beyond the vision of the Old Testament authors." Raymond Brown, *The Virginal Conception and the Bodily Resurrection of Jesus* (London, 1973), p. 15.

dom and resurrection. Further information about this Christology appears in Romans 1.3-4, which may have evolved from a Jewish Christian confession of faith:

> The Son of God... according to the human nature he took, was a descendant of David... Jesus Christ our Lord... was proclaimed Son of God in all his power through his resurrection from the dead.

But how could the Son of God have taken a human nature without sacrificing his divinity? Since the Father proclaimed his divinity at the resurrection, had he lost it during his human life? No. The letter to the Colossians, written in the mid-sixties and by Paul no doubt, states: "In his body lives the fullness of divinity" (2.9). Nevertheless, Paul does not differentiate very thoroughly between his human and divine natures. About his pre-existence, moreover, he has little to say: "Before anything was created, he existed" (Col. 1.17), and even fails to distinguish between the pre-existent Christ and the Holy Spirit. Harry Wolfson observes that the existence of a Pauline trinity before the birth of Christ depends "on whether the Holy Spirit is distinct from the pre-existent Christ or... identified with [him]."[37] Paul's faith hinged on the resurrection, from which he looked back, as in Romans 1.3-4, to the incarnation and forward, as in 1 Corinthians 16.22, to the second coming. All three of these events are supernatural. At the end of 1 Corinthians (mid-fifties), 16.22 presents a salutation in which Paul, as he says himself, wrote in his own hand along with his signature to the letter dictated by him. It contains the Aramaic "marana tha" meaning, most probably, "Lord, come!" still another remnant of the Jewish Christian liturgy. The Jewish Christians had apparently converted Jesus' recommendation to pray God, "Your kingdom come" (Lk. 11.2; Mt. 6.10)! into a plea for Christ himself to return.[38] Here is some of the earliest evidence that, after Jesus' crucifixion, his followers reinterpreted his unrealized prophecy of an imminent kingdom of God as a promise to return in supernatural splendor. Paul's nearly exclusive interest in supernatural manifestations shows that he had embraced a Christology which mostly ignores Jesus' humanity and exalts his angelic supremacy.

[37] *The Philosophy of the Church Fathers* (Cambridge, Mass., 1970), p. 182.

[38] Whether this term referred to the Eucharist or the second coming is controversial. Richard Hiers, *The Historical Jesus and the Kingdom of God* (Gainesville, 1973), attributes the conflict to conflation between the Eucharist and the messianic banquet which was expected to accompany either the kingdom of God or the second coming. Matthew Black tends to support this thesis: "Perhaps the popularity of the formula was its ambiguity and hence flexibility: it could be fitted into different contexts." "The Maranatha Invocation," *Christ and Spirit in the New Testament* (Cambridge, 1973), p. 196.

Before the destruction of the Temple in Jerusalem (70 A.D.), a Jewish Christian composed the homily traditionally misentitled Letter to the Hebrews and misassigned to Paul. This author assumed that he was writing "in the last days" (He. 1.2), those preceding what Jesus had called the kingdom of God. Apparently, therefore, his fellow Jewish Christians were still looking forward to an imminent realization of this prophecy. "When he appears a second time," says the author, "it will not be to deal with sin but to reward with salvation those who are waiting for him" (He. 9.28). The only explicit reference to the second coming in the New Testament, this reinterpretation of Jesus' prophecy reveals the dissociation of his redemptive martyrdom from the kingdom of God, a dissociation forced upon his posthumous followers by the failure of the original prophecy to materialize then as he had expected.

The author describes Jesus as a high priest who had come to resemble his brothers or fellow Jews so closely that he was able to sacrifice his life to redeem their sins.[39] Although this interpretation of Jesus' death does not in general harmonize with the synoptic version, it tends to confirm the hypothesis that he realized his prophecy of his own death by deliberately provoking the Saducees in Jerusalem (see p. 43). The author of Hebrews likewise refers to him by the use of two images that establish a very close relationship between him and God: "He is the radiant light of God's glory [shekinah] and the perfect copy of his nature" (He. 1.3). Evidently the author saw no contradiction between these mixed metaphors. To him they meant the Son represents the Father so perfectly that he is virtually, though not actually, identical to him. Such representation probably did not, in his opinion, confer divinity on Christ, a violation of his monotheism, but this difficulty would not ordinarily occur to Gentile Christian readers of his homily. Christ's resemblance to his Father as well as his brothers, on the other hand, was a step in the direction of the two natures, still remote from the author's thinking.

Synoptic Gospels

Thus the only extant documentation to have originated before the writing of the synoptic gospels tells us little of Jesus' human life.[40] Without any evidence of other such documentation, one must assume

[39] "It was essential that he should in this way become completely like his brothers so that he could be a compassionate and trustworthy priest of God's religion, able to atone for human sins" (He. 2.17).

[40] An important exception: the institution of the Eucharist in 1 Co. 11.23-25.

that whatever facts eventually turned up in the four gospels survived by oral transmission. Since the style of most gospel texts betrays homiletical or liturgical origins, the information they convey must have been selected for its apologetic rather than its historic value. Much and perhaps most information lacking in proselytic appeal may well have disappeared. The majority of scholars believe the earliest composite oral tradition to be what they call "Q" after the German *Quelle*, a collection of sayings attributed to Jesus which subsist in portions of text common to Luke and Matthew, but not Mark. "M," another oral source, may have appeared in writing for the first time as Mark, while Luke and Matthew include later developments of it. Aside from these two major traditions, a few minor ones have been identified, such as the nativity stories independent of each other in Luke and Matthew. All but the most conservative scholars, however, have rejected them as tardy legendary accretions (see p. 57). Yet Q and M undoubtedly contain authentic material. They circulated in Aramaic before translation into Greek, which appears to have preceded their being written down in the three gospels. This translation as well as pious enthusiasm, proselytism, ambition, and polemic seem to have wreaked havoc on traditions guaranteed only by reverence for their origin and the memory of men for whom written documentation was a luxury. The proportion of truth and the degree of accuracy eventually preserved raises unending controversy, but few if any scholars still cling to the literal perfection advocated by Voltaire's contemporary Calmet. Even after Mark had based his gospel on M, the latter continued to develop orally so that Luke and Matthew, each unaware of the other, appropriated more advanced versions of it. Consequently, the three gospels often disagree on points, and sometimes important ones, in basically the same passages from M. Although each gospel is traditionally known by the alleged name of its author, none of these designations withstands critical objections. Specialists nonetheless, for convenience, persist in calling them and their authors Mark, Luke, Matthew, and John.[41] Study has uncovered some information about the identity and motivation of the true evangelists as well as the time and place of redaction. Mark seems to have been written just before, but Luke and Matthew well after 70 A.D., when a Roman army crushed a Zealot revolt in the Jewish War and destroyed the Temple in Jerusalem. The Romans practically annihilated the Jewish Christian community in Palestine, so that nearly all the extant documentation of Christianity originated elsewhere and

[41] John's gospel is also called the fourth gospel.

probably from inferior sources. Writing in Rome, the Gentile author of Mark sought to divorce Jesus from Judaism at a time when the Romans were persecuting the Christians, whom they took for a radical Jewish sect connected with the Jewish Zealots. After these tensions had subsided, another Gentile composed Luke together with the Acts of the Apostles, originally a part of the same work. Having reviewed the traditions available to him, as he says in his prologue, he "decided to write an ordered account for" (Lk. 1.3) one Theophilus, apparently an interested official. There is no firm indication of any particular place of redaction. Roughly contemporaneous with Luke, Matthew appears to be the work of a Syrian Christian. It probably served as an official manual of instruction, for it obviously promotes the interests of priestly authority. Exegetes date Matthew and Luke in the eighties, but John in the late nineties. Mark, Luke, and Matthew, which contrary to John have M in common, constitute the synoptic gospels; it is generally convenient to examine them together and John separately.

Of all the works in the New Testament, only the synoptics inspire any confidence as potential sources of substantial biographical information. Attempts to extract Jesus' authentic deeds, words, and thoughts from them have proliferated since Reimarus initiated the quest for the historical Jesus. There would be little use in reviewing the vicissitudes of this inquiry here (see p. 5), but it has produced some agreement on points appropriate to the present study: Jesus' reputation as a Galilean teacher, healer, and exorcist; his prophecy of an imminent kingdom of God; his allusions to a son of man and his crucifixion by the Romans in Jerusalem.

The Judaism of Galilee

Superstition, anachronism and xenophobia characterized the Judaism of Galilee, a remote province infested with Gentiles. Here was the homeland of the *hasidim*, rural holy men like Honi Ha-Me'aggel ("Circle-Drawer") in the first century B.C. and Hanina ben Dosa in the first century A.D., whom Jesus resembled in many ways.[42] They claimed as he did an intimate and exclusive father-son relationship with God which, however, neither to them nor to their followers meant anything like divine status. That would have been blasphemous. They healed invalids and the infirm, they exorcized devils, and so did Jesus. Jews and especially Galilean Jews believed that sin, which they understood as disobedience to God's law, causes mental and physical disorders. Under Assyrian and Babylonian influence, they

[42] See Geza Vermes, *Jesus the Jew* (London, 1973), *passim*, pp. 65-85.

had begun to blame the symptoms of what we recognize as mental infirmity on possession by demons, whom they also held responsible for accidents. The *hasidim* therefore healed by obtaining forgiveness of sins from God and cast devils out by rebuking them in his all-powerful name, just as Jesus did. They did not value material wealth, but rather reliance on God, and they preferred moral to ritual or legal standards, like Jesus. Except for his celibacy, he was one of them.

Jesus also echoed the apocalypse, a movement that had begun after the disappearance, according to Jewish belief, of prophetic inspiration since the return from the Babylonian exile (ca. 538 B.C.). In order to recoup the prestige thus denied to them, the apocalypticists attributed their own works to prophets long dead and sought to detect mysterious allusions to future events in the Old Testament. They indulged in imaginative speculations on the end of the world, a subject that fascinated many Jews, and committed themselves to a variety of eschatological expectations which did not always harmonize with each other. While some embraced visions of a final catastrophe, others like Jesus foresaw merely a period of tribulations, preceding a last judgment of the living and the newly resurrected dead. This event would inaugurate the kingdom of God, who would reign over bodily subjects living a life of complete submission to his will. Thus Jesus taught his disciples to pray God:[43] "May... your kingdom come" (Lk. 11.2; Mt. 6.9-10). The only apparent originality in his interpretation of this apocalyptic dream consisted in the imminence of its realization, for he expected it even sooner than John the Baptist. He sometimes described it as if it had already begun.

Another aspect of his apocalypticism is less clear and more controversial. The phrase *son of man* occurs frequently in the synoptic gospels, but only in sayings ascribed to Jesus and often in connection with the kingdom of God. Whether Jesus actually used it, whether he used it to refer to himself and what he might have meant by it are all in dispute. A convincingly heterogeneous majority of critics nonetheless answer the first two questions in the affirmative. Unattested in extra-biblical literature, the awkward Greek original (*huios tou anthropou*) appears to have served as a literal translation of the Aramaic *bar nasha*. This phrase resembles others in Aramaic designating one who accomplishes an action or exists in a state as the son of the action or the state. Hence, according to examples given by Cullman,[44] *son of the lie*

[43] "May he establish his kingdom during your life" is part of a prayer still current in Jewish worship, according to William Davies, *Invitation to the New Testament* (London, 1967), p. 156.

[44] Oscar Cullman, *The Christology of the New Testament* (London, 1963), p. 13.

in Aramaic means *liar* and *son of wealth, rich man*. Jesus may have meant merely *the man* and he may have been referring to himself in the third person, for *bar nasha* could be used as a circumlocution for the speaker like the indefinite pronoun *man* in German. The term never seems to impress Jesus' listeners or arouse their curiosity. Unsatisfied with such a simple explanation, however, many scholars trace Jesus' son of man back to an apocalyptic vision in Daniel: "I saw, coming on the clouds of heaven, one like a son of man" (Dn. 7.13). The author of Daniel (ca. 165 B.C.) explains that this supernatural figure would assume sovereignty over all nations, but later he identifies him as "the saints of the Most High" (Dn. 7.18). Since concurrent singulars and plurals are typical of Old Testament style, he probably intended *son of man* to mean the chosen people of God or Israel.[45] In later apocalyptic speculation, the son of man developed into a judge who would appear at the end of time to separate the just from the unjust. In all probability, however, Jesus called himself *son of man* without any intention of claiming such status, a presumption foreign to his character in the synoptics. After his death, as in other connections, his followers must have altered his contexts in order to justify reference to Daniel 7.13 or the eschatological interpretation of the passage. He did not, in any case, consider the son of man divine.

Baptism

The earliest event in Jesus' life that one can assess with any confidence was his baptism by John the Baptist, for sources independent of the Bible confirm John's missionary activity around 30 A.D. Unfortunately, they tell us little about Jesus himself,[46] nor do the gospels offer much convincing information about his baptism. In all four, the Baptist prophesies that, while he baptizes with water, someone more powerful than he will soon be baptizing with the Holy Spirit. The three synoptics then report his baptism of Jesus, which the fourth gospel nonetheless omits.

[45] "The hero of the Daniel narrative is a human being elevated above the wicked beasts [a lion, a tiger, a leopard, etc.] and granted everlasting dominion over all things, a symbolical representation, according to the interpretative conclusion, of the eschatological triumph of the historical Israel" (Vermes, p. 170).

[46] The most significant extra-Biblical source is Flavius Josephus' *Antiquities of the Jews* (ca. 94 A.D.). Josephus attests John's baptismal activity (18.5.2) and the stoning of Jesus' brother James (18.9.20). A passage about Jesus is almost unanimously considered a fraudulent insertion, which Voltaire himself detected: *"Quelle absurdité de faire parler Joseph en chrétien!"* ("Christianisme," *Dict.*, p. 109).

Afterwards, Mark relates:

> No sooner had [Jesus] come up out of the water than he saw the heavens torn apart and the Spirit, like a dove, descending on him. And a voice came from heaven, "You are my son." (Mk. 1.9-11)

Throughout his gospel, Mark describes Jesus as a messiah anxious to conceal his identity, despite constant betrayal of this secret. Here he presumes to narrate a vision experienced and known only by Jesus himself. How then did Mark find out what had happened? Probably he or his informant embroidered the bare fact of Jesus' baptism by John with speculation. Surely the question of authenticity never occurred to him, preoccupied as he was with amplifying his interpretation of M, the oral tradition he had received. Was he aware, moreover, that he was making Jesus appear subservient to a less powerful prophet? Did he perceive the contradiction in purifying the messiah of a sin he was incapable of committing? Apparently not, for he seems interested only in stressing the promptness with which God approves Jesus' act. Thus God in his haste tears a hole in the solid heavens of ancient belief and sends the Holy Spirit fluttering down in the form of a dove. Following the dove through the hole is the echo of God's voice or *bath quol* (*daughter of the voice*),[47] a chirping or moaning sound[48] that replaced prophecy when prophecy ceased. God borrows his own language from Psalms 2.7, "You are my son," which the psalmist nonetheless intended to express Yahweh's traditional adoption of a Hebrew king. The intervention of God in Mark is perhaps the remnant of a more primitive Christology, according to which Jesus resembled other men until God adopted him as his son, thus renewing his adoption of kings. But Mark himself seems to have reinterpreted this vision as a confirmation of Jesus' original Sonship. He implies that God baptized Jesus with the Holy Spirit in order to designate him as the subject of John's prophecy. Thus Jesus was the one mightier than John who would baptize with the Holy Spirit instead of water, a convenient insinuation since there is no evidence of Jesus baptizing anyone with water.

In borrowing the passage from Mark, Luke retained this pregnant insinuation, which probably does not reflect John's true thought. Luke did make changes, however. After the baptism, he depicts Jesus at prayer, an attitude announcing an important event in his gospel.

[47] "If a critical situation were developing, the noise could be interpreted as supporting... the main actor in a significant way." J. Duncan Derrett, *Jesus' Audience: The Social and Psychological Environment in Which He Worked* (London, 1973), p. 121.
[48] Like the call of a dove!

He then stipulates that "the Holy Spirit descended on [Jesus] in bodily shape, like a dove" (Lk. 3.22), thus eliminating the possibility of hallucination. The bodily state of the Holy Spirit confirms the as yet material conception of this divine attribute. Luke converted the vision perceived in Mark by Jesus alone into a miracle witnessed by all who are present, for he believed the miracle was intended to edify them. Already in this gospel the annunciation has established the congenital Sonship of Jesus. Already his explanation, when still a child, of his conversation with the theologians in the Temple as attending to his "Father's business" (Lk. 2.49) has proved his self-awareness, and so God intervenes not to inform him, but others. The apologetic intentions in Luke's modifications inspire even greater scepticism than those in most of Mark. Nor does Luke attempt to overcome Mark's failure to remove the contradictions of Jesus' subservience to John and the necessity for cleansing God's own son of sin.

Matthew, who habitually leaves no questions unanswered, tries to answer these by inserting a conversation between Jesus and John before the baptism takes place. Here John recognizes Jesus' superiority and objects that Jesus should be baptizing him. But Jesus insists that he wants to "do all that righteousness demands" (Mt. 3.15). Matthew's constant concern for reinforcing church discipline no doubt persuaded him that Jesus was merely setting a useful example. Since the practice of Christian rites began only after Jesus' death, however, this explanation hardly eliminates the contradictions in question. Otherwise Matthew follows Mark.

The author of the fourth gospel does not mention Jesus' baptism, and yet he confirms John's prophecy of one mightier than himself and the descent of the Holy Spirit in the form of a dove. Did he simply drop the baptism of Jesus? He respects history even less, far less than the synoptists, although his source, independent of theirs, apparently contained some valid information. He makes no secret of his determination to convince us of Jesus' divinity, a point he belabors from one end of his gospel to the other. The baptism of Jesus by John would obviously impede the accomplishment of this goal and he apparently left it out of his gospel for this reason. His inclusion of materials traditionally associated with it tends to prove that he knew of it. He takes evident liberties with John's expectation of a more powerful figure and God's identification of Jesus as his son:

> The Baptist declared, "I saw the Spirit coming down on him like a dove. [God] had said to me, 'The man on whom you see the Spirit come down... is the one who is going to baptize with the Holy Spirit.'" (Jn. 1.32-33)

Of all the evangelists, the fourth alone ties the two themes together in a syllogistic knot to persuade us that Jesus was indeed the subject of John's prophecy. The process of midrash attains the ultimate apologetic goal inherent in the materials originally furnished by oral tradition when the Baptist recognizes Jesus as "the chosen one of God" or "the son of God" depending on the manuscript consulted.

In all likelihood, therefore, pious speculations accumulated around one or two facts concerning Jesus' baptism. The most certain and the most embarrassing of the two was ignored, explained away and eventually suppressed. The accretion and the accretion alone then provided basic ingredients for a more sophisticated speculation. Hellenistic theology, having found the divinity of Jesus already stated here and elsewhere, expanded on it and eventually elaborated a trinity. All three elements of this dogma happened to figure in the vision appended to the baptism of Jesus in Mark.

Exorcism

The mythical temptation of Jesus by Satan follows his baptism in the synoptics. The Jews believed that, prophecy having ceased, Satan owned the world and his demons possessed a great many people. The exorcism of many demons, they thought, would herald the kingdom of God, which would bring Satan's reign and the Roman occupation to an end. When Jesus convinced Jews in rural areas[49] of Galilee that he was casting demons out of people believed to be possessed by them, he drew crowds. He also convinced them that he was healing the infirm, but this sort of thing was by no means unusual. When he prophesied an imminent kingdom of God, they believed him just as they had believed others and, when it failed to materialize, they abandoned him, so that only a small number of followers remained. During the religious and national feast of Passover, he led these to Jerusalem where the Romans, who suspected him of inciting them to revolt, crucified him. The Romans knew from experience that Galilean proselytism and enthusiasm often took the form of rebellion.[50] John neglects the Galilean ministry and, though the synoptists recognized its importance, they either ignored or more probably were ignorant of its duration, chronology, and itinerary. Yet the details they

[49] Vermes emphasizes the rural character of Jesus' speech, his comparison of sins to weeds in the parable of the sower and his avoidance of cities like Sephoris, only four miles from Nazareth (p. 48).

[50] "It is a normal reaction to autocratic government in premodern societies to express political and economic dissatisfaction in terms of religious enthusiasm" (Derrett, p. 79).

furnish conform to historical knowledge of this region before the Jewish War and Jesus' activity there qualifies as historically probable.

In the early chapters of the synoptics, numerous episodes about Jesus' exorcism of demons demonstrate that he owed most of his popularity as a Galilean holy man to this ability. The symptoms of epilepsy and hysteria, in particular, suggested the subjection of body and mind to a hostile power. Most of the demoniacs in the synoptics appear to have been suffering from one of these. Often fear of demons no doubt resulted in hysteria diagnosed as possession, which then excited further fear. Such a self-propagating cycle would account for the virtual epidemic of demonianism confronted by Jesus in Galilee. The phenomenon also had social repercussions, because the family and the community of a demoniac in Jewish society considered his affliction an evil affecting the entire group. Thus the entire group sought to eliminate the blight on its reputation and exorcists being welcome, exorcists appeared.

What actually happened when a demon was thought to be cast out? Epilepsy may have provided the most convenient opportunities, for most epileptic convulsions eventually cease anyway and the next seizure comes after a delay, sometimes a long one. Presumably exorcists had more permanent success in eradicating hysteria and physical ailments of psychosomatic origin. In these cases, belief at a more or less profound level caused the disorder,[51] belief skillfully manipulated could eliminate it as well, hence Jesus' emphasis of faith.[52] He needed only to bring the subject to a sufficiently intense emotional crisis by heightening his expectation of a cure and then suggest dramatically that the cure was effectively taking place.[53] If we can trust the synoptists, he did not use an elaborate rite for the first phase as others did, but rather relied on his reputation. For the second, he simply ordered the demon to come out, as if it dared not disobey him. What witnesses then admired as authority, a great virtue, readers may now recognize as self-confidence, a powerful illusion. Nevertheless, when exorcists

[51] "The high incidence of acute mental ill-health in Jesus' time is [probably because of] unbridled religiosity and sin-fantasies... The conditions evidenced the presence of evil spirits" (Derrett, p. 155).

[52] "Just as the state of possession is due to a man's belief in the power of demons who can enter into him, so exorcism is the result of a man's belief that they can be, and are being cast out by the exercise of superior power." Edward Langton, *Essentials of Demonology: A Study of Jewish and Christian Doctrines* (London, 1949), p. 162.

[53] "From my own experience I can testify that behavior and certainly attitudes can be changed instantly by the application of the right emotional force (rational or irrational) at the right time and in the right way, and rational argument is powerless in comparison with it" (Derrett, p. 116).

tried to cast demons out of someone suffering from a uniquely physiological infirmity or form of insanity immune to this kind of treatment, they must have failed. Perhaps they admitted too great an obstinacy on the part of the demon in order to explain their failure. Significantly, the synoptists neither mention failures nor claim infallibility for Jesus as an exorcist.

His success in casting demons out did not particularly distinguish him.[54] Apologists found more spectacular evidence in acknowledgment of his distinction by the very demons he was about to exorcize. They report incidents in which the demon cries out in fear at Jesus' approach, identifying him as "the holy one of God" or "the son of God."[55] The evangelists, who had a Hellenistic background, took such expressions to be titles conferring supernatural status on Jesus. The Greek *hagios* or holy one, however, was probably meant to translate the Aramaic *hasidh* or holy man, neither a title nor a supernatural figure. *Son of God* in all likelihood originally designated Jesus the holy man, who enjoyed the favor of God without sharing in his divinity, an idea entirely foreign to the Galilean Jews following him. Nor was any demon likely to have cried out to him, but rather the alleged demoniac himself who, as many patients, feared the doctor coming to heal him.[56]

The synoptists also narrate a number of cures by Jesus that involve forgiveness of sins and not exorcism. Physical disability such as blindness or paralysis seems particularly to have fallen into this category. Again, the group deplored the injury to its reputation because of the individual's affliction and encouraged any available holy man to restore its integrity by healing the invalid in its midst. Like other holy men, Jesus willingly performed this service. His technique, a variant of the one he applied in exorcism, consisted of convincing the patient that his sins were forgiven. When the disability had come from trauma over sin, as frequently it must have, the patient no doubt recovered more frequently than otherwise. But Jesus apparently had no competence for distinguishing between this kind of infirmity and others such as genetic defects, for which his folk psychiatry could have done practically nothing. He could only have failed in such cases and perhaps he explained his failure by insufficient faith on the part of

[54] In Mk. 9.38-40 paralleled by Lk. 9.49-50, he refuses to try to prevent another man from casting out demons in his name: "Anyone who is not against us is for us" (Mk. 9.40).

[55] Mk. 2.12; Mt. 4.6, 8.30; Lk. 4.4, 10.

[56] Known as "the dentist chair jitters," according to Robert Lundin, *Principles of Psychopathology* (Columbus, Ohio, 1965), p. 93.

the patient. For when he succeeded, according to the synoptists, he praised the greatness of the patient's faith for having made a cure possible, as indeed it probably had.

Kingdom

But Jesus did not heal invalids and exorcize demons merely to alleviate individual suffering and collective anxiety in rural Galilee. These activities, which he saw as removal of sin and evil from the world, were part of his preparation for the reign of God. They dramatized the immediacy of this reign and attracted many Jews, so that he could exhort them to repentance for the sinful past and dedication to a righteous future. Yet he intended this moral reform, which has since become the Christian ethic, only as a discipline preliminary to the kingdom of God. The urgency with which he anticipated the kingdom proves his sincerity, for it made the continuation of his popularity contingent on the early realization of his prophecy. He took no refuge in a procrastinating future: "There are some standing here," he dared to tell his disciples, "who will not taste death before they see the kingdom of God" (Mk. 9.1; Lk. 9.27).[57] He did not know, however, exactly when it would come and he had the courage to admit it: "As for [the] day [and] hour, nobody knows it, neither the angels of heaven, nor the son; no one but the father" (Mk. 13.32; Mt. 24.36). Since this admission detracted from his authority over his followers, it tends to substantiate his sincerity. But it also raises another obstacle to the claims of divinity and equality with God that would be made for him long after his death. The synoptists even furnish evidence, unwittingly no doubt, that on at least one occasion he committed an obviously human error. In all three gospels, he sends his disciples out to the surrounding countryside with instructions to prepare the people there for the kingdom of God. In Matthew, he makes his most specific prophecy on the subject: "You will not have gone the round of the towns of Israel before the son of man comes" (Mt. 10.23). Thus the son of man should have inaugurated the kingdom of God before the disciples came back to Jesus. While Matthew omits their return, they reappear in his text (Mt. 12.1) and the other two synoptists report this

[57] Mt. 16.28 is similar: "There are some of these standing here who will not taste death before they see the son of man coming with his kingdom." Matthew appears to have inserted *son of man*, so that the passage would conform to Dn. 7.13. Werner comments: "What of the situation when *all* the faithful of that supposedly privileged last generation had died, without having lived to see the *Parousia*? When this happened the expectation of the *Parousia* must itself finally have become a problem" (p. 40).

return (Mk. 6.30; Lk. 9.10). The intervening text offers not the slightest hint that the strangely sectarian and provincial version of the kingdom preached by Jesus occurred.[58] Nor does any passage in the New Testament claim that a kingdom of God ever materialized.

Messiah

The failure of this prophecy to come true within the limits set by Jesus himself convicts him of nothing worse than succumbing to self-delusion, an entirely human error. To the extent that he can be extricated from the presumption attributed to him by his apologists, he deserves the sympathy given anyone sincerely and courageously devoted to a selfless cause. The contrast between his devotion to the kingdom of God and apologetic exploitation of his memory emerges particularly from a comparison of synoptic texts treating a conversation he had with Peter. When he asks the disciples who they think he is, Peter gives various answers:

> You are the messiah. (Mk. 8.29)
>
> The messiah of God. (Lk. 9.20)
>
> You are the messiah... The son of the living God. (Mt. 16.16)

Since messianic expectations and pretentions were numerous and varied in Galilee then, Peter may well have come to the conclusion cited by Mark. Obviously, however, Luke has added a phrase redundant to Jewish ears and Matthew, an idea removed from their conception of the messiah. In Mark and Luke, Jesus neither confirms nor denies Peter's statement, but orders the disciples "not to tell anyone" (Mk. 8.30; Lk. 9.21), thus preserving the public secret of his messiahship. Mark himself appears to have superimposed this secrecy on his source material with the intention of persuading his readers that Jesus was indeed the messiah expected and yet, somehow, unrecognized by his fellow Jews. In view of Mark's efforts to detach Jesus from Judaism, however, one must discount both the messianic secret and Jesus' command not to repeat Peter's identification of him. Once this command is deleted, nothing remains in Mark and Luke except Peter's

[58] "Jesus... tells [the Twelve] in plain words [Mt. 10.23] that he does not expect to see them back in the present age. The Parousia of the son of man, which is logically and temporarily identical with the dawn of the kingdom, will take place before they shall have completed a hasty journey through the cities of Israel to announce it... It is equally clear... that this prediction was not fulfilled. The disciples returned to him; and the appearing of the son of man had not taken place." Albert Schweitzer, *The Quest of the Historical Jesus* (London, 1931), p. 357.

remark that he was the messiah, which Jesus neither confirmed nor denied. Matthew's version of his reply to Peter raises even greater suspicions: "You are a happy man! Because it was not flesh and blood that revealed this to you but my father in heaven" (Mt. 16.17). The substitution of an affirmative response for a noncommital one and the addition of the claim that God had inspired Peter to identify him as the messiah impugn Jesus' modesty. Neither Matthew nor Luke nor Mark produce any serious evidence that Jesus on this or any other occasion accepted the title of messiah. Matthew's attribution of such an acknowledgment to Jesus, in fact, suggests that only a messiah could serve his purpose. This purpose is unmistakable in his continuation of the praise he has Jesus lavish on Peter at the expense of the other disciples: "You are Peter and on this rock I will build my church" (Mt. 16.18). The Aramaic equivalent of *Peter* being *kepha* or rock, Voltaire protests that God would never build a church on so flimsy a pun.[59] Without parallel in Mark or Luke, the favoritism in this passage contradicts Jesus' usual policy of treating the disciples as equals[60] and scholars suspect that a partisan of Peter has tampered with the tradition. The very desire to found a church, moreover, betrays Matthew's own concern to provide his church with an illustrious founder despite Jesus' steadfast fidelity to Judaism.

While founding a church probably never occured to Jesus, sectarianism definitely beckoned. His native Galilee had a traditon of messianic unrest. Galilean countryfolk like those who gathered around him wherever he went found chauvinistic insurrection and eschatological revival to be much the same temptation. In 6 A.D., a reputedly messianic leader, Judas the Galilean, who had founded the Zealots together with the Pharisee Saddok, led a revolt against the Romans and their Jewish collaborators.[61] The revolt was crushed, as one might expect, but Zealotism lived on and eventually erupted in the Jewish War. The vast majority of Jews expecting a messiah yearned for a triumphant Judas. Zealotism, moreover, had much in common with Pharisaism, since both appealed, like Jesus, to the poor

[59] "Mélanchton... ne pouvait concevoir que Dieu eût employé un pareil jeu de mots... et que la puissance du pape fût fondé sur un quolibet" ("Pierre," *Dict.*, p. 348). Voltaire is using Melanchton to express his own opinion, a habitual tactic.

[60] In Mk. 9.33 and Lk. 9.46-48, Jesus settles a dispute between the disciples over who is to be the greatest in the kingdom of God. His answer in Luke is explicit: "The least among you, that is the one who is great" (Lk. 9.48). He implies the same answer in Mark and in a parallel in Matthew (18.1-5), but Matthew omits the quarrel between the disciples.

[61] S.G.F. Brandon is convinced that "Judas and Saddok... believed that the kingdom of God was at hand." *Jesus and the Zealots* (Manchester, 1967), p. 51.

and humble. Both had the same goal: rededication of the Jewish people to God by isolating them from the corruption of the Gentile world. Their methods differed: The Zealots sought to liberate them from Roman rule and restore their sovereignty over the promised land. The Pharisees strove to tighten the discipline of moral and ritual obedience to God which distinguished them from the Gentiles. Repentance for sins, they thought, would likewise hasten the kingdom of God. While Jesus himself does not appear to have been a Zealot or Pharisee, the synoptists, Gentiles all as irony would have it! obscured his tolerance of Zealots and exaggerated his rivalry with Pharisees in order to separate Christianity from Judaism. In reality, he shared total reliance on the will of God with the Zealots and unquestioning faith in the advent of God's kingdom with the Pharisees. He may have differed with the Zealots over the legitimacy of violence and with the Pharisees over the immediacy of the kingdom, but these differences are unlikely to have been extreme. In all probability, the only messiahship practically available to him had to approximate Zealot and Pharisaic expectations. Since there is little evidence, however, that he admitted to any kind of messiahship,[62] one can only note the messianic aspects of his role. Among these one must include exorcism, healing, preaching, the urgency of his message, and the large crowds he attracted. But he never exploited the opportunity implicit in Peter's identification of him as the messiah.

Atoning Martyrdom

Instead, he devoted himself almost exclusively to the illusion of the forthcoming kingdom of God. Despite his expectations, God had not established the kingdom during his Galilean ministry, not even, according to his prophecy, when he had sent his disciples out to "the towns of Israel." To accredit the absence in the synoptics of any disappointment, embarrassment, or impatience on his part would be naïve. They do indicate implicitly that he changed his mind about what would be necessary to obtain the kingdom. His conduct of the Galilean ministry suggests the belief that the conversion of many Jews would bring it about. His prophecy and accomplishment of death in Jerusalem, on the other hand, implies the necessity for an atoning

[62] After the feeding of the five thousand, "Jesus, who could see they were about to come and take him by force and make him king, escaped" (Jn. 6.15). *King* was a Gentile synonym of *messiah*. If this episode is authentic, it attests the refusal by Jesus to lead a Zealot uprising.

martyrdom.[63] His popularity in Galilee, the rumor of his messiahship repeated by Peter and the Galileans who accompanied him to Jerusalem were enough to revive fears of Zealotism there. He needed only to provoke the authorities in order to accomplish his prophecy, for one could count on the Romans to deal rapidly and ruthlessly with any challenge to their hegemony. His Galilean ministry proves his sincerity, courage, and determination. How many others have sacrificed their lives for their nation?[64] There is no need to suspect Mark's essential testimony to the first prophecy of his passion:[65]

> He began to teach them that the son of man was destined to suffer grievously... and to be put to death, and after three days[66] to rise again. (Mk. 8.31)

Luke converts nearly the same wording into a direct quotation, while Matthew adds a few words to Mark's indirect question and substitutes *he* for the *son of man*. Both return to the passive voice, *to be raised up*, as in Paul, instead of reproducing Mark's active voice. Mark continues to use the active voice in Jesus' second and third prophecies of his passion, mere rhetorical echoes, no doubt, of the first one. The active voice reappears in Matthew's versions of the second and the third, and in Luke's version of the third, Luke having omitted reference to the resurrection in the second. This vacillation between the passive and active voice in the later synoptics suggests a lingering hesitation between the Pharisaic and the Hellenistic conceptions of resurrection. The Pharisees taught that God would restore all bodies to life for the last judgment, while Hellenistic resurrection consisted in the reanimation of the body by its soul, separated from it by death. Thus Paul, a former Pharisee, speaks of God raising Christ and the Gentile Mark assumes that Jesus rose on his own. If Jesus himself prophesied his resurrection, however, he could only have foreseen a Pharasaic, not a Hellenistic event. Nor could such a prophecy have surprised his

[63] The theory exposed here follows Hiers in his partial endorsement of Schweitzer and Johannis Weiss, *Die Predigt Jesu vom Reiche Gottes* (1892).

[64] "The gospels present us with a Jesus dominated by a concern for the redemption of his people Israel." G.H. Boobyer, *Jesus and the Politics of His Time* (Salisbury, Rhodesia, 1968), p. 12.

[65] The deleted phrase *is* suspect, however: "to be rejected by the elders and the chief priests and the scribes." Bultmann appropriately dismisses such details as *vaticinia ex eventu*. Many scholars reject the entire prophecy and all others like it on the same grounds. Yet Jesus could scarcely have been unaware of what would happen to him in Jerusalem if he behaved as he intended.

[66] The Jews believed that the soul lingered for three days and then left as the corpse began to decay.

Jewish listeners, since they shared his belief that the kingdom of God would bring the resurrection of the dead.

Something in the prophecy disturbed Peter so greatly that "he started to remonstrate with [Jesus]" (Mk. 8.32; Mt. 26.22). Nowhere else in the synoptics does Jesus meet with such resistance from his own followers and nowhere does he answer them with such strong language: "Get behind me, Satan!... The way you think is not God's way but man's" (Mk. 8.32; Mt. 16.23). Matthew even inserts, "You are an obstacle [*scandalon* in Greek!] in my path." Apparently, Matthew took the passage for a fine example of church discipline, while the delicate Luke suppressed it because it detracted from Jesus' dignity. Mark's interpretation deserves more serious consideration: Peter represents the Jewish opinion that an executed and therefore defeated messiah cannot be the true messiah wielding the power of God. Mark and most Christians after him assumed that Jesus was a different kind of messiah, a spiritual rather than a military deliverer. "As often as this is maintained," says Bornkamm, "so seldom do we find it confirmed by the sources."[67] One cannot escape the fact that Christianity owes the very concept of spirituality to Hellenistic influences virtually unknown to Jesus. Over the years, critical analysis of his sayings in the synoptics has stripped away much of the Hellenistic alluvion of apology to reveal a thoroughly Jewish Jesus.[68] In all probability, when Peter protested against a prophecy dashing his hopes of following the messiah to victory, Jesus rebuked him, not because he misunderstood the spiritual nature of messiahship, but because he opposed a divine prerequisite for the kingdom of God.

In the synoptics, the reader finds most of Jesus' sayings about the son of man after Peter calls him the messiah. Immediately after Peter's declaration, in fact, Jesus evokes the suffering and exaltation of the son of man for the first time: he "was destined to suffer... and to rise again" (Mk. 8.31). Nearly all of the remaining son-of-man passages in the synoptics include at least one of these two predictions. For once, synoptic chronology appears to convey an authentic sequence of events. The synoptists, in any case, are testifying that Jesus preferred to be known as the son of man rather than the messiah, even though they want to show that he was, in effect, the messiah. Jesus nonetheless, according to them, actually defined the son of man as one who, in

[67] Günter Bornkamm, *Jesus of Nazareth* (New York, 1960), p. 172.

[68] "That Jesus' understanding of the kingdom of God was 'purely spiritual' is extremely doubtful. Synoptic sources report that, in the new era, both he and his disciples would be sitting on thrones and drinking at tables with the patriarchs" (Hiers, p. 82, n. 22).

contrast with the messiah, undergoes first human defeat and then divine vindication. This sequence has nothing in common with conceptions of the messiah current at that time, hence Peter's protest. It does belong to an entirely different tradition, that of the atoning martyr who dies for the Jewish nation.[69] The example given by Jesus when his disciples quarrel over precedence among them tends to confirm this interpretation. The son of man, he says, did not come "to be served but to serve, and to give his life as a ransom for many" (Mk. 10.45; Mt. 20.28). The superiority of the disciples should consist in their service to their fellow Jews. They should follow the example of the son of man who, by his suffering and death, would atone for the sin of the Jews which caused their bondage to the Romans. Only when he had removed this sin would God establish his kingdom in Palestine.

Jerusalem

He therefore set out for Jerusalem, the most appropriately symbolic place for a martyrdom redeeming the entire Jewish nation. To the Temple in the holy city, all Jews, except a few dissident sects,[70] owed allegiance, most paid the half-shekel tax, and many made pilgrimages. All the evangelists say that Jesus himself, like so many others, was going to Jerusalem for Passover, but John says that he had been there before and for other feasts. Neither Jesus' reputation nor his approach are likely to have escaped the Romans and the Sadducees, the Jewish sacerdotal aristocracy collaborating with the Romans to preserve their prestige, power, and wealth. Since the rise of Zealotism, both had much to fear from a Galilean leader descending on Jerusalem with his followers, however peaceful they may have appeared. At least one, perhaps several of Jesus' disciples were Zealots[71] and the synoptists give little evidence of disagreement between him and this revolutionary sect. A discreet entry into the city followed by

[69] According to Second Isaiah, the Suffering Servant (Israel) of Yahweh, the Redeemer, atones unto death for the sins of his fellow men (see especially Is. 53). Yahweh will reward Israel with "Salvation... The least among you will become... a mighty nation" (Is. 60.18, 22). W.H.C. Frend's analysis of Jewish martyrdom during the second century persecution of Antiochus IV yields the following points: (1) refusal to abandon the law; (2) representation of Israel; (3) precipitation of judgment and the resurrection of the martyr; (4) docile submission to suffering and death (see pp. 45-47). Frend, *Martyrdom and Persecution in the Early Church* (Oxford, 1965), amply illustrates these points with examples, most of them from the period preceding the crucifixion of Jesus.

[70] The Essenes, the Samaritans, the sectarians of Qumran, the followers of John the Baptist.

[71] Simon the Zealot, Judas Iscariot, and Peter. Judas' betrayal of Jesus may be an anti-Zealot fabrication.

docile behavior might have reassured the Romans and the Sadducees, but all four evangelists tell us just the opposite.

They all agree that he deliberately entered Jerusalem, to the acclamation of many people, riding on a colt or donkey.[72] Had Zecharia not prophesied, "Your king comes to you... triumphant, humble and riding on a donkey" (Ze. 9.9)? This prophecy was widely accepted as messianic in character and the evangelists mention no other occasion on which Jesus used such a beast for transportation. The crowd, most of whom had no doubt accompanied him from Galilee (Luke), not only shouted their acclaim, but also laid their cloaks (John) across his path. Surely they believed that he was the king in Zecharia. Surely the Romans thought he had made just this claim, since the placard over his head on the cross read "king of the Jews." Nor could his followers have talked him into this role, for time and again in the gospels he insists on making his own decisions. He must have known of the Roman garrison in the city and the Roman hostility to anyone pretending to royal sovereignty over a country occupied by them. His triumphal entry resembles a calculated provocation.

In Mark, Jesus leaves the city after a brief visit to the Temple, while in Luke and Matthew he expels the vendors and money changers there, an act set by Mark on the next day and by John, during a previous Passover. John furnishes the most detailed account:

> [Jesus] found people selling cattle, sheep and pigeons, and the money changers sitting at their counters... Making a whip out of some cord, he drove them all out of the temple, cattle and sheep as well, scattered the money changers' coins, knocked their tables over and said to the pigeon sellers, "Take all this out of here and stop turning my father's house into a market." (Jn. 2.16)

This market provided worshipers with animals for sacrifice and Temple money in exchange for Roman coin, an obviously useful service. To be sure, one can scarcely deny the validity of Jesus' protest in John or the probable validity of his protest in the synoptics: the merchants were turning "a house of prayer" into "a robbers' den."[73] Proper evaluation of the latter claim, however, depends on the fact that the Sadducees, who governed the Temple, profited from this commerce. Thus Jesus' assault on the Temple market challenged their authority and momentarily suspended their earnings. The four evangelists

[72] A colt according to Mark and Luke, a colt and a donkey according to Matthew! the colt of a donkey according to John!!

[73] Mk. 11.17; Lk. 19.46; Mt. 21.13.

refer to their anger in various ways.[74] Mark and Luke, for instance, say they wanted to do away with him, but dared not try because of his popularity with the people. Here is the only allusion to any possible accomplices of Jesus. As Voltaire protests, Jesus could scarcely have disrupted the Temple market on his own.[75] The Temple boasted its own police force and Roman soldiers were stationed in the Antonia fortress, which overlooked it, for the very purpose of quelling any disorder that might break out. If Jesus' assault on the market succeeded to the extent claimed by the evangelists, he must have planned it secretly, enlisted the aid of many Galileans, led a sudden attack, and beat a swift retreat. Brandon even supposes that he coordinated this operation with a Zealot uprising elsewhere in the city which diverted the attention of the Roman garrison.[76] During his narrative of Jesus' trial before Pilate, Mark inadvertently refers to "the uprising" (Mk. 15.7) as if to a recent and well-known event which he has nonetheless otherwise concealed from us. The disruption of the Temple market apparently survived his editing because it seemed harmful to the Sadducees and not the Romans. In reality, the Sadducees buttressed Roman power by their collaboration and therefore impeded the rededication of the Jewish nation to God which would have to precede the kingdom. Thus Jesus' motivation in the Temple incident must have been far closer to Zealotism than the pious outrage of evangelical and Christian propaganda. The incident likewise threatens another apologetic myth perpetrated by the evangelists, that of the nonviolent Christ. Even if Jesus had accomplished what they tell us he did, he was certainly not furthering the cause of nonviolence.[77]

[74] In John the "Jews" demand a sign to justify his act. Jesus replies, "Destroy this sanctuary [the Temple], and in three days I will raise it up" (Jn. 2.19).

[75] "Il entre...dans cette cour où de petits marchands étaient autorisés par la loi à vendre des poules, des pigeons, des agneaux à ceux qui venaient sacrifier. Il prend un grand fouet, en donne sur les épaules de tous les marchands, les chasse... eux, leurs poules, leurs pigeons, leurs moutons et leurs boeufs mêmes, jette tout leur argent par terre, et on le laisse faire! Et si l'on en croit le livre attribué à Jean, on se contente de lui demander un miracle pour prouver qu'il a droit de faire un pareil tapage dans un lieu si respectable." *Examen important de milord Bolingbroke* (1767), M. XXVI, 224. M. designates Louis Moland, ed., *Oeuvres complètes de Voltaire* (1877-1882).

[76] "The operation in the Temple apparently took place about the same time as an insurrection elsewhere in the city, which the Romans suppressed. This uprising was undoubtedly instigated by the Zealots, and it is difficult to believe that it was quite unconnected with Jesus' action in the Temple." Brandon, *Jesus and the Zealots*, p. 351.

[77] In all four gospels, one of Jesus' followers draws his sword upon Jesus' arrest and strikes off the ear of the high priests' servant. John identifies this follower as Peter. In Luke, the swordsman asks Jesus, "Shall we use our swords?" (22.50) thus implying that others were armed. Although Jesus repudiates this violence, the fact that one or more of his disciples were armed conflicts with his condemnations of violence.

Trial

They have also obscured the two trials of Jesus, if indeed there were two and if both amounted to what we call a trial. How much information have they suppressed and how much of what they have preserved can we trust? As they relate them, the trial before Pilate, the Roman procurator, and especially the trial before the Jewish Sanhedrin dominated by the Sadducees raise unceasing scepticism and controversy. Yet we have no other significant sources,[78] a fact suggesting that most of Jesus' contemporaries, even in Palestine, did not consider his fate unusual or important.[79] Although the evangelists as usual disagree over some essential details, they are all preoccupied with shifting the responsibility for Jesus' crucifixion from the Romans to the Jews.

They reveal sufficient evidence to persuade most critics that at least some members of the Sanhedrin, the ecclesiastical high court in Jerusalem, questioned Jesus after his arrest. The critics nonetheless suspect polemical intentions behind many of the circumstances given and complain about the absence of others that would tend to identify the procedure with that of the Sanhedrin. Either a legitimate trial did not take place or the source material has been altered to the point that only a few clues to the actual trial remain. The most exasperating discrepancy of all is the lack of reference to the only act of Jesus in the gospels that could have provoked the intervention of the highest Jewish court in Palestine, his assault on the Temple market. Among the accusations against him, which the synoptists dismiss as false and contradictory, they specify only one, the threat to destroy the Temple. Apologists have always hastened to draw a parallel with Jesus' prophecy that "not a single stone [in the Temple] will be left on another."[80] But this conspicuous prophecy after the event betrays the hand of Mark, forever anxious to obscure the Jewish origin of Christianity because of the Jewish War. Brandon supposes that, originally,

[78] In his *Annals*, Tacitus merely states that *Christus* was executed by Pontius Pilate (15.44).

[79] The fraudulent insertion about Jesus in Josephus' *Antiquities* (18.3.3) may have replaced a derogatory remark about him: "Jesus [was] a wise man, if it be lawful to call him a man; for he was a doer of wonderful works, a teacher of such men as receive the truth with pleasure. He drew over to him both many of the Jews and many of the Gentiles. He was [the] Christ. And when Pilate, at the suggestion of the principal men among us, had condemned him to the cross... he appeared to [those that loved him] alive again the third day, as the divine prophets had foretold these and ten thousand other wonderful things concerning him" (Philadelphia, n.d.). The context frequently expresses Josephus' contempt for such figures.

[80] Mk. 13.2; Lk. 21.6; Mt. 24.2.

Jesus had expressed the desire of many Jews for reform of the Temple administration,[81] which the Zealots eventually accomplished, in 66 A.D. at the outbreak of the war. One can well imagine the Sadducees' resentment.

Jesus' responsibility for the disruption of the Temple market must have been evident, yet John alone mentions the high priest's curiosity "about his disciples and his teaching" (18.19), essential points in the investigation of subversion. According to Mark, Luke, and Matthew, the high priest asked Jesus if he was the messiah and the son of God. A large majority of critics reject the second question as a Gentile insertion. To Jesus and his Jewish contemporaries, *son of God* did not mean, as it did to the evangelists, a congenital relationship with God, for such a concept would have violated their monotheism. "He in no sense claimed for himself the identity of son of God," declares Schmaus in his reformulation of Catholic dogma.[82] While the high priest almost certainly saw no connection between a son of God and the messiah, he may well have wondered if Jesus accepted the latter title, a subversive one from his viewpoint. Mark, Luke, and Matthew each attribute a different answer to Jesus: "I am" (Mk. 14.62); "If I tell you... you will not believe me" (Lk. 22.67); "The words are your own" (Mt. 26.64). The confirmation in Mark raises suspicion, since he obviously intended his gospel to demonstrate, among other points, that Jesus was the messiah. The messianic secret, which ends with this affirmative answer, is an attempt to explain the lack of evidence. The noncommital answers in Luke and Matthew contradict Mark and the one in Matthew resembles Jesus' reply to an equivalent question by Pilate. Matthew must have had a good reason this time for resisting the temptation to which he had succumbed in reporting Jesus' reply to the same identification by Peter. Vermes concludes that Jesus rejected the title.[83]

In Mark and Matthew, Jesus immediately adds: "You will see the son of man *seated at the right hand of* [*God*] and *coming* [*on*] *the clouds of heaven*" (Mk. 14.62; Mt. 26.64). The first italicized phrase (my italics),

[81] "By making some pronouncement of his intention to destroy the present ordering of the Temple and replace it by another more pure and holy, Jesus anticipated what the Zealots achieved in A.D. 66" (*Jesus and the Zealots*, p. 335). Brandon is referring to a saying by Jesus which he believes to be behind the false accusation before the Sanhedrin in Mk. 14.58 and Mt. 26.61 and his saying in Jn. 2.19: "Destroy this sanctuary [the Temple], and in three days I will raise it up."

[82] Michael Schmaus, *God and His Christ*, *Dogma*, 3 (1971), 8.

[83] "If the gospels have any coherent meaning at all, [Jesus'] comment on Peter's confession and the answers to the high priest and Pilate are only to be understood as a denial of Messiahship" (p. 144).

which comes from Psalms 110.1, has nothing in common with the apocalyptic son of man, but Jesus' Jewish contemporaries did consider it messianic. The second italicized phrase, which Luke omits, concerns the son of man in Daniel. All three evangelists nonetheless associate the apocalyptic son of man with the reputedly messianic phrase from Psalms, an innovation traditionally hailed as proof of Jesus' originality. Mark's Gentile ignorance and presumption are a more plausible explanation. In Mark and Matthew, the high priest condemns Jesus' answer as blasphemy, a probable insertion by Mark to substantiate Jewish responsibility for Jesus' death. The high priest is unlikely to have considered anything the evangelists quote Jesus as saying on this occasion as blasphemy.[84] What little documentation of his appearance before members of the Sanhedrin has survived suggests that they tried to induce him to confess to a claim of messiahship, the kind of messiahship they feared, and that he replied by prophesying the immediate advent of the son of man. If God had established the kingdom he expected, there would have been no need for a messiah.[85]

The Sadducees who had questioned him seem to have concluded that they had enough evidence to persuade the Romans to crucify him as a Zealot leader. When they turned him over to Pilate, therefore, they must have accused him of pretending to Zealot messiahship. All four gospels testify that Pilate asked him, "Are you the king of the Jews?"[86] a Roman equivalent of the messiah. According to the synoptists, Jesus replied, "It is you who say it" (same references), as noncommital a reply as he makes to the high priest's question about his messiahship in Luke and Matthew. One must discount John's version of his reply to Pilate: "Mine is not a kingdom of this world" (18.36). This remark implies both the messiahship of Jesus and the divinity of the messiah, both unacceptable to him. Although the evangelists have left us an incomplete and distorted account of the trial before Pilate, they do express the convincing probability that he did not admit to claiming messiahship for himself. Yet the Romans crucified him on this charge anyway, since all four gospels cite the placard above his head on the cross as reading, "king of the Jews."[87] Roman law stipulated capital punishment for the crime of causing injury to the majesty

[84] Unless he understood "I am" in Mk. 14.62 as a usurpation of Yahweh's sacred name (see p. 7), but it seems very improbable that Jesus would have said such a thing.

[85] "When the kingdom of God comes, God will bring it. God, not the messiah, will overcome the enemies of the Jews" (Hiers, p. 82).

[86] Mk. 15.2; Lk. 22.3; Mt. 27.11; Jn. 18.33.

[87] Mk. 15.26; Lk. 23.38; Mt. 27.37; Jn. 19.19.

of the emperor and the Roman authorities in Palestine customarily crucified Zealots on this charge.[88] Other passages in the gospels tend to confirm that they executed Jesus on a conviction of Zealotism: allusions to a recent uprising in Jerusalem, the release of a prisoner named Barrabbas arrested because of it, and references to him and the two men crucified with Jesus as *brigands*, the Roman term for Zealots.

Centurion

The synoptists were careful to preserve a remark made by a centurion at the foot of the cross, apparently the one in charge of the detail sent to crucify Jesus and the two Zealots condemned to die with him. But Luke's version differs from Mark and Matthew's:

> In truth this... was a son of God. (Mk. 15.39; Mt. 27.54)
>
> This was a great and good man. (Lk. 23.47)

As Mark suggests in the preamble to his gospel,[89] he intended to persuade his readers that Jesus was the Son of God. For lack of human testimony, he has recourse to demons and the voice of God to prove the suitability of this title. He also apparently inserted it in the high priest's question about Jesus' identity and converted Jesus' non-commital reply to an affirmative one. He interprets it as proof of genetic descent from God and hence Jesus' divinity. For Jesus' Jewish contemporaries, however, it designated, among other things, a fellow Jew who, though entirely human, enjoyed the special favor of God. As a Galilean holy man claiming, with public approval, the intimate paternity of God, Jesus certainly qualified as a son of God in this traditional sense. If the centurion actually did apply the title to him, he must have understood it to mean something quite different, even though the context implies that he had borrowed it from Jesus' followers. Since the Romans took the precaution of recruiting troops for the occupation of Palestine from the Gentile population, he probably interpreted it as the privileged offspring of a union between a pagan god and a beautiful mortal, for his religion admitted many such sons

[88] "Under Roman law, a claim to be a king of a province under Roman rule was tantamount to insurrection and high treason: it was by the *Lex Julia maiestatis* originally enacted by Caesar in 46 B.C. and re-enacted by Augustus in 8 B.C. a capital offence known as *crimen laesae maiestatis*, the crime of causing injury to the majesty of the emperor. [It includes] practically everything that... a governor might consider harmful to the interests of Rome." Haim Cohn, *The Trial and Death of Jesus* (New York, 1971), pp. 171-72.

[89] "The beginning of the good news about Jesus Christ, the Son of God" (1.1).

of gods. One can well imagine a soldier's superstitious admiration for a man who had died bravely, especially when he had been given the unpleasant task of putting him to death. His understanding of the term could hardly have satisfied Mark and the temptation to place it in a context implying divine filiation must have been great. Mark yielded to the temptation and Matthew followed suit, while Luke either opted for caution or chose a more cautious tradition. Yet Luke's apparent suspicion of a pagan testifying in favor of Christianity makes his version seem even less convincing. Christians have usually taken recognition of Christ as the Son of God by the centurion for convincing evidence because it comes from a normally unsympathetic source. This is almost certainly an error.

Resurrection

Once the gospels have been purged of probable distortion and accretion, they yield little evidence of a divine nature in Jesus during his lifetime. But his resurrection is even more suspect. Paul answered Corinthians denying the resurrection by impassioned assurances that the activities of Christian missionaries like him would be useless without it.[90] Nowhere, however, does he make any allusion to Jesus' tomb discovered empty, according to the four gospels, by women who had accompanied Jesus from Galilee. Would he have omitted such evidence, had he known of it? Alarmed by a challenge to the fundamental article of his faith, he could not conceivably have rejected the empty tomb. Discrepancies between the four gospel versions of the story as well as apologetic and polemical elements in them convince most scholars that they originated well after the death of Jesus.[91] Christians must have invented it to rebuke such sceptics as the Corinthians faced by Paul and especially orthodox Jews. In view of his early conversion to Christianity, the resemblance between the risen Jesus' appearance to him and the other resurrection appearances in the gospels once passed for proof of the resurrection. Christ, he argues, "was raised to life on the third day in accordance with the Scriptures" (1 Co. 15.4). Since this sentence nonetheless belongs to a creedal formulation, which he had no doubt memorized in the indoc-

[90] "If Christ has not been raised then our preaching is useless and your believing is useless; indeed, we are shown up as witnesses who have committed perjury before God" (1 Co. 15.14-15).

[91] "The empty tomb is a later legend introduced by Mark for the first time in the narrative." Reginald Fuller, *The Formation of the Resurrection Narratives* (London, 1972), p. 52. "Attempts to establish a historical kernel of the empty tomb story are not very convincing." C.F. Evans, *Resurrection and the New Testament* (London, 1970), p. 76.

trination following his conversion, one cannot value its factual probability very highly. The refrain that Christ in rising from the dead had realized Old Testament prophecy is simply false, as we have seen (p. 25). After his resurrection, according to 1 Corinthians, he appeared (1) to Cephas, (2) to the twelve (disciples), (3) "to more than five hundred of the brothers... most of whom are still alive" (15.6), (4) to James (his brother), (5) to all the apostles, and (6) to Paul himself. The addition of his miraculous encounter with Christ seems to have been motivated by the condescension of the other apostles. Since he did not see Christ, but only heard his voice speaking from heaven long after the resurrection appearances had ceased, it does not really qualify as a resurrection appearance. Consequently, one had best eliminate it from the list before comparing appearances noted by Paul with those in the gospels.

Compiled in the second century, the canonical yet spurious long ending of Mark would not serve any useful purpose in such a comparison either. The abrupt ending of the authentic text has raised much speculation about a lost ending which, like the long ending, would have contained resurrection appearances. Only the discovery of this ending or some likely allusion to it, however, could efface the definite possibility that Mark knew of no specific resurrection appearances. The angel who greets the women in the empty tomb tells them to inform the disciples that the risen Christ will precede them to Galilee: "It is there you will see him, just as he told you" (Mk. 16.7). The latter phrase apparently refers to the prophecy of the kingdom of God, which seems pathetic here. One finds two appearances in Matthew. In one (7) the risen Christ appears to the women as they leave the empty tomb and, since they grasp his feet, he must be in bodily form. He tells them to send the disciples to Galilee where he will rejoin them. There (8) he meets the eleven (after Judas' suicide) on a mountaintop and tells them to "baptize [all nations] in the name of the Father... the Son and... the Holy Spirit" (Mt. 28.19). Few scholars still maintain that Jesus actually proclaimed this trinitarian formula, the only one of its kind in the New Testament. Either Matthew borrowed it from his community or later Christians inserted it in his text. Baptismal formulas invoking Christ alone,[92] Christ who seems never to have baptized anyone, appear in Acts. Since creedal evolution usually involves elaboration, one may therefore assume that this formula was probably unknown to Jesus and late, perhaps very late.

[92] "An earlier, pre-Matthean monadic form of the tradition, which Matthew edited to produce the triadic form... continued to exist side by side [with the triadic] until the Council of Nicaea" (Fuller, p. 88).

According to Luke, Christ appeared (9) to two of his followers on the road to Emmaus, an unidentified town near Jerusalem. But once the apparent literary, apologetic, and fabulous elements have been removed from this story,[93] which occurs nowhere else in the New Testament, little substance remains. Having seen the risen Christ in Luke, these two followers return to Jerusalem where the disciples inform them that Christ has appeared (10) to Peter. Luke gives no circumstances for (10) just as Paul gives none for (1), thus one cannot determine whether they are the same tradition. In his gospel, Christ appears (11) to the eleven in Jerusalem, while, according to Matthew, he appears to the eleven in Galilee (8). In Luke's text, Christ demonstrates his bodily state by asking the disciples to touch him and by eating in front of them. Like Matthew and John, Luke apparently inserted this demonstration in the tradition to answer adversaries of Christianity who disputed the reality of the resurrection. To the disciples, the risen Christ explains that the prophets had foreseen the resurrection of the messiah, but no passage in the Old Testament says anything of the kind. Christ tells them to preach to all the nations in his name "beginning with Jerusalem" (Lk. 24.47), then goes out in the countryside and ascends into heaven. In the opening verses of Acts, the continuation of his gospel, Luke declares that "for forty days [Christ] had continued to appear to them" (Ac. 1.3), but he does not add to the three appearances he has already cited.

According to John, he appears (12) to Mary of Magdala, one of the Galilean women, in the tomb where she has found his body missing. Since he tells her not to cling to him, she must be clutching at him as in Matthew (7): he must be in the flesh. Later, he passes through closed doors into a room in Jerusalem to appear (13) to the disciples when Thomas is absent. Afterwards when Thomas returns, he refuses to believe in this appearance. Christ therefore reappears (14) to all twelve disciples[94] in the same room a week later and asks Thomas to put his hand into the wound in his side.[95] Thomas exclaims, "My Lord and my God"[96] (Jn. 20.28)! Since the Aramaic equivalent of Lord (*mar*) is the title disciples customarily applied to their teacher, Thomas may well have used it to address Jesus before his death. Unlike Paul,

[93] "There are many indications that Luke intervened at a number of... places in this story, though to what extent is a matter of controversy." Willi Marxsen, *The Resurrection of Jesus of Nazareth* (Philadelphia, 1970), p. 54.

[94] Including Matthias apparently.

[95] Further evidence of bodily resurrection. The risen Christ is no phantom.

[96] *Lord* is pre-Johannine, according to Fuller, and *God*, Johannine: "The earlier strata of the New Testament never designate Jesus unequivocally as God. The practice begins in the later writings of the New Testament" (p. 143).

on the other hand, John must have meant *Kyrios* in the Old Testament sense of *Adonai* designating Yahweh. Needless to say, Thomas was no more likely to confuse a resurrected man with his unique God than any other Jew, not even in a moment of enthusiasm. Evidently John put these words into his mouth to support his doctrine of Jesus' divinity. Christ's spirituality, moreover, in passing through the closed doors conflicts with the corporality of the wounds he exposes to Thomas' doubting fingers. Johannine propaganda so pervades all three of the appearances in John that one can scarcely hope to salvage any truth from them. The canonical appendix, which describes further appearances, is known to be late in origin.

Most reports of appearances are in sum isolated and unsupported by any details. Others are isolated, but supported by suspicious detail. Lacking in detail, the reports of an appearance or appearances to Peter in Paul (1) and Luke (10) may or may not be the same tradition. Paul gives no detail for his report of an appearance to the twelve (2), while John lavishes detail on two such reports (13 and 14), but this detail, which is loaded with Johannine propaganda, inspires little confidence. Furthermore, Christ allegedly appears to the eleven in Galilee according to Matthew (8) and in Jerusalem according to Luke (11), hence these reports have nothing in common except the number and identity of the witnesses. Together with "hosts of minor discrepancies"[97] (p. 5), Fuller raises two major contradictions: (1) between Jerusalem and Galilee; (2) between the spiritual manifestations in Matthew (Galilee), John 21, and even Mark by implication perhaps and the material manifestations in Matthew (near the tomb), Luke, and John 20.[98] Though fond of miracles, one might add, Mark reports no appearances at all, unless the end of his gospel has been amputated, which is possible but unlikely. Paul and the three evangelists prove little more than the existence of belief in appearances by the risen Christ after his death. "The resurrection," Schmaus acknowledges, "is not an event within history [and cannot] be established by means of historical research"[99] (III, 31).

[97] "The precise words of the risen Christ in Matthew, Luke, and John are heavily stamped with the characteristics of each particular evangelist." Gerald O'Collins, *The Easter Jesus* (London, 1973), p. 26.

[98] Evans finds that it is "quite impossible to harmonize the resurrection traditions" (p. 128).

[99] In C.H. Dodd's opinion, the resurrection "is the central belief [from] which the church itself grew... So much the historian must affirm; upon the truth or falsity of the belief he is not obliged or indeed entitled to pronounce." C.H. Dodd, *The Founder of Christianity* (London, 1971). Perhaps not *obliged* but certainly *entitled* and especially when he tries to ascertain the probability of such an event.

But one can go even further than this important concession. The efforts of the canonical authors to persuade their contemporaries that a dead man had returned to life on no more solid grounds than hearsay convict them of a proselytism devoid of any respect for truth. In this case, moreover, the plea for tolerance and perspective is a guilty plea for, while a climate of faith legitimized then what we condemn as fraud today, truth does not change. To be sure, some kind of truth must have produced the hearsay that formed the traditions in the New Testament. Since no one, despite many massive efforts, has found more solid evidence of this truth, however, probably no one will without the unlikely chance discovery of decisive new documents.[100] The synoptics nevertheless provide the elements of at least a hypothetical solution in conformity with scientific standards. As of the crucifixion, the son of man had not inaugurated the kingdom of God in Palestine, despite Jesus' urgent expectations throughout his ministry. His Galilean followers must have taken these expectations seriously. Even the shock of his crucifixion could not have erased from their minds the one great prophecy that had characterized his ministry and, in fact, drawn most of them to him. Nor would they have forgotten his prophecy or prophecies of the son of man's impending death and resurrection, especially when his death had just taken place. He had nonetheless had some difficulty in shifting their attention from messianic liberation in the Zealot style to the kingdom of God as he foresaw it. Despite his prophecy of his death, the crucifixion must have had a traumatic effect on them since it disqualified him as the messiah. Once their hopes had been dashed, however, nothing further could have kept them from more serious expectation of what Jesus himself had prophesied. As his exorcism of demons in Galilee indicates, expectation of miracles produces miracles, a well-known hysterical phenomenon.[101] The Pharasaic belief in the resurrection of the dead on the day of judgment, the first day in the reign of God, impregnated Jesus' faith and hence that of his followers. Under the circumstances, hallucinations in which they saw and heard Jesus

[100] The discovery of the Dead Sea Scrolls in 1947 raised hopes that such documents might soon be available. These hopes have been dashed: "Do the Dead Sea Scrolls confirm the New Testament? The two bodies of material are moving in different orbits. Not a single person, date, or event is mentioned in common in both sets of documents, hence there is no occasion for either to confirm or deny the other... The similarities have been examined and can be explained in nearly all cases by the Jewish origin of the movements. The differences are such that they seem to require independent development of the two movements." William La Sor, *The Dead Sea Scrolls and the New Testament* (Grand Rapids, 1972), p. 254.

[101] See especially p. 37.

would be perfectly understandable. The accumulation of frustrations and the shock of losing the beloved leader on whom they had pinned all their hopes were probably enough to provoke these hallucinations. Such men in such a day could scarcely have interpreted this kind of psychotic experience as anything other than resurrection appearances. Only permanent alienation, on the other hand, could have convinced them that the son of man, who was appearing to them, had actually established the kingdom of God. New expectations therefore arose and developed into the belief, forever condemned to postponement, in the second coming. When the men who had experienced the resurrection appearances involved themselves in persuading others who had not, imaginative elaboration was inevitable. The temptations of testifying to an event which has emotional repercussions in the witnesses themselves are great. Later and more deliberate apologists converted the rumors born of such testimony into more effective propaganda. They added such refinements as commands by the risen Christ to preach to the Gentiles whom Jesus had generally ignored,[102] his demonstrations of corporality designed to prove that he really had returned to a bodily life, the incomprehension and astonishment of the witnesses, a standard device in miracle stories.

Miraculous Conception

How much of the original truth did they piously obliterate? The fragmentary state of the surviving documentation implies that most of the evidence did not suit their purposes. Did they also attribute a miraculous conception to Jesus without the remotest justification in their sources? The material in the birth narratives of Luke and Matthew resembles mythology too closely to be taken for history. These narratives, which appear nowhere else in the New Testament, agree only on the manner in which this conception supposedly occurred. When, according to Luke, Mary asked the angel Gabriel how she, a virgin, could conceive a son, he answered, "the Holy Spirit... will cover you with its shadow" (Lk. 1.35). This shadow, which would vaguely imitate a mortal lover, was the Old Testament glory, the fiery cloud of God's presence. According to Matthew, "the angel of the Lord" or God's personal messenger appeared to Joseph in a dream to reassure him that Mary was pregnant, "because she [had] conceived

[102] Exceptions: Jesus' cure of the centurion's servant (Lk. 7,1-10; Mt. 8.5-13; Jn. 4.48-53), his brief incursions into the Decapolis at Gadara or Gerasa (Mk. 5.1-20; Lk. 8.26-39; Mt. 8.28-34) and the region of Tyre and Sidon (Mk. 7.24-30; Mt. 15.21-28), and Jesus' visit to Samaria in Jn. 4.

what [was] in her by the Holy Spirit" (Mt. 1.20). Both evangelists therefore imply that God himself was impregnating Mary by means of the Holy Spirit, which served as a seminal instrument in a curious transposition of human reproduction. Both likewise maintain, in the context, that Mary remained a virgin, the implication being that Joseph was not Jesus' real father. God's conception of Jesus confirms, and in all likelihood deliberately, the genetic interpretation of the title Son of God. While Paul proclaims Christ's eternal pre-existence, therefore, Luke and Matthew trace his existence back no further than his divine conception in the body of his human mother. More than any other episode in the Bible, the trinitarian participation in this conception inspired the enormous controversy from which the Augustinian Trinity eventually emerged. Yet the trinitarian performance in Luke and Matthew clearly involves subordination of Christ to God and the impersonality of the Spirit, a mere instrument of procreation. Wolfson observes (p. 176) that this trinity begins, as in Paul and John, with the birth of Christ; only two divine persons exist previously. The miraculous conception also furnished the raw material for another great controversy which would produce the dogma of the two natures in Christ, the human and the divine, although Luke and Matthew give no indication of having thought such a mystery possible or necessary. These dogmatic developments nonetheless invest the search for the origins of the myths in their gospels with special interest. The fact that the two synoptists concurred in the virginal conception of Jesus, even though they were unaware of each other's work, suggests the existence of a tradition originating in some obscure event or events, rather than outright fabrication by an unscrupulous apologist. Probably the real birth of Jesus, rather than the apologetic need to complete his biography by a birth narrative, was at least one of these events. But it also seems likely that Gentile apologists Hellenized the Jewish belief about human conception in general, which had been applied to Jesus. The Jews believed that the Holy Spirit attended the conception of every Jewish child, although the mother and father actually performed the function normally expected of them. It would not be difficult to imagine this belief being connected with the birth of Jesus, especially if he was born, as he probably was, of a Jewish couple named Mary and Joseph under perfectly natural circumstances. In the Hellenistic mind, however, the attendance of the Holy Spirit at the birth of an extraordinary man like Jesus must have been transformed into the impregnation of Mary by the Holy Spirit. Such a mind teamed with myths depicting the seduction of earthly women by the gods and the birth of divinely conceived human beings. Such a mind would likewise see the necessity for preserving Jesus from the taint of conception by a human father.[103]

John

Although the Hellenistic writer called John does not seem to have known of the virgin birth, he shared the mentality which had produced it. His versified prologue,[104] which he may have adapted from a hymn sung in his church, introduced one

> who was born not out of human stock
> or urge of the flesh
> or will of man
> but of God himself. (Jn. 1.13)

In the next verse, he identified this being as "the only Son [*monogenes*] of the Father" (Jn. 1.14), which he evidently understands in the congenital sense. Uninterested in authenticity or even verisimilitude, he dedicates his gospel to the illustration of Christ's divine Sonship and "remembrance" of his earthly career in apologetic retrospect. Other than disconnected facts, he therefore transmits little genuine information from his source, which was apparently independent of the synoptists'.

His prologue opens with a grandiloquent echo of Genesis 1.1: "In the beginning was the Word." The following verses indicate that the Word, which appears in only two other New Testament texts,[105] refers to the pre-incarnation Christ. Critical opinion disagrees as to whether Jewish or Hellenistic sources prevail in this concept. On one hand, God creates in the first chapter of Genesis by giving orders: "God said, 'let there be light,' and there was light" (Gn. 1.3). Although the phrase *Word of God* does not appear, God's Word is clearly active in accomplishing his will. The wisdom literature, which reflects Hellenistic influences, abbreviates and personifies the expression as *the Word*, which in fact resembles *the Wisdom*, since both are allegorical attributes of God. On the other hand, the Hellenistic Logos predominates in Stoicism, which defines it as a fiery vapor pervading and ordering the universe, in short a materialistic god. An Alexandrian Jew and contemporary of Jesus, Philo was apparently the first to

[103] C.K. Barrett supports this theory: "The Virgin Birth idea was an error of the Greek-minded leaders of the early Church in the second century." C. K. Barrett, *The Holy Spirit and the Gospel Tradition* (London, 1966), p. 15.

[104] Much of the information in this section comes from Raymond Brown, ed., *John* (New York, 1970) in *The Anchor Bible*.

[105] 1 John 1.1, probably by the same author, and Revelations 19.13.

attempt a deliberate synthesis of the Greek Logos and the Jewish Word. John professes the earliest known incarnation of such a synthesis, but he does not seem to have had direct knowledge of Philo.

The substitution of "the Word was" (Jn. 1.1) for "God created the heavens and the earth" in the first sentence of Genesis demonstrates John's belief that Christ was already in existence before creation took place. John adds:

> the Word was with God
> and the Word was God. (Jn. 1.1)

In the first line, he distinguishes between two separate beings in existence before the creation. In the second line, one should probably construe the noun *theos* (without the definite article *o*) as an adjective, thus "the Word was divine" would be a legitimate translation. John's commentary on the hymn in 1.18 includes one of two phrases depending on the variant one prefers, either "the only son" or "God the only son." But the second phrase enjoys more solid attestation and explicitly confirms that "the Word was God." Neither this phrase, however, nor any other in the prologue justifies consubstantiality at the expense of subordination. Nowhere, in other words, does the unity of the Father and the Son within the Godhead exclude the superiority of the Father over the Son. Subordinationism is far the more likely meaning in John and in John's day, but such critical scruples hardly burdened the conscience of fourth-century theologians bent on replacing the traditional subordinationism by an innovative consubstantiality.

The rest of John nonetheless confronted them with more obvious difficulties, as the following sayings ascribed to Jesus demonstrate:

> The Father is greater than I. (Jn. 14.28)
>
> I am in the Father and the Father is in me. (Jn. 14.11)
>
> The Father is in me and I am in the Father. (Jn. 10.38)
>
> The Father and I are one. (Jn. 10.30)

The sentences from Chapter 10 belong to a sermon given by Jesus to hostile Jews in the Temple during the Feast of the Dedication[106] and those in 14, to a farewell discourse delivered by him to his disciples before his last Passover. In neither case, therefore, can one elude the importance of his message. The contradiction between the first passage, one of Voltaire's favorite quotations, and the other three is apparent. Yet the first passage probably applies to the Hellenistic

[106] Or Hannukkah, which commemorates the rededication of the Temple in 165 B.C. after profanation by Syrian invaders.

criterion of being and the other three to the Jewish criterion of function. In John's mind, the subordination of Christ to God did not conflict with his representation of God, as in the hymn quoted by Paul (see p. 25). Nowhere, moreover, does John authorize the Patristic reconciliation of the apparent contradiction by distinguishing between two natures in Christ. The following passages from the farewell discourse elucidate Christ's representational function:

> If you know me, you know my Father too. (Jn. 14.7)
>
> To have seen me is to have seen the Father. (Jn. 14.9)
>
> Anyone who hates me, hates my Father. (Jn. 15.23)

While the following emphasize his subordination:

> The Son can do nothing by himself;
> He can do only what he sees the Father doing. (Jn. 5.19)
>
> I have come from [God];
> not that I came because I chose,
> no, I was sent, and by him. (Jn. 8.42)

The representational passages have always been used to justify the orthodox Trinity, while the subordinationist passages have been explained away from the fourth century on. John 14.28, "The Father is greater than I," has, on the other hand, justified adversaries of consubstantiality ever since the Arians.[107] There can be little doubt, in any case, that John subordinated the Son to the Father.

He also confirmed the proclamation of Jesus' divinity in his prologue by a series of four *I am* statements in imitation of Yahweh's self-identification in the Old Testament, in Exodus 3.14, for example: "God said to Moses, 'I am who I am!'" The Johannine Jesus refers to himself in this way three times in answering the hostile "Jews" (Judeans) in the Temple at Tabernacles and once on the eve of his passion in speaking to his disciples:

> If you do not believe that I am, you will die in your sins. (Jn. 8.24)
>
> When you have lifted up the son of man, then you will know that I am. (Jn. 8.28)
>
> Before Abraham ever was, I am. (Jn. 8.58)
>
> I tell you this now, before it happens, so that when it does happen you may believe that I am. (Jn. 13.19)

[107] According to Brown, Jn. 14.28 "has been the subject of much Christological and Trinitarian debate. The Arians called upon this statement to justify their Christology, and subsequently it has often been used as an argument against the divinity of Jesus" (*John*, II, 654).

In John 8.24, Jesus is threatening his listeners with eternal death, should they reject him as a redeemer. In John 8.28, the phrase *to lift up* refers to his crucifixion, his resurrection and his ascension, for all three belong to one continuous exaltation in Johannine thought. John 8.58 is Jesus' reply to hecklers who mock his assertion that Abraham rejoiced in anticipation of his coming.[108] He existed even before Moses because he preceded the creation itself. John 13.19 refers to his quotation of Psalms 41.9[109] as a prophecy of Judas' betrayal. His realization of this prophecy, he insinuates, will prove his divine status. John attributed seven other statements to him in which *I am* takes a predicate indicating a service offered to his listeners. Before his resurrection of Lazarus, for instance, he proclaims, "I am the resurrection" (Jn. 11.25). These metaphorical usurpations of Yahweh's name tell us much about John and almost nothing about Jesus.

The gospel that offers the least reliable information about Jesus supplies more raw material for theological speculation than all the other three together. If John's intentions had been respected, however, the definitive Trinity would never have evolved, since the Father, in his opinion, is greater than the Son and the Holy Spirit does not always qualify as a person. Nevertheless, he did emphasize the divinity of Christ and increase the documentation tending to support the eventual Trinity and Christology of the Church, a documentation already begun by the synoptists and Paul. Although his gospel may not have been accepted by most Christians before the middle of the second century, it had become the predominant Scriptural authority of the Church by the fourth and has remained so ever since.[110] Perhaps its greatest defect is its distortion of the synoptic Jesus. The presumptuous antagonist of the worshipers in the Temple bears little resemblance to the Galilean holy man. His bombastic and redundant sermons differ entirely from the dynamic sayings preserved by the synoptists. Like Paul, John obscured Jesus' memory more than he preserved it. Although Paul may have confused the pre-existent Christ with the Spirit, they were both preoccupied with a divine figure in existence before the creation and destined to return to heaven after an earthly interlude, which Paul neglects and which John uses to illustrate his divinity despite the incarnation.

[108] At this point, they begin picking up stones, but he leaves before they throw them.

[109] Jesus says this at the Last Supper.

[110] "In the patristic age, it was taken for granted that texts from this gospel were to be regarded as primary data of the problem which had to be solved" (whatever that problem might be). John Robinson, "The Use of the Fourth Gospel for Christology Today," *Christ and Spirit in the New Testament* (Cambridge, 1973), p. 61.

FATHERS

The New Testament in general consists of propaganda in one form or another and most of it distorts the historical truth to some extent. On this shaky foundation, the post-canonical theologians would build with surprising confidence and, during the second and third centuries, somewhat independently of each other. I do not intend to cover the entire development of Trinitarian and Christological doctrine during this period, but rather briefly to expose the doctrines of several major Fathers.

Ignatius

Ignatius of Antioch, a second-century bishop and martyr (died ca. 115 A.D.), left a number of letters in which he opposed the Docetists, who believed that Jesus had been incapable of suffering. While Ignatius defended the reality of Jesus' human life, his passion and his death, he also stressed his divinity. An important anti-Docetic passage appears in his Letter to the Ephesians:

> There is only one Physician, both carnal and spiritual, born and unborn, God become man, true life in death; sprung both from Mary and from God, first subject to suffering and then incapable of it—Jesus Christ Our Lord. (8)[111]

Physician refers to the Savior and by no means the healer.[112] Some of the paired phrases associating divine and human attributes indicate consecutive relationships and delimit the three phases in Christ's existence: *God become man, true life in death*, and the anti-Docetic *first subject to suffering and then incapable of it*. Others describe the simultaneous coexistence of godhood and manhood: *carnal and spiritual, born and unborn*, and *sprung both from Mary and from God*. In this way Ignatius combines the human birth of Jesus in Matthew and Luke with his divine origin in Paul and John (provided he knew John) without trying to determine how they interrelate. The passages citing God and Christ alone in his letters are far more numerous than those mentioning the Holy Spirit with them. Like John, he emphasizes the identity of the Father and Son at times and the difference between them at others. He definitely understood the Son to represent the Father and, probably in the same sense as John:

[111] James Kleist, trans., *The Epistles of St. Clement and St. Ignatius of Antioch* (London, 1961).

[112] In Mt. 9.12, Jesus explains why he is dining with tax-collectors: "It is not the healthy who need a doctor, but the sick."

> There is one God, who manifested himself through Jesus Christ, his son—who, being his Word, came forth out of the silence into the world and won the full approval of him whose ambassador he was. (Magnesians 8)

Thus the son, who embodies some of the Father's essence, power, and will, acts on his behalf and obeys his orders. One must not forget Christ's subordinate role as God's ambassador and especially when Ignatius calls Christ God: "God Jesus Christ" (Trallians 7). One finds a text evoking all three divine persons in his Letter to the Ephesians, whom he describes as

> stones of the Father's temple... to be taken aloft by the hoisting engine of Jesus Christ, that is the cross, which the Holy Spirit serves... as a rope. (9)

This metaphorical contraption implies a trinity in which each person specializes in a salvific function. It suggests the successive subordination of the Son to the Father and of the Holy Spirit to the Son. Ignatius in fact confirmed the first element of this hierarchy in his Letter to the Magnesians whom he exorted to submit to their bishop "just as did Jesus Christ... to the Father" (13). The relegation of the Spirit to the function of a mere rope in the salvific hoist tends to rank him third as one would expect, yet Ignatius appears to have considered him a person rather than a thing. He told the Philadelphians that "the Spirit is not led into error, since he proceeds from God" (7). Like Paul, he identifies the pre-existent Christ with the Spirit, so that his trinity begins with the incarnation. Without having given it any special attention, he believed in a functional and hierarchic trinity of divine persons. He looked upon Christ as both human and divine, but only during his earthly life, and he did not try to explain how the two natures could coexist in a single person.

Justin

Beheaded in 165, Justin was a more productive theologian than Ignatius. Of his substantial works, however, only two *Apologies*—the second is probably a supplement to the first—and the *Dialogue with Trypho*[113] have survived. A converted pagan, he spurned "the things too disgraceful to mention" attributed to the gods he had abandoned. Instead, he had come to worship "the unbegotten and impassible God" (1 *Apology* 25) which he found in Christianity. But middle Platonism rather than Judaism had persuaded him that this God is so

[113] Quotations in this section will come from Thomas Falls, trans., *Writings of Justin Martyr* (London, 1961).

remote from his creatures that he needs an intermediary to communicate with them. Before Jesus' conception, the pre-incarnation Word, whom Justin identified with the Spirit, assumed this role in his theology. "It is not right to understand the Spirit and the power of God as anything else than the Word, who is also the first-begotten of God" (1 *Apology* 33). Having made this statement, Justin paraphrases the fertilization of Mary by the Spirit in Luke 1.35. This task accomplished, the Spirit "rests" or "ceases" (*Dialogue* 87) until Christ bestows him on his followers after the ascension.[114] Justin therefore believed in a trinity, albeit a subordinationist one: "We... believe [the son of God] to be in the second place and the prophetic spirit in the third" (1 *Apology* 13). The prophetic spirit was of course the one who had inspired the prophecies of the Old Testament, but Justin assigns the same function to the Word further on.[115] In the *Dialogue* he even tries to persuade Trypho, a Jew, that all the appearances by God in the Old Testament were really the work of the Word. In fact Justin was anxious to exonerate God of the anthropomorphic activities assigned to him in the Pentateuch.[116] To explain another effect common to the Spirit and the pre-incarnation Word, he adopts the "seminal Word" (2 *Apology* 13) from Stoicism. The Word sowed the seed of reason in philosophers like Socrates who, since they lived before Christ, had no opportunity to embrace his teaching. In this way, Justin sought to repair an oversight loudly deplored by Voltaire (see p. 190).[117] He likewise explored the evolution in the relationship between divinity and humanity in Christ which Ignatius had neglected. Like Ignatius he did not shrink from calling Christ God: "The Father of all has a Son, who as the first-born Word of God, is also God" (1 *Apology* 63). From all eternity, the Word was "with" (2 *Apology* 6) God, he existed in other words as a "rational power" (*Dialogue* 61) within God. Before the creation, God begot the Word as "when one fire kindles another

[114] "In strict logic, there is no place in Justin's thought for the person of the Holy Spirit, because the logos carries out his functions." L.W. Barnard, *Justin Martyr: His Life and Thought* (Cambridge, 1967).

[115] "The prophecies... were [not] spoken by the inspired prophets of their own accord, but by the Word of God who prompts them" (*1 Apology*, 6).

[116] "The ineffable Father and Lord of all neither comes to any place, nor walks, nor sleeps, nor arises, but always remains in his place, wherever it may be, acutely seeing and hearing, not with eyes or ears, but with a power beyond description" (*Dialogue*, 127).

[117] In his *Pucelle* (begun 1731), the Franciscan Grisbourdin arrives in hell: "Sépulcre où gît la docte antiquité, / Esprit, amour, savoir, grâce, beauté / ... / Les meilleurs rois sont avec les tyrans / [exemples] / Et vous, Socrate, enfant de la sagesse, / Martyr de Dieu dans la profane Grèce / ... / Tous malheureux morts sans confession" (B., VII, 348).

without losing anything, but remaining the same" (*Dialogue* 61). When the Spirit impregnated Mary, "Christ... became the whole Word, namely, Word in body and soul" (2 *Apology* 10). Justin therefore not only retains the metaphysical engenderment of Christ in Paul and John, but also his physical conception in Luke and Matthew. The first operation produced the Word or Spirit, differentiated from each other only by modal distinctions before the incarnation. The second separates them, although the Spirit remains inactive during the life of Christ. Consequently, all three elements in Justin's trinity are active only from the bestowal of the Spirit after the ascension onward. He assigns power to each of the three persons relative to their rank in the hierarchy[118] and this power, which he compares to fire,[119] assures the unity of the Godhead.

Irenaeus

Another native of Asia Minor, Irenaeus immigrated to Western Europe and became bishop of Lyon in 177-178. *Against Heresies*, his most important work, reveals the mind of a polemicist, not a theologian. With Justin and Ignatius he shared the transcendent God of middle Platonism: "One cannot know God" (4.20.1).[120] But his conception of "the Son eternally coexisting with the Father" (2.30.9) excludes the metaphysical engenderment of the Word in their theology. How then, according to him, did the Father beget his "uncreated" (3.8.3) Son? "No man knows" (2.28.6), answered Irenaeus, who distrusted theological speculation. He conferred the title of God on the Son as well as the Father, but not on the Spirit.[121] He identified the pre-incarnation Son with the Word and the pre-incarnation Spirit with Wisdom. Since "no man is above his master" (2.28.6), he subordinated the Son to the Father. He reinforced this subordination by reference to Psalms 33.9:

> [Yahweh] spoke and [the world] was created;
> he commanded, and there it stood.

[118] "The first power after God the Father and Lord of all things is the Word, who is also his Son, who assumed human flesh and became man" (*1 Apology*, 132).

[119] "This power was generated from the Father, by his power and will, but not by abscission, as if the substance of the Father were divided... I cited the example of fires kindled from a fire" (*Dialogue*, 128). Here is a partial anticipation of consubstantiality.

[120] John Keble, trans., *Five Books of Irenaeus, Bishop of Lyons, Against Heresies* (London, 1872).

[121] "The Spirit [has] sealed both with the title of God:... the Son [as well as] the Father" (3.6.1).

"Who therefore did he command?" asked Irenaeus. "The Word, no doubt" (3.8.3). His interpretation of the incarnation depends on Paul's theory that Christ, a second Adam, redeemed the offspring of the first.

> The Word of the Father and the Spirit of God, having united with the ancient substance of Adam's formation, rendered man living and perfect. (5.1.3)

The Word and the Spirit therefore impregnated Mary together, but Irenaeus did not explain how they could both participate in this operation. Contrary to what one might expect, moreover, he saw it as divinity *swallowing* humanity *up* (3.20.1). The incarnation thus removed the curse of Adam's sin and bestowed the promise of salvation on mankind. Furthermore, the incarnate Son was both God and man, "God summing up anew in himself the old formation of man" (3.18.7) or recapitulation as Irenaeus called it. He does not seem to have anticipated the difficulty involved in combining divinity and humanity in a single person. Concerning the relationship between the incarnate Son and the Father, he derived a striking formula from John 14.9, "He who has seen me [Jesus] has seen the Father": "The Father," commented Irenaeus, "is the invisible of the Son and the Son the visible of the Father" (4.6.6). Presumably he did not mean this literally, that the Father was merely a phantom replica of the Son's human body! However enigmatic, his interpretation of John would lend itself to speculation on the consubstantiality of the Father and the Son. Irenaeus, who appears to have had no idea of this doctrine, definitely believed in a subordinationist and functional trinity:

> God... having been seen... prophetically through the Spirit and... adoptively through the Son... shall also be seen paternally in the kingdom of heaven, the Spirit truly preparing man [for] the Son of God, and the Son leading him to the Father, while the Father, too, confers [upon him] incorruption for eternal life, which comes to everyone... seeing God. (4.20.5)

Preparing, leading, and *conferring* clearly build a hierarchy of increasing powers, hence subordination. The Spirit's inspiration of prophecy during the Old Testament era simply repeats Justin and the contemporary tradition. But the adoptive function assigned to the Son refers to his recapitulation of human nature by means of the incarnation, an original interpretation by Irenaeus. The ambiguous chronology and omissions such as the pre-incarnation role of the Son show that Irenaeus did not concern himself very much with thoroughness. Engrossed no doubt in his war on heresy, the bishop of Lyon ignored some of the gaps in his theology and covered others by rhetoric apparently devoid of conceptualization. Consequently, he seems particularly unreliable for a Church Father and, according to some churches, a divinely inspired source.

Clement

Unlike Irenaeus, Clement of Alexandria, who fled from Egypt during the persecution of Christians in 202-203, was a true philosopher and theologian. In accordance with middle Platonism, he conceived of God as transcendent unity. He therefore included "the One is indivisible" (5.12)[122] among his *Carpets* of loosely related thoughts and declared God "ineffable by his power" (5.65). Yet middle Platonism likewise required divine immanence and omnipresence, so that God could communicate with his creation. Clement naturally turned to the Son for this mediation: "God... cannot be the object of knowledge; but the Son is wisdom and knowledge and truth" (4.165). The Word was a far more adequate intermediary than Jesus, for he penetrated everywhere like the rays of the sun, as the Stoic Logos had before him. Clement was probably thinking of the Word rather than Jesus when, from his scholarly viewpoint, he entitled one of his works *The Instructor*. Assuming God to be mind (Gk. *nous*), he deduced from 2 Corinthians 4.4, "Christ... is the image of God," that God reproduced an image of himself in generating the Word. The second mind resembled the first so closely that Clement called him "God" (1 *Instructor* 4), "really God" (*Exhortation* 10.10) and even "all-powerful God" (3 *Instructor* 39). Must one in fact interpret "Both are one God" (1 *Instructor* 8) as proof of monarchial (modal) unity? No, since Clement distinguished between the essential Logos or Nous itself and the offspring of the essential Logos which he usually referred to simply as the Logos. Before the creation, the Word (Logos) issued from God (Nous), but without separating from him, so that he remained a part of the divine substance. Although Clement looked upon the Father and Son as consubstantial, a word that appeared only later, he adhered to the subordinationism typical of his day. In a prosopopoeia imagined by him, the Word allegorizes himself as "the arm of the Lord... the will of the Father" (*Exhortation* 12.120). The subordinationism suggested by these phrases seems difficult to reconcile with consubstantiality in a trinity. Having accomplished the creation, the Word appeared as Yahweh in the Old Testament, spoke through

[122] William Wilson, trans., *The Writings of Clement of Alexandria* (Edinburgh, 1867, 1869).

the prophets and became Jesus. Each of these three actions constituted a degree of incarnation according to Clement, who considered the flesh merely a visible manifestation of the spirit. Despite his opposition to Docetism, he looked upon the third and most complete incarnation as nothing more than role-playing: "The Word... enacted the drama of human salvation" (*Exhortation* 10.10). Jesus did not eat, he argued, to nourish his body, but rather to show other men that he was no Docetic phantom. Clement does not seem to have realized that this conduct amounted to deceit unworthy of such a divine being. He further submitted that the Savior "was... inaccessible to any movement of feeling, either pleasure or pain" (6 *Carpets* 9.71), the fundamental tenet of Docetism. Consequently, he only divorced himself from this heresy by his rhetorical opposition to it. His Platonic preoccupation with the superiority of spirit over matter may have led him astray. Like other early Fathers, he often spoke of the Spirit and the Word before the incarnation as if they were the same figure: "The Lord Jesus, that is the Word of God, the Spirit incarnate" (1 *Instructor* 6.43). He nonetheless professed a trinity: "The universal Father is one, and one the universal Word, and the Holy Spirit is one and the same everywhere" (1 *Instructor* 6.42). This sentence leaves important questions unanswered, such as the subordination and consubstantiality of the Spirit. Clement's writings are in fact more ambiguous than the foregoing exposition suggests, for he was unable to formulate a coherent doctrine. He did render Christianity a great service, however, by his instruction of a student who would more than make up for his deficiencies.

Origen

Origen, the student in question, was one of the most dynamic thinkers ever to profess Christianity. Unfortunately, the Church repudiated much of his doctrine long after his death and most of his phenomenal written production was destroyed on the pretext of heresy. Voltaire remembered him as the ascetic who had castrated himself in order to concentrate exclusively on theology.[123] Origen directed Clement's school in Alexandria until 231 when, persecuted by the archbishop, he founded a new school in Caesarea of Palestine where he died in 253. The transition from Clement's middle Platonism to Origen's Neoplatonism altered neither the transcendent unity of the Father

[123] "Il y avait sans doute une grande dose de folie dans la philosophie d'Origène, puisqu'il s'avisa de se couper les testicules," *Examen important de milord Bolingbroke*, M. XXVI, 260.

nor the universal immanence of the Son. Origen adhered to Clement's Platonic conception of God:

> Since... the God of the universe is mind... [he] is not comprehended by any being other than [what is] made in the image of that mind. (*Against Celsus* 7.38)[124]

The Logos therefore remained "the archetypal image" (*On John* 2.2)[125] of the divine Nous. Origen followed the earlier Fathers and John in professing both the unity of the first two persons and the distinction between them. But he also introduced two words into the discussion of this mystery which, after semantic evolution, would figure in the Trinitarian controversy of the fourth century. In his works, *hypostasis* designated a separate divine existence, while *homoousios* or *consubstantial* indicated that they consisted of the same divine substance. With these two concepts in mind, he did not shrink from speaking of two Gods as well as a unique God in the same passage.[126] He distinguished between them by subordinating the Son to the Father as the following sentence demonstrates: "The Son is not mightier than the Father, but inferior to him" (*Against Celsus* 8.15). The substance common to Father and Son, on the other hand, consisted in their "identity of will" (*Against Celsus* 8.12), for Origen considered willpower a substance. Not only did the Father and the Son want the same thing, but the Son actually obeyed the Father's commands. The Son even owed his existence to the Father's will: His "birth from the Father is... an act of [the Father's] will proceeding from the mind" (*On Principles* 1.2.6).[127] Origen agreed with Clement that the Father needed merely to wish something in order to create it spontaneously. But he further believed that the substance of the Father's will was perpetually reproducing itself as the Son: The Father "continually gives existence to"[128] the Son. On this score, he unwittingly anticipated a reply to Arianism when he wrote, "There is no time when [the Son] did not exist" (*On Principles* 4.4.1). He probably borrowed eternal generation from Stoicism and from Platonism the pre-existence of souls, among which he included

[124] Henry Chadwick, trans., *Contra Celsum* (Cambridge, 1953).

[125] My translation: *Commentaire sur saint Jean* (Paris, 1966).

[126] "Origène dit: 'N'est-il pas vrai alors qu'il y avait un Dieu fils de Dieu, qui est fils unique de Dieu, *le premier né de toute la création*, et que nous ne faisons pas scrupule d'affirmer, en un sens, deux Dieux, d'affirmer en un autre sens, un Dieu unique.'" Jean Scherer, trans., *Entretien d'Origène avec Héraclide* (Paris, 1960), pp. 55-56. The italicized phrase tends to support Arius.

[127] G.W. Butterworth, trans., *Origen on First Principles* (London, 1936).

[128] Fragment from a homily on Jeremiah 9.4, quoted from T.E. Pollard, "The Exegesis of John 10.30 in the Early Trinitarian Controversies," *New Testament Studies*, 3 (1956-1957), 93, n. 2.

Jesus'. Before Jesus' conception, his soul combined with the Word, an association by which it became divine, as iron becomes fire (red hot) over flames. When his body had attained fully human form in Mary's womb, this Word-soul joined it in turn. Origen was the first to speak of this God-man, a combination that resulted in the subsequent deification of the human component:

> His mortal body and the human soul in him received the greatest elevation not only by communion but by union and intermingling, so that by sharing in his divinity he was transformed into God (*Against Celsus* 3.4.1)

The Creator, explained Origen, could assign any qualities he wished to matter and substitute some for others whenever convenient. Despite the successive deification of Jesus' soul and body, he retained his human nature, for Origen initiated the distinction between his human and divine natures. Nor did he doubt that Jesus' human nature had suffered and died. His human body, he further specified, "was born of a virgin and the Holy Spirit,"[129] a sentence that reveals his belief in the separate existence of the Holy Spirit before the conception. Like the other early Fathers, however, he neglected the Spirit in favor of the Father and especially the Son. He did suppose that the Spirit proceeds from the Father and through the Son, the subject of a dispute between the East and the West many centuries later. In his trinity, the Spirit depends on the Son for existence just as the Son depends on the Father.[130] Subordination is explicit in his doctrine:

> The power of the Father is greater than that of the Son and of the Holy Spirit, and that of the Son is more than that of the Holy Spirit. (*On Principles* 1.3.5)

Between the persons, he lessened the functional distinctions, thus anticipating the eventually orthodox Trinity. "There is no difference in the trinity," he said, "but that which is called the gift of the Spirit is made known through the Son and operated by God the Father" (*On Principles* 1.3.7). The immateriality of the three persons, a steadfast element of Hellenistic Christianity, subsisted in his theology.

Tertullian

The Latin polemicist and apologist Tertullian, who embraced Christianity ca. 193 and Montanism (a Christian sect) ca. 207, believed

[129] *On Principles*, I, Preface, 4.

[130] "Nul autre que le Père n'est sans origine... Si toutes choses furent par le Verbe, le Saint-Esprit a plus de dignité que tout le reste... Il ne porte pas... le nom de Fils de Dieu... il semble que le Saint-Esprit ait besoin [de l']intermédiaire [du Fils] pour subsister," Cécile Blanc, trans., *Commentaire sur saint Jean*.

every existing person and thing to be corporeal, even the Deity. "Nothing lacks bodily existence" (*On the Flesh* 11),[131] he wrote; "God is a body" (*Against Praxeas* 1).[132] Unlike Origen, he conceived of an initial time when "God was alone" (*Against Praxeas* 5), though not strictly speaking, for he had divine reason within him. Thought being potential discourse, "he... put forth the Word" (*Against Praxeas* 5), thus generating the Son from his own substance. Even though Tertullian called this divine substance spirit, he considered it a rarefied form of corporality: "Spirit has a bodily substance of its own kind" (*Against Praxeas* 1). Nor did he admit any division in this substance separating the Father from the Son: "Nothing... is alien from the original source whence it derives its own properties" (*Against Praxeas* 8). That "Christ is Spirit of Spirit and God of God" (*Apology* 1) seemed perfectly logical to him. Yet the first two persons in his trinity remained entirely distinct in his mind, because "the Father is the entire substance, but the Son is a derivation and portion of the whole" (*Against Praxeas* 9). Consequently, he insisted that they were "two separate beings" (*Against Praxeas* 4). Although he needed only to follow his predecessors in assigning the usual creative and prophetic roles to the Word, the incarnation would seem to have confronted him with a problem because of his materialism. How could the indivisible substance of his divinity become in part a human being walking about freely on earth without division? This question might have daunted a lesser mind. Tertullian submitted that a protrusion of the divine substance identical to the Son penetrated into Mary's womb where it was clothed in flesh descended from Adam. In this way, the divine substance joined with human substance to form Jesus: "the powers of the Spirit proved him to be God, [while] his suffering attested the flesh of man" (*On the Flesh* 5). Tertullian's designation of the divine substance as spirit may have caused him to hesitate, as he did, between binitarian and trinitarian rules of faith. Occasionally, he equated the Spirit to the Word: "the two are one" (*Against Praxeas* 26). Elsewhere, however, he proclaimed a "third name in the Godhead and [a] third degree of the divine majesty" (*Against Praxeas* 30). He likewise anticipated Roman dogma by deriving "the Spirit from... the Father through the Son" (*Against Praxeas* 4). The successive derivation of each person in the trinity from the preceding one confirmed the traditional subor-

[131] *The Writings of Quintus Sept. Flor. Tertullianus* (Edinburgh, 1869-1870): all quotations except those from *Against Praxeas*. Wolfgand Bender, *Die Lehre über den Heiligen Geist bei Tertullian* (Munich, 1961), was particularly useful in the preparation of this section.
[132] Ernest Evans, trans., *Tertullian's Treatise Against Praxeas* (London, 1948).

dinationism in his opinion: "Everything which proceeds from something else must needs be second to that from which it proceeds" (*Against Praxeas* 8). He defined trinitarian economy as forcefully as trinitarian unity: this economy consists in the relationship between the persons. To the continuity of substance he added the unity of will or rule known in those days as monarchy. For the first time, moreover, he explicitly bestowed divinity on the Spirit as well as the other two persons.[133]

Both Tertullian in the West and Origen in the East therefore advocated a trinitarian hierarchy. During the second and third centuries, in fact, the subordinationist trinity had predominated. For reasons known and unknown, however, this venerable orthodoxy suddenly became radical heresy in the early fourth century.

Arius

Towards 320 the presbyter Arius disagreed with his bishop, Alexander of Alexandria, before fellow clergymen in a church. Arius was defending the supremacy of God and Alexander, the divinity of Christ. Alexander called a synod of bishops under his jurisdiction in Egypt and Libya, allowed Arius to argue his case before them and, once a heavy majority had voted against him, excommunicated him and his followers. Alexander then wrote letters to foreign prelates, informing them of his action and explaining why he had taken it. But Arius countered with a letter-writing campaign of his own and won considerable support in the East. He already enjoyed popularity with the people of Alexandria. Eventually forced to flee into exile, he first received the hospitality of the learned Eusebius of Caesarea and then that of the influential Eusebius of Nicomedia, a fellow student of Lucian in Antioch.[134] The Arian party tried to force Alexander to reinstate the exiles, but he steadfastly refused. This dissension came at a time when, after two and a half centuries of sporadic persecution, the emperor Constantine was giving Christianity his protection. Irritated by the controversy, he sent Hosius, bishop of Cordova, to Alexandria with a letter of reprimand for Arius and Alexander. Much admired by Voltaire (see p. 186), this letter shows that Constantine thought the controversy little more than a pedantic bickering over

[133] "The Father is God, and the Son is God, and the Holy Spirit is God" (*Against Praxeas*, 13).

[134] Little is known of Lucian's teaching, a probable source of Arius' doctrine. His literal exegesis of the Bible contrasts with Origen's allegorical interpretation. Origen is another probable source of Arius' opinion.

theological minutia. Upon arrival in Alexandria, however, Hosius discovered, if he did not already know it, that Alexander's position resembled that of the western Church, while Arius' did not. After a fruitless attempt to arbitrate the conflict, probably by exhorting the Arians to yield, he reported to Constantine that scolding both parties would not end the dispute. He and Alexander apparently persuaded the emperor to call a council of all the prelates in Christendom, so as to condemn Arius and establish a dogma acceptable to them. Although few western bishops attended and the pope merely sent representatives, the Council of Nicaea was later designated as the first ecumenical council in history.

What was then the doctrine that convinced them of such a necessity? Unfortunately, little documentation has survived other than what the enemies of Arius transmitted with the intention of denigrating the movement. How can we be sure they have chosen the most significant texts and refrained from altering them? Not only do ancient and even some modern historians treat Arius with a contempt unwarranted by the evidence, but also they tend to hold the founder of the movement responsible for its later extremism. The ideas expressed in Arius' letter to Eusebius of Nicomedia appear archaic rather than innovative. According to this text, God created the Son and did not engender him:

> Le Fils n'est ni engendré, ni partie de l'inengendré [Dieu] de quelque manière que ce soit, ni tiré d'un sujet préexistant, mais par volonté et par dessein [de Dieu] il commence d'exister avant les temps... Dieu monogène, immuable. (Boularand I, 44)[135]

By setting the creation of the Son in a pre-temporal era and hailing him as unchanging God, Arius makes unwitting concessions to future orthodoxy. The word *monogenes*, on the other hand, is only an apparent concession, for the Arians did not distinguish between such terms as *gentos*, made, and *genntos*, engendered, but understood them both in the sense of originated. Thus Arius believed, as Origen had, in a second God, though a second God created and adopted by the first one. However soon the Father made the Son, in his opinion, there had to be a time when the Son did not exist:

> Avant d'être engendré ou créé... il n'était pas, car il n'était pas inengendré [*agenntos*]. On nous persécute pour avoir dit: Le Fils a un commencement. Dieu est sans commencement. (Boularand I, 44)

Arius contradicts Origen's assertion that there never was such a time,

[135] Quoted from Ephrem Boularand, *L'Hérésie d'Arius et la "foi" de Nicée* (Paris, 1972). Translation by Boularand.

because he does not admit the doctrine of eternal generation. He is more concerned with the priority of the Father than the status of the Son anyway, as a letter from him to Alexander demonstrates. From both a grammatical and a theological viewpoint, the Father is the subject and the Son, the object in this text. To his earlier concessions, Arius adds recognition of the Son as a "créature de Dieu parfaite, mais non pas comme une des [autres] créatures" (Boularand I, 49). Yet he rejects the possibility of two eternal and unbegotten Gods, a belief he implicitly ascribes to Alexander and his allies. "Dieu est avant tout," he argues, "même avant le Fils, comme nous l'avons appris de toi qui le prêchais au milieu de l'Eglise" (Boularand I, 50). Since Alexander had inherited perpetual generation from Origen, however, he could believe in the priority of the Father without sacrificing the coeternity of the Son. Another third-century innovation that offended Arius is consubstantiality. If the Son "était une partie de [Dieu] consubstantielle et comme une émission, le Père [serait] composé, divisible et changeant" (Boularand I, 50), all of which, in his opinion, weaken the deity. He apparently could not conceive of a spiritual existence to which one may add or from which subtract without alteration. He insisted on a materialistic interpretation of consubstantiality which made it impossible for him to accept it. His commonsense objections suggest that, despite his reputation as a dialectician, his reactionary theology resulted from a lack of imagination. His enemies' complaints of his success with the uneducated tend to support this hypothesis. In order to propagate his teaching among them, he composed a poem in the Alexandrian equivalent of light verse, entitled *Thalia*, meaning banquet or drinking song. If fragments from this work preserved by Athanasius can be trusted, Arius completes his description of the Son's cosmic birth by the opinion that "le Verbe de Dieu... a été tiré du néant" (Boularand I, 57). The creation of the Word from nothingness effectively follows from the rejection of consubstantiality. According to other fragments, the Father adopted the Son, who has an imperfect knowledge of the Father and even of his own substance. Athanasius paraphrases still another fragment as follows:

> Les essences du Père et du Fils et du Saint Esprit sont divisées par nature, étrangères, séparées, incompatibles et ne participent pas l'une de l'autre. (Boularand I, 81)

Would the Trinity have subsisted if the Church had endorsed this opinion? Perhaps the threat to what has come to be a fundamental dogma has caused Arius' persistent notoriety as a heretic. In reality, he was merely a reactionary theologian in a day of progressive theology and the founder of a movement that soon left him behind. The word "heretic" derives from the Greek *hairein*, to choose: Arius made the mistake of choosing the past instead of the future.[136]

Nicaea

At the Council of Nicaea (325), he distinguished himself rather as a scapegoat than a leader. Eusebius of Nicomedia had already assumed the leadership of his faction, while Eusebius of Caesarea was maneuvering for a compromise acceptable to both sides. Nor did Alexander of Alexandria lead the opposition, a responsibility that Hosius may well have reserved for himself even before his trip to Egypt. More than any other prelate, he enjoyed the confidence of the first Christian emperor who, for his part, appears to have intended the council to unify his empire in a unique faith. Like his pagan predecessors, he was backing a religion more to consolidate his authority than to satisfy his spiritual needs. He knew enough about theology, nonetheless, to preside over the council occasionally and, though prompted no doubt by Hosius, to propose consubstantiality. In all likelihood, Hosius adhered to the monarchianist interpretation of consubstantiality prevalent in the West. More proficient in the theological semantics of the Greek language than Constantine, a fellow westerner, Hosius was in a position to acquaint the emperor with *homoousios* or consubstantiality. Having approved a Caesarean creed submitted as a compromise by Eusebius of Caesarea, Constantine recommended the insertion of *homoousios*. The Arians opposed the term on the grounds that it was not in the Bible, that it implied a division of God's substance and that it raised the Son to the uncreated status of the Father. They especially feared any lessening of God's supremacy. Typically, however, their very resistance persuaded their enemies to include it in the creed eventually adopted, one different from Eusebius'. In this one, they also inserted anti-Arian clauses and appended anathemas of Arian opinions. The clauses against Arianism occur in the second section devoted to Christ:

> We believe... in one Lord Jesus Christ, the Son of God, begotten from the Father, only-begotten, that is, from the substance of the Father, God from God, light from light, true God from true God, begotten not made, of one substance [*homoousion*] with the Father.[137]

[136] "If the newly developing Catholic Church be measured by the same rule by which it condemned other groups and tendencies as heretical, it is itself nothing other than a heresy, but certainly the most pregnant, which ultimately had driven triumphantly all others from the field" (Werner, p. 52).

[137] Quoted from John Kelly, *Early Christian Creeds* (London, 1963), p. 215.

True God from true God assures full divinity to the Son, a point denied by the Arians. *From the substance of the Father* prevented them from equating *begotten* to *created*, an unwanted distinction also forced upon them by the addition of *begotten not made. Of one substance with the Father* reinforces *from the substance of the Father*, so that the Son continues to be that from which he comes. The framers of this creed thought such redundance necessary to confront the Arians with language they could not construe in a sense favorable to them. They in fact continually accused them of twisting the meaning of Scripture, a most revealing complaint! They had wanted to draft their creed in Scriptural language but, when they saw they could not confound the Arians with such language, they resorted to the term *homoousios*. It not only resumed the anti-Arian position, but also offended the Arians. Arius had rejected it in the profession of faith he sent Alexander, and Eusebius of Nicomedia had done likewise in another which he read to the council, only to hear it shouted down. The appearance of *homoousios* in the creed forced bishops who did not want to condemn Arius to decide either for or against him. Hosius, whose western theology the creed accommodated, could expect the support of only four other western bishops and the two priests representing the pope. Alexander and most of the other eastern bishops hostile to Arius might have preferred to stop short of consubstantiality, for they professed no more than the perfect likeness of Father and Son. Subordinationists in the Origenist tradition like Eusebius of Caesarea were more or less sympathetic to Arius. Unfortunately, it is impossible to determine the relative strength of these two factions, which formed the vast majority of the council. Led by Eusebius of Nicomedia, the supporters of Arius apparently numbered seventeen, but only two dared refuse to sign the creed and Constantine immediately exiled them along with Arius and others. It mattered little what some three hundred bishops really thought!

During the next quarter century, the decisions of the council seem to have been ignored throughout the empire. Neither did its creed replace local formularies, nor its catchword appear in the new professions of faith proliferating in the East. Although no one, for the time being, dared to challenge a dogma sanctioned by the emperor, the two Eusebii and their friends scarcely accepted it as definitive. In synod after synod, they not only promulgated creeds of their own, but also condemned bishops who had opposed them at Nicaea. These creeds, which say nothing of consubstantiality, shy away from Arianism and condemn Sabellianism, an extreme form of monarchianism. The Eusebians also contrived to have Arius recalled from exile, but they publicly denied that as bishops they needed to consult a mere priest in formulating theology. They brought false witness against each of the principal collaborators at Nicaea on moral grounds, so that the gullible Constantine banished them one by one. With some difficulty, they even talked him into inflicting the same punishment on Athanasius, who had succeeded Alexander as bishop of Alexandria. Five times this fate would befall the eventual champion of Nicaea. At first, the western Church paid little attention to this agitation, but, as exiles like Athanasius began to complain of mistreatment for beliefs similar to those in the West, sympathy grew. After Constantine's death in 337, each of his three sons inherited a portion of the empire. Later, one was killed, then another died, and finally Constantius extended his rule over the whole empire. These vicissitudes brought shifts in power between East and West that favored Athanasius and his western allies at times and the successors of the Eusebii at others. An attempt (ca. 340) to settle the issue by an ecumenical council at Serdica (the modern Sofia), situated near the border between East and West, produced no more than separate eastern and western synods opposed to each other. Thus the arbitration of the quarrel between partisans of Arius and Alexander at Nicaea, which rewarded the expectations of neither Hosius nor Constantine, eventually resulted in the division of the empire along sectarian lines.

Athanasius

If it were not for Alexander's successor Athanasius, the many indecisive synods in the third century might have buried the Council of Nicaea in forgetfulness. By his writings and other activities, he raised the Nicene doctrine from the status of an arbitrary decree to that of an acceptable precedent. At Serdica, for instance, he dissuaded Hosius himself from submitting a new profession of faith to the western bishops on the grounds that the Nicene creed was sufficient. The proliferation of Eusebian professions of faith, which he diagnosed as a symptom of heterodoxy, may have helped to convince Hosius. Athanasius' faith actually resembled Arius' insofar as he believed that "God is a whole and not separate parts."[138] He differed from him by his belief that "God… is Father of the Son without partition."[139] Since "God is spirit,"[140] God's creatures partake of his infinite substance in

[138] *Against the Heathen*, 21, in Robert Thomson, trans., *Contra Gentes and De Incarnatione* (Oxford, 1971).

[139] *Letters Concerning the Decrees of the Council of Nicaea*, II, in John Newman, trans., *Select Treatises* (London, 1895).

[140] *Discourses against the Arians*, 1.15, in Newman.

the form of grace without diminishing him. "God's image" (*Discourses* 2.35) the Son, who is of this substance, can distribute it too. Athanasius often uses the traditional analogy of the sun and its radiation to describe the relationship between the Father and the Son. It suggests, in fact, the eternal generation of the Son by the Father which Athanasius inherited from Origen. But he did not accept the Origenist definition of consubstantiality which the Eusebians, in their subordinationism, specified by the word *homoiousios*, designating an identity of nature between Father and Son. Instead, he defended the Nicene *homoousios*, descriptive of a continuous divine substance, which in his theology implied equality between the first two persons.

The Arian relegation of the Son to creaturehood, Athanasius thought, would deprive him of the power to accomplish creation and redemption: "We do not worship a creature; we worship the Lord of creation" (to Adelphius).[141] Since his creatures degenerated with Adam, however, the Son had to use "the body as a human instrument"[142] in order to save them. "He offered to death the body which he had taken to himself, and immediately abolished death from all who were like him" (*The Incarnation* 9). Thus Athanasius shifted to the redemption the accent which, in pre-Nicene Christology, had fallen on the creation. Furthermore, he argued not from common sense as Arius had, but rather from faith, faith in the redemption. Redemption required a divine redeemer and so the Son had to be fully divine. But Athanasius had a tendency to neglect the question of how divinity and humanity could combine in Jesus. He was content to follow the Origenist tradition of distinguishing between superhuman feats like the resurrection of dead men and human weaknesses like suffering on the cross. Instead of refuting the Arians, he merely contradicted them when they cited the human shortcomings of Jesus as evidence against his equality with God. For he shared with them and with the pre-Nicene tradition the assumption that the Word served as a soul in Jesus' body, which had no real human soul. Assuming that he embraced the immortality of the human soul as other Christians did, his distinction between the immortal and mortal elements of Jesus in the following passage convict him of this future heresy:

> The Lord himself being immortal, but having a mortal flesh, had at his own free will, as God, to become separate from the body and take it up again when he would. (*Discourses* 3.57)

The Word therefore animated the body of Jesus by dwelling in it and

[141] Quoted from Johannes Quasten, *Patrology* (Westminister, Maryland, 1960), III, 75.
[142] *The Incarnation of the Word*, 44, in Newman.

deprived it of life by leaving it, the effect Christians have always attributed to the human soul. Athanasius asserted in fact that the Word deifies this human body: "The Word was not impaired in receiving a body... but rather he deified that which he put on" (*Discourses* 1.42). Unlike the human soul, however, the Word remained impassible, whatever happened to the body it inhabited. Athanasius even declared that the Word "was harmed in no respect" (*The Incarnation* 54) by the crucifixion, but rather "let his body suffer" (*Discourses* 3.58). This doctrine hardly explained the human psychology of Jesus in the gospels; worse, it gave the impression that the redeemer's vicarious suffering was little more than a gratuitous simulation.

While this defect recalls earlier theology, other aspects of Athanasius' theology anticipated future dogma, such as his interest in the Holy Spirit. Voltaire chortled over the brief sentence in the creed of Nicaea treating the Spirit as an afterthought (see p. 141). We have already seen that Athanasius considered God himself a spiritual substance. To establish the divinity of the Spirit,[143] he had recourse to many of the arguments he had already used to prove the Son's divinity. If the Spirit were merely a creature, he could only transmit the divine substance and not impart it on his own initiative. But he belongs to the divine substance

> because he is one, and still more, because he is proper to the Word who is one, he is proper to God who is one, and one in essence with him [*homoousios*]. (*Letters* 1.27)

To avoid the implication that the Spirit was a second son or grandson of the Father, Athanasius asserted that "the Spirit... proceeds from the Father" (*Letters* 1.2) and implied that he proceeds from the Son as well, thus foreseeing the eventual Roman dogma concerning the generation of the Spirit. As a whole, his trinity foreshadowed Augustine's: "The whole triad is one God" (*Letters* 1.17), one in nature and one in activity. Thus the persons in this trinity had lost their pre-Nicene autonomy, and henceforth all three would act in unison: "The triad is creator" (*Discourses* 1.18). This conception represented an obvious break with tradition.

The West, where conformity prevailed over curiosity, adhered to this doctrine which, in part, had evolved from its own belief. In the East, the Eusebian majority continued to prefer *homoiousios* to *homoousios*, even though subordinationism was declining among them. But a radical Arian minority had won the allegiance of the emperor

[143] Adolf Laminski, *Der Heilige Geist als Geist Christi und Geist der Gläubigen... Athanasios von Alexandrien* (Leipzig, 1969), proved useful in the preparation of this paragraph.

who, like most of his predecessors, saw nothing more in the religion of his subjects than a political tool. In influence rather than numbers, they predominated until, eventually, they lost their imperial support and split into two factions. The succession of emperors ruling over the eastern half of the empire brought further shifts in favor, thus disrupting the efforts of Athanasius to reconcile East and West on the basis of Nicaea. At the simultaneous councils of Rimini in the West and Seleucia in the East, Arians backed by the emperor Constance actually imposed a formulary implicitly revoking Nicaea. Yet the extorted signatures of unwilling bishops had even less effect than in the earlier council. In 362 Athanasius held a small, but more significant synod in Alexandria to promote reunification. It facilitated the conversion of Arians to Nicaenism, declared the Spirit consubstantial with the rest of the Trinity and authorized the use of *hypostasis* to mean either substance or individual. Contrasting interpretations of this word had been impeding agreement on the Nicene creed. The synod likewise adopted a resolution assigning a human soul to Jesus, even though Athanasius himself did not accept this opinion. His friend Apollinaris would soon earn a reputation for heresy by continuing to preach the traditional substitution of the Word for a human soul in Jesus. Apollinarianism and Macedonianism, the denial of divinity to the Spirit, would eventually eclipse Arianism as a reactionary threat to the reunification through tacit innovation pursued by Athanasius and, after his death, by Basil of Caesarea in Cappadocia (Anatolia).

Basil

Basil, who faced persecution for his resistance to Arianism, proceeded with an extreme discretion which he called "economy," much to Voltaire's amusement.[144] Instead of proclaiming the Spirit's divinity, he treated the third element of the Trinity with the same honor as the other two. On one solemn occasion,[145] he even alternated the innovative "Glory be to the Father with the Son together with the Holy Spirit" and the traditional "Glory be to the Father through the Son in the Holy Spirit"[146] while reciting the litany in his cathedral. In answer

[144] "C'est une expression consacrée aux Pères de l'Eglise... elle signifie, 'parler selon les temps et selon les lieux'... Ce style économique doit être manié avec la plus grande circonspection, et... il n'appartient pas aux profanes d'imiter... ce que les saints ont hasardé... dans la naïveté de leur style." "Economie de paroles," *Questions sur l'Encyclopédie* (1771), M. XVIII, 468.

[145] Sept. 7, 374 A.D., feast of St. Eupsyquius.

[146] Quasten, III, 210.

to inquiry by friends and enemies afterwards, he wrote *On the Holy Spirit*. Nowhere in this work did he designate the Spirit as God, nowhere did he declare him consubstantial with the Father and the Son, but he left his readers with both impressions. Matthew 28.19, "Baptize... in the name of the Father and of the Son and of the Holy Spirit" had inspired the innovative doxology he recited in the cathedral. He commented:

> The Spirit is spoken of together with the Lord in precisely the same manner in which the Son is spoken of with the Father... The relation of the Spirit to the Son is the same as that of the Son to the Father. (17.43)[147]

Basil had no reason to suspect the passage in Matthew of tardy insertion as exegetes do today (see p. 53), and so he assumed it to be an integral part of a divinely-inspired text. The naming of the Spirit along with the Father and the Son in such a passage convinced him that the Spirit had the same relationship with the Father as the Son. How then could he have avoided the conclusion that the Spirit was also consubstantial and equally divine? His friend Gregory of Nazianze, on whom one must depend for sure knowledge of his theology, effectively confirms that Basil publicly preached and privately confessed, "The Spirit is God" (Oration 43.69).[148] Basil's conception of the Trinity made it difficult for him to conclude otherwise: "Identity of operation in the case of Father and of Son and of Holy [Spirit] clearly proves invariability of nature" (Letter 189.7). Whatever one member of the Trinity does, the others do it too, a far cry from the specialization in Ignatius' hoisting machine. Identity of nature, which Basil inferred from identity of function, was nothing new to Trinitarian theology after Origen, but he reinforced it by the coincidence of each element with the entire substance of the Godhead: "The whole Son is in the Father and has all the Father in himself" (Letter 38.8). Thus the distinctions between the three members of the Trinity grew more tenuous in Basil's theology: "The hypostasis of the Son becomes as it were the form and presentation by which the Father is known" (Letter 38.8), a reflection of the Son's revelatory role. Although Basil retreated to modal distinctions of this sort, condemned as heresy in earlier theologians like Sabellius (third century), he nonetheless in-

[147] Blomfield Jackson, trans., *The Treatise De spiritu sancto, SLNPF*, 2d Series, VIII (Grand Rapids, 1955). *SLNPF* designates *A Select Library of Nicene and Post-Nicene Fathers*.

[148] Charles Browne and James Swallow, trans., "Orations of Saint Gregory Nazianzen," *SLNPF*, 2d series, VII (Grand Rapids, n.d.).

sisted that the three elements were distinct from each other. His most important contributions to the definitive dogma of the Trinity were his contrasting definitions of *ousia* (substance) and *hypostasis*:

> *Ousia* is common, like... Godhead... while *hypostasis* is contemplated in the special property of Fatherhood, Sonship or the power to sanctify. (Letter 214.4)

Beginning with Basil, the individuality of each Trinitarian element would depend on the mysterious content of its *hypostasis*, a concept he had standardized as the designation of what distinguished it from the others.

Gregory of Nazianze

A great preacher, Gregory of Nazianze clarified some of Basil's innovations and proposed a few of his own. He not only confirmed Basil's promotion of the Spirit to Godhood, but also distinguished between the generation of the Son and the procession of the Spirit. "I must coin a word for the sake of clearness," he said of *procession*, "for... the Spirit [is not] changed into... Son because he proceeds" (Oration 39.12). This is how he answered the Macedonians, who had been objecting that a consubstantial Spirit would be a second son or grandson of the Father. Only the derivation of the second and third hypostases in Basil's Trinity distinguished them from each other and their source. Thus Gregory sought to establish a distinction between the relations of the Son and the Spirit to the Father. The generation of the Son and the procession of the Spirit implied such a distinction, but he could not say how one differed from the other. Under the cover of a semantic solution, he was really introducing a new mystery into Trinitarian theology, just as Basil had. For the distinction between *generation* and *procession* was as mysterious as the content of *hypostasis*. Gregory likewise expanded Basil's semantic standardization of the Trinity to the combination of divinity and humanity in Christ. The Trinity consists of three hypostases, he declared, but only one nature, while Christ, who is one of the hypostases, has two natures, the divine nature of the Trinity and the human nature of Jesus. Gregory went a step further than Athanasius by declaring the human nature deified by the divine (perichoresis). In answer to Apollinaris, he completed Christ's human nature by providing it with a human soul: "There are two natures in [him], God and man, since there is a soul as well as a body in him" (Letter 101).[149]

[149] Quasten, III, 252.

In 381, Gregory presided over a council of eastern bishops at Constantinople, until dissension drove him to resign. The creed which, for reasons still obscure, came to be associated with this council, confirmed the procession of the Spirit from the Father and the equal honor of the Spirit with the Father and the Son. Although no certain reference to this creed between 381 and 451 is known, the Council of Chalcedon (451) endorsed it along with the creed of Nicaea. The Constantinopolitan creed, commonly known as the "Nicene," has enjoyed widespread acceptance by Christians ever since. The Council of Constantinople also condemned Apollinarianism, Macedonianism, and various kinds of Arianism. It had the effect of silencing the Arians and Macedonians, but the problem raised by Apollinaris continued to plague the Church.

Augustine

Augustine's *On the Trinity*[150] (400-416) consolidated the doctrine that had evolved from opposition to these "heresies." Continuing the trend in the West, he so tightened the unity of the Godhead that no person in the Trinity had any independence of will or action from the other two, with the exception of Jesus in the incarnation. After Jesus' baptism,

> the whole Trinity together produced the voice of the Father, the flesh of the Son and the dove of the Holy Spirit... The Trinity, inseparable in itself, can be manifested separately through the form of a visible creature. (4.21.30)

By the time of Augustine, Christian theologians had convinced themselves that Romans 9.5, "Christ who is above all, God for ever blessed!" and John 1.1, "The Word was God,"[151] proved the unity and equality of the first two persons. They had so much confidence in this evidence that they could further persuade themselves that the Spirit enjoyed the same privileges as the Son. Augustine admitted none of the subordination that had characterized the trinity of earlier centuries, but merely an order of priority independent as usual of any temporality. He dismisses John 14.28, "The Father is greater than I," as a reference to Jesus' humanity: "In the form of God he himself is even greater than himself, but in the form of a slave[152] even less than

[150] Quotations will come from Stephen McKenna, *On the Trinity* (Washington, 1963). Michael Schmaus, *Die psychologische Trinitätslehre des heiligen Augustinus* (Münster, 1967), was especially useful in the elaboration of this section.
[151] See pp. 26 and 60.
[152] A reference to Ph. 2.7. See p. 24.

himself" (1.7.14). In the pursuit of an ideal equality, he does not hesitate to advance an additional mystery after the precedents of Gregory, Basil, and others:

> So great is the equality of this Trinity that... [no] person whichever of the three it may be [is] anything less than the Trinity itself. (8, Preface)

Thus affirming the equality of any part to the whole, he carries the triumph of mysticism over the commonsense reaction initiated by Arius to an excess that makes the Trinity more incomprehensible than ever. Having reaffirmed this idealized equality elsewhere, he congratulates himself: "the sensual man does not perceive this" (7.6.11). Writing in Latin, Augustine translates *hypostasis* as *person* and *ousia* as *essence*. He naturally maintains "three persons of the same essence," but he also eliminates any possibility of a fourth person: "no other person... can exist... from the same essence" (7.6.11). While three or more statues could be made of gold, the divine essence only consists of three persons. He derives the nature of this essence from Genesis 1.27, "God made man in the image of himself," whose meaning he restricts to mental resemblance. The Trinity is therefore mind and the persons resemble memory, understanding, and will working together in the human mind. Even more than the Cappadocians, Augustine emphasizes unity at the expense of individuality, so that little but derivative relations remain to distinguish between them. The Father can qualify for this title only by having a Son and the Son, by having a Father, even though the relationship is eternal. To Gregory's distinction between the generation of the Son and the procession of the Spirit, he merely adds that "the Holy Spirit came forth not as one born, but as one given" (5.14.15). This explanation shows that Augustine's Trinity escapes absolute unity by a contradiction implying mystery. Only in heaven "shall we discern, by a mind that contemplates, why the Holy Spirit is not a Son, although he proceeds from the Father" (15.25.45). Even so, Augustine has to recognize an exception to the inseparable activity of his Trinity. While all three persons accomplished the incarnation, "the Son alone... was made flesh" (15.11.20). The union of divinity and humanity in the person of Jesus altered neither ingredient, yet the divine as usual predominated. For Jesus could not bring himself to sin, even though he had a human soul and free will, another enigma: "Was not his free will... so much the more free in proportion to the greater impossibility of his becoming a slave of sin?"[153] Augustine further refines traditional doctrine by the

[153] *On the Predestination of the Saints*, 15.30 in *A Work of the Predestination of Saints* (London, 1550).

argument that the man Jesus came into existence upon his union with the Word: "From that time when he began to be man... he was also God" (13.17.22). To describe this union, which he compares to that of body and soul in ordinary men, he uses a formula that would emerge from the fifth-century controversy over Christology as the eventual dogma: "The mediator appeared, uniting both natures in the unity of one person" (*Letters* 137.3.9).[154] Two natures, one person. In sum, Augustine's contributions to Christological and Trinitarian theology consisted especially of contradiction masquerading as mysticism.

Theodore of Mopsuestia

In the East, where Christology had replaced the Trinity as a source of controversy, Apollinarians were exalting the divinity of Christ at the expense of his humanity. The Antiochian Theodore, bishop of Mopsuestia from 392 on, resisted this tendency by promoting the integrity or, as he put it, economy of Jesus' human nature. Christ could never have redeemed mankind, he argues, unless he had a complete human nature:

> Il est un homme parfait, celui qui fut assumé et en qui demeura le Verbe de Dieu,—lui qui fut parfait en tout selon la nature humaine et dont l'état résultait d'un corps mortel et d'une âme intelligente, car c'est "pour l'homme et pour son salut qu'il descendit du ciel." (*Catechetical Homily* 5.17)[155]

Since the rational soul in other men carried the taint of Adam's sin, the Redeemer could not do without one, although his had to be pure. The divine nature so thoroughly assumed the human that his death on the cross did not separate them. Theodore illustrates this union by the metaphor of the assuming nature that dwelt in the temple of the assumed, a confusing one for the modern reader.[156] The distinction between the active and the passive voice in *assuming* and *assumed* as well as *dwelling in* and *dwelt in* prove that he did not depart from the traditional predominance of divinity over humanity as his enemies would charge. Yet both natures remained intact, despite the indestructible bond uniting them: "We show both the difference of the

[154] Wilfred Parsons, trans., *Letters 131-164* (New York, 1953).

[155] Raymond Tonneau, trans., *Les Homélies catéchétiques de Théodore de Mopsueste* (Vatican, 1949). See Robert Devresse, *Essai sur Théodore de Mopsueste* (Rome, 1948) for a defense of his orthodoxy.

[156] Jn. 2.19-21 inspired the metaphor: Jesus tells the Jews that if they destroy "this [Temple]," he will "raise it up" in three days. They object that it took forty-six years to build the Temple. "But he was speaking of the [Temple] that was his body."

natures and the unity of the person."[157] *Person* in this quotation translates the Greek *prosopon* which, in Theodore's writings, neither retains its previous meaning of mask or role nor provides an equivalent of the Latin *persona* used by Augustine. It probably means *manifestation*, for after the union of the natures, he says, "there were no longer two prosopa, but one."[158] Although he defines the prosopon of the united natures as "honor, greatness and worship,"[159] the term remains vague. Despite the integrity of both natures, Theodore shared the contemporary belief that their conjunction authorizes reference to one by epithets appropriate to the other, a practice known as the communication of idioms. He explains Philippians 2.7, for instance, as follows:

> L'adoration fut accordée à la forme de l'esclave qui par sa nature ne la possédait pas... Cela fut dit de la nature humaine, [Paul] le dit cependant, par communication, de la nature divine. (*Catechetical Homily* 6.6)

He also approves the attribution of divine epithets to Jesus' human nature, including the title Mother of God, provided one understand it to mean that Mary gave birth only to the temple in which the Word dwelt.[160] This restriction shows that he does not subscribe to the opinion of his enemies, according to which an exchange of properties actually took place between the two natures. He anticipates posthumous calomny, moreover, by explicitly denying the possiblity of two sons (or persons) in Christ:

> Ce n'est pas... parce que nous disons deux natures que nous sommes contraints de dire deux... fils, ce qui serait d'une naïveté extrême. (*Catechetical Homily* 8.14)

Over a hundred years after Theodore's death, the Second Ecumenical Council of Constantinople (553) either ignored this passage or made little effort to discover it, since it condemned him for the heresy of teaching two persons in Christ. Unaware of his posthumous career as a scapegoat, he took the trouble to integrate his Christology into the by then orthodox Trinity with the best of consciences:

[157] *On the Incarnation*, quoted from Richard Norris, *Manhood and Christ: A Study in the Christology of Theodore of Mopsuestia* (Oxford, 1963), p. 223.

[158] *On the Incarnation*, Norris, p. 228.

[159] A fragment from *Against Eunomius* quoted from Aloys Grillmeier, *Christ in the Christian Tradition* (New York, 1965), p. 252.

[160] "Ce ne fut pas la nature divine du [Fils] unique [que les pères de Nicée] pensent être née d'une femme, comme si de là elle eût eu [son] commencement... car elle n'eut pas de Marie son commencement" (*Catechetical Homily*, 6.3).

En disant Fils, nous disons la nature divine de l'Unique et nous comprenons aussi l'homme assumé pour nous... en qui il est sans que s'en éloignent le Père et l'Esprit-Saint, parce que la trinité même ne se divise pas. (*Catechetical Homily* 8.17)

Nestorius

Theodore died in 428, the year Nestorius became patriarch of Constantinople. Having received his theological training in Antioch, Nestorius preached a Christology very similar to Theodore's. In Constantinople, he promptly made enemies among the people and at the imperial court by persecuting dissidents. Intolerant of deviation at home, he nonetheless welcomed dissident refugees from the West and Egypt. He received Pelagians pending an inquiry addressed to Pope Celestine and Egyptians complaining of mistreatment by Cyril, patriarch of Alexandria. The relations between Rome and Constantinople had been indifferent, but Alexandria rivaled Antioch over doctrine and Constantinople over politics. Cyril was a dangerous man in a powerful position. After irritating Cyril and Celestine, Nestorius exposed himself by taking sides in a theological dispute. The cult of Mary among the people of Constantinople brought censure of the title Mother of God from an Antiochian preacher in a Constantinopolitan church. Nestorius, who was present, approved this censure and elaborated on it in his own sermons. Both he and his enemies disseminated these sermons and soon they were in the hands of Celestine, who could not read the Greek text, and Cyril, who could. Cyril therefore had little trouble convincing Celestine of Nestorius' "heresy."[161] Celestine appears to have understood that Nestorius rejected the title Mother of God and advocated two sons in Christ. He called a synod at Rome, probably had Nestorius condemned on these two counts and informed Cyril of this action. Cyril in turn convoked a synod in Alexandria and, having obtained a more comprehensive condemnation of Nestorius, sent him an ultimatum. Although he claimed to be representing the pope, his letter exposed his own Christology, not Celestine's, and included twelve *Anathemas* calculated to provoke Nestorius. As if on behalf of the pope, Cyril ordered Nestorius to sign within ten days. Needless to say, Nestorius did nothing of the kind. He did deny that he believed in two sons and withdrew his opposition to Mother of God, but made the same restriction as Theodore had. Meanwhile, Cyril had written a long letter advocating his

[161] Grillmeier finds that Nestorius' doctrine "could compete with any Christology" of his time (p. 380).

opinion to each member of the royal family at Constantinople in an effort to undermine Nestorius' authority. Theodosius II, the emperor in the East, resented the letter, which he took for an attempt to divide his family. In the expectation that Cyril would be disciplined, he called a council at Ephesus in 431 to settle the issue. Seeing the danger, Cyril arrived promptly with a delegation of Egyptian bishops far in excess of the number prescribed by Theodosius. Resentment against Nestorius enabled him to win the support of most bishops present by the date set for the opening of the council. Neither the delegation under John of Antioch nor the legates sent by Celestine had arrived, but Cyril persuaded the bishops who had arrived to open the council anyway and presided over it in the name of the pope. The accused then became the accuser. Having expelled a protest delegation, the council summoned Nestorius and, when he refused to appear, convicted him of heresy in a single session. A week later, John arrived with his delegation and held a rival council, deposing and excommunicating Cyril. Both parties appealed to Theodosius, who ordered each to send eight representatives to meet with him at Chalcedon, across the Bosphorus from Constantinople. He also had Nestorius (who now wished to retire to his monastery in Antioch) and Cyril confined to their quarters in Ephesus. At this point, however, the wealthy patriarch of Alexandria seems to have showered Theodosius' courtiers with extravagant gifts. At Chalcedon, the Antiochian delegation, which had forgotten Nestorius, enjoyed initial success with the emperor in attacking Cyril's *Anathemas*. But Cyril's munificence soon began to sap their favor and Theodosius, finding them increasingly obstinate, withdrew across the Bosphorus with the Cyrillian delegation, leaving the Antiochians to draw their own conclusions. Cyril was allowed to escape and he returned to Alexandria in self-proclaimed triumph, while Nestorius was taken to his monastery. The controversy raged on until 433 when John and Cyril agreed to a *Formulary of Reunion* which, at the price of a few concessions, implicitly refuted the *Anathemas* and left Theodore's Christology nearly intact. The only major concession was the substitution of union for conjunction as an explanation of how the two natures were joined, a point now accepted by the Antiochians themselves. The *Formulary* nonetheless maintained Theodore's qualification of the title *Mother of God*. In order to obtain Cyril's signature, however, John sacrificed Nestorius to Cyril's revenge. The scapegoat, who could have signed the *Formulary* himself, was relegated to a remote exile under his worst enemy's jurisdiction. The *Formulary*, moreover, satisfied neither the Antiochians who wanted to see Nestorius vindicated nor the Alexandrians who took the *Anathemas* seriously.

Cyril

The latter pressed Cyril for an explanation: How could the author of the *Anathemas* have signed the *Formulary*? Politics were his primary motive, but he had more palatable excuses. He had persuaded the Antiochians to accept the Trinitarian idea of consubstantiality in formulating Christology, a move they had been resisting. The *Formulary* therefore stated that Christ was "consubstantial with the Father according to his divinity and consubstantial with us according to his humanity" (Denz., n. 272).[162] On the other hand, Cyril had agreed to the Antiochian demand that he recognize two natures in Christ, even though he defined the Greek *physis* (nature) differently from them and in a manner comparable to Theodore's *prosopon*. This is one reason why he had accused Nestorius of teaching two sons, while he himself spoke of two natures becoming one through the incarnation.[163] This semantic obstacle must have been detected during the negotiations after Ephesus, for the *Formulary* proclaimed "a unity of two natures" (Denz. n. 272), a compromise preserving both the Antiochian definition of *physis* and Cyril's preference of union over conjunction. The Antiochians' acceptance of union largely as he taught it was his best argument in justification of having signed the *Formulary*. Although he declared "the mode of union" "wholly incomprehensible,"[164] he restated the traditional view that both the humanity and the divinity in Jesus remained intact after the incarnation and that neither mingled with the other in any way. From the life-giving power attributed to the Eucharist, he presumed that the Word infused Jesus' body with this power,[165] although his humanity included a rational soul.[166] To the communication of idioms, he added the actual exchange of properties between the humanity and the divinity without any alteration of their integrity.[167] Not only did Jesus impart the "Spirit by a material breath,"[168] but also the Word underwent "the

[162] Heinrich Denziger, *The Sources of Catholic Dogma*, trans. Roy DeFerrari (St. Louis, 1957).

[163] "The two natures are united, but... after the union there is no longer a division into two [natures]; we believe, therefore, in one nature of the Son, because he is one, though become man and flesh." (*Epistle*, 40, to Acacius, in Quasten, III, 140).

[164] *That Christ Is One* in *A Library of the Holy Catholic Church* (Oxford, 1881), p. 264.

[165] "If you remove the life-giving Word of God from the mystic and true union with his body and sever them utterly, how can you show that it is still life-giving?" *Five Books against Nestorius* (4.5) in *A Library*.

[166] "His... body has been ensouled with a reasonable soul." *Treatise against Diodore*, 9, in *A Library*.

[167] In Aristotelian terms, one might speak of two subjects exchanging their accidents.

[168] *Scholia on the Incarnation*, p. 695, in *A Library*.

suffering of the flesh."[169] Cyril defended unrestricted reference to Mary as the Mother of God on the grounds that the Word "gathered up man's birth through himself."[170] "The holy virgin," he insisted, "brought forth... God personally united to flesh" (*Letter* 17.11).[171] This opinion, which clashed with the one on this subject in the *Formulary*, confirmed that his signing of the document was especially the result of political expedient. By no means did he relegate Christology to the status of a mere political tool, however. In fact, he shared a fundamental concern with Theodore, the desire to safeguard the credibility of redemption: If the Word "had not been born as we according to the flesh... he would not have freed man from the blame [contracted] in Adam."[172]

Monophysites

His prestige as a theologian far outweighed his reputation for unscrupulous politics, and his numerous writings, in which he systematized his interpretation of tradition, were widely accepted as the standard of "orthodoxy" he intended them to be. Yet the least sincere of his works, the *Anathemas*, had become a second bible to the monophysites, who believed in a unique, divine nature in Christ.[173] Among these dissidents were Dioscorus, his successor as patriarch of Alexandria and Eutychius, the abbot of a large monastery near Constantinople.[174] Eutychius had distinguished himself by his persecution of "Nestorians," priests accepting the *Formulary*. His godson the eunuch Chrysaphius, who was Theodosius II's chancellor, assured him the support of the court. But Chrysaphius had made an enemy of the co-empress Pulcheria, Theodosius' sister, by persuading him to exile her. She had been an obstacle to Chrysaphius' ambitions. In a synod under Flavian, the patriarch of Constantinople, Eusebius of Doryleum, who owed his see to Pulcheria, attacked Eutychius' orthodoxy. When they finally succeeded in forcing Eutychius to appear for questioning, he answered evasively, while Chrysaphius applied pressure to have him acquitted. They nonetheless convicted him of heresy and he angrily appealed to the people, the court, and all the

[169] *Five Books*, 1, Prologue.

[170] *Five Books*, 1, Prologue.

[171] Quasten, III, 142.

[172] *Five Books*, 1, Prologue.

[173] The human nature with its rational soul is completely absorbed by the divine nature.

[174] The unfortunate, but inevitable proliferation of proper names in the rest of this paragraph will at least illustrate the nature of Byzantine intrigue.

high prelates in Christendom, including Pope Leo I. After receiving an official account of the verdict from Flavian, Leo had his secretary Prosper of Aquitaine write a work known as the *Tome to Flavian*. Although it condemned Eutychius alone, Leo apparently intended it as a reasonable mediation between the two extremes, as he understood them, of Eutychianism and Nestorianism. It advocated a union or communion, as Prosper called it, of two natures, each of which continued to do what was proper to it.[175] Yet the monophysites were repudiating as Nestorian any such distinction between natures. Dioscorus, who presided over a council at Ephesus arranged by Chrysaphius, refused to allow Leo's legates to read the *Tome* before it. The assembly reinstated Eutychius and deposed Flavian as well as Eusebius of Doryleum. When he heard what had happened, Leo branded it as the "Robber Council," a name that delighted Voltaire (see p. 211). A year later, Theodosius fell from a horse and died, thus leaving Pulcheria to reign alone. Having removed Chrysaphius, she "married" (without abandoning her vow of virginity) Marcian, a senator, in order to reinforce the power of the throne with a masculine ruler. In 451 he called an ecumenical council to be held at Chalcedon under the control of imperial commissioners. Sensitive to the shift in imperial power, most of the bishops who had collaborated with Dioscorus now voted with the majority to depose him and confirm the condemnation of Eutychius. The council also allowed Leo's legates to read the *Tome*, which it approved. The five hundred bishops, most of them from the East, would have preferred to limit themselves to such "unfinished" business, but Pulcheria was determined to obtain a Christological dogma applicable to the entire empire. The imperial commissioners prodded them relentlessly until a representative committee had produced a statement which they could sign. Its principal sources were a letter from Cyril to Nestorius adopted by the Council of Ephesus in 431, the *Formulary* and the *Tome*. The following is an extract:

> We confess... Christ... perfect in human nature... with a rational soul and a body... consubstantial with the Father according to the divinity and consubstantial with us according to human nature, like... us in all things except sin... born of the Father before the ages according to divine nature, but in the last days... born of the virgin Mary, Mother of God according to human nature... for our delivrance, one and the same Christ... acknowledged in two natures without mingling, without change... the distinction of the natures nowhere removed on account of

[175] See E.H. Blakeney, trans., *The Tome of Pope Leo the Great* (London, 1923).

> the union but rather the peculiarity of each nature being kept, and uniting in one [*prosopon*] and [*hypostasis*]. (Denz. n. 148)

Thus Chalcedon established a definitive Christological formula, two natures in one person, just as Constantinople I (381) had established a definitive Trinitarian formula, three persons in one substance. Both are monuments to the triumph of mystery over rationalism. The Apollinarians and the monophysites as well as the Arians had been trying rationally to reconcile variety with unity instead of resigning themselves to faith in a reconciliation inaccessible to reason. Such mystery tended to discourage Christians from thinking for themselves by removing doctrine from their rational jurisdiction. It therefore increased their dependence on the Church, which had usurped the exclusive authority to formulate orthodoxy. Over a century of controversy had taken Christianity even further from the reality behind the New Testament than the speculations of the earlier Fathers. Whatever the proportions of Jewish and Hellenistic influence, the abstraction of Christianity from the world of experience, which the synoptists had described with some accuracy, accelerated in the second and third centuries. In the fourth and fifth, intellectual arrogance and political ambition in most cases supplanted the joy of speculation, thus provoking violent twists in the Christian line as "orthodoxy" shifted back and forth with imperial power and Church politics. Yet the relative corruption of the second period seems no less typical of human psychology than the relative innocence of the first. Despite persistent affirmation by apologists, such ordinary history lacks anything like a divine signature.

ERASMUS

While Trinitarian and Christological doctrine continued to develop from the fifth century on, no fundamental additions or changes occurred and no significant challenge took place before the sixteenth century. Nor did the Lutheran and Calvinist sects, which prided themselves on their more ancient orthodoxy, deviate from dogma in these respects. But renaissant curiosity and reforming zeal exposed the Bible to critical scrutiny for the first time since Jerome, who had died in 420. When Erasmus published his Latin version of the Bible in 1516, the italicized words in the following quotation from 1 John 5.7 were missing: "There are three witnesses *in heaven: the Father, the Word and the Spirit, and these three are one*." Having found them in none of the older manuscripts, he dared to eliminate the only complete statement of the Trinity in Scripture.[176] Although pious reaction forced him to restore them in later editions, he did not really change his mind and Biblical erudition in the nineteenth century confirmed the inauthenticity of "the Johannine comma."[177] Convinced that the Trinity could neither be founded on Scripture nor rationally demonstrated, he followed the example of earlier nominalists[178] by taking refuge in a fideistic submission to the authority of dogma:

> Quomodo Filius sit alius a Patre... noli scrutari: tibi satis est credere Patrem, Filium et Spiritum Sanctum tres personas, sed unum Deum.[179]

Their attitude was apologetic, however, and his was critical.

SERVETUS

Fideism, on the other hand, did not neutralize scepticism about the Trinity in the minds of increasingly numerous scholars more radical than him. Michael Servetus seems to have thought that, despite the inquisition in his native Spain, the Jews and the Moors had resisted conversion to Christianity because of their repugnance to this dogma in particular. Nor could he find much support for it in Scripture, which he knew unusually well in a day of intensive Biblical scholarship. In editing Sante Pagnini's Latin translation of the Bible, he noted that the Hebrew *almah* in Isaiah 7.14 meant "young woman" and not "virgin" as in the Greek Septuagint, a point much belabored by Voltaire. This correction ruined the traditional assumption that Isaiah had prophesied the virgin birth of Jesus. Servetus also discovered that the pre-Nicene fathers taught a trinity more faithful to Scripture than their successors. He deplored the introduction of unscriptural terms like *homoousios* into Christian theology, because they sophisticated and thus distorted it. How could one so much as imagine three beings in one God?[180] "There can be nothing in the mind," he

[176] Mt. 28.19, "Baptize them in the name of the Father and of the Son and of the Holy Spirit," enumerates the three persons, but does not declare their unity. It is probably a late insertion.

[177] "On falsifia bien davantage une épître attribuée à ce même Jean. On lui fait dire qu'il y en a trois qui rendent témoignage dans le ciel, le Père, le Verbe, et l'Esprit-Saint; et ces trois sont un." Voltaire, *Dieu et les hommes par le docteur Obern*, M. XXVIII, 207.

[178] William of Occam, in particular.

[179] Erasmus, *Paraphrasis in epistolas Joannes* (Basel, 1540), p. 7.

[180] "I... prove not only that the three beings cannot exist in one God, but that they cannot even be imagined." Michael Servetus, *On the Errors of the Trinity* in *The Two Treatises of Servetus on the Trinity*, trans. Earl Wilbur (Cambridge, Mass., 1932), p. 50.

objected, "that was not first in the senses" (*Errors* p. 52), an Aristotelian apothegm. To the fideism of Erasmus and his fellow nominalists, Servetus replied:

> If you say... that it is enough to believe [in Trinitarian dogma]... you expose your foolishness even in the fact that you accept a matter beyond your understanding without sufficient warrant of Scripture. (*Errors* p. 52)

His confidence in the authority of the Bible equaled that of the Reformers, who nevertheless rejected his theology for fear of an uncontrollable assault on dogma. Having met with more suspicion than interest in Basel and Strasburg, he published *On the Errors of the Trinity* (1531) and *Two Dialogues on the Trinity* (1532) in hopes of making contact with Protestant theologians elsewhere. But these books stirred so much anger among them that he fled to France, changed his name to Michel de Villeneuve, and devoted himself to medicine, a profession that brought him fame. Meanwhile, his works were circulating far and wide among clandestine admirers, many of whom opposed the Trinity even more radically than he did.

His reinterpretation of it seems deceptively orthodox, for he accepted three persons in one Godhead. But he defined person as a manifestation, the pre-Chalcedonian connotation of *prosopon*. "The difference between the persons," he explained, was "to be judged in their ways of appearing" (*Errors* p. 132). He likewise distinguished between person and being, a word he much preferred to the unscriptural hypostasis. His God did not consist in three beings, a configuration he deemed inconceivable: How could there be "a multiplication of beings without a multiplication of essence"[181] (*Errors* p. 52)? He thus rejected the mystery implied by an abstraction combining unified and triple conceptions of the deity, a mystery which had gone nearly unchallenged for twelve centuries. He scorned the mystery as tritheism and the abstraction as a quaternity. Since his own trinity consisted in three manifestations of itself, he qualified as a modalist or Sabellian in ancient terminology. Yet he subordinated the three persons to each other in a manner reminiscent of the fathers hostile to Sabellianism. From them, for instance, he borrowed the analogy of the sun and its rays. To describe the generation of the Word "without body" (*Errors* p. 81), he frequently had recourse to the more obvious analogy of an utterance. Both analogies suggested to him the con-

[181] Solana interprets such statements as proof that Servetus did not understand the distinction between *ousia* and *hypostasis*. This opinion implies an abusive underestimation of his intelligence. See n. 188.

tinuity of spiritual substance uniting the Word to God, who shared power with him equally. According to the *Errors*, "Christ... came down from heaven and assumed flesh as a man" (p. 3), a traditional opinion revised in the *Dialogues*. Here he interpreted John 1.14, "The Word was made flesh," as an event previous to Jesus' human conception: "He and his flesh came down from heaven,"[182] like the bread which fed the children of Israel in the Sinai desert.[183] His body was "the express image of the Godhead" and "consubstantial with the Father" (*Dialogues* p. 200), for even in the flesh Christ consisted of a single divine substance. In the *Errors*, Servetus described him rather as "one who [shared] both substances" (p. 92), the flesh of man and the spirit of God. When writing his work, he was content to admire the

> mystery that... joins God to man and man to God. [How] wonderfully has God made the body of Christ his own, that it might be his own tabernacle for him to dwell in. (p. 93)

Despite this union, he admitted the communication only of God's qualities to man, not man's to God, and stressed the humanity of Jesus, "the miraculously born Son of God in fleshly form... not a hypostasis but an actual Son" (*Errors* p. 3). God therefore had a human Son, "a son by nature"[184] (*Errors* p. 16), the Word incarnate miraculously born of Mary, the Mother of God. Jesus was "not God in nature, but in appearance" (*Errors* p. 21), and Servetus denied that this "double use of the term God" (*Errors* p. 3) implied two Gods. The Spirit, on the other hand, neither deserves to be called God nor to figure in the Trinity, a doctrine unauthorized by Scripture anyway. The Spirit was "not a separate being, but an activity of God"[185] (*Errors* p. 3) and hence no more than a divine manifestation like the other two "persons" in Servetus' own trinity. The components of his theory

[182] Michael Servetus, *Two Dialogues on the Trinity* in *The Two Treatises of Servetus on the Trinity*, p. 199.

[183] Jn. 6.51; Ex. 16.4, 14-16.

[184] "Take this as an illustration: if powers were given me to beget a son in a woman by the breath of my mouth instead of by the seed of a man, then if I withdrew after the breath was emitted I would say to the woman, I have begotten a son, I leave a son in you who, when the fulness of time comes and he has become a man, will be born of you. And although that is absurd to say, my breath is a son, nay my word will be a son to me; yet we say that a son was then begotten by reason of the power of the seed, not because there was a real begetting of the breath or of the word uttered by God, but the begetting of the flesh took place in the outward uttering of the word." *Errors*, p. 107.

[185] "By Holy Spirit [Scripture] means now God himself, now an angel, now the spirit of man, a sort of instinct or divine inspiration of the mind, a mental impulse, or a breath; although sometimes a difference is marked between breath and spirit." *Errors*, p. 35.

taken from the fathers seem strangely archaic beside the more original ones derived from his interpretation of the Bible. He nonetheless demonstrated that the most orthodox sources could produce a very radical heresy.

Though successful in medicine and scholarly editing, he had returned to theology by 1746 when he began to correspond with Calvin about the Trinity. Why he thought Calvin, whom he had known in Paris, might appreciate his original thinking on this subject is an enigma. In their exchange of writings, he sent him much compromising material, including the manuscript of a new work entitled *The Restoration of Christianity*. A year later, Calvin broke off the correspondence without returning these papers and, in a letter to his colleague Farel, even vowed that if Servetus ever came to Geneva, he would not leave alive. The emanationist modification of Servetus' theology in the *Restoration* must have contributed to Calvin's attitude. For Servetus had reintroduced into Christian theology the Neoplatonic harmonization of transcendence and immanence characteristic of Origen, long since repudiated as a "heretic." He now defined God as the universal source of reason, by means of which all things were made. "Solus Deus," he added,

> est ipsa simplicitas, forma et essentia; a quo reliqua compositionem, constitutionem, formationem et dependentiam habent. Solus ipse est vita reliqua vivificans.[186]

But Yahweh's Pentateuchal appearances in a fiery cloud encouraged Servetus in his belief that the divine substance or spirit was really a kind of light: "Spiritus et lux sunt unum in Deo" (p. 162). The radiation of this light from its source provided the Neoplatonic transition from transcendence to immanence. Servetus, who typically identified this radiation as the Word, confirmed the Word's continuously creative function in the Hellenistic tradition. He also advanced a theory explaining the interaction between divine and ordinary light: "Lucem solis penetrat et sustinet intus lux illa Dei, omnes mundi formas penetrans, et sustinens, ut forma formarum" (p. 121). Elsewhere, however, this emanationist penetration and support of the creation became an identification of the creation with a modified portion of the divine substance itself: "Non solum in luce omnia repraesentantur, sed in luce omnia consistunt" (p. 145). The fine distinction that absolved Servetus of pantheism, which pious enemies hastened to allege, was precisely the implication that creation by no means absorbed the

[186] Michael Servetus, *Christianismi Restitutio* (n.p., 1553), p. 97.

source of the radiation.[187] It did include the radiation itself, nonetheless: "Verbum illud, in quo omnia consistunt, lux est" (p. 145), a sentence that appears to justify Solana's verdict of "pancristianismo."[188] The unity of Christ and the creation depended on his role as the versatile procreative agent of the Creator, a revival of the seminal Word. Consequently, Servetus' panchristianity supposed the tenuous unity of parent and offspring in a "family" of universal diversity! In this context, the divine conception of Jesus seems almost routine: "Verbum Dei... erat Christi semen" (p. 145). With the birth of God's human Son, the *Restoration* returned to the theology of the *Errors* and the *Dialogues* which, in general, it otherwise continued. In sum, Calvin's angry protest was naïve: "Voici un homme... qui voudra inventer une religion nouvelle."[189] Servetus had not tried to invent a new religion, but rather, as his title indicated, to restore an old one.

He was living in Vienne (near Lyon) when he secretly published the *Restoration* (1553) and soon Calvin had obtained a printed copy. With Calvin's cooperation, if not on his initiative, a Genevan friend of his betrayed Servetus to a Catholic correspondent in France and even furnished proof on request. Arrested in Vienne, Servetus escaped and eventually came to Geneva[190] on the way to Naples, a Spanish possession in those days. Recognized and arrested, he underwent a trial in which Calvin acted as the prosecutor and obtained the death penalty. Servetus was burned at the stake on a verdict of blasphemy against the Trinity and advocacy of adult baptism. In a letter to Melanchton printed with the *Restoration*, he had in fact called the Trinity "a three-headed Cerberus" (p. 700). While Swiss Protestant leaders approved the execution, others and particularly Italian antitrinitarians in exile raised such a storm of protest that Calvin felt obliged to publish a self-justification condoning the liquidation of heretics.[191]

[187] This distinction also absolves Spinoza of pantheism, and Malebranche as well, of dissolving all souls in the divinity as in Buddhism.

[188] Actually "pantéismo en forma de pancristianismo," inaccurate in my opinion. Marcial Solana, *Historia de la filosofía española en el siglo XVI* (Madrid, 1941), I, 667.

[189] Jean Calvin, *Commentaire sur Deutéronome* in *Joannis Calvini Opera* (Brunswick, 1860-1900), XXVII, 261.

[190] Why he took so obvious a risk is an enigma.

[191] *Déclaration pour maintenir la vraie foi touchant la trinité contre les erreurs de M. Servet, par Jean Calvin, où il est montré qu'il est licite de punir les hérétiques et qu'à bon droit ce méchant a été exécuté par justice en la ville de Genève* (Genève, 1554).

SOCINIANISM

Until two years before Servetus' death, these antitrinitarians had been active in northern Italy. Voltaire himself credited the legend of an antitrinitarian synod at Vicenza in 1546, but Socinian writers, anxious no doubt to endow their movement with an interesting origin, appear to have invented this event more than a hundred years after it supposedly took place. The synod boasted an impressive list of delegates, including Lelio Sozzini who, in Voltaire's day, enjoyed the reputation of having founded Socinianism. Later writers converted the synod into an antitrinitarian academy, the Collegia Vicentina, over which Lelio presided at the age of twenty-one.[192] When local authorities, according to this account, discovered and suppressed the assembly, the members who escaped formed new congregations in Switzerland, and Lelio founded the Socinian church in Poland. This legend may have emerged from a confusion of antitrinitarian activity in Vicenza with an antitrinitarian council that actually took place at Venice in 1550. This Venetian council drew some sixty delegates, some even from as far as Basel and Saint Gall, but not Lelio. The radical wing of the assembly persuaded all but two of the delegates to accept an agreement in ten points, the first being: "Christ is not God but man, born of Joseph and Mary, [and yet] filled with all the powers of God."[193] The council appointed two ministers to instruct distant congregations in the ten points. A year later, however, one of these men betrayed the whole movement to the Inquisition. Only then did the leaders flee to the North and eventually the Northeast, but Lelio and others had already preceded them.

Nor was he the most influential of these Italian antitrinitarians, as Voltaire and others believed. While his travels took him as far as England, Wittenberg, and Poland, he settled in Zurich under the protection of the Protestant leader Bullinger. After much consultation and correspondence with Calvin, his insatiable curiosity and subtle reasoning finally irritated this dangerous theologian. Like so many others, Lelio discreetly objected to Servetus' execution and Calvin began to suspect him of sharing his victim's doctrine. When other Reformers echoed this suspicion, Bullinger asked him for a confes-

[192] Both Cantimori and Williams nonetheless credit the possibility of an antitrinitarian fellowship of some sort in Vicenza: Delio Cantimori, *Eretici italiani de cinquecento* (Florence, 1967), p. 53, and George Williams, *The Radical Reformation* (Philadelphia, 1962), p. 561.

[193] Quoted from Earl Wilbur, *A History of Unitarianism* (Cambridge, Mass., 1947), p. 85.

sion of faith and he complied. This document, one of the few extant from his hand, is clever. He for instance rebukes ignorant and obstinate opponents of Trinitarian terms in use for over thirteen hundred years. Since he was writing in 1555, however, this facetious attack on antitrinitarians implied that these terms appeared over 200 years after Jesus' death. He then expresses a preference for dogma "in the words of Christ, the apostles and the evangelists" (Hulme p. 216),[194] thus implying scepticism about the testimony of the Fathers. Further on, he spins the following web of negatives:

> I do not assert that the Father is the same as the Son and the Holy Spirit. I do not suppose there to be three Jehovahs, coessential Gods; I do not divide the one person of Christ into two Christs, nor accept any confusion of his natures. (Hulme p. 217)

This sentence did not prevent him from believing the Father alone to be God, the Son, only a man and the Spirit, a mere attribute of the divinity. But Lelio knew better than to admit such opinions, especially after the example of Servetus, from whose doctrine he dissociated himself. Bullinger, who probably knew his mind better than Calvin had ever known Servetus', was only too anxious to approve his confession. Lelio died at the age of thirty-seven and his nephew Fausto Sozzini inherited his papers.

In 1579, Fausto came to Poland where he confederated several antitrinitarian sects to form a Socinian church. These sects had been loosely associated under the title of the Minor Church since 1565, when they broke away from the (Calvinist) Reform Church. They agreed with each other on two points only: the superiority of the Father to the Son and the unquestionable authority of the Bible. Among other influences, they had been exposed to the preaching of Pietro Goniadzki, a posthumous disciple of Servetus. As Lelio before him, however, Fausto rejected Servetus' theology, which in fact had won few adherents. He probably realized that still another doctrine would further complicate the task of synthesizing those already in competition with each other. This was the task he took upon himself, for he shared the two convictions the members of the Minor Church had in common. In his *Sum of the Christian Religion* he wrote, "ostendum fuit, si Deus unus est, non potest esse trinus aut binus."[195] This statement effectively demonstrates his confidence in the authority of the Bible and excludes any essential equality between the Father and

[194] Edward Hulme, "Lelio Sozzini's Confession of Faith," *Persecution and Liberty* (New York, 1931), pp. 211-25.

[195] *Fausti Socini Senensis opera omnia* (Irenopolis, 1656), I, 282.

the Son. There could be no fewer substances than persons, he argued, and, besides, a person was the same as an individual rational substance anyway. He even revived Arius' objection to consubstantiality: "partibus aliquo modo sit ipsa Dei essentia... sit absurdam adeo impium."[196] Thus Fausto believed the ancient assumption that Godly perfection required indivisibility and the commonsense notion that multiplying persons necessitated division of substance. Nowhere did Scripture justify Christ's status as the Son of God on the grounds "quod ex ipsa Dei substantia sive essentia sit generatus."[197] Fausto denied the existence of any Son of God before the human birth of Jesus, thus eliminating the independent existence of the Word before his conception. Curiously, he saw no necessary contradiction between the virgin birth and the natural fatherhood of Joseph, which he also advocated: "Christum revera ex Josepho natum fuisse."[198] He doubted the authenticity of the birth narratives in Luke and Matthew, denied that Jesus ever thought of founding a religion and recognized his preoccupation with the imminent kingdom of God. He conceded that Jesus could have foreseen messiahship for himself, but only during the kingdom, and observed that the Romans understandably took his activity for rebellious agitation. His assessment of the historical Jesus was therefore strikingly realistic after so many centuries of idealism in the service of metaphysical speculation. His scrutiny of the New Testament inspired scepticism about a divine nature in the Son and a denial of equality between him and the Father, except in the dignity, power, etc., with which the Father rewarded him after the resurrection:

> Jesus... hominem scilicet illum, qui vere crucifixus fuit, esse Dei viventis filium, cui omnia tradita sint a Deo in manis, quemque nos colere, et ab ipso vitam aeternam expectave oporteat.[199]

Reason and the Bible convinced Fausto, on the other hand, that the Holy Spirit deserved no such individual veneration, for it was merely an attribute of God. He explained how the concept had evolved from a metaphor of God's power as a mighty wind or breath and objected to personification of such attributes, "alioque multo plures etiam,

[196] *Defence of... Fausto Sozzini... against Gabriel Eutropius* (written 1584, published 1618), II, 653.

[197] *Christianae Religionis brevissima Istitutio* (unfinished text posthumously incorporated in the *Racovian Catechism*), I, 284.

[198] *Sacred Readings* (unfinished), I, 315.

[199] *On the Nature or Essence of Jesus Christ* (1588), II, 382.

quam tres."[200] He reminded his readers that God was unique and his substance, neither divisible nor communicable.

The *Racovian Catechism* (1605), published shortly after his death, codified his doctrine for the benefit of the Minor Church, which he had courageously defended for twenty-five years against relentless persecution by Reformers and Catholics alike. The secret of his success was a rare virtue in theologians, tolerance of other people's opinions. Although the requirement of adult baptism prevented him from joining the Minor Church himself, he managed to reconcile their divergent beliefs in a manner that allowed reasonable variation within the church. He did not try to convert the Polish Trinitarians, but rather pleaded in favor of mutual understanding, though in vain. Unfortunately, none of the antitrinitarian leaders who survived him could replace him and the Trinitarian alliance liquidated the Minor Church in 1658. Socinianism nonetheless spread to Holland, England, and North America where it now prospers under the name of unitarianism. It also had a subtle yet profound influence on intellectuals belonging to other Christian sects, such as Englishmen like Newton and Clarke and Calvinists in Geneva. It was in these two countries that Voltaire came into contact with Socinianism.

CONCLUSION

In sum, the critics of the orthodox Trinity in the sixteenth and seventeenth centuries might have expected tolerance or sympathy from their fellow Protestants. They shared the dream of a return to primitive Christianity and agreed on the right of each Christian to found his belief on the evidence of the Bible. Yet the Reformers' hostility to Servetus' theology, the approval of Calvin's retaliation against him by the Swiss Protestants, the suspicions of Lelio by Calvin and the Swiss Reformers, and the alliance of the Reform Church in Poland with the Catholics against the Socinians were cracks in the sincerity with which they professed these principles. Most Protestants did not really approve of exposing the Trinity and the two natures to the test of Scriptural authenticity, for they could dream of primitive purity without sacrificing fond habits. The hypocrisy of exempting these dogmas from the standard applied in all its rigor to more recent inventions like transubstantiation suggests that, despite secession from the papacy, the new priesthood continued to feel the need for cloaking its

[200] *Istitutio*, II, 284.

authority in mystery. Nor did the sixteenth- and seventeenth-century critics of the Trinity seek to endanger this authority, but rather sincerely to rediscover and re-establish the purity of an original faith.

Only in the eighteenth century did clerical authority and the illusions of original purity themselves come under attack. One reason for this radical mutation was the foolish suppression of warnings by scholars like Erasmus and Richard Simon, all the more suspect because of their disinterest! The Protestant clergies, who pretended to know better, joined the Catholic, ever faithful to its reactionary tradition, in sweeping the dust under the carpet. One might argue that the threat to essential dogmas, solutions of difficult problems obtained at the cost of great effort and much turmoil, justified the hostile reaction to irresponsible scholarship as well as Trinitarian and antitrinitarian heresy. The foregoing study nonetheless demonstrates that the heresies of Nicaea and Chalcedon are in large measure the orthodoxy of earlier times; that only two passages in the New Testament, both of them suspected of late insertion, clearly designate the three persons in the Trinity (Mt. 28.19; 1 Jn. 5.7-8); that, while some passages support the two natures, others contradict them and even in the same gospel (John); that the difficult problems served as a pretext for settling political scores within and without the Church; that the efforts to solve them involved cynical maneuver and the arbitrary exercise of power; that the turmoil arose because one faction was determined to impose its will on another and rarely in the interest of all Christians.

If the true interest of all Christians lies in the search for the authentic Christ, however, they are doomed to the pursuit of a chimera. As sincere as any Christians, the Socinians, fortunately for them, lacked the critical tools to peel back the layers of history in their quest for primitive purity. Some of these tools were available by the eighteenth century, but already the operation proved useful only in exposing the gap in the documentation between Judaism and Hellenistic Christianity. The Jewish War seems to have all but obliterated the memory of Jewish Christianity, the crucial transitional stage between Jesus, the Galilean holy man yearning for a Jewish kingdom of God, and Christ, the Hellenistic myth of an incarnated and resurrected God. The contrast between rudimentary materialist monotheism, on one hand, and sophisticated spiritualist polytheism in the form of a subordinationist or consubstantial triunity, on the other, is staggering. It seems likely that the religion we call Christianity actually crystalized from Hellenistic ignorance of its origin amputated by the Jewish War, which gave the Jews an evil reputation in the Roman Empire, thus stimulating anti-Semitism among Gentile Christians. Without this break in the tradition and this anti-Semitism, Christianity might have remained a Jewish sect with consequences open to speculation.

Just as Christianity grew out of Judaism and coexisted with it, deism grew out of Christianity and coexisted with it, yet deism never resulted in the foundation of anything like a church. Deists like Voltaire received a Christian education, continued to abide by many Christian customs and borrowed heavily from Christianity in formulating their various doctrines, as Becker demonstrates.[201] Despite the impact of deism, the vast majority of Europeans remained Trinitarian Christians in the eighteenth century. The faith continued to draw its strength from the ancient conviction that the Son of God, tantamount to God himself, had lived a human life and died a human death, so that men might live a life of eternal compensation after death. The constant and ubiquitous presence of the Holy Spirit (likewise tantamount to God himself) since Christ had left the earth undoubtedly reinforced this faith. The three persons and the two natures persuaded most of Voltaire's contemporaries and many of his readers that the deity was both accessible and available. The two dogmas therefore satisfied an urgent human need, which even Voltaire, the deist, seems to have felt.

[201] Carl Becker, *The Heavenly City of the Eighteenth-Century Philosophers* (New York, 1960).

VOLTAIRE'S ANTITRINITARIAN POLEMIC

Voltaire's fundamental antagonism to the Trinity and the two natures bears a remarkable resemblance to that of the Jews. The numerical sophistication and the anthropomorphic adulteration of the divinity offended him no less than it offended them. Yet his monotheism sprang from the eighteenth-century liberation of reason, while theirs continued to flow from a very ancient tradition. The gratuitous abstractions imposed by the political machinations of the Church convinced him that the Christian priesthood had stolen the deity from universal reason and enshrined it in a mystery to which they pretended to control the access. The natural light reveals his God spontaneously to all men, even those who neglect or ignore it, and even those who bury it in metaphysical illusion.[1] This deism nonetheless underwent an evolution during his long career. From his early youth, high intelligence afforded him an unusual independence of mind, which in turn kindled an insatiable desire for freedom of expression, a freedom somewhat fully enjoyed only late in his life. He soon recognized Christianity as the greatest obstacle to his self-liberation, but he was already an old man before he realized that the liberty to say and write what he pleased had little value without the emancipation of his listeners and readers. Until the return from England, therefore, his satire served to enhance his reputation as a daring poet rather than promote freedom of expression.

[1] In the chapter of *Zadig* (1747) entitled "Le Souper," the hero terminates disagreement between representatives of several ancient religions by obtaining unanimous consent to the worship of one supreme Being. Even the oversubtle Greek, a slyly indirect representative of Christianity, agrees.

Until the Return from England

The Jesuits of Louis-le-Grand completed their education of Arouet by 1711. Had he already begun to use what they had taught him against Christianity? One cannot definitely say. Since nobody could then foresee the value of information about him, the evidence is insufficient and probably unreliable. Yet it does conform to the pattern of behavior among boys attending sectarian boarding schools for the indoctrination of an elite: alternating revolt and dedication without profound conviction, and especially to attract attention. One report suggests that he angered a Jesuit teacher by a deistic remark[2] and, according to another, a classmate thought he might be tempted to become a Jesuit himself.[3] The sparse documentation of the years after he left Louis-le-Grand does not suggest rebellion against the convenient Christianity the fathers had tried to instill in him, but rather the impertinent iconoclasm of a gifted adolescent. Pomeau designates "Le Vrai Dieu" of 1715 as his earliest extant satire of Christian mysteries. Although the critic bases this description of the ode on the irony he perceives in it, the poet does not signal any ironical intentions by means of incongruous terms in strategic places, the usual Voltairian technique. The older poet denied having written this poem, a denial we need not take seriously, and even attributed it to someone else[4] as if embarrassed by some unusual deficiency in it. Otherwise, why would he have repudiated proof of a precocious talent? Perhaps he thought the irony too equivocal. The fideistic profession of Christianity in the poem tends to overshadow the illogic in the content of belief exposed by it.

The poet's persistent reference to Christ as God himself, a favorite Voltairian device, is certainly a deliberate confusion of the first two persons in the Trinity. But the dogma stipulates unity as well as distinction, thus taking this unity literally does not, by itself, dramatize the logical contradiction in the dogma. Having begun the ode by an orthodox attack on polytheism and idolatry, Arouet heralds the estab-

[2] In *La Vie de Voltaire* (Genève, 1781), Théophile Duvernet tells of a clash between young Arouet and Father Lejay: "Le père Lejay, dans sa colère... le prend au collet et en le secouant rudement, lui crie à plusieurs reprises: 'Malheureux, tu seras un jour l'étendard du déisme en France'" (p. 16). This anecdote resembles the sort of retrospective apocrypha that often clutter the biography of a famous man.

[3] A letter dated July 23, 1711, from Voltaire to Fyot de La Marche reveals that a certain Blanchard asked Voltaire if he and de La Marche had not come to such a decision together. Voltaire denied the rumor (Best. D5).

[4] A note appended to the *Dialogue de Pégase et du vieillard* (1774), signed M. de Morza (Voltaire himself), denies his authorship of several works, including the following: "Une ode intitulée le Vrai Dieu, qui est d'un jésuite nommé Lefèvre" (M. x, 200, n. 2).

lishment of the true religion on the ruins of such error, now that "Sur la terre un Dieu vient de naître" (M. VIII, 415). He then emphasizes the inability of men to seize the opportunity for belief occasioned by the coming of Christ: "Ouvre les yeux, homme infidèle" (M. VIII, 416). Thus the first five stanzas do not lend themselves to irony at the expense of Christianity, but the last four can be given such an interpretation. Since God has become mortal, for instance, men are able to kill him:

> Vous semblez, de vos maux complice,
> Oublier que vous êtes Dieu. (M. VIII, 417)

How can creation survive the Creator? Arouet tells the sun:

> Va te cacher au sein de l'onde:
> Peux-tu donner le jour au monde
> Quand ton Dieu cesse d'en jouir? (M. VIII, 417)

During the cataclysmic events following the crucifixion,

> La Terre, en abîmes ouverte,
> Avec regret se voit couverte
> Du sang d'un Dieu qui la forma. (M. VIII, 417)

Thus the creation becomes the scene of the Creator's death. Neither these passages[5] nor their context, however, contain any device intended to trigger an ironical reaction. Although each presents an ironical situation, the poet does not exploit it. Instead of appealing to reason, he simply exposes contradictions which like all contradictions are vulnerable to it. Since Christian mysteries consist of logical contradictions, Christian readers need not take offense. Only Christians conscious of the critical attitude which no doubt motivated the young poet would detect his irony. Consequently, the ode could not have made much of an impact on the public or satisfied the ambitions of the author. Arouet probably resorted to invisible irony in order to avoid pious retaliation, but the results must have seemed pusillanimous to Voltaire.

The old man no doubt remembered his performance in the libertine society he had frequented with greater pleasure. From this audience he had nothing to fear and wit at the expense of Christianity brought him the applause he craved, whether in conversation or, perhaps, in writings since lost. The most convincing evidence of his daring is retrospective in nature. Gloating over his imprisonment in

[5] The following lines are also noteworthy: "L'homme est heureux d'être perfide, / Et, coupables d'un déicide, / Tu nous fais devenir des dieux" (M. VIII, 417).

1726, an informer named Beauregard wrote the lieutenant de police, "Vous venez de mettre à la Bastille un homme que je souhaitais y voir il y a plus de 15 années" (D 277). Since this claim takes us back to the period of Louis-le-Grand, the possibility of exaggeration necessitates a shift of emphasis from the duration of the complaint to the persistence of the offence.[6] Among other sins, the informer accuses Arouet of preaching deism to young noblemen, declaring himself an "ennemi de Jésus-Christ"[7] and belittling the apostles as "de bonnes gens idiots, simples et crédules" (Best. D 277). Although he obviously thinks he has enough evidence to convict an enemy of Christ, one regrets that neither he nor anyone else goes into greater detail about what Arouet was preaching exactly. The simplicity and credulity of the apostles would nonetheless become a perennial Voltairian argument against the value of their testimony. Upon it, he realized, stands or falls the divinity of Christ as well as the latter's relations with the other two persons in the Trinity and therefore the Trinity itself. Destroy the credibility of the apostles and the entire Trinity collapses, a commonsense observation. Apparently ignorant of these consequences, however, the informer is protesting rather against Arouet's disrespect for the apostles.

He had no respect for the Holy Spirit either, as he demonstrated in "La Bastille," a satire in verse inspired by his first incarceration there in 1717. Arrested the day after Pentecost, the satirist pretends to have mistaken the unexpected arrival of the police for a recurrence of the Spirit's miraculous intervention in Acts 2.1-4 (see p. 8). That morning, he testifies, "Un bruit étrange en sursaut m'éveilla." A valet given to drink announces that "le Saint-Esprit est là," for he has read in his Bible "Qu'avec vacarme il entre chez les gens" (M. IX, 353). The poet tells himself,

> "Gentil puîné de l'essence suprême,
> Beau Paraclet, soyez le bienvenu;
> N'êtes-vous pas celui qui fait qu'on aime?" (M. IX, 353)

Instead of a pigeon or a dove, however, a score of crows appear. "The

[6] "Il y en a 10 à 12 qu'étant allé voir à Saint Sulpice M. l'abbé d'Albert, je me plaignis à lui du métier que faisait l'homme en question, prêchant le déisme tout à découvert aux toilettes de nos jeunes seigneurs" (D 277). "D" refers to a letter in *Correspondence, The Complete Works of Voltaire*, ed. Theodore Besterman (Banbury, 1968-). I will use Besterman's numbering when he has been unable to date a letter precisely.

[7] "Je suis excusable de ne me pas nommer ici; cet homme peut sortir de prison, c'est le même qui conduisit en fiacre quatre coupejarrets jusqu'à la porte du chevalier de Rohan et d'ailleurs on est assez fondé à craindre ceux qui osent bien s'attaquer à Jésus-Christ même, le fils unique du tout puissant" (D 277).

younger son of the supreme essence" in this passage implies that the third and second persons of the Trinity do not belong to the same essence as the first, an error the older Voltaire would not have made. Further on, the satirist assimilates the royal family to gods on earth, thus completing his metaphor, since Christ, once a God on earth himself, had sent the Spirit to the apostles. Arouet has assembled this metaphor from choice elements of the Pentecostal miracle in Acts, the dogma of the Trinity, the Paraclete passages in John, and the descent of the Spirit on Jesus after his baptism in all four gospels (see p. 33). Except for the Trinity, he borrows from these sources so accurately and blends his borrowings so skillfully that one can only wonder whether he was relying on his education[8] or a more recent perusal of the New Testament. Although resentment of the Regent, the god on earth who had imprisoned him,[9] outweighs contempt for Christianity as the motive behind this satire, he does not forget Christianity. The appearance of "vingt corbeaux" where "une colombelle" (M. IX, 353) was expected sparks the irony of a police raid masquerading as the miraculous intervention of the Holy Spirit. This is the kind of device lacking in "Le Vrai Dieu." Arouet focuses our attention on several ironical contrasts, those between Christian myth and the reality of life under a Christian monarch, the promise of divine inspiration, and the fact of repression by fellow men, the doctrine of love and the effect of the Regent's ruffled vanity. Despite the subtlety of these considerations, the example of his personal experience provides common sense with a means of access to them all. Surprisingly, therefore, "La Bastille" has much more to offer than mere circumstantial satire. For this very reason, no doubt, it survived while other poems from this period disappeared.

The poem Voltaire particularly intended for immortality, though in vain, was of course *La Henriade*. In bidding for immortality, he took pains to offend as few of his contemporaries as possible, a precaution that dampened his enthusiasm. His efforts to win even pious approval for his epic exposed him to the kind of theological distinctions that he would later ridicule. In *La Ligue*, an early version of the poem begun in 1715, he published the following naïvely obsequious lines:

[8] "La mémoire de M. de Voltaire était prodigieuse. Il m'a dit cent fois: *Voyez dans tel ouvrage, dans tel volume, à peu près à telle page, s'il n'y a pas telle chose?* et il arrivait rarement qu'il se trompât, quoiqu'il n'eût pas ouvert le livre depuis douze ou quinze ans." Jean-Louis Wagnière, *Additions au Commentaire historique sur les oeuvres de l'auteur de La Henriade* in Sébastien Longchamp and Wagnière, *Mémoires sur Voltaire* (Paris, 1826), I, 53.

[9] He had apparently not written the satirical Latin inscription attacking the Regent for which he was imprisoned.

La puissance, l'amour avec l'intelligence,
Unis et séparés, composent son essence [celle de Dieu]. (B. II, 614)[10]

These verses nonetheless provide further evidence that he had not yet mastered the essential elements of Trinitarian dogma. Instead of three persons, he cites three abstractions, none of which adequately represents the person to which it apparently corresponds. Tradition, for instance, ascribes love to the Father as well as the Son and wisdom to the Father as well as the Holy Spirit. Too obviously a contradiction, a united and separated Trinity, moreover, can only be construed, according to theological semantics, as tritheism, which the main stream of Christianity had always rejected. Having detected this flaw, Voltaire replaced *unis et séparés* by *unis et divisés* in the first edition of the *Henriade* in 1728, an improvement tightening the relations between the three abstractions. Yet this expression is still defective, as a correspondent of the *Mémoires de Trévoux* complained in 1731, because the three persons are not *divisées* according to dogma, but rather *distinguées*.[11] Distinction between them does not imply division between them. Although *distinguées* would have provided the poet with the three syllables he needed for his verse, he never bothered to bring it up to theological standards of accuracy. Perhaps he disdained a concession that would veil from reason the fundamental contradiction he saw in the doctrine. Pomeau has discovered another anti-trinitarian allusion in the *Henriade*. The poet is relating the appearance of various non-Christian sects at the last judgment:

Le dervis étonné d'une vue inquiète,
A la droite de Dieu cherche en vain son prophète. (B. II, 515)

These lines convey two meanings, an obvious one intended to satisfy Christians and a subtle one more welcome to deists. They reassure Christians that God will hold infidels responsible for their error and insinuate, for the benefit of deists, that no one, Christ or Mohammed, shares any power with God. Yet what was to prevent shrewd and alert Christians from ferreting out the deist message? This danger may well have prompted Voltaire to drop the verses from the editions of

[10] "B." refers to Theodore Besterman, ed., *The Complete Works of Voltaire* (Banbury, 1968-).

[11] Florida quotes as follows: "On cite une définition de la Trinité, et cette définition est très mauvaise: ...Car il faut dire que les trois personnes adorables de la Sainte Trinité sont, non pas unies, mais une seule substance, un seul Dieu, quoiqu'elles soient, non pas *divisées*, mais distinguées. On ne se sert des termes *unis* et *divisés* qu'à l'égard des substances différentes. Ces termes sont donc impropres à l'égard de la Trinité, et plus propres à altérer le dogma qu'à l'établir et l'enseigner" (p. 78).

the *Henriade* published between 1730 and 1733 when, having returned to Paris from his English exile, he had good reason to stay out of trouble. These isolated allusions to the Trinity in the epic are propaganda in favor of a Jesuit-deist God.

Since the "Epître à Uranie" (1738) presents the same propaganda, the "Epître à Julie," the original version of the same work, must have done so too, but the text has been lost. Having composed "Julie" in 1722, however, Voltaire read it to his future enemy Jean-Baptiste Rousseau, who later threatened to divulge the contents in a letter tentatively dated 1725 by Besterman (D 248). He carried out this threat in a letter to the *Bibliothèque française* in 1736, yet without sufficient detail to satisfy scholarly curiosity. He deplores a work

> remplie d'horreurs... contre la personne même de Jésus-Christ, qui y était qualifié partout d'une épithète dont je ne puis me souvenir sans frémir. (D 1078)

Despite his habitually distorted representation of Voltaire's works,[12] remembrance of the horrible epithet has the ring of truth and one wishes that he had overcome his scruples. What indeed was this epithet? One must take further testimony by Rousseau into account:

> L'avis charitable que je lui avais donné... l'engagea à changer le titre de son "Epître à Julie" en celui d'"épître à Uranie" et d'en convertir les blasphèmes en ceux qu'il y a substitués. (D 1078)

Elsewhere in the same letter, one finds an explanation of what Rousseau means by such conversion: "Il a mitigé les expressions" (D 1078). Thus Voltaire had apparently substituted a milder blasphemy for the horrible epithet. Assuming that Rousseau is referring to the same text as that of the 1738 edition, examination reveals only one passage likely to have replaced the most shocking kind of blasphemy against Christ that Voltaire would cultivate in later years:

> Le fils de Dieu, Dieu même, oubliant sa puissance,
> Se fait concitoyen de ce peuple odieux [les Juifs];
> Dans les flancs d'une Juive il vient prendre naissance. (Wade p. 1110)[13]

Even the last of these verses does not contain any epithet blasphemous enough to make a pious hypocrite shudder. Since Voltaire, according to Rousseau, substituted milder blasphemies for those in "Julie," it is entirely possible that this epithet appeared in a line changed to read

[12] Rousseau's letter to Lasseré on Aug. 11, 1725, contains an appraisal of *Hérode et Mariamne* (1725) which is so biased that one can hardly recognize Voltaire's tragedy.

[13] Ira Wade, ed., "The Epître à Uranie," *Publications of the Modern Language Association*, 47 (1932), 1066-112.

"Dans les flancs d'une Juive [Dieu] vient prendre naissance." The miraculous conception of Jesus in the body of Mary would later bear the brunt of his assault on the nativity stories. His common sense told him that women do not become pregnant without male semen and it suggested that the miracle veiled a pregnancy unworthy of Jesus' reputation. Nor must one forget that Voltaire himself believed his natural father to be the poet Rochebrune and not his legal father, his mother's husband.[14] The horrible epithet may have been *bâtard* or something of the sort. Less taboo in French than English, this word would have met Voltaire's standard of poetic elegance,[15] yet it still qualified as an epithet, and not something worse, in Rousseau's vocabulary. Its association with Jesus' name, however, would certainly have explained the newly pious Rousseau's outrage. To be sure, proof that Voltaire called Jesus a bastard in "Julie" would require more conclusive evidence, providing it exists. The rest of the passage in the 1738 edition treats Jesus with contempt rather than scorn in referring to his childhood, his trade, and his mission. Having mentioned "un Dieu mourant," a theme already developed in "Le Vrai Dieu," he elaborates further on:

> Le fils d'un charpentier expira sur la croix.
> Je ne reconnais point à cette indigne image
> Le Dieu que je dois adorer. (Wade p. 1110)

Probably this early in his life, Voltaire's experience offered no example of tradesmen's sons rising to celebrity and his bourgeois prejudices prevented him from seeking any.[16] Middleclass common sense often implies the assumption of a lesser intelligence in the lower class, a motive in his eventual hatred of Jean-Jacques Rousseau. In his 1775 revision of the text, he re-entitled the poem "Le Pour et le contre," although the *pro* stanza comes only after the *con* stanza and contains many fewer lines. It begins with a vision which in 1738 read as follows:

> Ciel! ô ciel! quel objet vient de frapper ma vue!
> Je reconnais le Christ puissant et glorieux.

[14] To Richelieu, June 8, 1744: "Je crains bien qu'en cherchant de l'esprit et des traits, / Le bâtard de Rochebrune / Ne fatigue et n'importune / Le successeur d'Armand et les esprits bien faits." Armand was Voltaire's elder brother. To Mme Denis (his niece), July 25, 1753: "J'en ai trop méprisé mes traverses... mais il n'en est point du tout de même de la colique, et du commencement d'une hydropisie. Je me souviens que Rochebrune dans cet état, ne pouvait seulement faire une chanson." To Mme Denis, Aug. 11, 1753: "Vous savez que Rochebrune... est mort [d'une hydropisie], et que j'ai quelques raisons de prétendre à son tempérament."

[15] He uses it to refer to himself in the letter to Richelieu quoted in the preceding note.

[16] Late in life, he would come to admire Beaumarchais, but not, so far as we know, because the playwright had once been a humble watchmaker's son.

....
Sous ses pieds triomphants la mort est abattue. (Wade p. 1111)

The poet soon reduces this mysticism to the status of a beneficial illlusion and concludes: "C'est un bonheur... d'être trompé par [le Christ]." In a final stanza, he introduces a third point of view coinciding with his own deism which, by implication, he recommends as a resolution of the dilemma.

Assuming that much of "Julie" survives in "Uranie," the latter poem suggests that by 1722 he had already begun to master the art of antichristological satire. After the timidity and perhaps the inadequate irony of "Le Vrai Dieu," the critical attitude denounced by Beauregard resulted in a playful yet skillful attack on the Holy Spirit in "La Bastille" and a daring assault on Christology in "Uranie." His contradictory motivation in writing *La Ligue*, on the other hand, and the ignorance of the Trinity in which the Jesuits had left him conspired to spoil his brief incursions into that area. This dogma, in fact, would not greatly tempt him until much later in his career, when he had mastered philosophical dialectics sufficiently to cope with it.

Lettres philosophiques

After his quarrel with the chevalier de Rohan, Voltaire obtained release from the Bastille by offering to accept exile in England. He was living in Wandsworth, near London, when he sought unsuccessfully to employ the Quaker Edward Higginson as an intellectual companion. An apprentice teacher in the Quaker school there, Higginson impressed Voltaire by his Biblical scholarship and, no doubt, his tutoring skill. Voltaire consulted him several times in pursuing studies especially intended to improve his knowledge of the English language. Higginson testifies that, after admitting his deism, Voltaire went too far, "deriding the account given by the four evangelists of the birth of Christ and his miracles."[17] Later, Voltaire seems to have received an initiation to criticism of the Trinity at the court of Caroline, Princess of Wales, who enjoyed the company of distinguished freethinkers. Bolingbroke testifies that she delighted in reopening the fourth-century dispute over the Trinity.[18] When Voltaire returned to France in 1729, he took several manuscripts in English

[17] Gustave Lanson, ed., *Lettres philosophiques* (Paris, 1924), I, 21-22.

[18] "Our learned queen... attends frequently to the controversy, almost 1400 years old, and still carried on with as much warmth and as little success as ever, about that profound mystery, the Trinity." Quoted from A.M. Rousseau, *L'Angleterre et Voltaire* in *SVEC*, 145 (1976), 91.

with him, among them drafts of essays eventually published in the *Letters Concerning the English Nation*, the preliminary version of the *Lettres philosophiques*. Harcourt Brown[19] includes the second, the third and the seventh letters, which concern us here, among those originally written in English.

One of the several entitled "On the Quakers,"[20] the third letter explains how, in Voltaire's satirical opinion, George Fox founded Quakerism, but the satirist obviously had the foundation of a more ancient sect in mind as well. "*Christ,*" he hints in the first sentence, "was the first Quaker." Over the next 1600 years, "a few Quakers concealed in the world" preserved "the sacred fire" of Christianity in its original purity, when finally, in 1642,[21] it spread to England. The noncommital style exposes the absurdity of the pretention rather than the falsity of the claim, for at this point Voltaire took little interest in the transmission and development of Christianity. His analysis of Fox's career, on the other hand, shows that he had given much thought and perhaps even some study to the historical Jesus. Although he never states the parallel between Fox and Jesus here (see p. 33), he constantly implies it. Fox, he tells us, was born of a humble father (a silk-weaver) in a remote region (Leicestershire) rife with sectarianism. At about 25—Jesus may have been 30—he began to preach "with all the requisites of a true apostle, that is, without being able either to read or write" (*Letters* p. 13), an error in the case of Fox,[22] but a probability in the case of Jesus. Voltaire's experience with the Jansenist convulsionaries in Paris persuaded him that illiteracy breeds enthusiasm, an observation which does not apply to all enthusiasm. Though morally irreproachable, Fox was "a holy madman [who] traveled from one village to another exclaiming against war and the clergy" (*Letters* p. 14). Thus Voltaire thought Jesus' ethic to be pacifist rather than eschatological, an illusion propagated by the synoptists. His slight sympathy for Jesus in later years would arise from a feeling of solidarity with a fellow adversary of the priesthood, although Jesus in reality may have supported the Pharisees in their opposition to the Sadducees. Voltaire attributes Fox's arrest to clerical

19 "The composition of the *Letters Concerning the English Nation*," *The Age of Enlightenment* (London, 1967), pp. 15-34.

20 *Letters* (New York, 1974).

21 An error detected by Lanson. William Sewel, Voltaire's source, sets the beginning of Quakerism in 1649 when Fox was twenty-five. Sewel, *The History of the Rise, Increases and Progress of the Christian People Called Quakers* (New York, 1844).

22 Sewel states, "[Fox] learned to read pretty well and to write so much as would serve him afterwards" (p. 20).

revenge, the reason for Jesus' arrest given by the evangelists. The arrest takes place in Derby, an equivalent of the provincial town Voltaire would always insist Jerusalem was. Having received a box on the ear for failing to remove his hat, Fox according to Voltaire offered the other ear for similar treatment. He was in fact slapped by the judge and, after a beating by a crowd, on another occasion, he invited a further beating.[23] But Voltaire is casting Fox in a role played by Jesus and assigning one of Jesus' sayings to him. Matthew and Luke formulate the saying as follows:

> To the man who slaps you on one cheek, present the other cheek too. (Lk. 6.29)
>
> If anyont hits you on the right cheek, offer him the other as well. (Mt. 5.39)

During the trial before the Sanhedrin, on the other hand, the synoptists report that the guards beat Jesus, while a guard in John, the prototype of Voltaire's officer, actually slaps him for answering the high priest improperly. Both the principle and the act seemed absurd to Voltaire, who nonetheless maintains that men incapable of reason cannot resist the persuasive power of such absurdity. After the slapping incident, Voltaire's Fox imitates Voltaire's Jesus less systematically, yet he imitates the apostles from time to time. Voltaire notes that Fox "ran up and down the country with a dozen proselytes [disciples] at his heels" (*Letters* p. 15). The jailors and auditors (tax collectors?) converted by him correspond to the ostracized members of Jewish society whom Jesus proselytized. Fox prophesies the death of a judge who is mistreating Quakers and the judge dies two days later, but he dies of apoplexy for having "besotted himself every day with bad beer and brandy" (*Letters* p. 16). Chance and nature explain, to Voltaire's satisfaction, all prophecies of Jesus, his followers, or anyone else, that may have been fulfilled. He was probably still thinking of Jesus and his followers, though less directly, when he described Fox's conception of inspired discourse:

> He began to writhe his body, to screw up his face, to hold his breath and to exhale it in a forcible manner, (*Letters* p. 16)

which Voltaire compares to the frenzy of the oracle at Delphi. "Inspiration soon became so habitual to [Fox]," Voltaire comments, "that he could scarce deliver himself in any other manner" (p. 16). The con-

[23] "As Fox was kneeling down to pray... [Justice] Bennet ran upon him, and *struck him with both his hands*" (Sewel, p. 38). Fox "stood up, and stretching out his arms, said with a loud voice: *strike again*" (Sewel, p. 70).

vulsionaries had taught him that delusion of the unthinking masses begins by the self-delusion of an unthinking individual convinced of his exceptional status. They had also taught him that "enthusiasm is an epidemical disorder" (*Letters* pp. 14-15). Fox, he observes, immediately communicated his "gift... to his disciples [who] aped very sincerely their master's grimaces" and soon "the vulgar" (*Letters* p. 16) were speaking through their noses too.

One cannot thoroughly evaluate this aspect of Letter 3 without comparing it to a passage in Letter 2 which describes a Quaker meeting attended by Voltaire.[24] There was a long silence, he says, then a man stood up and removed his hat.

> After making a variety of wry faces and groaning in a most lamentable manner, he partly from his nose and partly from his mouth threw out a strange, confused jumble of words (borrowed as he imagined from the gospel) which neither himself nor any of his hearers understood. (*Letters* p. 10)

Voltaire's elderly Quaker companion admits that they must tolerate such babbling because they never know whether madness or the Holy Spirit moves a fellow member to preach.[25] Implicitly Voltaire, who credits the Spirit only in the form of a superstition, diagnoses the madness as self-delusion or even self-hypnosis perhaps. The speaking with tongues he had witnessed in the Quaker meeting house not only resulted in the description in Letter 2, but also the speculation in Letter 3. Reflection on this experience suggested a likely secret of Jesus' success and an explanation for part of the Pentecostal miracle in Acts. Perhaps Jesus had used a similar technique to convince himself and his followers of inspiration by the Holy Spirit.

Another letter originally written in English is number 7, "On the Socinians, or Arians, or Antitrinitarians." Voltaire, who uses these words together with *unitarians* as synonyms, was thinking of English antitrinitarians in particular. At this point in his career, he seems to have known little of fourth-century Arianism or sixteenth- and seventeenth-century Socinianism. As an organized movement in Poland, Socinianism had long since disappeared, but the legend of such a movement lived on in Christian polemic. Both *Socinian* and *Arian* were convenient epithets traditionally hurled at opponents whose theology could be twisted into some vague resemblance to these

[24] In the Quaker meeting house, Gracechurch St., in the City.

[25] Voltaire is exaggerating. Lanson documents Quaker efforts to throttle a fellow Quaker given to unreasonable preaching (see I, 28-29).

defunct heresies.[26] A number of seventeenth- and eighteenth-century Englishmen, however, including Locke, Newton, and Clarke, do qualify variously as Socinian and Arian. *Unitarianism*, a more recent word,[27] and *antitrinitarianism* are affirmative and negative synonyms describing the same tendency from a technical viewpoint. In fact, theological controversies in the seventeenth and eighteenth centuries blurred distinctions between all four of these terms in the public mind. The text of the seventh letter suggests that Voltaire himself, who had not undertaken the research of the Cirey period, did not know how to distinguish between them precisely. Yet he must have been aware that they do not coincide semantically. This insight enabled him to exploit the confusion of the concepts in common experience, so as to persuade his readers that the Trinity had encountered constant and widespread resistance ever since its inception.[28] But he limits the amplification of this assumption to two brief passages, each of which occurs at the end of a paragraph on a subject more familiar to him. He inserts the following transition between an illustrative anecdote and a discussion of Newton and Clarke's unitarianism: "The principles of Arius began to revive, not only in England but in Holland and Poland" (*Letters* p. 37). This sentence reveals the full extent of his ignorance on this subject. Further on, he places a more effective transition between a synopsis of Clarke's career and allegations of an antitrinitarian sect in England: "Arianism after having triumphed during three centuries, and then forgot twelve, rises at last out of its own ashes" (*Letters* p. 38). Yet the present tense of the final verb clashes with the sum of three and twelve centuries, which takes us back to Socinianism in the fifteenth. Voltaire evidently wanted to bridge the gap between ancient and modern Arianism, but leaping from the seventh century to the fifteenth and then from Poland to

[26] "En France on appelle sociniens tous ceux qui passent pour incrédules sur les mystères de l'Evangile, quoique la plupart de ces gens-là n'aient jamais lu ni Socin ni ses disciples." Pierre Bayle, "Spinoza," *Dictionnaire historique et critique* (Genève, 1969). The gospel mysteries are probably for the Huguenot Bayle the portion of the dogma accepted by Protestants of the Calvinist type.

[27] In 1687, Locke's friend Stephen Nye published the first title to include this word: *A Brief History of the Unitarians, Called also Socinians*. He defines the word as a synonym of both Socinian and Arian.

[28] Florida shows that Voltaire is merely taking Christian apologists at their word: "Both Anastase and Maimbourg... imply a continuity between the ancient rejectors of orthodoxy and the post-Reformation figures who also parted from the doctrinal norm. Both of them however emphasize the dormancy of the heresy for several centuries and do not try to show any actual historical link between the ancient Arians and the later heretics" (p. 19). See Louis Anastase, *Histoire du socinianisme* (Paris, 1727) and Louis Maimbourg, *Histoire de l'arianisme* (Paris, 1686).

England does not accomplish this purpose. The rebirth of the Socinian Phoenix nonetheless illustrates his premise that reasonable men will always refuse to believe in flagrant illogic. A more confident demonstration would have to await his studies at Cirey.

He begins the seventh letter by taking advantage of the subversive connotation with which polemicists had loaded the terms *Socinian* and *Arian*. For his claim that English antitrinitarians formed a small sect confirmed worst fears in pious quarters. This sect consisted, he says,

> of clergymen and a few very learned persons among the laity who, though they don't call themselves Arians or Socinians, do yet dissent entirely from St. Athanasius. (*Letters* p. 36)

In their opposition to the great partisan of the Nicene Trinity, they cited a prooftext that would later become a Voltairian favorite: "The Father is greater than the Son" (Jn. 14.28: "than I"). There could be no more powerful appeal to the natural light than confession by the Son himself of his inferiority to the Father. Despite this pregnant slogan, no antitrinitarian sect is likely to have existed in England then, but Voltaire was thinking of intellectuals like Clarke who met regularly in London at the house of William Whiston. This was a circle, not a sect.[29] Yet the fear of conspiracy raised among the orthodox by any hint of sectarianism made the seventh letter exciting for Voltaire's readers. If uncontrolled, however, this effect might have defeated his purpose of insinuating a recommendation of unitarianism, and so twice, towards the end of the letter, he curtails it. In the first instance, he reports that the sect was formed at a time of indifference to sectarianism in England and that it was declining. In the second instance, he reassures his readers that sects founded by philosophers like Newton, Clarke, Locke, and Le Clerc, have never drawn many followers. In other words, they are unlikely to threaten the state religion.

Voltaire seems to have obtained most of his information about English unitarianism from a conversation he had with Samuel Clarke, an Anglican minister and theological disciple of Newton.[30] Newton had

[29] "Whiston... formed a society for the study of primitive Christianity [in his own house]. In this he was joined by a zealous Quaker; by Gale the leader of the General Baptists; by young Talbot, son of the Bishop of Durham; and by Rundle, afterwards Bishop of Derry. Clarke and Hoadly had also some connection with the society." John Hunt, *Religious Thought in England* (London, 1873), III, 20.

[30] "Je ne crois pas qu'il y ait de démonstration proprement dite de l'existence de cet être indépendant de la matière. Je me souviens que je ne laissais pas en Angleterre d'embarrasser un peu le fameux docteur Clarke, quand je lui disais, on ne peut appeler démonstration un enchaînement d'idées qui laisse toujours des difficultés." To Frederick, ca. April 25, 1737 (D 1320).

died soon after Voltaire's arrival in England and, since he had published none of his voluminous theological writings, Clarke was a valuable source for anyone interested in them. Recent study of these manuscripts and publication of selections from them[31] confirm that Newton subordinated the Son to the Father, but they leave his attitude towards the divinity of Christ unclear. He nonetheless describes Jesus as "a true man born of a woman [and] crucified by the Jews" (p. 54). "Equality with God" in Philippians 2.6, he argues, does not mean "the congenit or natural divinity of the savior, but his glory and exaltation which he acquired by his death" (p. 131). Clarke's *Scripture Doctrine of the Trinity* (1712) indicates that, while he also believed in the subordination of the Son to the Father, he considered Christ to have been divine already in a pre-existent state, a characteristic of fourth-century Arianism.[32] Yet Clarke differs from Arius in that he implicitly excludes an initial period during which the Son did not exist: "The Son... existed with the Father from the beginning" (p. 279). Did Voltaire nonetheless explore such details in his interview with Clarke? The seventh letter makes no subtle distinction in this area. Concerning Newton, Voltaire merely mentions an inclination to Arianism and Socinianism as well as his approval of the unitarian tendency to "argue more mathematically than we do" (*Letters* p. 37), *we* being French Catholics. In Clarke he recognizes a "sanguine stickler for Arianism" (*Letters* p. 37), yet a virtuous man of mild disposition, little given to passion and absorbed in abstract calculations. These simple observations undermine the myth that heresy breeds monsters. Voltaire also pays homage to the *Scripture Doctrine*,

> a work containing all the testimonies of the primitive ages, for and against the unitarians, and [leaving] to the reader the counting of the voices and the liberty of forming a judgment. (*Letters* p. 38)

While the disinterest impressed him at the time of the *Letters*, one would further expect him to appreciate, in later years, a useful source of patristic quotations concerning the Trinity, but the catalogues of the Ferney library do not list it.

31 Frank Manuel, *The Religion of Isaac Newton* (Oxford, 1974) and Herbert McLachland, ed., *Sir Isaac Newton, Theological Manuscripts* (Liverpool, 1950).

32 "The Son... is evidently subordinate to the Father [and] derives his being and attributes from the Father, the Father nothing from him" (p. 304). "The Scripture... always supposes and affirms [the Son] to have existed with the Father from the beginning and before all worlds" (p. 279). "The Son in the New Testament is sometimes styled God... upon account... of his relative attributes and divine authority over us" (p. 296). Samuel Clarke, *The Scripture Doctrine of the Trinity* (London, 1712).

Voltaire's apology of unitarianism in the seventh letter also includes an anecdote which Lanson has traced to Sozomen (VII, 6) and Theodoret (V, 16), although the author, he says, has borrowed it from an intermediate, English source.[33] In this anecdote, a father-son relationship in possible experience parallels the most important Trinitarian relation, which is inaccessible to experience. The bishop[34] tweaks the prince's nose in front of the emperor, so that the emperor's anger may serve as a token example of the Father's wrath should anyone fail to respect the Son. A comparison of variants from this anecdote yields evidence supporting Brown's opinion that Voltaire originally wrote the seventh letter in English:

> The emperor was going to order his attendants to throw the bishop out of the window. (*Letters* p. 37)
>
> L'empereur allait se fâcher contre l'évêque. (Jore 1734; Lanson I, 78)
>
> L'empereur allait jeter l'évêque par les fenêtres. (subsequent editions; Lanson I, 78)

Voltaire's unsuccessful efforts to obtain a tacit permission from the French government for the Jore edition included a version of this passage ascribing to the emperor greater patience with the bishop and therefore implying a higher regard for the Church. Anxious for official approval and the public acclaim he thought would follow, he may well have made the first change to avoid any compromising parallels with corresponding figures in France. Having failed to obtain tacit permission, however, he had no further reason to moderate the provocative original statement. Why would he otherwise have missed the opportunity to make a point neglected by his source? He finds the bishop's argument inconclusive and submits that the emperor should have answered:

> There are two ways in which men may be wanting in respect to me: first, in not doing honor sufficient to my son; and secondly, in paying him the same honor as to me. (*Letters* p. 37)

This appendix to the ancient anecdote exploits the error of trying to explain a supernatural belief by analogy with a natural situation, in which it appears as mere self-contradiction. Voltaire's reinterpretation of the story not only reveals the greater credibility of subordinationism, but also undermines the apologetic value of parallels between the natural and the supernatural. He designed the seventh

[33] After rejecting several French possibilities, Lanson settles for George Bull's *Defensio Fidei Nicaenae* in *The Works of the Right Reverend George Bull* (London, 1725), III, 36.
[34] Amphiloquius according to Theodoret.

letter as an appeal to three different notions in the common experience of his readers: first the subversive reputation of antitrinitarianism; secondly, the standard of moral and intellectual excellence, and thirdly, the innocuity of weak and declining influence. Since the second category corresponds to his basic intention of promoting sympathy for unitarianism, he concentrates on that one, using the anecdote to demonstrate intellectual solidity and the profile of Clarke to exemplify a reassuring morality. In presenting this material, moreover, he refrains from any indication of his own attitude towards it. One must infer this attitude from the preponderance of evidence favorable to antitrinitarians.

Voltaire's ostensible detachment did not deter the censor abbé Rothelin from condemning an expurgated version of the thirteenth letter, one of those Voltaire had composed in French after his return to France. Yet the original version, probably written in 1732, had the effect of challenging Catholicism even less subtly. Voltaire published this text only in 1738. Contending that philosophers pose no threat to society, he cites several examples of their acquiescence in religious beliefs which the context exposes as unreasonable:

> Le mystère de la trinité et celui de l'eucharistie ont beau être contraires aux démonstrations connues, ils n'en sont pas moins révérés chez les philosophes catholiques, qui savent que les objets de la raison et de la foi sont de différente nature. (Lanson I, 201)

The final clause contains an apologetic commonplace to which, in itself, the abbé Rothelin could hardly have objected. Yet the perfunctory reverence of "Catholic" philosophers for the two articles in which they cannot reasonably believe is a different matter. Their indifference for a form of alleged truth contrasts with the association of philosophy in general and the pursuit of truth. This indifference therefore implies a lack of confidence in the truthfulness of the Trinity and the Eucharist. Furthermore, the abbé Rothelin must have objected to the idea that one could demonstrate the contrary of these dogmas. Christian propaganda has always insisted on placing them "above" the possibility of demonstration or on a level inaccessible to reason, a level at which the contradiction implied by each of them is supernaturally reconciled. Voltaire has simply found another devious way of insinuating that no such level exists. Although common sense cannot reproduce the foregoing critical analysis, all of the elements analyzed condition the commonsense scepticism desired by Voltaire, who nonetheless continues to conceal his own opinion.

The playful display of journalistic disinterest in the first twenty-four letters disappears in the twenty-fifth, where he subjects extracts from Pascal's *Pensées* to a critical commentary. He seems to have written the *Remarques* in 1732 and 1733. He did not originally conceive of the project as a part of the *Lettres philosophiques*, but decided to include them in the work in 1733 and they first appeared only in the Jore edition of 1734.[35] Despite Desné's efforts to justify the insertion of the *Remarques* in the *Lettres*,[36] the two works obviously have little in common. The most plausible explanation advanced so far by critics remains the hypothesis of an attempt to flatter the government's anti-Jansenist bias in order to obtain an official endorsement of all twenty-five *Lettres*. The twenty-third letter, "Sur la considération qu'on doit aux gens de lettres," eloquently reveals Voltaire's longing for the public recognition given English writers. Unfortunately, Cardinal Fleury, the French prime minister, overturned abbé Rothelin's approval of the *Lettres* and one suspects that the deism behind Voltaire's attack on Pascal was his principal motive. One can readily imagine his reaction to Remarque XII which reopens the ancient controversy over why Jesus' fellow Jews failed to acknowledge his messiahship. Pascal typically converts this weakness into a strength by affirming that only a race as avaricious as the Jews could have mistaken messianic prophecy for a promise of wealth: "Il n'y avait qu'un peuple aussi charnel que celui-là qui s'y pût méprendre" (II, 197).[37] Instead of outrage over Pascal's anti-Semitism or contempt for his dialectic, Voltaire makes a devastating reply which tends to suggest both considerations: "Le peuple le plus spirituel de la terre l'aurait-il entendu autrement" (II, 197)? God would not have equipped us with the natural light if he had any use for perfidious circumlocution. The political servitude of Jews under Roman occupation, Voltaire comments, and their yearning for a military liberator, who would win respect for Israel from all nations, were enough to mislead any people:

> Comment avec les lumières de leur raison [les Juifs] pouvaient-ils voir ce vainqueur, ce monarque dans Jésus pauvre et mis en croix? (II, 198)

Beginning with the 1748 edition, he would emend as follows:

> ...dans un de leurs concitoyens, né dans l'obscurité, dans la pauvreté et condamné au supplice des esclaves? (II, 198)

[35] Thiériot, who was overseeing the first edition of the *Letters* in London (1733), did not follow his instructions to include the twenty-fifth letter.

[36] Roland Desné, "The Role of England in Voltaire's Polemic against Pascal," *Eighteenth-Century Studies Presented to Arthur Wilson* (Hanover, 1972), pp. 43-57. Skillfully, but unsuccessfully, in my opinion, Desné promotes a unity of theme.

[37] Louis Lafuma, ed., *Pensées* (Paris, 1962), n. 502. Although Voltaire used the faulty 1714 edition of the *Pensées*, the sentence is the same as in the excellent 1670 edition.

First-century Jews could not have differed from eighteenth-century Frenchmen who expected their king to meet the standards of dignity, wealth, and triumph. Jesus in any case exemplified the opposite extremes and his Jewish contemporaries were merely using their heads in refusing to recognize a messiah in him. But the author of Remarque XII is less interested in justifying them than in proving them to be right. Towards the end of XII, therefore, he shifts the accent from justification to proof:

> Comment un peuple si attaché à sa loi pouvait-il, sans une lumière supérieure, reconnaître dans les prophéties qui n'étaient pas leur loi, un Dieu caché sous la figure d'un Juif circoncis, qui par sa religion nouvelle a détruit et rendu abominable la circoncision et le sabbat, fondements sacrés de la loi judaïque! (II, 198)

This sentence begins by exculpating the Jews for having failed to interpret the prophecies as Christians do and ends by exposing the irony of an anti-Semitic religion founded by a Jew. Voltaire thus implies that Christianity not only betrayed its Jewish source but also its Jewish founder. He reinforces the irony in the sentence by inserting an allusion to the Christian God in the figure of a circumcised Jew, an obvious absurdity. Cardinal Fleury could scarcely have failed to understand that such a phrase did not impugn Jansenism alone, but rather Christianity in general. Although Voltaire intended the *Remarques* as a refutation of Pascal in particular, he saw in him the most prestigious of all Christian apologists and neglected no opportunity to strike at his Christian background.[38]

Pascal's anti-Semitism had given Voltaire the opportunity to exploit the Jewishness of Jesus, an enigma which may well have dawned on him in England. In the Leningrad Notebooks, written between 1735 and 1750, one finds, on this subject, a brief anecdote concerning Mme Acosta. Voltaire had suffered heavy losses when her husband declared bankruptcy in 1726, but he forgave him and continued to see his family. The anecdote, whose authenticity we have no reason to suspect, reports a conversation that must have taken place during one of these visits:

> Mme Acosta dit en ma présence à un abbé qui voulait la faire chrétienne, votre dieu est-il né Juif? Oui. A-t-il vécu Juif? Oui. Est-il mort Juif? Oui. Eh bien, soyez donc Juif. (B. LXXXI, 365)

Not only does Voltaire indicate that the experience is a personal one, but also he does not use it, or at least not without extensive transfor-

[38] "Quel est l'homme sage qui sera prêt à se pendre parce... que sa raison ne peut débrouiller le mystère de la trinité?" Remarque VI, Lanson, II, 193.

mations, anywhere in his published works. This discretion likewise suggests that he actually witnessed such a conversation. One can well imagine why he did not forget it, for the Jewess was demonstrating in his very presence that Jesus' alleged intention of founding Christianity could not withstand analysis.

"Examen de la Genèse"

During his liaison with Emilie du Châtelet (1733-1749), he helped her apply such an analysis to the Bible. The proceedings of their collaboration, entitled "Examen de la Genèse," subsist in the form of two manuscripts,[39] which may have circulated among friends of the couple. Despite a thorough study of the work by Wade, the extent of Voltaire's contribution remains obscure. In a letter to Mme du Deffand in 1759, Voltaire implies that Emilie is the author: "Mme du Châtelet... avait bien commenté [l'Ancien Testament] d'un bout à l'autre" (Sept. 17). He apparently did not mention the New Testament, also commented on in the "Examen," because he had only the Old Testament in mind at the moment. He certainly wanted Mme du Deffand to think that Emilie had written the "Examen" and he may have regarded it as her work himself. He cared neither for sustained scholarly routine nor a reputation as a scholar and he lived in fear that works beneath him might be attributed to him. None of the text in the "Examen" reappears anywhere in collective editions of his works and he makes no further allusions to it in his correspondence. Wade has even found evidence suggesting that a manuscript of the "Examen" in Emilie's handwriting existed as late as 1829.[40] Yet these points in favor of her authorship are not conclusive. Grimm testifies in the *Correspondance littéraire* of 1776:

> On nous a assuré que [*La Bible enfin expliquée*]... était le fruit des loisirs de Cirey où on lisait tous les matins, pendant le déjeuner, un chapitre de l'Histoire Sainte, sur lequel chacun faisait ses réflexions à sa manière. (XI, 348)[41]

Voltaire, he adds, was the one who recorded these reflexions. Now Voltaire's *Bible enfin expliquée* is obviously a different text from the

[39] Troyes 2376-2377. Another manuscript sold in Paris in 1829 was entitled more appropriately "Examen de la Genèse et des livres du Nouveau Testament," according to Ira Wade, *Voltaire and Mme du Châtelet: An Essay on the Intellectual Activity at Cirey* (Princeton, 1941), p. 43.

[40] The manuscript sold in Paris in 1829; see preceding note.

[41] Grimm, Melchior, Denis Diderot, etc., *Correspondance littéraire, philosophique et critique* (Paris, 1877-1882).

"Examen." Since *on* in Grimm's passage almost certainly refers to Voltaire and Emilie, the "Examen" rather than the *Bible* would appear to have resulted from these conversations. Although one can imagine a simultaneous composition of the two works, the detached commentaries in the "Examen," each of them devoted to a single chapter of the Bible, resemble the product of a daily routine far more evidently than the sections in the *Bible enfin expliquée*.[42] Yet this daily routine itself raises a problem. Mme de Graffigny, the most informative witness of the couple's life at Cirey, records Emilie's entire daily schedule. She says nothing of lunch with Voltaire or, for that matter, any meal involving study of the Bible. She in fact observes that, while the couple invite her down to late-morning coffee with them, they do not accompany her and others to lunch, which Voltaire and Emilie apparently forego. And Mme de Graffigny visited Cirey in 1739 when their Biblical scholarship had probably already begun.[43] In contrast with Voltaire's Genevan period, not a trace of this activity appears in the extant correspondence of 1742-1743, when volume IV of the "Examen," on the gospels, was being composed.[44] But nearly all of the correspondence between Voltaire and Emilie, where allusions to their mutual study of the Bible would be likely to occur, has been lost. Despite the confusing impression conveyed by this extratextual evidence, one almost has to suppose that Emilie (despite Grimm) was the redactor of the "Examen," that Voltaire contributed some of the contents, and that they kept this activity confidential because she typically feared the reaction of the authorities.

If Voltaire collaborated with Emilie to any extent, his language may have affected her style, for she fully recognized his superiority as a writer. In one instance, she actually quotes a comment by him on conflicting events in the Bible: "Mais je dirai comme M. de Voltaire, ce n'est pas ma faute" (III, 119). Having found this phrase only twice in all of Voltaire's works, Wade plausibly concludes that Voltaire used it in conversation rather than writing.[45] Yet one can go further: The insertion of such a customary conversational remark in this critical

[42] I will discuss the *Bible enfin* in a later section (see p. 237).

[43] According to Wade, the activity began in 1736-1738 and continued until 1746-1749.

[44] According to Wade, p. 126.

[45] "Ce n'est pas ma faute si le curé Jean Meslier [edité par Voltaire] et le prédicateur des cinquante [Voltaire] ont été de même avis à deux cents lieues l'un de l'autre. Il faut que la vérité soit bien forte pour se faire sentir avec tant d'uniformité à deux personnes si différentes. Plût à Dieu que le genre humain eût toujours pensé de même, le sang humain n'aurait pas coulé depuis le concile de Nicée jusqu'à nos jours pour des absurdités qui font frémir le sens commun." Voltaire to the Duchess of Saxe-Gotha, Oct. 18, 1762.

commentary on the Bible suggests that it had become a satirical refrain causing smiles when it recurred. The constant repetition of "Il est plaisant que..." introducing events in which the Lord of Ferney would later take delight no doubt implies the couple's amusement. But unmistakable traits of Voltaire's style also appear, such as the frequency of superlatives and the habit of assigning his own opinions to others. The commentary on Matthew 9 emphasizes Jesus' epithet for the Pharisees, "*sépulcres blanchis*,"[46] a Voltairian tic. An allusion to the miraculous cure of Mme La Fosse (1725), a miracle Voltaire had investigated in person, further attests his collaboration on the "Examen" (Mt. 9).

In reading the commentary on the life of Jesus in Matthew, one can scarcely ignore his contributions. Anyone familiar with Emilie's competent but conventional style could hardly find her capable of describing the descent of the Holy Spirit on Jesus after his baptism by John as follows:

> Quelques commentateurs ont trouvé de l'indécence à faire venir le Saint Esprit sous la forme d'un pigeon, et ils ont prétendu que la colombe qui parut alors n'était qu'un symbole, mais le sentiment contraire a prévalu et le plus grand nombre a trouvé que la colombe était un animal doux, chaste et fécond, était très propre à loger le Saint Espirt, lequel, à ce qu'on prétend, est tout cela. (Mt. 3.16)

The vague source (*quelques commentateurs*), the mundane standard (*de l'indécence*), the choice of a vulgar bird (*un pigeon*), the facetious similarity between the dove, an object of experience, and the Holy Spirit, a mythical being, all belong to Voltaire's satirical arsenal of later years. Perhaps the redundancy of the first two clauses ("ont trouvé... et... ont prétendu") and the unexplained use of *pigeon* and *colombe* as synonyms come from Emilie, but the rest probably belongs to Voltaire. Wade shows that most of the "Examen" consists of borrowings from Calmet's *Commentaire littéral*. In the passage above, the confirmation of the traditional interpretation by the majority of scholars in Calmet becomes a display of their wishful phantasy in contrast with the sober minority of dissenters. Voltaire achieves this effect by his use of the adjectives *doux, chaste* and *fécond*, particularly the last two, which present a ludicrous contradiction. For all her intelligence, it is hard to believe that Emilie could have composed this passage by herself, but other commentary on the same chapter does seem to have been within her reach: Incapable of sin, Jesus had no need of baptism. How could the sky have split open? Did the pigeon speak? Who heard

[46] The commentary on the gospels is in Vol. IV of the manuscript.

the voice? Whom did they think the voice was designating? Probably John, who was better known than Jesus. Either Emilie or Voltaire could have made such objections.

The drowning of 2000 pigs in Matthew 8 naturally appealed to their curiosity.[47] After scepticism over the existence of swine in what they mistakenly thought a Jewish land,[48] they sympathize with "ces deux mille pauvres cochons qui en étaient bien innocents" and their owners "qui, moyennant ce miracle, durent être ruinés" (Mt. 8.32).[49] Irony over the economical loss suits Voltaire more convincingly than irony over cruelty to innocent animals, which Emilie may have contributed. The former appears frequently in Voltaire's works and the latter, practically never. Surprise over the docility of the herdsmen, another Voltairian theme, inspires a further remark:

> Si un enthousiaste en faisait autant de nos jours, il serait sûrement puni; ainsi... sans leur poltronnerie Jésus eût été pendu ce jour-là... Voilà une plaisante manière d'instruire et de sauver les hommes. (Mt. 8.32)

In the minds of his Christian contemporaries, his habitual substitution of *pendu* for *crucifié* tended to convert a sacred martyrdom into a criminal execution. The injustice of destroying the innocent herdsmen's livestock and the irrelevance of a supernatural distraction from Jesus' professed mission would always irritate Voltaire. He must have said this passage, therefore, and Emilie must have written it down.

Somewhat the same procedure seems to have produced the following observation as well:

> Il est plaisant que le fils de Dieu vienne se faire crucifier publiquement dans ce monde, et qu'il ressuscita incognito. (Mt. 28)

The contrast between the public humiliation of Jesus' execution and his private vindication by appearances to his followers never failed to excite Voltaire's suspicions. His common sense told him that many disinterested witnesses had confirmed the ordinary result of a radical career and that a few ambitious disciples had recouped the loss of

[47] Matthew situates this exorcism in Gadara, where two demoniacs, rather than one as in the other synoptics, are on the rampage. Jesus transfers the devils to a herd of swine which stampede into the lake and drown.

[48] The incident, according to the synoptics, occurred in the Decapolis, a pagan country.

[49] Voltaire borrowed his principal objections here from Thomas Woolston, *First Discourse on the Miracles of our Saviour* (London, 1727). "The Jews are forbidden to eat swine's flesh; what should they do with swine?... The proprietors of the swine were great losers and sufferers; and we don't read that Jesus made them amends, or that they deserved such usage from him" (pp. 33-34).

their benefactor by propagating the myth of his resurrection. He was probably the one who borrowed *dans ce monde* from the New Testament, for he would find Biblical parody irresistible later in his career. When Emilie wrote "Il est plaisant..." here, however, she must have been expressing her reaction to what he was saying. Their commentary on John 20 evokes the disciples' difficulty in recognizing the risen Christ. After puzzling over the evidence, Voltaire—for how could Emilie have thought of it?—concluded: "Je crois effectivement que rien ne change plus que d'être crucifié." Experience tells us, in other words, that the definitive change of death precludes a temporary return to life. In his treatment of the risen Christ's ability to pass through walls, Voltaire again imitates Calmet's practice of recording scholarly opinions, but one will not find the following opinion in Calmet: "Jésus... passa par le trou de la serrure" (Jn. 20.19). Voltaire could not care less whether keyholes existed in first-century Palestine. Since his contemporaries knew they were not always used to unlock doors, he proposed this inelegant explanation of the mystery. Rather than explain the mystery of the conception, on the other hand, he simply removes its taboo by describing it in vulgar language. Gabriel told Joseph "qu'il avait l'honneur d'être cocu du Saint-Esprit" (Mt. 1). Everyone knew that being a cuckold was no honor and that mere spirits do not endanger the virtue of men's wives. He thus returns obliquely to the insinuation that the miracle of the conception camouflages an illegitimate birth.

Was it he who also exploited contradictions between the two natures in Luke? Noting that Jesus prays to God in Luke 6.12, the commentator reasons:

> Sa personne humaine ne priait pas sa personne divine, mais sa nature humaine priait sa nature divine; ce qui fait une explication bien lumineuse. (Lk. 6.12)

This naïve analysis of Scripture in terms of dogma followed by exaggerated admiration for the concordance is too clever a caricature of Calmet for Emilie to have thought of it. The technique definitely resembles one used in the war on the infamous. Elsewhere, the commentator wonders why Jesus' divinity did not dispell the fear of his humanity in the garden of Gethsemane: "Assurément il avait une humanité très poltronne" (Lk. 22). In *assurément*, one recognizes another Voltairian favorite and the wit is obviously his too. An anecdote illustrating the conflict between the two natures confirms his authorship:

> Il fallait... dire [à Jésus] comme M. de Mazarin qui tremblait encore de peur après avoir gagné un gros coup. "Mon ami, dis à ton humanité que ta divinité est là." (Lk. 22)

Voltaire, not Emilie! Nor does he spare the Trinity. How could Emilie have supposed "le Saint Esprit fort piqué" over Jesus' declaration in Matthew 11.27 that only the Father and the Son know each other? Surely it was he who likewise added, "Ce qui fait du Saint Esprit un 0 en chiffre." A mathematical joke reducing the Trinity to two persons and the third person to zero could scarcely have come from the glum and passionate Emilie who, in all probability, depended on Voltaire for comic relief. There are many passages in the "Examen" that expose the divinity of Christ and the Trinity to criticism as sharp as any of the quotations above, and yet without the slightest hint of irony. Might one not conclude that it was she, and not Voltaire, who contributed them to the work? The following hypothesis also beckons: Emilie devoted a limited amount of time each day at the same hour to a chapter of the Bible and the corresponding commentary in Calmet. Voltaire attended many of these sessions and perhaps even read aloud from the daily text. He made comments which she recorded along with her own. Yet the bulk of the work was hers and he considered it as such, even after her death. He had no reason to retrieve comments deposited in the manuscript of a sorely regretted friend, for he was never at a loss to produce others.

Examen important

Since the "Examen de la Genèse" covers the entire Bible from Genesis to Revelation, Voltaire and Emilie must have begun with the Old Testament well before 1742. The material developed from analysis of the Bible in the first nineteen chapters of the *Examen important de milord Bolingbroke* suggests the tentative plausibility of the phrase "écrit sur la fin de 1736" on the title page of this work. But the last eighteen chapters reveal a competence in Church history and patristic theology that Voltaire acquired only after Cirey. An "Avis aux éditeurs," prefacing the work from 1767 on, also contradicts the date line mentioned above:

> Ce précis de la doctrine de milord Bolingbroke, recueillie tout entière dans les six volumes de ses Oeuvres posthumes, fut adressé par lui, peu d'années avant sa mort, à milord Cornsbury. (M. XXVI, 196)

But Torrey convincingly refutes the authorship of Bolingbroke, whose *Philosophical Works* in five, not six, volumes appeared in 1754-

1755.[50] The Englishman died in 1751, thus "peu d'années avant sa mort" refers back to at least 1749, the latest possible date of work on the "Examen de la Genèse" according to Wade. In support of the hypothesis that Voltaire composed the *Examen important* in the late forties, one might argue that he dated his *Sermon des cinquante*, another antichristian work related to the "Examen," 1749. The "Avis aux éditeurs" in the *Examen important*, on the other hand, which includes the attribution to Bolingbroke, appeared only in the 1767 edition as if by afterthought.[51] While the text presents little evidence of composition in the late forties, Wade[52] exposes several allusions to events more or less contemporaneous with 1736. The most significant are those in the "Avant Propos" referring to Meslier, "mort depuis peu" as well as another, unnamed rebel priest in Dorsetshire.[53] Wade testifies that the only other texts in which he has found the story of this Anglican divine are Voltaire's *Extrait* of Meslier and two of the other "Extraits" of the same author in manuscript. Voltaire believed Meslier to have died in 1733,[54] and so it would have been logical to refer to this year as *depuis peu* in 1736. Wade also cites echoes from the *Lettres philosophiques*, such as disapproval of Pascal ("Avant-Propos" and Chapter 13) and George Fox (Chapter 10). Nor does he neglect the appearance of Lady Blackacre (Chapter 2) whom Voltaire identifies in a 1767 footnote as a character in Wycherley's *Plain Dealer* (1674), adapted by him in 1740 as *La Prude*. Nevertheless, the large number of textual similarities between the *Examen important* and the "Examen de la Genèse" detected by Wade favor 1736 as the date of composition less than the whole Cirey period. While most of the comparisons he makes concern the Old Testament, three involve the New Testament,[55] which Voltaire and Emilie studied between 1742 and 1749.

[50] "He read Bolingbroke's *Philosophical Works* [in 1758-1759]. His remark that he found in Bolingbroke many leaves and little fruit was... the result of patient reading... In the volumes at Leningrad, Voltaire has left an abundance of markers and stickers which indicate his patient search and which reveal... [his] reactions." Norman Torrey, *Voltaire and the English Deists* (New Haven, 1967).

[51] The "Traduction d'une lettre [actually two letters] de milord Bolingbroke à milord Cornsbury," (M. XXVI, 301-06), in reality a preface by Voltaire, likewise appears for the first time in the 1767 edition.

[52] Ira Wade, *The Intellectual Development of Voltaire* (Princeton, 1969), pp. 550-56.

[53] "J'ai vu en Dorsetshire, diocèse de Bristol, un curé renoncer à une cure de 200 livres sterling, et avouer à ses paroissiens que sa conscience ne lui permettait pas de leur prêcher les absurdes horreurs de la secte chrétienne" (M. XXVI, 198).

[54] Meslier actually died in 1729.

[55] (1) Zachariah, son of Barachiah: *Examen important*, M. XXVI, 233; "Examen de la Genèse," IV, 88. (2) The money-lenders expelled from the Temple: *Examen important*, M. XXVI, 225; "Examen de la Genèse," IV, 76. (3) The Roman census associated with Jesus' birth: *Examen important*, M. XXVI, 236; "Examen de la Genèse," IV, 139.

Consequently, Voltaire may well have made an early draft in 1736, but he must have added to it at other times during the Cirey period. The examination of Bolingbroke's works a few years before the Englishman's death may concern a revision in the late forties. Did he give it the present title then and rework the contents accordingly? Perhaps.

Nevertheless, Pomeau's interpretation of a letter from Voltaire to Mme du Deffand in 1759 not only threatens this hypothesis, but also Wade's entire theory that he wrote the first nineteen chapters at Cirey. In this letter, Voltaire told Mme du Deffand, "Je voudrais que quelqu'un eût élagué en France les *Oeuvres philosophiques* de feu milord Bolingbroke" (Oct. 13). Pomeau seems to conclude that Voltaire meant an as yet unwritten work,[56] but the writer almost never gave advance notice of his antichristian projects in his correspondence. Usually such language in letters from him, which could be intercepted by the police and which would probably be read by friends of the addressee, hinted that he had already written the work and that it would soon appear in print. Still, he did not publish the *Examen important* for another seven years. Did he consider publishing it in 1759? Was he fishing for trial reactions from his pious enemies in Paris? Président Hénault, the queen's favorite, who faithfully attended Mme du Deffand's salon, was on good terms with many of them. Yet, nothing seems to have come of any plans to publish in 1759 a work he had probably been keeping to himself since Cirey. Pomeau's further objections to Wade's theory are also vulnerable: The first nineteen chapters exhibit information unknown to Voltaire at Cirey because he no doubt inserted it when he revised them again between 1759 and 1766. Such frequent revision conforms to his habits as a writer. Nothing would have prevented him from adding, at the same time or earlier, an attack on Abbadie whose *Traité* he knew (only?) in a 1750 edition and from changing the date of the *Toldoth Jeschu* from the ninth century to the first century.[57] Pomeau shows that he held the former opinion as late as 1741, but the Leningrad

[56] He prefaces his quotation of the letter by the following remarks: "Sous la forme où nous le lisons, l'*Examen important* est certainement postérieur à la publication des *Oeuvres* posthumes de Bolingbroke (1754-1755). L'idée de l'ouvrage apparaît pour la première fois dans une lettre de 1759 à Mme du Deffand" (*La Religion*, p. 181).

[57] Pomeau cites a note to the "Epître à Mme la marquise du Châtelet" published in a 1741 edition ("41R") of Voltaire's *Oeuvres*: here Voltaire sets the *Toldoth* in the ninth century. For 41R, see my "Survey and Analysis of Voltaire's Collective Editions," *SVEC*, 67 (1970), 114. Joseph Klausner, *Jesus von Nazareth* (Jerusalem, 1952), p. 65, states that the only *Toldoth* extant since the Middle Ages originated in the tenth century. In *Against Celsus*, Origen refers to a *Toldoth* cited by Celsus which has been lost.

Notebook (1735-1750) proves that he soon changed his mind.[58] Pomeau, on the other hand, discounts Wade's massive evidence that the same critical thinking conditioned both the *Examen important* and the "Examen de la Genèse." Voltaire, he argues, could have taken the same material from Calmet at Ferney that Emilie had at Cirey. But Voltaire no doubt, as we have seen, actively participated in the work Emilie recorded in the "Examen." Would anyone as busy as he was at Ferney bother to duplicate what he had already done? Probably not and certainly not Voltaire. Pomeau's final concession to Wade seems particularly damaging to his position: "Ici, comme dans les autres pamphlets bibliques de Ferney, Voltaire utilise les matériaux de Cirey, enrichis par ses recherches ultérieures" (p. 177). This admission reduces Pomeau's disagreement with Wade to an argument over the nature of these unknown materials. One suspects that he is thinking of the disconnected passages in Voltaire's notebooks, but the evidence furnished by Wade clearly demonstrates the existence of a substantially developed text as early as Cirey.[59]

While it was certainly more coherent than the notebooks, one cannot say whether Voltaire had a manuscript ready for publication. One may nonetheless expect the first nineteen[60] chapters to reflect the Cirey environment and the last eighteen together with the footnotes published in later editions, the Ferney environment. Once Voltaire had published the work in the *Recueil nécessaire* of 1766, clandestinely edited by him, he called the attention of the landgrave of Hesse-Cassel to "un ouvrage de milord Bolingbroke qui m'a paru ce qu'on a jamais écrit de plus fort contre la superstition [le christianisme]" (Aug. 25, 1766). While one must always allow for exaggeration in reading an author's evaluation of his own work, Voltaire undoubtedly wanted the landgrave to know that he considered it devastating. His attempt to pass it off as the thought, if not the style, of a dead Englishman confirms his appreciation of the risk involved in publishing it. Why then did he consider it so potent? Perhaps the answer will evolve from analysis of the antitrinitarian and antichristological contents of the work.

Chapter 10, "De la Personne de Jésus," which illustrates the second category, begins with scrutiny of the situation in Palestine in Jesus'

[58] "L'histoire de Panther [le *toldoth*] est beaucoup plus ancienne qu'on ne le dit. Celse en parle comme d'une chose de notoriété publique" (B. LXXXI, 428).

[59] "There is no reason in the world not to accept Wade's proofs that Voltaire's Biblical criticism was concentrated in the Cirey years." Owen Aldridge, Review of Wade's *The Intellectual*, *Comparative Literature*, 89 (1971), 189.

[60] Except Chapter 11, added in 1776.

day. Voltaire is insensitive to Jewish resentment of the Roman occupation and ignorant of Pharasaic xenophobia. He does understand the political and military significance of Jewish messianism along with its disastrous consequences for the Christian doctrine of a uniquely spiritual deliverance. He even realizes the importance of sectarianism in the backward province of Galilee:

> Plusieurs fanatiques s'ingérèrent de prêcher le bas peuple, surtout dans [le petit canton barbare de] Galilée, où les Juifs étaient plus grossiers qu'ailleurs. (M. XXVI, 221)

Only the pejorative bias of the vocabulary distorts the truth of the fact that Jesus cultivated the ignorant and volatile rural population of his province. According to the synoptic gospels, he avoided the larger towns of the region where he might have encountered stiffer intellectual opposition. "Bolingbroke" has legitimate grounds for his comparison of Jesus with his compatriot Fox: "Un misérable paysan établit de nos jours la secte des quakers parmi les paysans d'une de nos provinces" (M. XXVI, 221). The sentence, which confirms his maneuver in the third *Letter concerning the English Nation*, reminds us that most of Voltaire's readers had little sympathy for the lower classes. Having named other sectarian leaders, Jean Leclerc (Arminians, Remonstrants), Muncer and John of Leyden (Anabaptists), he mentions the Jansenist convulsionaries of Paris. This movement was urban, however, and since it grew out of miracles performed on the tomb of a dead holy man rather than the evangelism of a living holy man, it does not parallel his other examples. He nonetheless feels that he has laid sufficient groundwork for a general conclusion:

> Ce sont pour la plupart des gueux qui crient contre le gouvernement, et qui finissent ou par être chefs de parti ou par être pendus. Jésus fut pendu à Jérusalem sans avoir été oint. (M. XXVI, 221-22)

The last phrase reminds us that he never received the indispensable consecration of a true messiah. The whole passage concludes a development intended to belittle him by casting him in the role of a failure according to a scenario composed of selected historical elements. The text illustrates Voltaire's technique of choosing and shaping facts that elicit the judgment he desires from his public. He strikes a final blow, moreover, with his ironical contrast between the hanging of Jesus and the successful leadership of his remote disciple Fox.

He elaborates on the parallel between Jesus and Fox in Chapter 11, which he inserted in the *Examen important* in 1776. But why does he give Judea as Jesus' native province this time? "Jésus est évidemment un paysan grossier de la Judée, plus éveillé, sans doute que la plupart des habitants de son canton" (M. xxvi, 227). Something he had read no doubt! The point remains that Jesus distinguished himself only because of the rustic mediocrity surrounding him. Voltaire's scorn for Jesus' class, which most of his readers shared, was a leitmotiv in his antichristian works. Though illiterate, Jesus founded a sect opposed to "celle des récabites, des judaïtes, des thérapeutes, des esséniens, des pharisiens, des saducéens, des hérodiens" (M. xxvi, 227), so many in fact that none could be important. Having changed his mind about the proliferation of sects, which had seemed healthy to him in the *Letters*,[61] he now deplored an insidious revolt against the centripetal consensus of reason. "Bolingbroke" reminds the reader that he has already compared Jesus to Fox,

> qui était comme lui de la lie du peuple, prêchant quelquefois comme lui une bonne morale et prêchant surtout l'égalité, qui flatte toute la canaille. (M. xxvi, 227)

His phobia against Jesus' alleged equalitarianism characterizes the period of Les Délices and Ferney, when wealth and authority over many stimulated a latent paternalism. The very exercise of authority inspires fear that obedience will cease, so that any independent influence capable of upsetting the routine of docility becomes suspect. For this reason, Voltaire treated Fox more severely in 1776 than he had in 1733. Like Jesus, Fox founded an inappropriate society, which soon deviated from his intentions. Like Jesus, he attacked the clergy, but English law treated him more leniently, while the Jewish priests forced Pilate "à... faire pendre [Jésus] à une potence en forme de croix, comme un coquin d'esclave" (M. xxvi, 227). The arrogance of one who has nothing to fear from such gibets undermines any justice we may find in this verdict of a punishment fitting the crime. The tone discolors the reputation of the man who had defended so many victims of judicial tryanny and the note is so vindictive that one must wonder if class solidarity assured him the usual applause in this case. He had a more delicate touch in the third *Letter* and even in Chapter 10 of the *Examen important*.

The *Toldoth Jeschu*, a life of Jesus inspired by Jewish resentment of Christianity, presented him with a finished narrative useful to this purpose, though legendary in nature.[62] The text available to him

[61] "If one religion only were allowed in *England*, the government would very possibly become arbitrary; if there were but two, the people would cut one another's throats; but as there are such a multitude, they all live happy and in peace" (*Letters*, p. 35).

[62] Klausner finds "dass diesem Buch nicht der geringste historische Wert beizumessen ist" (p. 63).

under this title, the same as the one extant today, dates from the tenth century. He nonetheless believed it to have originated in the first century, because Origen refutes pre-existing elements of the story, which Celsus had taken from the Talmud.[63] According to the *Toldoth*, the soldier Panther seduces the menstruant and therefore reluctant Mirja under the cover of darkness by impersonating her betrothed Jocanam. Thus Mirja conceives (per impossibile!) Jeschu, whom Jewish customs doubly condemn, not only for his illegitimate birth, but also for his conception during the menstruation of his mother. Voltaire omits both the obscene circumstance and the circumstance mitigating Mirja's responsibility. The following sentence in the *Examen important* is in fact misleading: "La conduite de Mirja la déshonorera; son fils Jésu ou Jeschut fut déclaré bâtard[64] par les juges de la ville" (M. XXVI, 223). He may be insinuating fuller responsibility on her part to discredit the exaltation of Mary in Catholicism, but this insinuation also worsens Jesus' illegitimacy from a general Christian viewpoint. From a Jewish viewpoint, it could scarcely be worse as the *Toldoth* actually describes it. The rest of the basic legend and the supernatural incidents woven into it do not concern us here. One need only observe that Voltaire seeks to extract authentic information about Jesus from the *Toldoth* on the strength of verisimilitude, the predominant standard of his historiography, as Pomeau notes.[65] Having summarized the text, Voltaire concludes:

> On y ajouta depuis des fables insipides, des miracles impertinents qui firent grand tort au fond... [Celui-ci] est bien plus croyable, plus naturel, plus conforme à ce qui se passe tous les jours dans le monde qu'aucun des cinquante *Evangiles* des christicoles.[66] (M. XXVI, 223)

[63] "Let us return... to the words put [by Celsus] into the mouth of the Jew, where *the mother of Jesus* is described as having been *turned out by the carpenter who was betrothed to her, as she had been convicted of adultery and had a child by a certain soldier named Panthera*" (*Against Celsus*, II, 32). Klausner comments: "Hätte sich nicht im Talmud und bei Celsus die Legende von Jesus illegitimer Geburt erhalten, die ja in Wirklichkeit nur der christlichen Ansicht entsprang, dass Jesus ohne natürlichen Vater gezeugt worden sei; dann hätte nicht der Verfasser von 'Toldoth Jeschu' auf dieser Talmudischen Erzählung seine Legende... aufbauen können. Niemand wäre dann auch auf den Gedanken gekommen, dass dieser Talmudische Bericht sich auf Jesus beziehe" (pp. 34-35).

[64] Evidence that Voltaire was not above qualifying Jesus by this epithet. See p. 112.

[65] "Il se fie généralement aux vraisemblances parce qu'il croit en la nature humaine... Voltaire souvent se trompe [en] définissant comme nature les habitudes de l'Europe contemporaine... Cette croyance à l'universalité naturelle de ses critères fait la force, peut-être, d'une civilisation. Mais elle égare les historiens qui ne savent s'en déprendre." "Introduction," *Essai sur les moeurs* (Paris, 1963), I, xxi.

[66] *Christicole* is Meslier's favorite epithet in his posthumous *Mémoire*.

The fifty gospels in question include the extracanonical gospels which are as valid, he insists, as the four canonical gospels, a claim no one makes today. The passage clarifies his conception of verisimilitude as believable and natural conformity with what happens every day, but he does not confine it, as we must, to the common experience of the leisured classes in Europe during the eighteenth century. According to this standard, he argues, the essential truth of the *Toldoth* is the illegitimacy of Jesus' birth, yet the real source of this conviction seems to be an awareness of his own illegitimacy and the suspicion that Jesus did not deserve his prestige. These motives tend to explain his fascination with the verisimilitude of a "mauvais ouvrage" (M. xxvi, 222):

> Il est plus vraisemblable que Joseph Panther avait fait un enfant à Mirja qu'il ne l'est qu'un ange soit venu par les airs faire un compliment de la part de Dieu à la femme d'un charpentier comme Jupiter envoya Mercure auprès d'Alcmène. (M. xxvi, 223)

The mundane vocabulary trivializes the intervention of a divine being in the life of a human. The natural explanation eclipses the supernatural, whether Christian or pagan, for neither meets the standard of verisimilitude. The association of the pagan explanation with the Christian behumbles the traditional scorn for the rival religion of antiquity. Thus the *Toldoth* provides Voltaire with several opportunities to exploit discrepancies between Christian belief and historical verisimilitude.

In turning to Christian sources, he first assaults God's inseminating agent:

> On fait venir je ne sais quel *agion pneuma*, un saint souffle, un Saint-Esprit dont on n'avait jamais entendu parler, et dont on a fait depuis la tierce partie de Dieu, Dieu lui-même, Dieu le créateur du monde; il engrosse Marie. (M. xxvi, 223)

The exotic appositions preceding the Holy Spirit and the following clause, which casts doubt on his previous existence, reduce the third person to absurdity. A parallel clause and further appositions spread this doubt to the Trinitarian God, of whom the Holy Spirit is both a part (a dogmatic error) and the whole. Voltaire then compresses these antecedents into the pronoun *il* and "he," in the last, anticlimactic clause, stoops to a banal masculine function. This stylistic performance did not completely satisfy his appetite for satire in 1742 and 1759, for he probably inserted the following questions from the Jesuit Sanchez on one or both of these dates:[67] "si Dieu eut beaucoup de

[67] He wrote Frederick in 1742 (ca. Nov. 5): "Il y a un casuiste qui examine si la vierge eut du plaisir dans la coopération de l'ombrombration du saint-esprit; il tient pour

plaisir avec Maria, s'il répandit de la semence et si Maria répandit aussi de la semence" (M. XXVI, 224). Quotations from Sanchez's *Disputationem de sancto matrimonii sacramento* (1602) in a note to the contemporaneous *Relation... du jésuite Berthier* confirm the latter two, but not the first.[68] Did Voltaire invent this one himself? Perhaps. In any case, it intensifies the absurdity of an immaterial being indulging in bodily copulation and emitting sperm. Speculation over his pleasure nonetheless implies some experience with intercourse, while the emission of semen by the female partner betrays partial ignorance of the same act. This odd mixture of truth and error suggests that Sanchez took his vow of chastity seriously and depended on lay consultants for his information. However respectable in his time and calling, such abstinence handicapped him ludicrously in his study of marriage and most of Voltaire's readers took the basic sexual experience he lacked for granted. Sanchez's monumental innocence delighted Voltaire, because it demonstrated how far Christian theologians could stray from common sense. After this insertion, one finds a sentence developing the idea exposed in the clause that precedes it, "il engrosse Marie": "Jésus devient donc un fils de Dieu et d'une Juive, non encore Dieu lui-même, mais une créature supérieure" (M. XXVI, 224). This assessment of Jesus accurately represents the opinion of the synoptists, but it contradicts John, who proclaims his deity from the beginning, and dogma as well.

The synopsis of Jesus' mission in Chapter 10 adds little to the exorcism involving the 2000 swine, but it does thicken Voltaire's dossier of the Temple cleansing. He remarks that the Temple merchants "étaient autorisés par la loi" (M. XXVI, 224), thus establishing Jesus' legal guilt in the matter. He emphasizes the violence of the act: "Il prend un grand fouet, en donne sur les épaules de tous les marchands, les chasse à coups de lanières" (M. XXVI, 224). Of the four evangelists, however, only John mentions a whip and even he says nothing about its size. The evangelist merely implies that Jesus uses the whip, without indicating whether he merely brandished it or actually lashed the merchants with it, as Voltaire tells us.[69] Nor does the

l'affirmative, et en apporte de fort bonnes raisons" (Best. D 2681). Besterman comments, "Sanchez is the Thomas Aquinas of sex."

[68] "Semen ubi femina effudit, an teneatur alter effundere, sive inter uxores, sive inter fornicantes" (9.17.8)? "An virgo Maria semen emiserit in copulatione cum Spiritu Sancto" (3.21.11)? Mac., p. 79, n. 2. Mac. designates Jean Macary, ed., *Voltaire: Facéties* (Paris, 1973).

[69] "Making a whip out of some cord, he drove them all out of the Temple" (Jn. 2.15). Such precise details in John support the theory that he had access to a more direct source than the synoptists.

businessman in Voltaire neglect the merchants' financial losses, perhaps the worst of the scandal in his opinion: "Il... jette leur argent par terre" (M. xxvi, 224). While his disapproval of "un pareil tapage dans un lieu respectable" (M. xxvi, 224) sounds like irony, his apparent irritation over the merchants' docility suggests that he would not have imitated them:

> C'était déjà un fort grand miracle que trente ou quarante marchands[70] se laissassent fesser par un seul homme, et perdissent leur argent sans rien dire. (M. xxvi, 225)

Here Voltaire unintentionally substitutes himself for Jesus as the object of satire. How many of his readers cared about the injustice done to Jesus' victims? Few of them, no doubt, had much sympathy with what they took for an inferior race, a suspect religion, and a parasitic trade. Perhaps he would have made a stronger impression on them by limiting himself to his indictment of Jesus' behavior. Convinced that Jesus deserved his fate, Voltaire reiterates his public execution, his secret resurrection, and his ascension witnessed only by disciples. This miracle, he objects, "était pourtant fort aisé à voir, et... aurait fait dans le monde une assez grande nouvelle" (M. xxvi, 226). To Voltairian common sense, secrecy in such matters almost necessarily implies fraud.

In view of the gospel evidence, the divinity of Christ seemed so fraudulent to him that he added a note to Chapter 10 in 1771 supposing the steps Christians had taken to convince themselves:

> Quelques adhérents du Juif Jésus se contentent, dans les commencements, de dire que c'était un homme de bien injustement crucifié... Puis on s'enhardit; on ose écrire que Dieu l'a ressuscité... enfin on en fait un Dieu. On fait trois dieux. On pousse le sophisme jusqu'à dire que ces trois dieux n'en font qu'un. (M. xxvi, 226-27)

He typically sees no more in this evolution, which may well have taken place, than clerical deception at the service of clerical ambition: "Puis on s'enhardit." But clerical ambition does not adequately account for religion in general and Christianity in particular. Nor does Voltaire register the decline of remembrance with the death of older generations and the increase of imagination to replace it among the younger ones in a society lacking written records. Although Voltaire the historian appreciates the importance of such conditions, Voltaire the polemicist forgets them by his preoccupation with cultivating his

[70] The gospels do not cite the number of merchants, but Voltaire's figure seems plausible.

readers' experience. Even as a historian, however, he had no access to information about the tradition of charismatic holy men in rural Galilee, hence his hostility to what he considered an ambitious rabble-rouser and fomenter of enthusiasm.

He usually relegates Paul to a similar category, but a note inserted in Chapter 12 in 1771 reveals a grudging respect for the negative implications of testimony by this fellow intellectual: "Il ne dit jamais que Jésus soit Dieu" (M. XXVI, 232). He seeks to prove the point by a brief survey and analysis of allusions to Christ by Paul that might be interpreted as recognition of his divinity. He even raises the dilemma of Romans 9.5 (see p. 26), "[le] seul verset dans tous les écrits de Paul où le mot de *Dieu* pourrait tomber sur Jésus" (M. XXVI, 232). Impatient with scholarly indecision over this passage, he declares that it separates Christ from God. In support of this choice, he cites the progressive but respectable authority of Grotius and Erasmus as well as one of the strongest traditional arguments: "Il serait trop étrange que Paul, reconnaissant Jésus pour Dieu, ne lui eût donné ce nom qu'une seule fois" (M. XXVI, 232). Otherwise, why such reticence about the most important point in his theology? Voltaire could not have given a reason more agreeable to good sense.[71] In the same note, he observes: "Pour le mot de *trinité*, il ne se trouve jamais dans Paul, qui cependant est regardé comme le fondateur du christianisme" (M. XXVI, 232). Since Paul never mentions it in letters about his theology, how could he have believed in it? Common sense concludes that he did not.

The last eighteen chapters added to the *Examen important* at Ferney demonstrate a knowledge of post-Biblical developments which he did not have at Cirey. In Chapter 21, he manifests his suspicion of a passage in Justin which formulates a trinity unknown to Christianity until the fourth century. Today the work in which it appears is no longer attributed to Justin, but rather to Theodoret, a fourth-century theologian.[72] In a note added to Chapter 25 in 1771, he observes that

[71] In 1771, he appended the following note to Chapter 14: "Dans les *Actes*... et dans tous les discours de Paul, [Jésus] n'est jamais regardé que comme un homme et... il n'y a pas un seul texte authentique où il soit question de sa prétendue divinité" (M. XXVI, 238, n. 2).

[72] Here is the passage: "Au commencement il n'y eut qu'un seul Dieu connu en trois personnes, qui sont le père, le fils et le saint esprit; car puisque le fils fut engendré de la propre essence du père, et d'icelle même procède le saint esprit... tous trois participent d'une même substance [et] ils sont dignes aussi d'être égaux en divinité." Ian de Maumont, trans., *Oeuvres de saint Justin philosophe et martyr* (Paris, 1554), p. 164. The work in question is no longer attributed to Justin, however: "On paraît d'accord pour y voir aujourd'hui une oeuvre de jeunesse de Théodoret écrite avant 431." Henri Marrou, trans., "Introduction," *Lettre à Diognète* (Paris, 1965), p. 25.

Lactantius, who converted to Christianity at the end of the third century, concerns himself exclusively with the Father and the Son, thus neglecting the Holy Spirit.[73] In the same note, he claims, "La trinité est un dogme de Platon... Jésus... n'en avait jamais entendu parler dans son village" (M. xxvi, 252). While one cannot deny the second statement, the first is an obvious exaggeration, for he knew very well that Judaism had contributed the major ingredients in the Trinity. Yet one cannot easily ascertain the relative contributions of Hellenism and Judaism, a complex and controversial question to say the least. Perhaps Voltaire simplified this problem for fear of risking obscure and uncertain arguments before the tribunal of reason.

In the text of Chapter 25, where he pursues the Platonic origin of the Trinity, "Bolingbroke" declares Origen "le premier qui donna la vogue au *nonsense*, au galimatias de la trinité, qu'on avait oublié depuis Justin" (M. xxvi, 260). The last clause simply broadcasts Voltaire's ignorance of the trinitarian development during the interim (Irenaeus, Clement, etc.). From the *Timaeus* of Plato, who does not mention a trinity as such, he extracts the following argument:

> Dieu conçut l'idée du monde, Dieu le fait, Dieu l'anime,[74] mais jamais Platon n'a été assez fou pour dire que cela composait trois personnes en Dieu. Origène... prit ce qu'il put de Platon, il fit une trinité à sa mode. (M. xxvi, 261)

The error is flagrant,[75] for Origen did not convert a trinity of divine functions borrowed from Plato into a trinity of divine persons. He did apply Neoplatonic philosophy to the trinity he inherited from Clement and his predecessors (see p. 69). His trinity resulted from

[73] "Du saint esprit comme entité propre, il n'est absolument pas question chez Lactance." Hans von Campenhausen, *Les Pères latins* (Paris, 1967), p. 95.

[74] It is not easy to determine which passage in the *Timaeus* Voltaire had in mind. The following is one of the most explicit: "It is necessary to consider three sorts of things: one, that which is generated; another, that in which it is generated; and the third, that from which the generated nature derives its similitude. But it is proper to assimilate that which receives to a mother; that from whence it receives to a father; and the nature situated between these to an offspring." Thomas Taylor, trans., *The Timaeus and the Critias or Atlanticus* (Washington, 1944), p. 169. Curiously, this passage describes a trinity that resembles the Christian Trinity more closely than anything Voltaire attributes to Plato.

[75] "'[Dans] le roi de l'univers... les plus belles choses ont... leur cause première; les secondes en perfection ont en lui une seconde cause; et il est encore la troisième cause des ouvrages du troisième degré.' On pourrait ne pas reconnaître dans cette lettre la trinité telle que nous l'admettons; mais c'était beaucoup d'avoir, dans un auteur grec, un garant des dogmes de l'Eglise." Voltaire, in "Platon," *Nouveaux Mélanges* (1765), is quoting a letter from Plato to Denis (M. xx, 228). Here he is making a more moderate claim, but his evidence resembles the Christian Trinity even less.

learned syncretism and not frivolous speculation, as Voltaire would have us believe.

After a paragraph on the moral ineptitude of such metaphysics, he summarizes the trinitarian doctrine of Origen in a manner calculated to make the Alexandrian appear as fanciful and unorthodox as possible:

> Origène attribue un corps délié à Dieu... et il dit que Dieu le Père et Dieu le Fils sont deux substances différentes; que le Père est plus grand que le Fils, le Fils plus grand que le Saint-Esprit... Le Fils n'est pas la vérité par rapport à son Père, mais l'image de la vérité par rapport à nous; qu'il ne faut pas adorer le Fils, mais le Père... que le Fils apporta du ciel la chair dont il se revêtit dans le sein de Marie. (M. XXVI, 262)

Voltaire creates an impression of idle fantasy by taking Origen literally: (1) *Diffused body*, a contradiction in terms, might have been rendered more accurately by *immanence*. (2) The deliberate confusion of the Son's connection with the truth ruins the Neoplatonic reconciliation of the dichotomy between transcendence and immanence by the intermediary of Christ. (3) Voltaire mutilates Origen's attempt to solve the problem of the fusion between the two natures by ascribing heavenly flesh to Jesus. All of these distortions expose Origen to the scorn of common sense. But Voltaire accumulates evidence of the Alexandrian Father's subordinationism in the same passage: (1) The difference in substance between the Father and the Son excludes the latter from any kind of unity with the former. (2) The Father greater than the Son greater than the Holy Spirit correctly reproduces the trinitarian hierarchy of Origen. (3) Since the Son should not be worshiped, he cannot be divine. Although Voltaire thus represents Origen with at least literal fidelity, he is evidently using him for a propaganda assault on the Trinity.

The same chapter (25) evokes the neglect of the Holy Spirit at Nicaea, a favorite point. And in a note of 1771, Voltaire ridicules the "*agion pneuma* dont les christicoles ont fait un troisième Dieu! Ce mot ne signifiait que souffle" (M. XXVI, 261). Having quoted John 20.22, where the risen Christ breathes on the disciples to bestow the Holy Spirit on them, he explains,

> c'était une ancienne cérémonie des magiciens, de souffler dans la bouche de ceux qu'ils voulaient ensorceler. Voilà donc l'origine du troisième dieu de ces énergumènes. (M. XXVI, 261-62)

He then protests, with tongue in cheek, against the blasphemy of deifying magicians' breath. The concept of the Holy Spirit did in fact evolve from belief in the breath of God (see p. 16), and so his essential objection has to be disputed on the grounds of the problematic distinction between magic and religion among the ancient Hebrews. With reason, magic has no standing whatsoever. Chapter 25 also contains a digression on the apocryphal insertion in 1 John 5.7-8, which Voltaire, Erasmus (see p. 93), and modern scholars reject because it appears in none of the older manuscripts. The authentic text reads: "There are three witnesses, the spirit, the water and the blood, and all three of them agree." The apocryphal version replaces the words following *witnesses* by "the Father, the Word and the Spirit, and these three are one." But Voltaire doubts the validity of the authentic text too and he ridicules the Trinitarian interpretation of both:

> Quel fruit en pourraient recueillir ceux qui admettent ces falsifications? comment pourront-ils entendre que l'esprit, l'eau et le sang font la trinité, et ne sont qu'un? est-ce parce qu'il est dit que Jésus sua sang et eau et qu'il rendit l'esprit? Quel rapport de ces trois choses à un Dieu en trois hypostases? (M. xxvi, 261)

According to Luke 22.44, Jesus sweated blood and water in the garden of Gethsemane. Aside from the impossibility of sweating blood (except figuratively), Voltaire probably refers to this passage because it emphasizes Jesus' human weakness. The same may be said for Matthew 27.50 and Luke 23.46 which report that Jesus yielded his spirit when he finally died on the cross. To Voltairian common sense, death is the ultimate proof of Jesus' exclusive humanity.[76]

Chapter 35, which he added to the *Examen important* in 1767, begins with a brief discussion of the fifth-century controversy between Cyril and Nestorius. No doubt deliberately, however, he confuses this quarrel with others:

> Il fallut savoir précisément si ce Jésus avait eu deux natures, deux personnes, deux âmes, deux volontés; si, quand il faisait les fonctions animales de l'homme, la partie divine s'en mêlait ou ne s'en mêlait pas. (M. xxvi, 291)

Before the semicolon, each pair refers, however vaguely, to a specific quarrel. *The Formulary of Reunion* and the Council of Chalcedon imposed the two natures. The two Sons, which Cyril accused Nestorius (unfairly) of professing correspond to two persons in Trinitarian terminology. Apollinaris, who denied a human soul in Jesus, believed that the Word performed this function. The question of whether

[76] Chapter 31 is a probable prototype of several essays on the Arian controversy of the fourth century, the most successful being "Arius" in the 1767 edition of the *Dictionnaire philosophique*. I will discuss this article in a later section (see p. 204).

Christ had one or two wills led to a seventh-century controversy omitted in "The Trinity and the Two Natures" above. Voltaire enumerates the dual concepts alone, not only because they became the eventual orthodoxy, but also because they, in contrast with the corresponding singular concepts, are absurd. The impossibility of knowing whether Jesus had a divine equivalent for each of these human attributes exposes the entire series to the ridicule of the alleged necessity for knowing them all precisely. The text following the semicolon raises the problematic communication of idioms which also embroiled Cyril and the Antiochians. The Antiochians and eventual dogma allowed only that we may apply to one nature the epithets pertaining to the other. Before the *Formulary*, however, Cyril insisted that the divine nature absorbed the human, thus deifying the human qualities. Voltaire reverses this argument by his question of whether the divine nature involves itself in animal functions belonging to the human nature, as if he were innocently exploring the consequence of an actual exchange of qualities. But the next sentence in the *Examen important* dismisses such questions as worthy of Rabelais, Swift, or Punch, and a note inserted in 1776 proposes:

> Appelons les choses par leur nom. On a poussé le blasphème jusqu'à faire un article de foi que Dieu est venu chier et pisser sur la terre... Et on disputait gravement si c'était la nature divine ou la nature humaine qui chiait ou pissait! (M. XXVI, 291)

Manifestly, Voltaire had lost all his inhibitions by the age of 82! He not only reduces the two natures to the absurd, but also to the most obscene form of absurdity possible. The least beautiful of bodily functions focuses attention on the slavery of human necessity, an impossible barrier to apotheosis. The old man finally dared to do what he had always wanted, to focus the natural light on this truth in its most unmistakable, inevitable, and unforgettable form.

A section in the final chapter, "Excès de l'église romaine," which he appended to the *Examen important* in 1771, provides a fitting conclusion to the Trinitarian and Christological criticism in the work. Here he assumes as usual that the Catholic hierarchy endorses the dogma without believing a word of it and in order to consolidate or aggrandize its power:

> Y a-t-il eu un seul pape qui, pour peu qu'il ait eu du sens commun, ait cru l'incarnation de Dieu, la mort de Dieu, la résurrection de Dieu, la trinité de Dieu?... Certes ils n'en ont rien cru. (M. XXVI, 298)

It is useful to note what Voltaire explicitly condemns in the name of common sense. Incarnation, death, and resurrection subject God to human conditions, thus depriving him of his divinity. Since our life begins with conception and ends with death, experience can tell us nothing of resurrection and therefore common sense cannot accept it. Nor can it condone a trinity, because the experience of the Newtonian age projects a unitary mind in ultimate control of the universe. It is the constancy of such general convictions that assures a measure of continuity between the Cirey and Ferney panels of Voltaire's antichristian diptych. His systematic satire evidently ran the risk of retaliation by church and state, whose power depended in large measure on respect for Christianity, though not necessarily belief in the dogma. Consequently, when Voltaire found he could not put Bolingbroke's works to the same use as Meslier's, he decided to attribute his own text to the dead Englishman, thus seeking to "répandre la lumière sans dire de quelle main cette lumière [est venue]" (M. xxvi, 196).[77]

Sermon des cinquante

He was just as anxious to hide the immediate source of the natural light in another work from the Cirey period. Pomeau agrees with Wade that 1749 is at least the approximate composition date of the *Sermon des cinquante*. This date appears on the title page of the first commercial edition of the work in 1762 along with a list of attributions including La Mettrie and "*un grand prince très instruit*" or Frederick.[78] When Rousseau wrote in the *Lettres de la montagne* (1764) that Voltaire had composed the *Sermon*, Voltaire denied the accusation in a letter to Rousseau's former hostess Mme de Luxembourg. He also told her that the work had been "imprimé depuis plus de quinze ans à la suite de l'homme machine de La Mettrie" (Jan. 9, 1765). The earliest edition of *L'Homme machine* appeared in 1748, but without the *Sermon*. The Beuchot collection in the Bibliothèque Nationale nonetheless includes an edition of Voltaire's work dated 1749,[79] while another, dated 1753, is in Voltaire's library in Leningrad. In 1754, his enemy La Beaumelle referred to a *Sermon des cinquante* by the author of the *Siècle de Louis XIV*[80] and he may have heard (of?) it being read at Frederick's court, perhaps by Voltaire himself—who else at Frederick's court?—in 1752

[77] "Avis aux éditeurs" (1767).

[78] On Sept. 5, 1762, Voltaire sent a copy to the duchess of Saxe-Gotha and described it as "un petit sermon qu'on a imputé au roi de Prusse quoiqu'à tort."

[79] Z Beuchot 856, according to Pomeau.

[80] In *La Religion* (p. 177, n. 117), Pomeau notes "la mention du *Sermon des cinquante* dans la *Réponse* de La Beaumelle au *Supplément du Siècle de Louis XIV*. Elle est dans le *Mémoire de M. de Voltaire apostillé par M. de La Beaumelle* imprimé à la suite de la *Réponse au Supplément du Siècle de Louis XIV*, Colmar, 1754... pp. 158-159."

when he was there. Grimm affirms that the *Sermon* "fut prononcé à Berlin pendant le séjour du patriarche à la cour du roi de Prusse."[81] The definite existence of the work as early as 1752 increases the probability that Voltaire composed it at Cirey. Wade, who again furnishes much textual evidence in favor of this opinion, refers for instance to the opening sentence:

> Cinquante personnes instruites, pieuses et raisonnables s'assemblent depuis un an tous les dimanches dans une ville peuplée et commerçante. (M. XXIV, 438)

Une ville peuplée which might tolerate such a deist organization suggests Amsterdam rather than Geneva, as a manuscript reported by Barbier indicated.[82] Pomeau quotes another sentence from the sermon tending to confirm Amsterdam as the place of delivery: "L'Angleterre, l'Allemagne, nos provinces sont pleines de docteurs sages qui ne demandent qu'à éclater" (M. XXIV, 452). Note the allusion to "*nos* Provinces Unies." Voltaire certainly would have included Geneva in this list if he had written it after 1758. The subsistence of the passage as it stands in all subsequent editions suggests that he never thoroughly revised the text written at Cirey, his policy with respect to such satires.[83] Still another sentence in the *Sermon* recalls the daily routine of Biblical criticism at Cirey: "Vous savez, mes frères, quelle horreur nous a saisis lorsque nous avons lu ensemble les écrits des Hébreux" (M. XXIV, 439). This would not be the first time that Voltaire had indulged in such playful transposition. Wade reinforces this evidence by eleven instances of textual similarity between the *Sermon* and the "Examen de la Genèse," four of which concern the New Testament.[84] Thus Voltaire almost certainly composed the work as early as Cirey, kept it under cover until Ferney, except for the no doubt limited edition represented by the copy in Beuchot's collection,

[81] *Correspondance littéraire*, VII, 147 (Oct. 1766).

[82] "Il paraît une pièce manuscrite intitulée *Sermon des cinquante*. On suppose dans le préambule qu'il se tient à Genève une assemblée de 50 gens de lettres qui tour à tour font un sermon, et que celui-ci est de Voltaire à qui ses ennemis prêtent cette pièce dont le style bien différent du sien décèle la méchanceté. Ce sermon est épouvantable... Si l'auteur était connu, on ne lui ferait pas faire de voyage autre part qu'à la [place de] Grève pour être brûlé." Edmond Barbier, *Chronique de la Régence et du règne de Louis XV (1718-1763)* (Paris, 1857), IV, 360. Voltaire probably had nothing to do with this preamble.

[83] His habit of constant and thorough revision concerns only those works in which he saw permanent value, such as his tragedies, epic and philosophical poetry, historical works, etc.

[84] The date of composition of the gospels, the genealogies of Christ in Luke and Matthew, the temptation of Christ by Satan, and his cursing of the fig tree.

and finally published it in 1762. In this year, he recommended it to the duchess of Saxe-Gotha as follows:

> On y déteste les erreurs humaines et l'infâme charlatanisme qui donne encore aujourd'hui tant d'honneurs et tant d'argent aux corrupteurs de la raison... Tous sont également les ennemis de dieu [et] du sens commun que dieu nous a donné. (Sept. 5)

The *Sermon*, in other words, exposes the errors and charlatanism of Christianity.

The rejection of Jesus' divinity serves as a persistent theme in this satiric sermon. The preacher follows tradition by opening with a prayer, although the content of the prayer is anything but traditional. Among other requests, he asks God, and God alone, to purge his religion of superstition, infamous mysteries, and absurd fables. Towards the end of the prayer, he recommends the worship of "un seul Dieu... un Dieu qui n'a pu naître ni mourir, ni avoir des associés" (M. XXIV, 438). The death and birth of Christ and the distinction between Trinitarian persons are therefore, by implication, elements of the superstitions, mysteries, and fables rejected. Towards the end of the "Premier Point," a critical review of Old Testament history, the preacher concludes:

> Sous le gouvernement sage des Romains, il naît un roi aux Hébreux, et... ce messie... qui ayant d'abord été mis dans le grand nombre de ces prophètes sans mission, qui, n'ayant pas le sacerdoce, se faisaient un métier d'être inspirés, a été au bout de quelques centuries, regardé comme un Dieu. (M. XXIV, 444)

The preacher of this highly unorthodox sect reflects Voltaire's suspicion of Jesus' unofficial and subversive vocation. An establishmentarian snobbery contemptuous of enthusiasm accompanies his advocacy of a church subordinate to the state. Few of his readers would have taken offense at what we see today as a contradiction between the political conservatism in this passage and the religious radicalism implied by the deism of the preacher. For Voltaire's public feared ecclesiastical influence in government far more than outright tyranny. They also shared his contempt for enthusiasm, the sacrifice of individual good sense to collective emotion. As a practical rather than a sacred proposition, they could not accept the divinity of a charismatic leader. The stated lapse of several centuries before Jesus became divine elicited from them the accusation of pious fraud, which Voltaire makes explicitly in other texts. At the beginning of the "Troisième Point," on the New Testament, he appeals to their class consciousness:

> Il y eut toujours chez les Juifs des gens de la lie du peuple qui firent les prophètes pour se distinguer de la populace: voici celui qui a fait le plus de bruit, et dont on a fait un dieu. (M. xxiv, 449)

The society to which Voltaire belonged resisted ascension from below, even though the members of that society, like Voltaire himself, constantly strove to attain higher levels. This hypocrisy bred the usual scorn for distinction among the lower classes, thus he describes Jesus' prophetic career as presumption. The profound dissimilarity of class structure between the societies of first-century Galilee and eighteenth-century Europe would scarcely have occurred to most of his readers. Even among specialists, the sociology of first-century Palestine developed much later.

It is interesting to note that the last two passages quoted from the *Sermon* do not name Jesus, but simply refer to him by periphrasis. Voltaire continues this practice in a short paragraph following scepticism over the miracles that accompany Jesus' death on the cross: "Après cela il ne coûte rien de se dire ressuscité, et de prédire la fin du monde, qui n'est pourtant pas arrivée" (M. xxiv, 451). This unaccomplished prophecy refers to the kingdom of God, which Voltaire had no means of understanding. Only in the next paragraph, however, does *Jésus* actually appear. Voltaire seems to have avoided naming him in order to deprive him of the customary reverence inspired by his name. The contempt for Jesus he hoped to inculcate in his readers would meet less resistance from those brought up to respect Jesus' name if this name did not appear. When it does appear in the next sentence, Voltaire uses it only in connection with the sect formed after his death and treats it as if it were obscure by placing a demonstrative adjective in front of it:

> La secte de ce Jésus subsiste cachée, le fanatisme l'augmente;[85] on n'ose pas d'abord faire de cet homme un Dieu, mais bientôt on s'encourage. Je ne sais quelle métaphysique de Platon s'amalgame avec la secte nazaréenne: on fait de Jésus le *logos*, le Verbe-Dieu, puis consubstantiel à Dieu son père. On imagine la trinité, et, pour la faire croire, on falsifie les premiers évangiles. (M. xxiv, 451)

The last sentence apparently alludes to the no doubt spurious trinitarian formulation in Matthew 28.19 (see p. 53). The entire passage invites comparison with the note added to the *Examen important* in 1771 setting forth a more precise and yet less accurate chronology of Jesus' deification (see p. 38). Voltaire achieves greater accuracy here

[85] In 1752: *s'augmente*.

by his description of this deification as an amalgamation of early Christianity with *Platonism*, although *Hellenistic philosophy* would be more accurate still. In the note to the *Examen*, we saw that he abusively attributed the entire Trinity to Platonism, a fact indicating a drift away from the truth over the years.

He expands on another theme present in the *Examen* by speaking "de l'arbre de la croix, de la potence qu'on a divinisée" (M. xxiv, 452). The instrument of a disreputable execution has become the object of worship. His preacher ends the *Sermon* by another prayer complementing the one at the beginning. He in fact elaborates on his invocation of "un Dieu qui n'a pu naître ni mourir" by referring to "ce Dieu qui assurément ne peut ni être né d'une fille, ni être mort à une potence" (M. xxiv, 453). The additions enrich the symmetry of the two terminal points of human life by attributes unworthy of the divinity. Neither can God undergo human birth and death, nor can he undergo them unworthily, without disqualifying himself as God. This formula alone would be enough to explain Voltaire's hesitation to publish the *Sermon* and his desire to dissociate himself from it, at least ostensibly, once it had appeared in print. Vehemence and the absence of any compensating humor explain the delay in publication of this work and the *Examen important* until the relative security of Ferney.

Notebooks

He kept other writings too risky for publication in notebooks, from which he sometimes took them later when he thought greater daring possible. A firm conviction that would later appear in print, for instance, is in the Leningrad Notebooks under the heading "Autres Fables":

> Dans toutes les disputes qui ont partagé les chrétiens, Rome a toujours pris le parti le plus opposé à la raison. Cela a un air de divinité. Trinité, 2 natures, une personne. Transsubstantiation. (B. lxxxi, 354)

To settle a dispute by imposing the solution most contrary to reason naturally raises the suspicion that the authority involved is seeking to discourage the use of reason. Voltaire interpreted the constant recourse of the Church to such arbitrary contradiction of the natural light as evidence of priestly deception and ambition. In later texts, he would study the history of this deception in the areas indicated at the end of the passage, the Trinity and the two natures. This kind of note would not have been very useful for the composition of the *Sermon* and the first half of the *Examen important*, in which Voltaire comments on the Bible instead of exploring the history of dogma. Yet he must have written it at the beginning of the Cirey period. One finds it on the verso of leaf 65 and, on the verso of leaf 66, one finds various data from Voltaire's study of Newtonian physics, which he was pursuing in the late thirties. Besterman, in fact, sets the beginning of the Leningrad Notebooks in 1735.

He sets the Piccini Notebooks in 1750-1755 and under the subtitle "Parallèle," Voltaire lists the following:

Atalide pouvait ressuciter et mourir tant qu'il voulait. Esculape avait ressuscité Hippolyte, Alcide, Alceste.	Jésus-Christ ressuscita, etc., etc., etc., etc.,
Rémus et Romulus fils d'une religieuse et d'un dieu.[86]	Jésus fils de Marie et du Saint-Esprit. (B.LXXXII, 523)

These parallels illustrate the tactic of comparing Christian beliefs to elements of pagan mythology, a tactic we have already seen (see p. 136). They imply the mythological origin of such beliefs as the resurrection and the conception. Several pages further on in the same notebook one encounters an ostensible quotation from the *Country-Journal* of March 28, 1752, a number which, according to Besterman's research, is not extant, but may have existed.[87] Looking forward to immortality in heaven, the journalist assumes:

> Nous aurons le plaisir d'éclaircir toutes les difficultés qui nous tiennent ici dans l'obscurité. Nous saurons pourquoi dieu est venu dans le monde se faire tourner en ridicule, se faire fesser, se faire pendre, et pourquoi il a paru à sa mort plus abattu, plus sensible, plus poltron qu'aucun homme mortel: il semble que sa douleur fût augmentée par l'excellence de sa nature. (B. LXXXII, 526-27)

The final sarcasm underlines the exclusive preponderance of Jesus' human nature in contrast with his alleged divine nature. This remark reminds one of Voltaire himself. The vocabulary and the style belong to him, for he delights in predicating Jesus to the verbs *fesser* and *pendre*, and in calling him a *poltron*. The idea of using the leisure of

[86] Voltaire borrowed most of these examples from Meslier: "Athalides fils de Mercure avait obtenu de son père le don de pouvoir vivre, mourir et ressusciter quand il voudrait... Esculape fils d'Apollon avait ressuscité des morts et entre autres... il ressuscita Hippolyte, fils de Thésée, à la prière de Diane, et... Hercule ressuscita Alceste, femme d'Admet, roi de Thessalie pour la rendre à son mari... Rémus et Romulus premiers fondateurs de la ville de Rome étaient miraculeusement nés d'une vierge vestale nommée Ilia, Sylvia ou Rhéa Sylvia." Jean Meslier, *Mémoire des pensées et sentiments de Jean Meslier, Oeuvres complètes* (Paris, 1970-1972), I, 181. Meslier does not mention Alcides.

[87] "No issue after September 1750 is recorded by the British union catalogue of periodicals" (B. LXXXII, 526, n. 1).

heaven to solve the mystery of God's life on earth betokens a sense of humor strangely similar to his. If he originated the passage himself, however, why did he give such a precise reference to the *Country-Journal*? Certainly he ran no great risk by writing such things in his notebooks. Perhaps the answer lies as usual in a mediate solution. The text in the periodical may have exposed the oddity of an immortal becoming mortal so that mortals may become immortal.[88] From such a basic schema, Voltaire could easily have developed the passage above, but unfortunately one can prove nothing without the missing number of the *Country-Journal*.

Besterman likewise sets the Pierpont Morgan Notebooks in 1752, when Voltaire was in Prussia. Here one finds a list of Christian sects differing fundamentally over the status of Jesus:

> Les ébionites disaient que Jésus n'était pas dieu, les docètes qu'il n'était pas homme, les ariens qu'il n'était pas comme son père, les nestoriens qu'il n'avait pas deux natures, Basilides qu'il n'avait pas été crucifié. En effet les Juifs ne crucifiaient pas. (B. LXXXI, 175)

Such a variety of disagreements tends to confirm his long-standing opinion that speculation on the empirically unknowable produces dissension rather than truth, an opinion elucidated in the early letters of the *Lettres philosophiques*. Rekindling ancient heresies and confronting them with an orthodoxy born of political expediency would become a Voltairian technique. A more general lesson to be learned from the foregoing survey of the notebooks, however, is the paucity of allusions to the Trinity and the two natures. The two volumes of Besterman's edition yield surprisingly little material on these subjects.

Before leaving 1752, the year of Voltaire's dispute with the Jew Hirschel, one must consider a curious passage in the *Défense de milord Bolingbroke* which appeared then. *Nous* evidently refers to "we Christians," a convenient sarcasm:

> Nous [ne] disons point [d'injures] aux juifs mêmes, qui ont fait mourir notre dieu par le dernier supplice; au contraire, nous commerçons avec eux, nous leur accordons les plus grands privilèges. (M. XXIII, 553)

Voltaire is thinking especially of the privileges accorded Hirschel by the Prussian state. It was because of these privileges that the scandal angered Frederick and brought temporary disgrace on Voltaire. Al-

[88] The preceding text reads as follows: "Dans le *Country-Journal* du 28 mars 1752... il est dit que, si Adam n'avait pas mangé la pomme, les hommes auraient été immortels sur la terre, mais que le crime d'Adam leur a valu beaucoup mieux, puisque par Jésus-Christ ils sont immortels dans le ciel" (B. LXXXII, 526).

though Frederick was no Christian, he found Christianity useful in governing his kingdom. At a deeper level, Voltaire's irony concerns the hypocrisy of claiming a Jewish founder for the religion of an anti-Semitic society.

Essai sur le moeurs

Begun in 1741, his *Essai sur les moeurs* appeared in its essentially definitive form in 1756. He intended it both as a sequel and a reply to Bossuet's *Discours sur l'histoire universelle*. Religious mores interested him most and he tried to situate them in their age and environment, especially when such perspective disadvantaged Christianity. One finds an example of this technique in a 1761 addition to Chapter 91, "De la Prise de Constantinople par les Turcs." The Catholic historians Maimbourg and Fleury,[89] he observes, claim that, when Mohammed II enthroned the Christian patriarch of Constantinople, he told him, "la sainte trinité te fait, par l'autorité que j'ai reçue, patriarche oecuménique" (I, 823).[90] Voltaire reacts disdainfully:

> Ces auteurs connaissent bien mal les musulmans. Ils ne savent pas que notre dogme de la trinité leur est en horreur; qu'ils se croiraient souillés d'avoir prononcé ce mot; qu'ils nous regardent comme des idolâtres adorateurs de plusieurs dieux. (I, 823)

Thus Maimbourg and Fleury provide him with an opportunity to oppose the strict monotheism of Islam to the de facto polytheism, as he sees it, of Christianity. He enlists the Turks, the "Russians" of Old Regime Europe, to teach Christians a lesson. The same kind of argument recurs in another passage which he inserted in 1761, in Chapter 148, "De la Conquête du Pérou." Here he detects a typical instance of the human tendency to deify exceptional individuals:

> Le premier de ces incas qui avait subjugué le pays... passait pour le fils du Soleil. Ainsi les peuplades les plus policées de l'ancien monde et du nouveau se ressemblent dans l'usage de déifier les hommes extraordinaires, soit conquérants, soit législateurs. (II, 355)

One can imagine his pleasure upon discovery of the term *fils du Soleil* which his readers, he knew, would associate with *fils de Dieu*. The early Christian propaganda deifying Jesus as a messianic legislator tends to justify his second category of candidates for godhood. His study of

[89] Louis Maimbourg, *L'Histoire du calvinisme* (1682) and Claude Fleury, *Histoire ecclésiastique* (1691).
[90] René Pomeau, ed., *Essai sur les moeurs* (Paris, 1963).

universal history furnished him with many such opportunities to ruin Christian claims to uniqueness.

In addition to these brief insertions on the Trinity and the divinity of Christ, he devotes an entire chapter to Calvin's revenge on Servetus in the name of Trinitarian orthodoxy. Since Chapter 134, "De Calvin et de Servet," appeared in print for the first time in the 1756 edition of the *Essai*, his arrival in Geneva may have sparked his curiosity. He begins this chapter with regrets that the Spaniard abandoned medicine, "un art utile" (II, 244), to which he had contributed the circulation of the blood before Harvey. In rededicating himself to

> sciences dangereuses, il traita de la préfiguration du Christ dans le Verbe, [etc.]; il adoptait en partie les anciens dogmes soutenus par Sabellius, par Eusèbe, par Arius, qui dominèrent dans l'Orient, et qui furent embrassés au XVIe siècle par Lélio Socini, reçus ensuite en Pologne, en Angleterre, en Hollande. (II, 244)

Servetus' trinity does resemble Sabellius', but not Arius' or Eusebius of Caesarea's. Like Sabellius, Servetus believed that *"God has manifested himself in three different persons"* (*Errors*, p. 131), a rational solution for the enigma of triple unity. Such modalism differs from Arianism, which Arius and Eusebius held in its milder form. The subordination of the Son to the Father in all Arianism necessarily implies a distinction between them incompatible with modal unity. While Arianism predominated for a while in the East during the fourth century, Sabellianism had some following in the third and fourth centuries without ever predominating in either the East or the West. Far from accepting Servetus' Neo-Sabellianism, Lelio Sozzini explicitly rejected it (see p. 100), although he disclosed little of his own belief. His nephew Fausto acknowledged Lelio's influence, but Fausto himself formulated Socinian theology, which owed little to Servetus, Sabellius, Arius, or Eusebius of Caesarea. The fragmentary and diversified tendencies labeled Socinian in Holland and England do not justify the last phrase in Voltaire's statement. Consequently, the quotation shows that, after the philosophical letter on antitrinitarians, he continued to accept the apologetic error of continuous and unified opposition to the orthodox Trinity ever since the early Christian centuries. The new errors he added to the old seem to have resulted more from innocent ignorance than design, but how many of his readers knew the subject well enough to challenge him or even cared about the accuracy of his information? Solidarity with so many centuries of antitrinitarians had the effect of flattering their eighteenth-century aversion to a theological abstraction inaccessible to experience.

Nevertheless, Voltaire wanted more from them than sympathy with Trinitarian heresy; he wanted them to regret that so intelligent a physician as Servetus should have wasted himself on useless and dangerous speculation. To demonstrate the degree of Servetus' deviation from the pursuit of useful knowledge, Voltaire fabricated a "quotation" from his *Errors of the Trinity* and inserted it in the 1761 edition of the *Essai*:

> Comme le germe de la génération était en Dieu, avant que le fils de Dieu fût fait réellement, ainsi le Créateur a voulu que cet ordre fût observé dans toutes les générations. La semence substantielle du Christ et toutes les causes séminales et formes archétypes étant véritablement en Dieu, etc. (II, 244)

Pomeau traces this text to two passages in the book which resemble it more than others, yet Voltaire cannot even be found to have paraphrased them, to say nothing of translation.[91] Voltaire at least preserves Servetus' conception of the Word's generation from the Father by a method similar to human reproduction. While the thought in the passage does not particularly misrepresent Servetus, the style of the second sentence caricatures medieval scholasticism rather than Reformation theology. Voltaire obviously wanted to make Servetus look ridiculous to his readers, but he might have found authentic passages to achieve this effect. In his commentary, he invites them to appreciate the similarity between his fake quotation and Origen, and even, excepting the allusion to Christ, Plato. Though Origen and Servetus are both subordinationists, Origen does not profess the genetic pre-existence of the Word within the Father as propounded by the *Errors*, but rather the eternal generation of the Word, which harmonizes with Servetus' panchristianity in the *Restoration*. Origen's Christian reinterpretation of the Neoplatonic Word apparently lies behind Voltaire's reference to Plato. What remains to be seen, however, is why he inserted this paragraph in 1761 to begin with. He seems to be attacking the theologian in Servetus and through him all theologians. Perhaps he intended his fraudulent quotation as a monument to the frivolity of dissertating on matters beyond the reach of reason.

In the next two paragraphs, he summarizes Calvin's double betrayal of Servetus. Here he mistakenly charges that Calvin obtained part of Servetus' *Restoration* "par trahison" (II, 245). Servetus had sent Calvin

[91] The absence of the work from the catalogues of his library suggests that he resorted to a compilation, perhaps a faulty one.

a manuscript copy a few years earlier. Voltaire qualifies Calvin's collaboration with the Catholic authorities in France as an "action qui suffirait pour le déshonorer à jamais dans la société." The quarrel had erupted, he remarks, when "Servet… écrivit à Calvin sur la trinité." He attributes Calvin's subsequent behavior to "[la] haine théologique, la plus implacable de toutes les haines" (II, 245), thus implying that Trinitarian theology drove Calvin to his revenge. He exaggerates Calvin's abuse of Servetus during the trial[92] and holds him responsible for the verdict:

> à force… de crier et de faire crier que Dieu demandait l'exécution de… Servet, il le fit brûler, et jouit de son supplice. (II, 246)

While the excesses committed by Calvin in prosecuting Servetus cannot be denied, he did ask, though in vain, that the sentence be commuted from burning to hanging. Voltaire rightly protests, on the other hand, that "cette barbarie… qui s'autorisait du nom de justice, pouvait être regardée comme une insulte aux droits des nations" (II, 246). Servetus was a Spaniard, he explains, and he had not disseminated his opinions on Genevan territory.

"Dans ses ouvrages publiés, [il] reconnaît nettement la divinité éternelle de Jésus-Christ" (II, 246). And so he did, although he described this divinity as tributary to the Father's. In 1761, Voltaire added:

> Il déclara dans le cours de son procès… que Jésus-Christ était le fils de Dieu, engendré de toute éternité du Père, et conçu par le Saint-Esprit dans le sein de la Vierge Marie. (II, 246)

While Servetus' testimony at the trial in Geneva does not include this specific declaration, he does imply that Jesus Christ is the Son of God in statements such as, "J.C. a sa divinité de son père."[93] The trial records, on the other hand, mention neither questions nor answers about the eternal engenderment of the Word or the conception in the virgin Mary's womb by the Holy Spirit, but the *Restoration* promotes them both. Consequently, Voltaire, who culled his information from secondary sources,[94] simplifies a very complicated matter. Through ignorance and negligence to some extent deliberate, he presents a neat summary of orthodox views supposedly professed by Servetus at his trial, in order to convict his prosecutor of cynicism. Actually, the

[92] "Quand son ennemi fut aux fers, il lui prodigua les injures et les mauvais traitements que font les lâches quand ils sont les maîtres" (II, 246).

[93] F. Trechsel, *Die protestantischen Antitrinitarier vor Faustus Socin* (Heidelberg, 1839), I, 286.

[94] Florida cites Anastase in this connection. See n. 117.

trial proceedings show that Calvin thoroughly questioned Servetus about his interpretation of the distinctions between the three persons in the Trinity. Servetus insisted that these distinctions are "personal" and not "real," an opinion implicating modalism, which Calvin understandably denounced as heretical. These details would not have strengthened Voltaire's indictment of Calvin and, if he knew of them, he ignored them.

By 1761, he had discovered a compromising passage in a letter written by Calvin in France many years before his dispute with Servetus:

> En cas que quelqu'un soit hétérodoxe et qu'il fasse scrupule de se servir des mots *trinité* et *personne*, etc.... nous devons le supporter, sans le chasser de l'Eglise, et sans l'exposer à aucune censure comme un hérétique.[95] (II, 245)

Voltaire's attitude towards the contradiction between this plea for toleration under persecution and Calvin's later abuse of power in seeking personal revenge is predictable:

> Calvin changea d'avis dès qu'il se livra à la fureur de la haine théologique: il demandait la tolérance dont il avait besoin pour lui en France, et il s'armait de l'intolérance à Genève. (II, 245)

While Calvin's egoism and hypocrisy remained excessive, hatred of Servetus made a fanatic of him. Voltaire underlines the hypocrisy of his shift from tolerance to intolerance by citing the book he published advocating the punishment of heretics like Servetus (see p. 98). In 1756, he had already quoted a letter attributed to Calvin which describes heretics as

> ces zélés faquins qui excitent les peuples à se bander contre nous. Pareils monstres doivent être étouffés comme j'ai fait de Michel Servet, Espagnol. (II, 247)

The criminal stands convicted on the strength of his own cynical testimony, since years before in France Calvin himself had incited the common people to revolt against Catholic orthodoxy. But did Voltaire know that this letter was apocryphal?[96] One cannot tell, yet, he clearly

[95] Voltaire has condensed a much longer passage in *Johannis Calvini Epistolae et responsa* (Geneva, 1617), VI (Pt. 2), 397.

[96] According to Jules Bonnet, ed., *Lettres de Calvin* (Paris, 1854), II, 588. Voltaire might have quoted another letter from Calvin to Antoine de Bourbon on Dec. 14, 1557 (four years after Servetus' death): "Il semble bien qu'on puisse remontrer par raisons favorables que ce n'est le repos et profit du royaume [de] procéder [contre les Huguenots] par exécutions violentes, d'autant que les feux ne font que multiplier le nombre de ceux qu'on persécute" (Bonnet, II, 167).

intended to ruin Calvin's reputation. On one hand, the vindictive Calvin served as an example of the evil that a theologian could do.

On the other, the deist Voltaire, recently settled in Geneva, wanted to make the dogmatic Protestantism of the past seem odious to the allies he was trying to cultivate among Calvinist ministers. "Il semble aujourd'hui," he thought wishfully,

> qu'on fasse amende honorable aux cendres de Servet: des savants pasteurs des églises protestantes, et même les plus grands philosophes, ont embrassé ses sentiments et ceux de Socin. Ils ont encore été plus loin qu'eux: leur religion est l'adoration d'un Dieu par la médiation du Christ. (ɪɪ, 247)

According to Florida, the greatest philosophes are Newton and Locke,[97] with whom many of the ministers in Geneva and Lausanne substantially agreed. Neither the philosophes nor the ministers, however, had embraced the theology of Servetus, but rather, to some extent, that of Fausto Sozzini. While repudiating nothing in Calvinism, they refrained from discussing dogmatic mysteries like the Trinity and the two natures, in which they did not really believe. Most of them not only worshiped God through the intermediary of Christ, as Voltaire says, but also kept their faith in redemption by him. This faith in particular separated them from deists like Voltaire, who underestimated the difficulty in his forthcoming campaign to convert them.

His treatment of "les anabaptistes anglais" in Chapter 136 confirms the persistence of this erroneous tendency:

> Ils n'étaient réellement que des déistes: car ils ne reconnaissaient Jésus-Christ que comme un homme à qui Dieu avait daigné donner des lumières plus pures qu'à ses contemporains. (ɪɪ, 262)

Everything indicates that he meant for his readers to take this *car* seriously, unlike others in his stories where the context is almost as illogical.[98] This divine enlightenment was more than enough to elevate Christ above other men in the minds of these anabaptists. As evidence of their "deism," Voltaire is nonetheless content to applaud their rejection of certain dogmas: "Ils ne reconnaissaient ni l'histoire de la chute de l'homme, ni le mystère de la sainte Trinité, ni par conséquent celui de l'incarnation" (ɪɪ, 262). Refusing to accept these

[97] "The greatest *philosophes* [are] always Newton and Locke in the Voltairian canon" (Florida, p. 175).

[98] A famous example from *Candide*: "Monsieur le baron était un des plus puissants seigneurs de la Vestphalie, car son château avait une porte et des fenêtres." Jacques Bénac, *Romans et contes* (Paris, 1960), p. 137.

articles of faith neither divorced them from Christianity nor brought them into the fold of deism. Chapter 189, "De la Pologne au XVIIIe siècle, et des Sociniens," reveals further evidence of this tendency to confuse antitrinitarianism with deism:

> Ces unitaires... prétendaient soutenir la cause de Dieu même, en le regardant comme un être unique, incommunicable, qui n'avait un fils que par adoption. (II, 743)

The diminutive in the final clause obscures the importance of this adoption, which occurs at the resurrection and exalts Christ to subordinate, but divine status as the Son of God. In view of these examples, one must wonder whether Voltaire was deliberately omitting the intermediary role of Christ. Although he amplifies the universality of the pseudo-deism he sees in Socinianism, the opportunity to contradict Maimbourg moves him to admit that, in Holland, "Jamais les unitaires et les sociniens n'... ont eu d'assemblée publique" (II, 743), a partial correction of an error in the *Letters* (see p. 118).[99] Otherwise, he develops his erroneous thesis as boldly as ever:

> Cette religion [socinianisme-déisme] s'est étendue sourdement en Hollande, en Transylvanie, en Silésie, en Pologne, mais surtout en Angleterre... Cette religion, qui a dominé dans l'Eglise à diverses fois pendant trois cent cinquante années depuis Constantin,[100] [s'est] reproduite dans l'Europe depuis deux siècles. (II, 743)

He seems to have reserved this explicit consolidation of scattered hints for the final pages of a late chapter in the *Essai* on purpose.

It was in fact the last page of Chapter 189 until shortly before his death in 1778 when he revised the work for the last time. On this occasion, he appended another paragraph reaffirming the supremacy of true deism over antitrinitarian as well as Trinitarian Christianity:

> Qu'importe... que les chrétiens reconnaissent dans Jésus-Christ un Dieu portion indivisible de Dieu, et pourtant séparée,[101] ou qu'ils révèrent dans lui la première créature de Dieu? Ces deux systèmes sont également incompréhensibles. (II, 744)

It would be hard to believe that he came to this conclusion because his campaign to convert the Calvinist ministers had failed twenty-one years before (see next section). It seems more likely that this failure

[99] Florida makes this point (p. 177, n. 9).

[100] Arianisme subsisted for this amount of time, but by no means predominated, especially after the fourth century.

[101] This is another awkward attempt to express the orthodox Trinity. Christ is not a portion, but the whole of the divine substance. He is not separate from the other persons, but distinct. The clause following *ou* refers to unitarianism.

had taught him the futility of pretending that implicit or explicit antitrinitarianism conforms to the natural light. In view of his dwindling life expectancy, he may well have wanted to leave a less polemical *Essai* to posterity. For lack of time or patience, he overlooked the discrepancy between the historiography of the last paragraph and the polemics of the preceding text. The paragraph nonetheless harmonizes with his primary intention in writing the *Essai*. One finds an interesting expression of this intention in the *Remarques pour servir de supplément à l'Essai* (1763):

> La seule arme contre ce monstre [le fanatisme], c'est la raison. La seule manière d'empêcher les hommes d'être absurdes et méchants, c'est de les éclairer. Pour rendre le fanatisme exécrable, il ne faut que le peindre. (II, 931)

Pretending that antitrinitarian Christianity amounted to deism did not enlighten his readers. Before his death, he therefore preferred to paint the "monster" in its true colors.

Calvin's Atrocious Soul

He had a very different attitude in 1756 when he attacked Calvin's atrocious soul in hopes of separating the more philosophic ministers of Geneva and Lausanne from Calvinism. Some of them were closer to what he called natural religion than others and even close enough to be guilty of hypocrisy.[102] Neither pious nor zealous, Polier de Bottens of Lausanne was content to do his clerical duties and avoid suspicion. Yet he originated the Encyclopedia article "Messie" edited by Voltaire, which treats Jesus as one of the several false messiahs of the age. Young Jacob Vernes of Geneva took his responsibilities as a minister even less seriously. His *Catéchisme à l'usage des jeunes gens de toutes les communions* (undated) mentions neither the divinity of Christ nor redemption and admits only his delegation by God. While Jacob Vernet, on the other hand, subordinated the Son to the Father, he retained his divinity as well as redemption and, having occupied the chair of theology at the University of Geneva in 1756, defended the authority of the Genevan church. The other ministers who frequented Voltaire varied in opinion and dedication between these three examples. To him, Vernet's implicit unitarianism did not seem

[102] This section and the next cover the same ground as Florida, whose work was very useful in preparing them. Rather than Voltaire's interest in Socinianism in the broad sense, however, they concentrate on his preoccupation with the resemblance between his deism and the unitarianism of some ministers.

very different from Polier's crypto-deism, an impression to which Vernet had unwittingly contributed by his efforts to convert deists and even Voltaire himself to his liberal Protestantism. In 1755, he had sent Voltaire a copy of his *Traité*, with its explicit appeal to deists, and written him:

> Il faut aux hommes une religion aussi bien qu'un gouvernement, et vous voyez que la nôtre est... si simple, si sage, si douce qu'un philosophe ne saurait en demander une plus raisonnable, ni un politique une plus convenable au bien public. (D 6146)

While this naïve hint could hardly have tempted Voltaire, obviously the philosophe in question, it certainly suggested that Vernet's religion bore tantalizing resemblance to his own. The letter nonetheless prescribes the necessity for the gospel and insinuates that Voltaire should leave the religion of Geneva alone. Though irritated by the latter point, Voltaire wrote a polite and noncommittal reply which may have persuaded Vernet to abandon his project, for he made no further appeals. But Vernet's letter may have persuaded Voltaire to undertake the conversion of the ministers to deism.

An event occurring in Geneva, apparently in February of 1756, manifestly encouraged him. On April 12, he wrote Cideville that the brothers Cramer, to whom he had submitted the *Poèmes sur la loi naturelle* and *sur le désastre de Lisbonne* for publication, had read them to an assembly of "les chefs du conseil et de l'église." These poems "ont été universellement approuvés dans tous les points." He probably exaggerated the number of councilors and church leaders (*des* rather than *les*?) as well as the degree of approval, but there is no reason to believe he made the story up. Had he in fact instigated this reading of his poems himself? Writings such as the twenty-third *Lettre philosophique* underscore his desire for public acclaim. Since he enjoyed the esteem of both ministers and magistrates at the time, he could count on their good will. Perhaps he did therefore ask the Cramers to arrange the reading. Though written in 1752, *La Loi naturelle* contains six lines on Calvin and Servetus which the assembled ministers and magistrates must have noticed:

> Calvin et ses suppôts, guettés par la justice,
> Dans Paris, en peinture, allèrent au supplice.
> Servet fut en personne immolé par Calvin.
> Si Servet dans Genève eût été souverain,
> Il eût, pour argument contre ses adversaires,
> Fait serrer d'un lacet le cou des trinitaires. (M. IX, 453)

Voltaire would soon correct his mistaken impression that Servetus was opposed to any kind of trinity. The epithets in the passage are mild and Calvin's guilt appears diminished by its association with the alleged likelihood that Servetus would have behaved similarly in similar circumstances. These lines also tend to shift the blame from Calvin to the spirit of the age, theological fanaticism by implication. The tolerance, if not the applause, of his elite audience therefore seems entirely possible. The controversy which broke out a year later would demonstrate the value he assigned to the least indication of approval by such men. In the letter to Cideville quoted above, his enthusiasm over the public endorsement of his poems sounds like triumph:

> Genève n'est plus la Genève de Calvin... Le christianisme raisonnable de Locke est la religion de presque tous les ministres, et l'adoration d'un être suprême jointe à la morale est la religion de presque tous les magistrats. (April 12, 1756)

Although the statement tells us nothing less than the truth, it leaves a wide margin of possible error, for worship of a supreme being is a broader term than reasonable Christianity.

Voltaire was collaborating with the *Encyclopédie* then in hopes of slipping his antichristian propaganda into that work. Less wary than Diderot, d'Alembert, with whom he was corresponding, did not particularly suspect that he might unintentionally expose the Encyclopedia to retaliation by the pious faction in France. On August 10, d'Alembert arrived at Les Délices for a euphoric five-week visit. He made no secret of his intention to gather information for an Encyclopedia article on Geneva, for Vernet actually furnished him with historical material for this purpose. It seems unlikely that he should have refrained from questioning the ministers about their religion and pressing them for the details of their belief which he would discuss in his article. While they customarily avoided such issues, one cannot imagine them allowing him in his conversations with them to attribute to them a doctrine they did not accept. Nor can one believe that he mistook the awe of inexperienced ministers for acquiescence, an excuse offered by Vernet several years later.[103] D'Alembert was no novice reporter on his first assignment and he was in contact with mature defenders of the faith like Vernet himself, who as a young man had frequented Parisian society for ten years. Nevertheless, the illusion of agreement where none existed evidently bedeviled d'Alembert's visit to Geneva. The atmosphere in fact fostered misun-

[103] "Souvent de jeunes ecclésiastiques, par respect ou par timidité, ne contredisent pas formellement des discours hardis et d'un certain ton, quoiqu'ils les désapprouvent en eux-mêmes." *Suites des Lettres critiques d'un voyageur anglais* (Utrecht, 1761), p. 28.

derstanding, for the ministers admired Voltaire, d'Alembert, and the Encyclopedia so much that they must have found it difficult to exercise their critical discretion. As Chaponnière observes, the mutual antagonism to Catholicism may well have resulted in enthusiastic agreement, thus diverting their attention from areas of profound disagreement.[104] Torn between their fascination with philosophy and the responsibility of their vocation, the ministers must have lavished vague assurances on d'Alembert and perhaps even, in moments of embarrassment, assurances less than vague. Surely indoctrinated by Voltaire, d'Alembert must have solicited evidence of deism from them and they must have yielded to the temptation of delighting him with ambiguous hints. Whatever the degree of their private heterodoxy, their position in Genevan society depended on a public semblance of Calvinist orthodoxy. Nor did the sacrifice of Jesus' divinity imply the abandonment of his intermediate role for most of them, as it did for Voltaire and d'Alembert.[105] In d'Alembert's article, they probably expected to find praise of their philosophy and morality with no mention of their doctrine.

Voltaire began to upset their complacency by the publication of the *Essai*, but they did not react immediately. On January 13, 1757, he wrote Vernes, "C'est une chose bien honorable pour Genève... qu'on imprime dans cette ville que Servet était un sot et Calvin un barbare." Chapter 134 in the *Essai* refers to Calvin's "barbarie" (II, 246), but one must seek an illustration of Servetus' *sottise* in Voltaire's counterfeit quotation of the *Errors* (see p. 153). Voltaire evidently wanted to call attention to the chapter in a letter to the minister with whom he had the greatest influence. He had apparently heard little or nothing from the successors of Calvin on this pregnant subject and was anxious to sound them out. What did he learn from them? Presumably the same kind of approval they had given his poems. When a famous author fishes for compliments, admirers who do not share his fundamental convictions usually praise less essential aspects of his work. The size of the *Essai* favored such polite subterfuge. Since Vernet had edited an early version of the work ending before the Reformation,[106] he could

[104] "Rien ne fait croire à la solidité d'une amitié nouvelle comme la lutte commune contre un même adversaire. Mais les pasteurs genevois ne connaissaient point... la force des liens qui les attachaient aux idées religieuses." Paul Chaponnière, *Voltaire chez les calvinistes* (Paris, 1932), p. 66.

[105] "Both d'Alembert and Voltaire were misled by their rarified contacts with Geneva's aristocracy and blinded by their Roman Catholic presumptions about the logically necessary movement of Protestantism to deism and therefore... misjudged the temper of Geneva as a whole" (Florida, p. 228).

[106] *Essai sur l'histoire universelle depuis Charlemagne* (1754).

compliment Voltaire on that part of it. On the other hand, Voltaire's patrician friends, who shared his convictions, had no reason to apportion their applause.

Since no one had condemned the *Essai* and many had voiced some kind of approval, he felt that he could safely hazard an exaggeration similar to the one he had used in connection with his poems. On March 26, he wrote Pierre Rousseau:

> J'ai fait imprimer à Genève avec l'approbation universelle que Calvin était un très méchant homme, altier, dur, vindicatif et sanguinaire.

Although Chapter 134 applies none of these epithets to Calvin, they do convey the author's intentions more or less accurately. In writing to a fellow philosophe, he uses stronger language and eliminates the equal treatment of Servetus. Rousseau, the editor of the *Journal encyclopédique*, which was less radical than its title implies, did not take the hint to announce Voltaire's success in his review. Voltaire therefore made another attempt to publicize his Genevan precedent on March 26 when he wrote Thiériot:

> Ce n'est pas un petit exemple du progrès de la raison humaine qu'on ait imprimé à Genève dans cet essai sur l'histoire, avec l'approbation publique, que Calvin avait une âme atroce aussi bien qu'un esprit éclairé. Le meurtre de Servet paraît aujourd'hui abominable.

Thus Voltaire contrasts Calvin's atrocious soul with his enlightened mind, a variation on the tactic of moderating an attack on him by a concession to Genevan sensibilities. The quotation comes from the text as printed in the *Mercure de France* in May, for the original letter has been lost. The style reflects the intent to publish rather than merely correspond with a close friend. Thiériot in fact wrote back to acknowledge that he had carried out a commission by Voltaire to have it printed.

Since the writer's previous correspondence betrays the itch to denigrate Calvin, one cannot accept at face value his subsequent complaints that his text had been altered. He made this claim in a letter to Vernes in mid-May and observed that *âme atroce* does not occur in the *Essai*: "Je vous prie de détromper vos amis." Yet what would have kept him from using the phrase in the letter to Thiériot in anticipation of this very excuse? Some of the ministers must have assumed as much, because they held him responsible for slandering the founder of Genevan Protestantism anyway. On May 20, Voltaire admitted to Thiériot, "qu'il y a dans le pays que j'habite trois ou quatre personnes qui sont encore du seizième siècle." For the sake of peace and his friends' tranquillity, he asked Thiériot to confirm his claim that the

Mercure had printed an unfaithful version of his letter and that he had actually written "âme trop austère," not "âme atroce." "Autant qu'il peut m'en souvenir, c'était là la véritable leçon." In view of his excellent memory, one cannot take this remark seriously. To make matters worse, the minister replying to his *Mercure* letter in the *Journal helvétique* (June of 1757) traces the expression *âme atroce* to a verse in an ode by Horace, Voltaire's favorite poet: "Atrocem animum Catonis."[107] This minister, who may well have been Vernet himself, chides Voltaire for translating Horace out of context to malign Calvin. He contends that *âme austère* renders Horace and describes Calvin more accurately. It is interesting that both he and Voltaire should propose the same alternative. Perhaps Voltaire chose the verse precisely because *atrocem* translates in French either as *atroce* (cruel) or *austère*, thus leaving room for maneuver.

But why had the author of the letter to the *Journal helvétique* taken such offense over the atrocious soul to begin with? The ministers, whom he obviously represents, had made no serious protest against worse abuse of Calvin in the *Essai* itself. He reserves his greatest resentment for Voltaire's boast of public approval: "C'est ce qui nous blesse le plus" (D 7272). Voltaire, he warns, is mistaking tolerance of his writings for an endorsement of them. He also rejects Voltaire's charge that a miscarriage of justice had taken place. Though regrettable, the execution of Servetus conformed to the laws and customs of the age and Voltaire is impugning the integrity of the magistrature. Thus the minister tries to involve the magistrates by ascribing injury to them as if they were not reacting vigorously enough to the letter in the *Mercure*. His awkward protest implies embarrassment as well as isolated and impotent outrage, for Voltaire had exposed the inability of the pastorate to control the press in Geneva. His published insinuation that progressive Protestantism prevailed over traditional Calvinism had disturbed the delicate equilibrium between public respectability and private freethought, thus jeopardizing the ministers' authority. Significantly, the minister skirts the basic theological issues that had pitted Calvin against Servetus: "Calvin ne pouvait regarder Servet... que comme un de ces hardis ennemis de la religion qui sont punissables par les lois." To this circumlocution, he adds no more than a misleading allusion to "ce qu'on appelle aujourd'hui le spinozisme" (D 7272). He does not even answer Voltaire's lethal and yet erroneous charge that the pastorate had abandoned Calvin's doc-

[107] Flaccus Horatius, *Odes and Epodes of Horace*, ed. Clement Smith (Boston, 1896), II, i, 24.

trine for Servetus'. His opinion closely resembles that of Vernet, who seems either to have written the letter or sponsored it.

He is the only prominent minister who persistently tried to obtain official censure of Voltaire before the publication of "Genève" in the Encyclopedia. The Vénérable Consistoire, the governing body of the Genevan pastorate, had already brought charges against Voltaire, though in vain, before the Petit Conseil[108] on May 21, shortly after the publication of the letter to Thiériot in the *Mercure*. When the Consistory decided to investigate the object of the protest in the *Journal helvétique*, Vernet served on the committee appointed for this purpose. While the committee found the letter excessive in places, a criticism that must have caused Vernet some chagrin, it approved the general text, proposed a refutation of Voltaire's antichristian polemic and encouraged Vernet to pursue this project. By the end of September, the Consistory had adopted the proposal, "pourvu qu'on le fasse en observant les règles les plus exactes de la modération et de la charité Xe [sainte]" (B. CII, 502). Eager to begin his refutation, Vernet requested communication of the Servetus dossier in the city archives, but the Petit Conseil, which included several of Voltaire's friends, refused (Sept. 12). He likewise asked Voltaire's doctor, Théodore Tronchin, to lend him a manuscript copy of Servetus' *Restoration* in his possession. Théodore turned him down too. Vernet then sent Théodore a list of questions about the work and sought to convince him and his cousin Jean-Robert Tronchin, the attorney general, of the necessity for an answer to Voltaire. Both tried to discourage him. To no avail.

Voltaire then undercut his enfeebled influence by providing Théodore with copies of the letters Vernet had written him. He had little difficulty in persuading Théodore that this once enthusiastic admirer, who had edited an early version of the *Essai* and had offered to re-edit it, should not attempt to refute chapters in the same work. Vernet had written these compromising letters at a time when he knew nothing of the chapter on Calvin and Servetus. Though stubborn, he was isolated and, as far as Voltaire was concerned, "Tous les honnêtes gens [dans la ville de Calvin] sont des déistes par Christ" (Aug. 29, 1757). By October 21, he was gloating over the Council's rebuff of Vernet in a letter to Bertrand, the more deist than Christian pastor of the French-speaking congregation in Bern.[109] If Vernet had seen the Servetus dossier,

[108] The highest and smallest assembly (20 members) in the Genevan government.

[109] Bertrand published a refutation of the letter against Voltaire in the August, 1757, issue of the *Journal helvétique*.

> il aurait vu, peut-être, qu'on brûla ce pauvre diable avec des bourrées vertes où les feuilles étaient encore. Il fit prier maître Jehan Calvin ou Chauvin de demander au moins des fagots secs et maître Jehan répondit qu'il ne pouvait pas en conscience se mêler de cette affaire.

Such playful variations on a name occur frequently in Voltairian satire.[110] He could have found nothing more harmful to Calvin's reputation than evidence that he had refused to intervene in the perpetration of an unusual excess of cruelty. However, this allegation is almost certainly legendary, since it appears in none of the documentation known to be authentic (see p. 154). In order to ruin the credibility of Calvin's defender, Voltaire told Bertrand, "c'est un antitrinitaire qui veut aujourd'hui justifier la mort de Servet," as if he believed Servetus hostile to any kind of trinity. This is unlikely, if Voltaire wrote Vernes on October 28, as Besterman believes, that "Servet avait déclaré nettement que la *divinité habitait en Jésus Christ*, et plus nettement qu'on ne le déclare aujourd'hui." To be sure, he aimed the final clause at Vernet. In imitation of the New Testament epistles, he concludes his letter with an invocation to the eternal being to have pity on Jehan Chauvin "pour un si grand crime."

"Genève"

His relentless praise of remorse for a crime most Genevans preferred to forget had caused embarrassment and perhaps even irritation, but little profound resentment, except for that of Vernet and a few others. In late November of 1757, however, "Genève" appeared in Volume VII of the *Encyclopédie*. Unaware of the Genevan reaction to Calvin's atrocious soul, d'Alembert quoted the entire passage from the *Mercure*, including the boast of public approval. Yet he had no intention of raking the pin across the prick. On the contrary, he wanted to hold Geneva up to France as an example to be followed, in the manner of the *Lettres philosophiques*.

Unwittingly, he made the article even more obnoxious to the ministers by his echo of Voltaire's erroneous assertion that they had adopted Servetus' doctrine:

> Plusieurs ne croient plus à la divinité de Jésus-Christ, dont Calvin, leur chef, était si zélé défenseur et pour laquelle il fit brûler Servet.[111]

[110] In the dialect of Picardie, Calvin's native province, "*K*... before *A* remained intact," W.D. Elcock, *The Romance Languages* (London, 1960), p. 366. Voltaire knew nothing of the French *chauvin* (xenophobic), the legacy of Sgt. Chauvin, a soldier of the Napoleonic era.

[111] "Genève," *Encyclopédie ou dictionnaire raisonné des sciences, des arts et des métiers* (Paris, 1751-1766).

Voltaire had evidently misled him into believing that Servetus did not regard Christ as divine, but Voltaire had since learned otherwise. D'Alembert at least limited the extent of this belief among the ministres to several of them, thus respecting the difference between them. Such precision belongs to science rather than common sense. He did not know of Vernet's limited defense of Calvin, for he affirmed that the ministers "n'entreprennent point de le justifier." Why had Voltaire failed to keep him informed? Perhaps Voltaire was more anxious to provoke the ministers than spare his disciple. D'Alembert observed that, when the ministers conversed with a Catholic, they compared Calvin's "action très blâmable" to the "abominable journée de la Saint Barthélemy." Though a Catholic only by background and expedient, he was speaking of himself, but he obviously borrowed the example of the Saint Barthélemy, Voltaire's great phobia, from Voltaire. He committed a further Voltairian error by assigning "un socinianisme parfait" to "plusieurs pasteurs de Genève," although these precautionary partitives improve on his source. He explained that they rejected "tout ce qu'on appelle *mystères*" and "s'imaginent"—a word intended to placate Catholic enemies of the Encyclopedia—"que le premier principe d'une religion véritable est de ne rien proposer à croire qui heurte la raison." Recalling the controversy over Vernet's *Traité*, he remarked that they substituted *utility* for *necessity* in characterizing "la révélation, ce dogme si essentiel au christianisme" (see p. 171). Thus d'Alembert construed Socinianism in the vague sense of Catholic polemic, in the sense of rational revolt against the mysteries of the dogma, while Voltaire retained the original connotation of unitarianism.

Like Voltaire, however, d'Alembert confused Socinianism with the religion of reason or, in other words, deism. He concluded his treatment of doctrine with a bolder statement than even Voltaire had dared to make in public:[112]

> La religion [chez les ministres] est presque réduite à l'adoration d'un seul Dieu, du moins chez tout ce qui n'est pas peuple; le respect pour Jésus-Christ et pour les Ecritures sont peut-être la seul chose qui distingue d'un pur déisme le christianisme de Genève.

In contrast with Voltaire, the co-editor of the *Encyclopédie* valued such words as *nearly* and *perhaps*. But no combination of adverbs would be enough to appease the ministers, once they had read that only respect for Christ and Scripture separated them from deism. D'Alembert's sentence openly conveyed his satisfaction with how little he thought

[112] Compare with *Essai*, II, 247; see p. 156.

that was. Would not his readers everywhere in Europe and especially his Catholic readers agree? He should have foreseen it, his espousal of the Catholic taunt that Protestantism fatally results in deism would offend the ministers. Furthermore, the alleged existence of true Christianity only among the common people of Geneva came as insult after injury.

D'Alembert was welcoming the ministers into the deist fold at a time when they had already begun to resist Voltaire's attempts to seduce them.[113] The evidence of the disciple's dependence on the master incited them to accuse Voltaire of responsibility for the article. Naves proves conclusively, however, that d'Alembert composed it himself, as he stubbornly insisted in the ensuing controversy.[114] Yet there can be no doubt that Voltaire had inculcated in him his own conception of Genevan religion, so that d'Alembert sought confirmation of Voltaire's ideas from the ministers. The disciple indubitably translated the master's thought into his own language but, since the master knew of the disciple's intention to write an article on Geneva, one can scarcely absolve Voltaire of manipulation. The ministers were right, therefore, to hold him responsible for it.

Having heard about the contents of "Genève" before receiving Volume VII, he wrote d'Alembert on December 2:

> Vous y louez la modération de certaines gens. Hélas! vous ne les connaissez point; les Genevois ne disent point leur secret aux étrangers. Les agneaux que vous croyez tolérants seraient des loups si on les laissait faire.

From his viewpoint, the secret they had kept from d'Alembert was their incompatibility with deism and their resistance to revelation of their heterodoxy. On December 6, he sent another letter to d'Alembert to thank him for his support "à propos du meurtre infâme de Servet... dans l'article 'Genève,'" which he had still not seen. "Des misérables," he lamented, "ont été assez du [seizième] siècle pour oser dans celui-ci justifier l'assassinat de Servet." After the story of Vernet's

[113] "Si nous voulons... une preuve décisive que l'article n'a pas été connu de Voltaire dans sa rédaction avant qu'il fût publié, il suffit d'y lire la citation de la fameuse lettre à Thiériot: on y voit l'*âme atroce* dans sa version la plus primitive. C'est que d'Alembert ignorait la rectification de Voltaire, et il cite le texte dans son intégralité sans se douter que la reprise du mot, origine de controverses et d'injures depuis plusieurs mois, était une maladresse énorme." Raymond Naves, *Voltaire et l'Encyclopédie* (Paris, 1938), p. 47.

[114] "La lecture suivie de l'article nous persuade qu'il a été écrit par un informateur consciencieux et didactique, épris à la fois de méthode et de prosélytisme, mais le plus souvent monotone et peu brillant: c'est désigner sans hésitation d'Alembert, et non Voltaire" (Naves, p. 48).

failure to obtain the records of the trial "qui rendra Calvin à jamais exécrable," he concluded:

> Des magistrats détestent le crime auquel le fanatisme entraîna leurs pères, et des prêtres veulent canoniser ce crime!

This distortion of Vernet's intentions apparently indicates Voltaire's anger with him for having dashed his hopes of winning the ministers over to an alliance with deism.

On December 9, the Petit Conseil talked itself out of taking action against "Genève," on the pretext that the French government might demand something undesirable in return for its cooperation. Though professing indifference in the matter, Voltaire wrote Théodore Tronchin and Vernes that the ministers had no reasonable objection to being described as believers in a single God. He knew they could not risk a public clarification of their position on the Trinity without shattering the Trinitarian façade behind which they professed their unitarianism. Their policy of silence on the former allowed them to avoid sincerity about their secret adhesion to the latter. In a letter to d'Alembert on December 12, Voltaire confirmed his authorship of "Genève":

> Quelques-uns m'accusent d'une confédération impie avec vous. Vous savez mon innocence... Laissez-les protester... Ils auront beau jurer qu'ils croient la trinité.

Their fellow Protestants in Switzerland, Germany, and Holland knew better, he added. In the same letter, he confirms that d'Alembert had obtained his information directly from them: "Vous qui êtes instruit de leur foi par leur bouche, ne vous rétractez pas."[115] For the first time since settling on the shores of Lake Léman, he associated the ministers with their Catholic counterparts and blamed both clergies for the murders of Servetus and Hus as well as the convulsions around the tomb of Deacon Pâris. The last accusation suggests a lapse in his self-control, for he must have remembered that Vernet shared his scepticism about the convulsionary miracles.[116] Anger erupts in the next sentence: "Fanatiques papistes, fanatiques calvinistes, tous sont pêtris de la même m... détrempée de sang corrompu." The abuse of both reveals his exasperation over the ministers' resistance to his deistic proselytism. He now realized, to his dismay, that one could not necessarily destroy hypocrisy simply by exposing it.

[115] Théodore Tronchin soon asked for a retraction, but in vain.

[116] Vernet likewise expresses scepticism over the cure of the La Fosse woman's hemorrhage in *Deux Lettres à M. l'abbé* (1726).

He had succeeded only in driving the ministers from flexibility to belligerence. At the meeting of the Vénérable Compagnie des Pasteurs on December 23, Professor de La Rive warned that "Genève" contained passages injurious to the pastorate. All the ministers were questioned to determine who had betrayed them, yet none admitted to having encouraged d'Alembert to believe what he had written in the article. The Compagnie then formed a committee including Vernet and, as lay secretary, Théodore. Meanwhile, Voltaire discovered that Vernet had asked a friend for information about the Calvin papers in the Bibliothèque Royale. "Son ami," he wrote Bertrand, "y a trouvé tant de choses *atroces* qu'il en est honteux." He added an ironical speculation at the expense of all clergymen: "Hélas! Jésus-Christ n'a fait brûler personne. Il aurait fait souper avec lui Jean Hus et Servet." On the same day, he exhorted all of Vernes' colleagues to detest "le meurtre abominable de Servet et les moeurs *atroces* qui ont conduit à ce meurtre." In the interest of his newly ecumenical anticlericalism, he reinforced the example of Servetus by those of Du Bourg, Barneveldt, and De Witt; "chaque nation a des horreurs à expier."

By December 27, he had finally received and read "Genève." Two days later, he sent a letter of congratulation to d'Alembert and a letter of conciliation to Vernes. He assured d'Alembert that all Genevans owed him their gratitude, even the ministers, who nonetheless

> sont assez lâches pour désavouer leurs sentiments que vous avez manifestés et assez insolents pour se plaindre de l'éloge que vous leur avez donné d'approcher un peu de la raison. (Dec. 29)

Between these lines, one reads his resentment over their rejection of his own sentiments, whose failure contrasted embarrassingly with the success proclaimed by d'Alembert in accordance with his earlier optimism. Despite the cordial tone of this letter, he may even have been irritated with his disciple for having exposed him to such embarrassment. The Genevan councillor Dupan wrote his friend Freudenreich, "Voltaire a été très fâché contre d'Alembert [à cause de] 'Genève'" (Florida, p. 266). If this information is accurate, however, Voltaire had the good sense to keep it from d'Alembert. He did describe the ministers' efforts to retaliate and lavished particular scorn on Vernet, whose name he cited. After this diatribe, he asked "N'avez-vous pas vingt fois entendu dire à tous les ministres qu'ils ne regardent pas Jésus Christ comme Dieu?" *All the ministers* means all of those d'Alembert had consulted, but Voltairian common sense ignores such niceties. What mattered most to Voltaire was that the co-editor of the

Encyclopedia had heard a representative elite deny the divinity of Christ. Even if they went back on their word, "il demeurera consigné dans un livre immortel qu'il y a eu des prêtres... qui ont osé ne croire qu'un dieu." For lack of something more durable, there had at least been a historical precedent.

In the letter to Vernes, he gently scoffed at the scandal over "Genève":

> Carissime frater in deo et in Servetto, êtes-vous bien fâché dans le fond du coeur qu'on dise dans l'*Encyclopédie* que vous pensez comme Origène et comme deux mille prêtres [ariens] qui signèrent leur protestation contre le pétulant Athanase?[117] (Dec. 29)

While *in Servetto* replaces the usual *in Christo*,[118] Voltaire continues to confuse Origenism with Arianism. The appeal to the young minister's intellectual pride seems awkward, for how could association with an ancient heresy dispell his colleagues' suspicion of his indiscretion about their modern heresy? The disclosures in the Encyclopedia had compromised him more than any other minister because of his enthusiasm for philosophy and his friendship with Voltaire. "Allez, vous n'êtes pas si fâché," Voltaire assured him, but Vernes must have regretted being unable to muster the anger Voltaire denied. Voltaire even jested that he should feel like Dorinne who loves Licas in Quinault's *Alceste*: "Licas s'en vanta, et Dorinne... en fut bien aise."[119] Surely the irony seemed more cruel than comic to Vernes, yet Voltaire appended an implacable postscriptum requesting support for his denial of any responsibility for "Genève"!

"Les prêtres hérétiques de Genève conspirent contre nous," he warned d'Alembert on January 3, 1758;

> il n'y a sorte d'atrocité que quelques-uns d'eux n'aient faite contre le mot *atroce*, mais je les attends à l'article "Servet."

He must have been thinking of the committee deliberating on "Genève." D'Alembert ignored the hint to let him contribute an article on Servetus to the Encyclopedia. But Voltaire also asked for d'Alembert's permission to speak for him in order to "finir cette affaire." His optimism stemmed from his friendly relations with the magistrates: "Mes amis et moi, nous les mènerons beau train; ils boiront le calice jusqu'à la lie." Would the magistrates nonetheless be willing to help him force the ministers to admit their unitarianism? That remained to

[117] See p. 203, n. 161.

[118] Perhaps he was also thinking of *in petto*.

[119] Voltaire quotes Dorinne as follows: "Licas est peu discret / D'avoir dit mon secret" (Act I, scene 4). *Dorinne* is usually spelled *Dorine*.

be seen. One of the friends he was counting on was certainly Théodore who, as secretary of the committee, could be very useful to him. How should we interpret his niece's new year greetings to Théodore two days after his proposal to d'Alembert? Mme Denis included an intriguing passage in this letter: "Mon oncle, après avoir lu l'article de Genève, en a été inquiet, trouvant que d'Alembert l'avait cité très mal à propos" (Jan. 5). She conveys Voltaire's promise not to write "une panse d'A" on the subject without Théodore's consent, a promise apparently intended for publishable material only. Although this concern tends to confirm his irritation with d'Alembert, it likewise supports his steadfast denial of responsibility for "Genève." He may well have wished to concede a truth for the purpose of crediting a falsehood.

Théodore had meanwhile been trying to persuade d'Alembert to retract, first by asking Diderot to intervene and then by sending his request directly to the author of "Genève." D'Alembert had refused, but he had announced his resignation as co-editor of the *Encyclopédie*, though mostly because of the Catholic reaction in France. In his reply to Mme Denis, which has been lost, Théodore mentioned both the resignation and his attempt to obtain a retraction. Threatened with the neutralization of his opinion as published in the Encyclopedia and the loss of his Encyclopedic agent, Voltaire immediately wrote Théodore, d'Alembert, and Diderot. He assured Théodore that d'Alembert would neither resign (wrong) nor retract (right):

> Si on se plaint trop fort, il citera un certain catéchisme de votre professeur de théologie où il est dit que la révélation a son *utilité* et où l'on ne trouve pas un mot de la sainte, adorable et individuelle trinité. (Jan. 8)

Voltaire had found the utility of revelation stated by Vernet in the second edition of his *Instruction chrétienne*, a copy of which the minister had sent him.[120] The work does not mention the Trinity. Having conceded the difficulty of Théodore's position, Voltaire submits that if he were a friend of the ministers,

> je leur conseillerais de faire eux-mêmes un article de Lélio Socini, pour la lettre L du tome prochain, d'expliquer la trinité bravement, et de dire qu'ils la croient, et qu'on s'est trompé à l'article "Genève."

He realized of course that he was proposing so reasonable a solution that neither the ministers nor the Encyclopedists would ever dare

[120] *Instruction chrétienne ou catéchisme familier pour les enfants* (La Neuveville, 1754), I, 72. On December 29, 1754, Voltaire had written d'Alembert: "Vernet... n'a-t-il pas imprimé, dans je ne sais quel catéchisme qu'il m'a donné et que j'ai jeté au feu... que *la révélation* peut *être de quelque utilité*?"

accept it. Though different in kind, hypocrisy kept them both in business. He seems to have hoped that Théodore would communicate his challenge to the committee. Perhaps a devious or pusillanimous response from them would weaken the doctor's resolve to press d'Alembert for a retraction. Voltaire knew that politics motivated Théodore's activity on their behalf and not sympathy.

In his letter to d'Alembert, he tried to dissuade him from either resigning or retracting, both of which, he said, would please enemies like Vernet; in reality, his own enemies. Unaware that Diderot had already turned Théodore down, he repeated many of the same arguments against a retraction and, more discreetly, a resignation. But he supplemented them by a new and more ambitious one:

> On touche à une grande révolution dans l'esprit humain... L'article dont on fait semblant de se plaindre est un coup important dont il ne faut pas perdre le fruit. (Jan. 8)[121]

Wishful thinking or willful exaggeration? Probably the latter at this point. He had nevertheless indoctrinated the author of "Genève" in hopes of bringing the ministers into an alliance with deism. Such an alliance might indeed have precipitated a revolution in human thinking, but this dream betrays a naïve psychology of adversary relations. "Genève" and the letter in the *Mercure* had ruined a slight chance of success by flaunting the ministers' hypocrisy and impotence, thus wounding their pride. Voltaire had probably realized upon reading the article that he could no longer hope to realize his dream. Presumably, he continued his campaign in the interest of aggravating a scandal injurious to a branch of Christianity. Nor did he fool Diderot, in his letter to him, by ascribing his own tactic to d'Alembert: "Il... force [les prédicants de Genève] ou à s'avilir en reniant leur créance, ou à convenir tacitement qu'on ne les a pas calomniés." Voltaire had been trying to force the choice on them for over a year without any success, but Diderot must have wondered why Voltaire thought either goal worth the effort.

Diderot regretted the publication of "Genève"[122] and suspected Voltaire of a willingness to sacrifice the Encyclopedia to his anticlerical crusade. Despite frequent professions of esteem for the project, Voltaire's correspondence tends to substantiate this suspicion. His letter

[121] Besterman is not sure of the date, but this relative uncertainty raises no special problem here.

[122] In answering a complaint from Tronchin on December 30, 1757, Diderot excuses d'Alembert as follows: "Sa faute est une inadvertence... un mot inconsidéré." Georges Roth, ed., *Diderot: Correspondance* (Paris, 1955-1970).

to Théodore on January 12 typically focused on the provocative passages in "Genève" rather than the overall value of Volume VII. Exaggerating the popularity of the article among their mutual patrician friends, he wondered, rhetorically, what Théodore was complaining about. In addition to other ideas, most of which we have already examined, he argued that d'Alembert had mentioned Christ and "dès qu'il y a du Christ, il n'y a plus personne à faire ardre." He likewise confirmed Mme Denis' news of his alarm over "Genève": "Je conçois que [d'Alembert] aurait pu se dispenser de faire la profession de foi des gens." This statement is less hypocritical than it sounds, because he did not mention Geneva and Lausanne in the *Essai* when applauding "l'adoration d'un Dieu par la médiation du Christ" (II, 247). There he had merely referred to "de savants pasteurs des Eglises protestantes" (II, 247), while d'Alembert in Volume VII has designated the ministers of Geneva. This indiscretion may indeed have irritated him, since it impinged on the ministers' pride and incited them to join the previously isolated Vernet in opposition to him. "Laissez faire dans l'esprit humain la révolution qui se prépare," he nonetheless exhorted Théodore, who by class and inclination had little sympathy with anything of this sort.

Increasingly concerned over the deliberations of the committee, Voltaire wrote him again on January 15. This time he sought to give the impression of being embroiled in a theological dispute unworthy of his intelligence. "Jamais," he recalled, "il n'y eut de sédition à Stamboul au sujet de la consubstantialité." And it was consubstantiality that so embarrassed the committee. Since sedition, though unreligious in nature, had broken out twice in Théodore's lifetime against the oligarchy controlled by his class (1718, 1734-1736), he knew what Voltaire meant. Voltaire reminds him that Théodore had made no secret of his contempt for "les hommes" whom he considered "des coquins et des bêtes."[123] Voltaire probably guessed correctly when he represented this contempt as inclusive of all clergymen:

> Je ne voudrais pas... rencontrer [les hommes] dans un temple après les assassinats de Jean Hus, de Dubourg, de Servet, d'Antoine, et de Barneveldt, après leurs autodafé et leurs Saint-Barthélemy.

He thus alluded to Théodore's fellow committee members, whose predecessors had burned Nicolas Antoine at the stake in 1632 for his conversion to Judaism and of course Servetus before him. Exaggerat-

[123] "Les hommes, dites-vous, sont pour la plupart des coquins et des bêtes. Vous ne voudriez pas les rencontrer dans un bois, et moi..."

ing his fear of Calvin's successors, he claimed to have had far less contact with them than d'Alembert:

> Tous vos ministres chez qui je n'ai jamais mangé, et chez qui d'Alembert dînait tous les jours se sont expliqués hautement avec lui.

Since the letter to Vernes above tells a different story, he obviously thought the amount of contact with the ministers subject to interpretation according to the addressee! D'Alembert must have dined with them often, nonetheless, for Voltaire knew Théodore could check his allegation at any meeting of the committee. He understood that "Genève" would have a greater impact on Genevan opinion if he could show that he had no part in it. He therefore dissociated himself from it: "J'aurais plus que personne le droit de me plaindre de M. d'Alembert... mais je suis loin de me plaindre." If he had collaborated on the article, he argued, he would share responsibility for a passage praising himself:[124] "Je ne mérite certainement pas ce ridicule." He was apparently trying to overcome the disadvantage of d'Alembert's resignation by seizing the initiative, but his attempts to influence the secretary of the committee seem unimpressive and they may even have hurt his cause more than they helped it.

Still another letter to Théodore on January 18 reveals Voltaire's willingness by then to settle for less than he had been bargaining for. As a basis for negotiation, he proposed a written statement from d'Alembert denying the implication that the ministers were not Christians, yet this formula neither retracted the offensive statements in "Genève" nor absolved the ministers of heresy. While offering to make peace with the Genevan pastorate, he continued to enjoy the good will of the ministers in Lausanne, his winter residence at the time. "Les magistrats et les prêtres sont venus dîner chez moi comme à l'ordinaire," he wrote d'Alembert the next day. Although he did not mention any names, Polier must have been among them. They could not have been very representative, because he admitted to Bertrand the same day that attitudes toward "Genève" ranged from enthusiasm to anger among the clergy. "Ce petit orage," he commented, "ne submergera pas ceux qui ne sont pas de l'avis de l'*omousios*." He neglected to add that they had not moved any closer to deism either; in reality, he was conceding the failure of his campaign.

He nevertheless congratulated d'Alembert on January 29 for having forced "les hérétiques à publier un catéchisme." From Théodore,

[124] After quoting the atrocious soul statement, d'Alembert had written, "Nous croyons que les éloges sont à partager également entre l'auteur, son siècle et Genève."

no doubt, he had learned that the committee would submit to the Compagnie a profession of faith answering "Genève." But the committee had already read their draft of the profession to the Compagnie on January 20 and the ministers had approved it for publication. Voltaire made a further comment in a letter to d'Alembert on February 5:

> [Les] sociniens honteux... ont consumé un grand mois à ce bel ouvrage. Voilà qui est bien long, disait-on; il faut un peu de temps, répondit [la Cramer],[125] quand il s'agit de donner un état à Jésus-Christ.

Voltaire and his friends therefore assumed, after a few hints from Théodore no doubt, that embarrassment and hypocrisy had protracted what should have taken these competent theologians far less time.[126] But they had brought an additional humiliation on themselves by trying, once again, to embroil the Petit Conseil in the affair: "Les prêtres... ont voulu parler au nom des magistrats comme au leur, et les magistrats ne l'ont pas souffert." The records of the Conseil date this refusal three days later (Feb. 8), an anomaly implying that at least one of the councillors had informed Voltaire in advance of the official act. Even more eloquently than their dissociation from the Compagnie's self-defense, this courtesy proves that "Genève" had not hurt his relations with the magistrates.

Their refusal to cooperate, however, did not discourage the ministers from publishing the *Extrait des registres de la Vénérable Compagnie* on February 10. The contents of this work confirm that their convictions could not sustain their resentment. It contains no allusions to the Trinity other than various treatment of the three persons. The Holy Spirit comes as an afterthought terminating much rhetoric about Christ designed to veil his subordination to "le seul vrai Dieu" (p. 4), who enjoys the privilege of the initial position. The text concerning the first two persons reads as follows:

> *La vie éternelle consiste à connaître le seul Dieu, et celui qu'il a envoyé, Jésus-Christ*, en qui *a habité toute la plénitude de la divinité... afin que tous honorent le Fils comme ils honorent le Père*. (p. 4)

Faithful to Protestant Scripturalism, Vernet and company borrowed the language of this statement almost exclusively from the Bible, and

[125] Voltaire attributed the remark, incorrectly, to the painter Jean Huber on February 5. In another letter to d'Alembert on February 13, he corrected his mistake: Mme Cramer had said it.

[126] The deliberations were in their sixth week by then.

just as exclusively from John, a more significant point.[127] Only in John could they perhaps have found language sufficiently ambitious and ambiguous for their purposes. The conjunction *et* separates the unique God from Christ whom he delegates. The entire fulness of the divinity could dwell in Christ without necessarily deifying him and one might honor the Son as one honors the Father without believing them equal or consubstantial. The text, which excludes neither adoptionism nor representation, must have resulted from a desperate attempt to conciliate conflicting opinions within the committee. Indignant over the relegation of their religion to a mere respect for Christ, they reject the term as "trop faible ou trop équivoque" (p. 4), but they manage to substitute no more for it than what Florida calls "a fulsome array of superlatives" (p. 204) without theological significance. They might have squelched the charge of deism once and for all simply by giving greater emphasis to Christ as "sauveur [et] médiateur," titles drowned in the flow of rhetoric. It was the redemption that separated a relatively sincere majority of them from deism. Otherwise, silence would have been the best possible answer to "Genève." Publishing the *Extrait* amounted to broadcasting their inability to reconcile their actual faith with traditional Calvinism, thus confirming Voltaire's allegation. Although they had neither repudiated their belief nor admitted their heresy as he had foreseen, he had clearly won his argument with them.

Eventually he began to brag of his partial victory in his correspondence, though without the usual exuberance. In a letter to Bertrand on February 18, he lamented, "Hélas! ce pauvre Servet aurait reconnu [la] divinité [de Christ], quoiqu'il n'adoptât pas l'omousion." On sending d'Alembert a copy of the *Extrait*, he made fun of the ministers' dissatisfaction with mere respect for Christ: "Ils ont de la passion, du goût pour lui." They might have accepted *passion*, but certainly not *goût*, since it implied homosexual love. Assuming on February 25 that d'Alembert had received "la profession *servétine*," he remarked, "Ceux qui ont fait brûler Servet pensent absolument comme lui et le disent." The repetition of this habitual comment reveals that he had not read the *Extrait* closely enough to detect its most glaring weaknesses. The name of Servetus continued to serve as a commonsense

[127] The italics as usual designate quotations from Scripture: "Eternal life is this: to know you, the only true God and Jesus Christ whom you have sent" (Jn. 17.3). "The Father is in me and I am in the Father" (Jn. 10.38). "He has entrusted all judgment to the Son, so that all may honor the Son as they honor the Father" (Jn. 5.23). "*Toute la plénitude de la divinité*" appears in Vernet's *Traité* (IV, 50; 1730 ed.). Florida finds that the *Extrait* "was completely consistent with Vernet's theology" (p. 204, n. 52).

catch-all for various degrees of antitrinitarianism. His letter to the comte de Tressan on March 3, however, reflects a more accurate knowledge of the ministers' heresy. Here he noted that their neighbors were accusing them of burning Servetus and carrying his doctrine even further than he had. Exaggerating as usual, he concluded, in a letter to d'Argental, that "la déclaration des prêtres de Genève justifie entièrement d'Alembert... Ils se déclarent en un mot chrétiens déistes" (Feb. 25). *Chrétiens déistes* recalls *déichristicoles* which Voltaire had borrowed from Meslier and used in the *Examen important*. *Deist Christians* applies appropriately to crypto-deists such as Vernes, Polier, and Bertrand, but not to subordinationists like Vernet. For the benefit of common sense, Voltaire had maximized the evidence of deistic temptations among the ministers, and he had goaded them into a compromising profession of faith by means of "Genève." He had used the Encyclopedia in a cunning and yet abortive attempt to convert the spiritual leaders of Geneva to deism, with the expectation that the masses would follow. But he had succeeded only in forcing the ministers to entrench themselves in hypocrisy. He had drawn so much attention to the contradictions among them, moreover, that anticlericalism, if not deism, fed on the issue, both in Geneva and elsewhere. Since the letter in the *Mercure*, he had avoided retaliation by printing nothing on the subject under his own name, yet letters to influential correspondents were enough to amplify his propaganda.

In 1759, he supplemented his *Mémoires pour servir à la vie de M. de Voltaire* by a summary of the affair. "Je regarde ce petit triomphe," he concluded, "comme le plus bel exemple des progrès de la raison dans ce siècle."[128] Although he intended *petit* as an expression of modesty, one must take it seriously in this context, for his victory did not precipitate a mass conversion to the religion of reason as he had hoped. The controversy continued in the form of published works by d'Alembert, Vernet, Voltaire himself, and Jean-Jacques Rousseau,[129] but one must look elsewhere for further development of Voltaire's antitrinitarianism. In 1758, he discovered that d'Alembert was planning a trip to Italy without passing through Geneva. "Quoi!" he protested,

[128] *Mémoires pour servir à la vie de M. de Voltaire* (Paris, 1965), p. 77.

[129] Rousseau, *Lettre à M. d'Alembert sur les spectacles* (1758); d'Alembert, *Lettre à J.-J. Rousseau sur l'article Genève de l'Encyclopédie* (1759); d'Alembert, *L'Article Genève de l'Encyclopédie* (1759); Voltaire, *Dialogues chrétiens ou préservatif contre l'Encyclopédie* (1760); Vernet, *Lettres critiques d'un voyageur anglais* (1761); Rousseau, *Lettres de la Montagne* (1764).

> parce que quelques marmottes du pays en manteau noir ont signé qu'ils sont d'accord avec vous dans le fond et ont un peu biaisé sur la forme, vous éviterez de passer par une ville où tous les honnêtes gens vous estiment! (June 7)

Once bitten, twice shy, d'Alembert did not change his mind.

"Messie"

In a letter to d'Alembert in 1757, Voltaire describes Polier de Bottens as "prêtre par état, incrédule par sens commun" (Feb. 29). Voltaire made better use of this disciple, who furnished the Encyclopedia with seventeen articles edited by him. He was so pleased with Polier's "Messie" that he revised it and published it himself in the *Dictionnaire philosophique* a year before the original appeared in Volume x of the *Encyclopédie*.[130] In soliciting the article, he probably saw no need for the discreet innuendo and show of detachment he must have used to influence the author of "Genève." Torrey and Wade believe he proposed the article to Polier, told him how to write it, and even referred him to specific passages in the Bible. Little wonder that the contents of the original often remind one of Voltaire himself!

Polier devoted the final pages of "Messie" to a review of false messiahs, among whom one might all too easily include Jesus himself. Voltaire needed only to substitute the *passé simple* for the *passé composé* to convert the following sentence to his style: "Il y [a eu] eut de ces *faux Messies* avant même la venue du véritable oint de Dieu."[131] Both writers obviously meant it ironically. The number of unsuccessful messiahs, such as Judas the Galilean in the first century and Bar Kokhba in the second, vexes the question of why one should distinguish Jesus from them. Christians have always argued that he differed from them by the spiritual nature of his mission. In the *Encyclopédie*, Polier and Voltaire parody this doctrine: "Il était dans le plan de la sagesse éternelle que les idées spirituelles du [vrai] *Messie* fussent inconnues à la multitude aveugle."[132] *Messiah* with the definite article was explicit in the mind of the minister, but not in that of the deist who modified it by the adjective *true*. Both saw irony in the proposition, but each conveys it in his own way. Polier continues:

[130] "The ponderous, bulky and somewhat overweighted article of Polier was reduced to the short, rapid and light proportions of a normal Voltaire article... When one considers how little was left of the original contribution, one must conclude that Voltaire was really publishing his own work." Norman Torrey and Ira Wade, "Voltaire and Polier de Bottens," *Romanic Review*, 31 (1930), 155.

[131] *Ency.*, XXI, 638; *Dict.*, p. 310.

[132] *Ency.*, XXI, 632; *Dict.*, p. 305.

> Elles le furent au point que, lorsque le Sauveur parut dans la Judée, le peuple et ses docteurs, ses princes même attendaient un monarque, un conquérant qui par la rapidité de ses conquêtes devait s'assujettir tout le monde; et comment concilier ses idées flatteuses avec l'état abject, en apparence, et misérable de Jésus-Christ? (*Ency*. p. 632A)

This sentence exhibits Polier's scholarly attention to detail, precision, and proportion beyond the needs of common sense. Dissatisfied with this style and thought, Voltaire supplanted the sentence by a more dynamic, though, for once, less interesting one:

> Elles le furent au point que les docteurs juifs se sont avisés de nier que les passages que nous alléguons doivent s'entendre du *Messie*. (*Dict*. p. 305)

Se sont avisés displays a mock annoyance with the Jewish "doctors" for their stubborn exercise of good judgment. But one regrets that Voltaire did not compress Polier's Voltairian idea into a Voltairian sentence with greater sharpness of bite.

A number of massive sentences, which Voltaire did not sufficiently prune, spoil the style of the Dictionary article. According to one of them, the combination of God's glowing promises and continual oppression by foreigners made the Jews yearn for a liberator. Consequently they are not to blame for having failed to recognize in Jesus the messiah they expected. Polier finishes the sentence as follows:

> d'autant plus qu'il est de l'homme de tenir plus au corps qu'à l'esprit et d'être plus sensible aux besoins présents que flatté des avantages à venir. (*Ency*. p. 632A)

Voltaire replaced this trite conclusion by "d'autant plus qu'il n'y a pas un seul passage dans l'Ancien Testament où il soit dit: 'Croyez au Messie'" (*Dict*. p. 305). This ending tends to revitalize Polier's sluggish sentence by giving it a more logical and forceful ending, one more satisfying to reason.

Elsewhere, Polier presents several Jewish objections to the idea of a messiah being both man and God. The prophets do not teach it, they distinguish between God and David, they declare God master and David his servant, etc. Here Voltaire inserted a one-sentence paragraph: "On sait assez que les Juifs, esclaves de la lettre, n'ont jamais pénétré comme nous le sens des Ecritures" (*Dict*. p. 307). This ironical impatience with the Jews for their failure to interpret their own writings in the Christian manner deliberately violates common sense. It also exploits Polier's erudition more skillfully than the similar device mentioned above. In both cases, however, the presumption of Christian exegesis exposes the special status of Jesus to a counterattack.

In another paragraph, Polier finds irony in the contrast between some of the figures called messiah in the Old Testament, "des rois idolâtres," and "l'oint véritable du Seigneur, ce *Messie* par excellence."[133] Voltaire cut his development short at this point and appended a triple sarcasm: "le Christ, fils de Dieu, enfin Dieu lui-même" (p. 305). Here one recognizes his tactic of taking the unity of the Trinity literally and associating Christ with people considered unworthy of him. The smoothness of the transition between Polier's text and his own suggests that he had recommended guilt by association in proposing the article to him.

Other traces of Voltaire's influence appear in Polier's text. He asks rhetorically, for instance, whether the inability of the Jews and some early Christians to "s'élever à l'idée de la nature divine de l'oint du Seigneur" should surprise us in view of their "idées si grossières sur la venue du *Messie* et sur son règne"[134] (p. 307). In Christian apology and anti-Semitic propaganda, the adjective *crude* or its equivalents have often qualified Jewish expectations of a temporal messiah. Following Voltaire's advice perhaps, Polier nonetheless reminds us that the earliest Christians, who remained faithful to Judaism, shared in the alleged ignorance of Jesus' divinity. This ignorance amounts to good sense, because they knew him as a fellow Jew and human being. In typical Voltairian style, Polier, who was thinking of the synoptic gospels, observes that neither the disciples nor Jesus himself were aware of his divinity. Such remarks, which occur frequently in Voltaire's works, always invite the inference that later Christians deified him. In short, while Voltaire adapted Polier's text to his purpose, advance recommendations facilitated the task. The editing consisted especially of stylistic improvements, but also a few significant additions transforming the minister's learned argument into a commonsense appeal. Polier's erudition furnished Voltaire with a lethal though, according to his standards, unsharpened polemical weapon against the divinity of Christ.

The Early Sixties

Editing the works of disciples, even when they had followed his advice, could not permanently satisfy Voltaire, who felt a compelling need to write for himself. In 1758, he purchased the estate of Ferney, just across the Genevan border in France and far from Paris. He must have found the security greater than ever before in his long and

[133] *Ency.*, XXI, 631; *Dict.*, p. 305.
[134] *Ency.*, XXI, 635; *Dict.*, p. 307.

hazardous career. The time had finally come, he decided, to declare war on Christianity, which he began to call "the infamous."[135] In addition to the usual polemic monographs, he initiated the production of small and prickly satires in a variety of forms. During the early sixties, he published the *Sermon des cinquante* (1762), which he had been holding back since 1749, and several other *rogatons* attacking, among other doctrines, the Trinity and the divinity of Christ.

Already in the *Conversation de M. l'intendant des menus... et M. l'abbé Grizel* (1761), there are allusions to the procession of the Holy Spirit and suspicion of Jesus' popularity with the common people. In ridiculing priestly intolerance of the acting profession, a habitual complaint, Voltaire pretends to have summarized a real conversation for the benefit of readers "qui ont le sens commun" (*Dial.* p. 81).[136] Further on, the intendant denounces the clerical hypocrisy of loyalty to the crown and persecution of people engaged in a profession approved by the king. A typical Voltairian straw man, Grizel betrays the Church by trying to defend it. He founds this defense on the frequency with which it has contradicted itself in the past, as if such a precedent justified continuation of the same practice. He even furnishes the following illustration:

> Pourquoi a-t-on excommunié, anathématisé pendant des siècles ceux qui disaient que le Saint-Esprit procède du Père et du Fils? Et pourquoi damne-t-on aujourd'hui ceux qui pensent le contraire? (*Dial.* p. 90)

This is a reference to the dispute over the *filioque* ("and the Son"), which caused the definitive schism between the eastern and western churches. Towards the end of the seventh century, the Latin church added it to the Nicene-Constantinopolitan creed to prescribe belief in the procession of the Holy Spirit from both the Son and the Father. Previously, the Spirit had been thought to proceed from the Father alone. Despite several abortive reconciliations based on acceptance of the *filioque* by the Greek church,[137] eastern Christians have never agreed to the innovation expressed by it. Grizel does not mention the

[135] "L'*Infâme*, ce monstre que représente toute religion établie, et en particulier, bien entendu, la religion chrétienne, dans ce qu'elle a de plus cruellement oppresseur." Jacques Van den Heuvel, ed., *L'Affaire Calas* (Paris, 1975), p. 7.

[136] Voltaire, *Dialogues et anecdotes philosophiques* (Paris, 1966), ed. Raymond Naves.

[137] Council of Lyon (1274): "The three representatives of Michael VIII Paleologus accepted the *filioque*, but the clergy and the people of Constantinople rejected it, despite the repressive measures of the emperor." The Council of Florence (1439): "The Latins and Greeks agreed that the Holy Spirit proceeds from the Father and the Son as from one principle and one spiration, but the agreement did not last." "Filioque," *The New Catholic Encyclopedia* (Washington, 1967).

Greek church because Voltaire wanted to insinuate that the Roman church considers itself unique. For the same reason, perhaps, the *abbé* speaks of their mutual excommunications and anathemas, as if they had emanated from only one church and before Rome included the formula in the creed. Although Voltaire does not explain this error, he clearly intended Grizel as a representative caricature of the Roman priesthood, so that readers would know what to think of their ambivalent attitude towards the theater.

Faced with increasingly embarrassing protests from the intendant, the priest diverts him from his argumentation by declaring some of his relatives excommunicant on the grounds that they hold public offices involved in the collection of taxes. Once the intendant's anger has cooled, Grizel concedes that Jesus denigrated tax-collectors[138] in order to cultivate hatred for them among the common people, who considered Roman taxes a tribute exacted by their foreign masters. Again, the *abbé* naïvely betrays his own Church:

> Criez au nom de Dieu contre les puissances et contre les impôts, vous aurez infailliblement la canaille pour vous... et quand vous aurez un assez grand nombre de canailles à vos ordres, alors il se trouvera des gens d'esprit qui lui mettront une selle sur le dos, un mors à la bouche, et qui monteront dessus pour renverser les Etats et les trônes. (*Dial.* p. 86)

Thus a mass of fanatics became the conqueror's horse. This capsule history of Christianity substitutes part of the truth, the imperialism of the crusades for instance, for the whole. It frees common sense of doubts with which it might not be able to cope, an objective of all propaganda. Unless one resorts to symbolic interpretation of a kind Voltaire himself disapproved, the horse-and-rider analogy distorts the true story. The political aspects of Jesus' mission, on the other hand, are not less certain than obscure, but Voltaire leaps to unlikely conclusions.

While the *Conversation* offers no more on our subjects than these two passages, the *Sermon du rabbin Akib*, published in the same year, contains a little less than two pages of pertinent material. Having pioneered the satiric sermon with the deistic *Sermon des cinquante*, Voltaire composed a Jewish sermon. He may have named his preacher after Rabbi Akiva ben Joseph, a scholar who annointed the rebel leader Bar Kokhba as the messiah in 132 A.D. The Romans crushed the rebellion and eventually tortured Akiva to death. Voltaire's Akib devotes his sermon to a plea for tolerance after a Lisbonne

[138] "If your brother does something wrong... and... refuses to listen to the community, treat him like a pagan or a tax collector" (Mt. 18.15, 17). In other words, like an outcast!

auto-da-fé in which thirty-two Jews were burned at the stake along with "Malagrida Jésuita."[139] Under the cover of Akib's protest, Voltaire censures Christianity from a Jewish viewpoint. Akib addresses the following reproach to Christians:

> Votre Dieu était de notre religion... Il naquit Juif, il fut circoncis comme tous les autres Juifs; il reçut, de votre aveu, le baptême du Juif Jean, lequel était une antique cérémonie juive... il accomplit tous les devoirs de notre antique loi; il vécut Juif, mourut Juif, et vous nous brûlez parce que nous sommes Juifs. (Mac. p. 156)

Worshipers of Jesus are burning his fellow Jews alive, while Calvinist ministers, according to Voltaire, endorse the theology of Servetus whom Calvin had sent to the stake. The faith of the victims, in both cases, has become the current belief of the persecuting sect. The tactic, which remains essentially the same, consists of confronting eighteenth-century Christians with a historical self-contradiction. Determined to block any escape from this trap, Voltaire exploits the rabbinic reputation for textual expertise. "J'en atteste vos livres mêmes," Akib insists: "Jésus a-t-il dit dans un seul endroit que la loi de Moïse était ou mauvaise ou fausse? L'a-t-il abrogée" (Mac. p. 156)? Asked by a rabbi, the question seems all the more embarrassing to Christians. A historical and textual critic in the tradition of his second-century namesake, Akib also refutes the persistent Christian incrimination of the Jews for the murder of Jesus:

> Il ne fut condamné que par les Romains... Nous n'avions pas alors le droit de glaive... Le supplice de la croix était inusité chez nous. (Mac. p. 156)

Since history records no incidence of crucifixion by Jews, they cannot be held responsible for the execution of Jesus. When Jesus provoked the Pharisees, the rabbi concedes, they accused him before Pilate, but "Est-ce une raison pour brûler des négociants juifs et leurs filles dans Lisbonne" (Mac. p. 157)?

Akib then turns to the Christian complaint that Jews do not recognize the divinity of Jesus. He answers this charge by an appeal "aux savants de l'Europe," his colleagues:

> Jésus, dans [l']Evangile, s'appelle quelquefois fils de Dieu, fils de l'homme, mais jamais Dieu; jamais Paul ne lui a donné ce titre. (Mac. p. 157)

[139] Paulo Mury states that the Jesuit Malagrida was strangled before his body was burned on the orders of the Marquis of Pombal. Fifty-two others were also executed in the repression of a conspiracy to assassinate Joseph I (1758), but none seem to have been Jews. See Mury, *Historia de Gabriel Malagrida* (Lisbon, 1875), pp. 178-80.

He explains that the son of God is a familiar Jewish expression meaning a just man. How could Jesus' fellow Jews detect divinity in a mere son of God? Christians are asking too much. Unfortunately, in a final argument against the divinity of Jesus, Voltaire could not entirely refrain from intervening in his rabbi's sermon and spoiling his record of respect for the truth. "Pendant trois cents ans," says Voltaire-Akib, Christians saw no more in Jesus than

> la plus parfaite des créatures. Ce ne fut qu'au concile de Nicée que la majorité des évêques constata sa divinité, malgré les oppositions des trois quarts de l'empire. (Mac. p. 157)

As Voltaire well knew, Christians began to worship a divine being in Jesus well before Nicaea and, in fact, from the end of the first century. It is curious, moreover, that he should have failed to suspect Constantine of forcing many bishops to vote against their will, directly or indirectly. His estimate that three-quarters of the empire were opposed to the Nicene decision is an exaggeration: one-third would have been more accurate. Voltaire-Akib concludes,

> Si donc les chrétiens eux-mêmes ont nié si longtemps [la] divinité [de Christ], s'il y a même encore des sociétés chrétiennes qui la nient, par quel étrange renversement d'esprit peut-on nous punir de la méconnaître? (Mac. p. 157)

Here one rediscovers the insinuation of continuous opposition to the Trinity in still another context, a Jewish context. Voltaire renewed this theme as one reframes a painting, a technique borrowed no doubt from his experience with drama.[140] The rigors of Jewish monotheism suggested by the identity of his spokesman reinforce the irony of the antitrinitarian contradiction within Christianity. Rabbi Akib, in sum, reinforces his protest against the Christian persecution of Jews by the Jewishness of Jesus, the predominant innocence of Jews in the crucifixion of Jesus, and the obscurity of Jesus' alleged divinity. Towards the end of the *Sermon*, he asks a final, unanswerable question: "[Si Jésus] réapparaissait aujourd'hui au monde, se reconnaîtrait-il dans un seul de ceux qui se nomment chrétiens" (Mac. p. 157)?

Voltaire asked another unanswerable question while reading François Pluquet's *Mémoires pour servir à l'histoire des égarements de l'esprit humain*, published a year later (1762). After underlining Pluquet's assertion that Jesus "*meurt, ressuscite et monte au ciel*" (I, 113), he wrote

[140] An example: variations on the theme of the venerable old man in his tragedies: Lusignan in *Zaïre* (1732), Alvarez in *Alzire* (1736), Zopire in *Mahomet* (1741), Cicéron in *Rome sauvée* (1750), Pammève in *Oreste* (1750), Sozame in *Les Scythes* (1767), Arzémon in *Les Guèbres* (1769).

in the margin, "l'as-tu vu?"[141] When Pluquet affirms, against all the evidence, that Jesus, during his Judean mission, "annonce un Dieu en trois personnes" (I, 113), Voltaire notes, "il n'en parla jamais" (Philips p. 65). Although he intended these remarks for no readers other than himself, they both register commonsense judgments.

That same year, he began the *Traité sur la tolérance* (1763), which he initially may have intended as a mere protest against the judicial murder of Calas. By 1763, however, he had accumulated many chapters that have little more in common with Calas than the need for tolerance. As the work grew, so did his ambition to obtain official approval for it in France, and he avoided the provocative language of his other works.

"The Father is greater than I" (Jn. 14.28), his favorite Biblical quotation, appears in two different chapters. One of these (16), the "Dialogue entre un mourant et un homme qui se porte bien," supposes the presence of a Jesuit or an ally of the Jesuits at the bedside of a Jansenist during the reign of Louis XIV. Yet Voltaire does not identify them as such, apparently because he wanted the dialogue to reflect other examples of doctrinal tyranny in the history of the Church. In exchange for last rites, the Jesuit is trying to force the Jansenist to sign the Formulary of 1665 condemning the five propositions said to be in the *Augustinus* of Jansenius. If the Jansenist wishes to die in peace, the Jesuit threatens him, he must endorse the following proposition too: "[Ces paroles] 'mon Père est plus grand que moi' signifient expressément, 'Je suis aussi grand que lui'" (M. xxv, 91). Here Voltaire ignores the traditional restriction of John 14.28 to Jesus' human nature, an exegesis leaving the Trinitarian relations of his divine nature intact. To the injury of his contradictory interpretation, the Jesuit adds the insult of a contradictory formulation: "Le Père communique tout au Fils, excepté la paternité" (M. xxv, 91). This ironical play on words respects the meaning, though by no means the intention, of Trinitarian dogma. The logic of metaphysics nonetheless justifies Voltaire's analysis, because, according to it, an engendered deity, who does not engender in turn, cannot do so. Voltaire was counting on the folklore of manhood to scorn such impotence as a sure symptom of inferiority. Common sense, in any event, infers the subordination of the Son.

The other quotation of John 14.28 occurs in Chapter 11 where Voltaire discussed Cardinal Duperron's successful attack, in the Etats Généraux of 1614, on a law establishing the independence of the

[141] Edith Philips and Jean Perkins, "Some Voltaire Marginalia," *SVEC*, 114 (1973), 66.

crown. On that occasion, he maintained that Arianism would constitute sufficient grounds for deposing a king. A steadfast royalist, Voltaire rejected this opinion. A king, he submits, might understandably take "Mon Père est plus grand que moi" seriously and become an Arian on the strength of Jesus' own testimony. "Si vous osiez vous soulever contre lui," he warns the ghost of the Cardinal, "et que je fusse un de vos juges, je vous déclarerais criminel de lèse-majesté" (M. xxv, 63). He not only defends the right of the crown to independence from the Church, but also the right of the king to reasonable belief.

Despite his disenchantment with Frederick the Great, his resurgent faith in the feasibility of enlightened monarchy exposed him to illusions about ancient as well as modern rulers. The letter in which Constantine scolded the partisans of both Alexander and Arius in the initial phase of the Arian controversy persistently fascinated him (see p. 73). One encounters a typical quotation from it in Chapter 21 of the *Traité*: "Vous êtes de grands fous de disputer sur des choses que vous ne pouvez entendre" (M. xxv, 103). His enthusiasm over this opinion of the dispute may have blinded him to Constantine's motives, which did not concern the welfare of the population, but rather the conservation of his power. A unified church served as a more useful instrument for the exercise of this power than a divided one, while religious dissension threatened to weaken his authority. Voltaire habitually suspected the Church of using the state and not the other way around. In the *Traité*, he imagined Constantine preaching good sense to "les chefs de l'ergotisme": "Avez-vous les titres de la famille divine? Que vous importe que le *Logos* soit fait ou engendré" (M. xxv, 103)? Such inquiry struck Voltaire as presumptuous, frivolous, and futile. In the preceding paragraph of Chapter 21, he adds the implications of cynicism and tyranny. Here an enemy of the Arians threatens to cut their throats if they cannot "distinguer *l'omousion* dans l'hypostase" (M. xxv, 103). Such confessional imperialism reminds one of the Jesuit in Chapter 16. For all the realism in such passages, however, it seems strange that so shrewd a historian as Voltaire did not detect the political maneuvering of clerical factions behind the façade of doctrinal controversy. Did he fall a victim to his own propaganda? Or was he pulling his punches in hopes of official approval for the *Traité*? One cannot say.

He had lesser inhibitions in writing the *Dialogue du douteur et de l'adorateur* (1763),[142] which contains a few pages of antichristological

[142] The first edition is undated. Beuchot gives 1763, Bengesco, 1766; Naves inclines to 1763 because of the resemblance with the *Catéchisme de l'honnête homme* published in 1763.

polemic. In defense of Voltaire's deism, the Adorateur objects to the abuse of the term *Son of God* in Christianity:

> Un sage, quand il dit que Dieu est son père, entend sans doute que Dieu est le père de tous les hommes: le sens dans lequel on a voulu l'entendre est impie et blasphématoire. (*Dial.* p. 139)

A wise man would not pretend to the exclusive filiation of God. This statement follows others in each of which the Adorateur finds that a wise man would not imitate acts attributed to Jesus: withering a fig tree because it bears no fruit in March, converting water into wine for people who have drunk too much, casting demons into 2000 swine in a country where there are no swine, transfiguring himself at night in order to have white clothes,[143] a classic Voltairian list. In advance of this series, the Adorateur declares: "On... impute [à Jésus] des choses qu'un sage n'a pu faire ni dire" (*Dial.* p. 139). This context fully clarifies his final objection to abuse of the expression *Son of God*: If Jesus deserved the confidence of the natural light, which comes from God, he did not consider himself a Son of God in the Christian sense, a usurpation of divinity and therefore blasphemy from a deist viewpoint. The Adorateur has already expressed the opinion that Jesus was a wise man who "déclamait contre les prêtres imposteurs, et les superstitions" (*Dial.* p. 139). Priests have distorted the figure of the wise man by veiling it in superstition useful to their selfish purposes. The Adorateur deplores the rivalry between the evangelists, among whom he includes the uncanonical evangelists, in seeking to inflate the wonder they ascribe to Jesus. In reality,

> L'histoire véritable de Jésus n'était probablement que celle d'un homme juste qui avait repris les vices des pharisiens, et que les pharisiens firent mourir. (*Dial.* p. 140)

Voltaire did not always see Jesus in such a charitable light. The wise man became a just man by exposing the vices of priests, who predictably exacted their revenge. But priests made a prophet of this man after his death and eventually even a God: "voilà la marche de l'esprit humain" (*Dial.* p. 140). A final series of protests broadens the scope of the Adorateur's polemic:

> Jésus a-t-il dit qu'il y avait en lui deux natures? Non; et nous lui donnons deux natures. Jésus a-t-il dit que Marie était mère de Dieu? Non; et nous la faisons mère de Dieu. Jésus a-t-il dit qu'il était trin et consubstantiel? Non; et nous l'avons fait consubstantiel et trin. (*Dial.* p. 140)

[143] Voltaire was apparently unaware of the ancient Jewish belief that divine grace momentarily whitened the person who received it as if it were a bright light.

Hence the perversion of his wisdom and the betrayal of his integrity. Jesus authorized neither the two natures, nor the divine maternity of his mother, nor the Trinity.

The Adorateur speaks with somewhat the same voice as the honest man in the *Catéchisme de l'honnête homme* (1763), a dialogue, as the subtitle indicates, between him and a *caloyer* or Greek monk belonging to the order of Basil. After the satiric sermon, Voltaire invented the satiric catechism. In typical Voltairian fashion, the monk starts the conversation by asking about the honest man's religion,[144] but the latter takes the opportunity to criticize Christianity. Voltaire's efforts to establish the man's sincerity tend to sharpen this criticism: "Je donne la torture à mon esprit pour comprendre comment un Dieu est mort" (Naves p. 124). When the monk cites Jesus' miracles as proof of his Godhood, the honest man counters with the futility of these miracles and particularly the futility of his power to ressuscitate:

> S'il eût opéré ces prodiges, c'eût été pour faire connaître sa divinité. Songez-vous bien ce que c'est que d'accuser Dieu de s'être fait homme inutilement, et d'avoir ressuscité des morts pour être pendu? (*Dial.* p. 131)

Voltaire seems to have infused the horror of blasphemy into the honest man so as to turn the tables on Christian apologists in the habit of condemning the least rebuke of their opinions as a manifestation of this crime. For him, however, it consisted in ascribing a violation of common sense to God himself, from whom the natural light shone forth. The humiliating death of an incarnated, immortal being, who can raise mortals from the dead, is blasphemy against the God of reason. Like Bossuet, the honest man hammers away at variations, but not the ones Bossuet had in mind. When the caloyer supposes that "Dieu a pu ordonner toutes ces variations," variations in Catholic dogma, the honest man loses his temper: "Dieu varier! Dieu changer! cette idée paraît un blasphème" (*Dial.* 129). An institution vacillating as chronically as Bossuet's Church could not be governed by God, whose perfections necessarily include permanence.

Behind this vacillation lies the implication of priestly deceit and lay gullibility. The honest man's subjunctives (*Dial.* p. 131) convey his doubt that Jesus ever performed any real miracle to begin with. He finds the incarnation and the resurrection indefensible, despite the efforts of apologists to justify them, at least partially, on the basis of redemption. He has lethal arguments against redemption too:

[144] In the first *Letter Concerning the English Nation*, Voltaire starts his conversation with the elderly Quaker by asking, "My dear sir... were you ever baptized?" (p. 3).

> Je me suis demandé pourquoi, étant Dieu, [Jésus] n'a pas usé des droits de la divinité; pourquoi, en venant nous délivrer du péché, il nous a laissés dans le péché; pourquoi en venant éclairer les hommes, il a laissé presque tous les hommes dans l'erreur? (*Dial.* pp. 123-24)

One detects a hint, however slight, of sincere regret in this eloquent passage, yet Voltaire is dealing the most destructive blow in the *Catéchisme*. Jesus could not have been God intervening in this life, because he did not eliminate the evils vulnerable only to divine power. By sin, however, the honest man does not mean sacrilege, but rather the cruelty of men to each other and, by error, not deviation from dogma, but closing one's eyes to the natural light. In the same paragraph, he regrets that Jesus did not unite the various sects and religions of his time,[145] as one would expect of God on earth. Neither did Jesus declare himself divine, nor does Scripture give any sure evidence of his divinity, on the contrary. Voltaire reiterates John 14.28 and adduces Mark 13.32-Matthew 14.36 which he paraphrases as follows: "Le père seul sait ce que le fils ignore."[146] Jesus' admission that he did not know when the kingdom of God would come proves, to the satisfaction of common sense, his at least partial ignorance of divine wisdom and hence his separation from the divine substance. Voltaire again ignored the traditional exegesis confining this weakness to Jesus' human nature.

He nevertheless rebutted the entire theory of the two natures in the *Catéchisme* along with other dogmas. If Jesus had wanted to found the Christian Church, the honest man argues,

> N'aurait-il pas dit: Je suis Dieu, engendré et non fait; le Saint-Esprit procède de mon père sans être engendré; j'ai deux volontés et une personne?... Il n'établit ni dogme, ni rite, ni hiérarchie; ce n'est donc pas lui qui a fait sa religion. (*Dial.* p. 127)

Since he said none of these things, others had to say them for him and how could they have known what he thought? How could these ordinary men have discovered such supernatural mysteries as his Godhood, his engenderment by the Father, his two wills, and the procession of the Holy Spirit? The natural light tells the honest man that they could not have indeed. After stressing the unlikelihood of divinity in a man of Jesus' social and intellectual mediocrity, he repeats the

[145] "J'ai cent fois souhaité que Jésus-Christ, en venant s'incarner en Judée, eût réuni toutes ces sectes sous ses lois" (*Dial.*, p. 123).

[146] In speaking of the kingdom of God, Jesus tells his disciples: "As for that hour or day, nobody knows it, neither the angels of heaven nor the Son; no one but the Father" (Mk. 13.32). Mt. 24.36 is very similar.

information given by Akib about his fidelity to Judaism. He even lapses into brief, but ugly exasperation: "Enfin comment puis-je reconnaître Dieu dans un Juif de la populace" (*Dial.* p. 125)? He can make no sense of his parables, whose mode of thought was inaccessible to him: "Est-ce ainsi que Dieu parle" (*Dial.* p. 125)? Such teaching does not cultivate human reason like that of Plato, Socrates, Antonius, Epictetus, Zaleucus, Solon, and Confucius: "Comment pouvons-nous juger autrement que par nos idées" (*Dial.* p. 125)? Voltaire did not realize to what extent the great thinkers of both Christian and pagan antiquity had moulded these very ideas. Though sensitive to the variety of ancient culture, he accepted what met his standards and rejected the rest, especially what violated them most flagrantly.

Thus the honest man asks the monk: "Que pouvez-vous avoir de commun avec [Jésus]" (*Dial.* p. 129)?[147] The monk, who seems suspiciously docile, agrees that Christianity has changed, though perhaps with God's blessing. The honest man protests that God would never authorize changes in his religion. Towards the end of the dialogue, he finally answers the monk's initial question by recommending to him "cette religion... que Dieu a gravée dans tous les coeurs; mais certes il n'y a pas gravé que trois font un" (*Dial.* p. 136). Then why have so many people been Christians for so long? A minor argument in the *Conversation* becomes a major argument here: Christianity thrives on the rabble roused by demagogic promises of equalitarianism. Lured by democratic illusions, the common people swallow whatever they are told, for they cannot read, not even the Bible: "Est-ce par la lecture qu'on persuade à dix millions de paysans que trois font un" (*Dial.* p. 128)? Whoever reads the New Testament will see that it does not support the Trinity.

Such strictures do not appear to trouble the monk, who, in fact, makes little effort to defend his faith. One is tempted to relegate him to the role of a figure intended merely to sustain the dialogue and acknowledge to some extent the errors of the religion he represents. But Naves perceives in him the noncommital reserve of the Genevan pastorate and he wonders if Voltaire was thinking of Vernet.[148] Voltaire himself alleges that another Genevan had translated the *Catéchisme* from an imaginary Greek original. In the heading of the work, he included the initials of the following phrase: "Dom Jean-

[147] "Je n'ai trouvé aucune trace du christianisme dans l'histoire de Jésus" (*Dial.*, p. 126).

[148] "Ce bon caloyer, qui parle si peu et écoute si bien, fait déjà la concession capitale, celle des dogmes, et ne retient que la morale. C'est à peu près ce que faisaient les protestants libéraux, et Vernet lui-même avant la brouille avec Voltaire" (Naves in *Dial.*, p. 495, n. 120).

Jacques Rousseau, ci-devant citoyen de Genève." Although Rousseau had made enemies of both Voltaire and Vernet by 1763, the author of the *Catéchisme* could not have found a more self-righteous and provocative model for his honest man. In 1762, Rousseau had published *Emile*, which contained the theist *Profession de foi du vicaire savoyard* greatly admired by Voltaire, despite his scorn for the rest of the book and the author. The theory that the *Catéchisme* represents an imaginary dialogue between impersonations of Rousseau and Vernet deserves serious consideration. One can certainly picture Voltaire amusing himself at his enemies' expense with the publication of a dialogue between these mutual enemies exposing his own opinion. His talent for adapting his own language and thought to such spokesmen taken more or less directly from real life is the most interesting lesson to be learned from this study of antichristological writings in the early sixties. While the *Catéchisme*, the *Dialogue*, and the *Sermon* treat roughly the same subject as the passages selected from the *Traité*, they are obviously more effective. In these humorous simulations of oral communication, Voltaire develops new ideas less than he renovates old ones by dressing them in new clothing.

Pot-Pourri

In 1765, he published a curious hybrid between the dialogue and the tale entitled the *Pot-Pourri*. But he classified it as a narrative work, since it appears in the volumes labeled "Romans" in the quarto (XIII, 1771) and *encadrée* (XXXII, 1775) editions of his complete works. It consists, in fact, of a basic narrative interspersed with digressions, mostly in the form of monologues or dialogues and these elements have little more in common than the Voltairian satire of Christianity. Yet somehow the work attains a satisfying literary unity, perhaps because the wit and style simply reveal his authorship in every part of it. The basic narrative begins with the two conflicting genealogies of Polichinelle, the adopted son of Brioché.[149] Both trace his lineage immediately to clowns on the seventeenth-century Parisian stage and ultimately to *le prince des sots* and *la mère sotte* of medieval farce.

Brioché tried to teach the humpbacked and potbellied Polichinelle to read and write, but he only learned to spell and sign his name, which no one could read. Polichinelle did have a good memory, though, and since Brioché was too poor to support him, he organized

[149] "Dès la fin du XVIe siècle, Paris possédait des théâtres de marionnettes, montrant les types purement français de Polichinelle, Pierrot et Dame Gigogne; le théâtre de Brioché, au Pont-Neuf, fut célèbre vers 1650." "Marionnettes," *Larousse du XXe Siècle* (Paris, 1931).

a marionette company. "M. et Mme Brioché admirèrent le bon sens du jeune homme" (Bénac p. 409).[150] Polichinelle and his companions established their show in a village on the road from Appenzell to Milan, where charlatans were prospering from the sale of nostrum. When they discovered that Polichinelle's marionettes were drawing their customers away, they brought several charges against him before a local magistrate: drunkenness, witchcraft, molesting a guinea pig merchant, and a particularly violent act: "Un jour il avait donné cent coups de pied dans le ventre, en plein marché, à des paysans qui vendaient des nèfles" (Bénac p. 409). Voltaire does not tell us what happened next, as if his "sources" did not say, but one of them "prétend [que Polichinelle] fut avalé par un crapaud" (Bénac p. 410), a fate contradicted by another.[151]

Further on, he resumes the narrative with the adventures of Polichinelle's companions after his disappearance. They move to the fifth floor of a house in a small town where they subsist on the sale of drugs. "Un jour ils entendirent du bruit sur leur tête, comme celui d'une brouette qu'on roule sur le plancher" (Bénac p. 415). On the sixth floor, they find a man named Bienfait making marionettes: "On n'entendait pas un mot de ce qu'il disait" (Bénac p. 415). One of them nonetheless deciphers a prediction by Nostradamus, the sixteenth-century French astrologer, to the effect that "*Bienfait ressuscitera Polichinelle*." He proposes, "Nous ferons valoir Polichinelle par Nostradamus et Nostradamus par Polichinelle" (Bénac p. 416). Bienfait therefore makes a marionette of Polichinelle. They all settle in Milan where, under the protection of Mme Carminetta, an Italian theater type representing temporal power, they show Polichinelle with much success. Taking advantage of the opportunity to sell nostrum, Bienfait becomes so rich that he assumes the leadership of the company. He begins to treat his patroness condescendingly and "un jour... il lui fit fermer la porte au nez" (Bénac p. 416). He expands the business to the point of showing Polichinelle in other cities, but only on condition that everyone call the marionette *Monsieur*. Although the narrative continues, the present study does not require further summary.

The conflicting genealogies obviously correspond to those of Jesus in Matthew and Luke, which Voltaire never tired of attacking.[152]

[150] Voltaire, *Romans et contes* (Paris, 1960), ed. Henri Bénac.

[151] These "sources": François Parfaict, *Histoire générale du théâtre français* (1734-1749) and Gabriel Daniel, *Histoire de France* (1696).

[152] Lk. 3.23-28 and Mt. 1.1-17. The honest man complains, for instance, "Que voulez-vous que je pense quand je vois deux généalogies de Jésus directement contraires l'une à l'autre; et [qu'elles] ne sont pourtant pas la sienne, mais celle de son père Joseph, qui n'est pas son père" (*Dial.*, p. 124).

They imply that the apologists of Jesus, in their haste to provide him with an illustrious ancestry, did not even bother to consult each other; that the motives for their admiration of Jesus determined the kind of ancestors they chose for him, and that this choice reflects the intellectual vulgarity of his admirers.

A thoroughgoing snob in theatrical matters, Voltaire also lavished his scorn on the lowest form of comedy and the actors who practiced it. In Jesus, he saw a kind of actor playing an enthusiastic role before a volatile populace and yet, eventually, failing in this contemptible career. Convinced that a great mind will inevitably communicate its thought in writing, he not only denied Jesus this distinction, but also assumed him to be illiterate and ignorant. His eighteenth-century intellect could not effectively separate these two concepts, as one must in order to understand first-century Galilee.

Thus Brioché (Joseph) fails to impart much of an education to Polichinelle (Jesus) who, nevertheless, by means of memory and good sense, succeeds at least momentarily in organizing a popular puppet show in a village on the road from Appenzell to Milan. Voltaire thus situates his career in a remote and mountainous region of eastern Switzerland, north of the linguistic frontier between Romance and German, a language he thought barbaric.[153] The village is Jerusalem and the country, ancient Palestine where Greek mingled with Aramaic, Hebrew to Voltaire. The charlatans selling nostrum are the Jewish priests who testified against Jesus before Pilate, the magistrate in Voltaire's satire. The charges, like most charges brought for devious reasons, have some measure of truth in them, as Voltaire sees it. Drunkenness resembles enthusiasm, he thought, and often results in violence, such as the assault on the peasants selling medlars, which, along with the molesting of the guinea pig merchant, evokes the cleansing of the Temple.

History taught him that accusing one's religious enemies of witchcraft or magic had often been an effective method of retaliation. Some of the events in the gospels may also have incited his suspicion that Jesus did indulge in sorcery, the transfiguration, for instance. The controversial hypothesis of Polichinelle's having been swallowed by a toad abruptly terminates the story of his life. In this way, Voltaire amputated Jesus' death and resurrection, the most crucial episode of all from a Christian viewpoint. He seems to have calculated that he had transposed enough details from the gospels to ensure identifica-

[153] Like many Frenchmen, he found it cacophonous, hence the name of the baron in *Candide*: Thunder-ten-tronckh.

tion of Polichinelle, that any treatment of the passion, however discreet or clever, would attach more importance to it than he felt it deserved, and that omitting an event confidently expected by nearly all his readers would convey his scorn more dramatically than anything he could write. Besides, being swallowed by a toad was a fitting end for a sorcerer. The wheelbarrow rolling across the ceiling of the upper room quaintly trivializes the Pentecostal miracle. Heaven, from which God sent the Holy Spirit down, becomes a higher story to which the disciples easily go up without further ado. Bienfait, who evidently made the noise, represents the human reality behind the mythology of the Holy Spirit. No one can understand him, because he is speaking in tongues as the Quakers in England had when Voltaire attended one of their meetings (see p. 116). Bienfait resuscitates the puppet master Polichinelle in the form of a puppet, just as Voltaire thought ambitious schemers had resurrected Jesus in the form of the Son and eventually God. Bienfait becomes the Church and later the pope. Nostradamus' prediction interpreted as applying to the reproduction of Polichinelle refers to Old Testament prophecy adapted to New Testament apology. Milan is Rome, of course, and the protection of Mme Carminetta symbolizes the imperial support of Christianity. Bénac thinks the slamming of the door in her face alludes to the humiliation of the emperor Henry IV by Pope Gregory VII at Canossa in 1077.[154] There is no reason to dispute this explanation, although it implies that Voltaire took some liberty with the chronology. Only in a later episode does Bienfait insist that his marionette be called *Monsieur*, a development almost certainly designating the deification of Christ, which occurred many centuries before Canossa.

Such is Voltaire's satire of Jesus in the *Pot-Pourri*. The work appears unusually malicious only from a Christian viewpoint, for satirists have ridiculed less sacred individuals and institutions just as ruthlessly. The transformation of Jesus' life into that of Polichinelle is not only daring, but also clever. The performance suggests that the New Testament lends itself to destructive as well as constructive interpretations of Christianity.

Questions sur les miracles

The importance of miracles to Christianity was the subject of a Genevan controversy in 1765. In answer to Rousseau's *Lettres de la montagne* (1764), the theologian David Claparède published his *Considérations sur les miracles*, which in turn provoked other writings, among them

[154] *Romans et contes*, p. 653, n. 569.

Voltaire's *Questions sur les miracles*. This work is a collection of make-believe letters, some of which appeared in print before the publication of the whole. As one might expect, Voltaire adopted most, if not all, of his "correspondents" from real life.

Before investigating his treatment of Jesus and the Trinity in the *Questions*, one should first examine other aspects of the work which are closely related to these. The postulant Théro addresses the first three letters to R, a professor of theology no doubt representing both Claparède and Vernet. An uneasy candidate for the ministry, Théro is seeking advice and reassurance: "Le coeur me saigne quand je vois des hommes remplis de science, de bon sens et de probité, rejeter nos miracles" (Mac. p. 236). From his continuing conflict with the ministers, Voltaire had learned that Genevan Christianity was oscillating between de-emphasis and repudiation of miracles. The temptation of philosophy, he realized, inclined them rather to repudiation. The first letter from Théro to R underlines this temptation, for the aspiring minister insinuates that he had read a long list of writers Voltaire classifies as deists. Among them, one finds such favorites as Socinus (Lelio and/or Faustus?), Locke, Bayle, Toland, Tindal, Collins, Woolston, Bolingbroke, Middleton, Spinosa, Boulainvilliers, Fréret, Dumarsais, Meslier, and La Mettrie. These writers, Théro complains, "croiraient insulter Dieu s'ils lui supposaient un fils qui ait fait des miracles dans la Galilée" (Mac. p. 222).

In his third letter, Théro tells R of his difficulties with a German count, who resembles Frederick:

> Je lui ai demandé ce qu'il risquait en soumettant sa raison. "Je risque, m'a-t-il répondu... d'offenser l'Etre des êtres, qui m'a donné cette raison." (Mac. p. 242)

In the present, therefore, Théro finds the same resistance to the religion he is aspiring to propagate as in the past.[155] Voltaire imagined that nothing would discourage an apprentice clergyman like the argument that his faith is opposed to the will of God. Since the *Questions* contain no answers from R, he must have intended for us to conclude that R makes none. The latter's silence suggests that he has no solutions for Théro's problems and shares in the ministerial hypocrisy of avoiding doctrinal entanglement.

[155] Having failed to move a mountain by faith, the countess "crut aussi peu aux miracles modernes que son mari; de sorte que je me trouve aujourd'hui le seul homme au château qui ait le sens commun, c'est-à-dire qui croie aux miracles" (Mac., p. 267), testifies Théro. In other words, according to Voltaire, the only one in the castle who does not have common sense.

The English Jesuit Needham, who was in Geneva in 1765, joined in the controversy over the miracles. Among other pamphlets on this subject, he published a *Parodie de la troisième lettre du proposant* which Voltaire reproduced in the *Questions* with a commentary by Théro. In his "Avis préliminaire," Needham expresses his irritation with the exaggeration of morality at the expense of doctrine in Théro's letters. "Il est ridicule," Théro-Voltaire replies,

> de comparer la raison universelle, qui inspire toutes les vertus, à des dogmes particuliers dont il n'a jamais résulté que du mal. (Mac. p. 256)

The note reveals the subtle evolution of Théro's faith under the influence of the German count, who has hired him as his chaplain. For one thing, he has nothing but praise for the count whose freethinking does not trouble him as it did before. For another, he no longer writes to R. but rather to Covelle, the fornicator who had won Voltaire's admiration for refusing to kneel in penitence before the Consistoire. In an unlikely letter to a fellow Genevan, the unintelligent and unrefined Covelle echoes Voltaire:

> Quel peut... être le but de ceux qui nous enseignent des choses que leur bon sens et le nôtre désavouent?... On n'a jamais fait croire des sottises aux hommes que pour les soumettre. (Mac. pp. 268-69)

Covelle therefore brings us back to the theory that dogmatic religion arises from the ambition of priests bent on subjugating their fellow men. Although it scarcely evolves in Voltaire's thought, he gives it new impetus by ascribing it to a rebellious victim of priestly arrogance. The foregoing discussion reveals that defense of the natural light serves as a unifying theme in the *Questions*, a more coherent work than it seems at first glance.

Among Théro's complaints, one finds the fundamental problem of New Testament exegesis: "Trois évangélistes semblent formellement opposés à Jean" (Mac. p. 235). The synoptists, he continues, end the biography of Jesus at Passover, three months after his baptism, while John terminates it three years later, on the third Passover after his baptism. Théro's first letter to R presents an odd synopsis of the baptism itself:

> Une preuve... publique et... éclatante de [la] divinité [de Jésus] c'est son baptême. C'est en présence d'une foule de peuple que, Jésus sortant nu hors de l'eau, la troisième personne de la Trinité descend sur sa tête en colombe; que le ciel s'ouvre, et que Dieu le père s'écrie au peuple: "Celui-ci est mon fils bien-aimé" [etc.] (Mac. p. 221)

It is not odd in itself, but rather as a product of Voltaire's pen. For once, this miracle has elicited not the slightest trace of irony from him, a rare exercise in restraint. He probably made this special effort in order to ensure the sincerity of his postulant from the beginning. The purity of Théro's motive for defending Christianity guarantees the value of his defeat. Yet later, Voltaire gave in to the temptation he had resisted. While annotating a copy of the 1765 Neuchâtel edition, he made the following comment in the margin: "Dieu le père parlait en hébreu, mais tous les romains, tous les étrangers durent se faire expliquer ces paroles."[156] This ironical remark is rather less impressive than the absence of irony in the original. It is just as well that Voltaire did not incorporate it in a revised edition, for which he intended this annotation, according to Philips and Perkins (*ibid.*).

In a very different effort to suppress textual irony, he had almost the same success. Unlike Théro, Covelle knows no other life than the sensual and material. For this very reason, Voltaire leaves judgment of the Gerasene exorcism to him. "Cela passe la raillerie," Covelle snorts over the drowning of the 2000 swine,

> surtout s'ils étaient engraissés. Un bon cochon gras vaut environ dix écus patagons: cela faisait vingt mille écus de perte pour le marchand. (Mac. p. 252)

One must admire Voltaire's restraint in expressing an objection so close to his heart, but he allowed himself one small break in his discipline here. For he invented the Patagonian crown, which a Covelle would never have dreamed of, in anticipation of a reply to Needham further on in the *Questions*. The Jesuit had used a Patagonian spokesman in his parody of Théro's second letter. The price of swine in first-century Palestine, where Jews banned the animal, seemed as fabulous to Voltaire as the Patagonian giants. Needham may in fact have reminded Voltaire of Maupertuis' speculations on them in the *Histoire du docteur Akakia* (1753), another satirical correspondence.

The final letter of the *Questions* relates the interrogation of Needham by the consistory of Neuchâtel, where he stops on the way to visit Théro's German count in hopes of converting him. They ask him why he saw a discrepancy between the three months of Jesus' career in the synoptists and the three years in John. Needham answers, "il fallait prendre trois mois pour trois ans" (Mac. p. 293). In other words, he simply ignores the discrepancy he has raised, a tactic he repeats in his more elaborate reply to the next question:

> Interrogé comment il avait expliqué l'apparition et l'ascension en Galilée selon Matthieu, et selon Luc à Jérusalem et en Béthanie, a répondu que ce n'était pas une chose importante, et qu'on peut fort bien monter au ciel de deux endroits à la fois. (Mac. pp. 293-94)

[156] Philips and Perkins, p. 361.

Having called him an imbecile, his interrogators ask him, "Est-il vrai que théologiens sont parfois gens absurdes" (Mac. p. 294)? Manifestly, Voltaire enjoyed parodying the abbreviated style of judicial interrogations. He imagined Needham undergoing such questioning so that he might convict him of infractions against common sense. But he also takes advantage of the opportunity to repeat the chronological discrepancy between the synoptics and John in another context and to recall the contradictions between the various resurrection appearances.

Covelle foreshadows Needham's cavalier reconciliation of contradictories in exegesis by his sarcasm in an earlier letter to a country parson. We need only agree, says Covelle, on an interpretation contrary to the true meaning of a given passage. As examples, he furnishes John 14.28, which we have already seen several times, and Romans 9.5:

> "Le don de Dieu s'est répandu sur nous par la grâce donnée à un seul homme, qui est Jésus"... veut dire sans difficulté: "Le don de Dieu s'est répandu sur nous par la grâce donnée à un seul Dieu, qui est Jésus." (Mac. p. 260)

In contrast with John 14.28, however, Romans 9.5 presents a problem of textual accuracy which Voltaire chose to ignore. Since the grammar of this verse does not indicate the relationship between *Jesus* and *God*, the relationship cannot be determined, because there is no punctuation in the oldest manuscripts (see p. 26). Yet Voltaire at least had the merit of placing a stumbling block across the path of apologists using the verse to prove that Paul thought Jesus divine. He marshals other arguments against Jesus' divinity in Théro's second letter. "Il ne semble pas raisonnable [aux incrédules]," he warns the professor,

> que Dieu se soit fait Juif plutôt que Romain, qu'il soit né d'une femme vierge [etc.], et que Dieu ait enfin fait tant de miracles pour être outragé, pour être supplicié, pour rendre le monde beaucoup plus méchant qu'il n'était auparavant. (Mac. p. 235)

Théro qualifies the last phrase by further Voltairian exaggerations concerning war and tyranny. Scientifically, one can scarcely argue that Jesus made life on earth either worse or better, an observation which has nearly the same polemical impact as Voltaire's. He contends rather that God could not have behumbled himself as Christians claimed he did unless he achieved results commensurate with such an act by such a being. The first argument in the quotation expressing Voltaire's prejudice in favor of the Romans and against the Jews also has its value. His education by the Jesuits, his classical culture, and his study of civilization all reinforced a natural tendency to prefer logic to inspiration. In the absence of such prejudice, however, one might legitimately ask how God could have preferred any race to the others.

Théro tells R of another problem raised by the deists mentioned in his first letter. Referring to the Pentecost miracle, he observes that the apostles, touched by the inverted tongues of flame, preached to the bystanders in their own languages and yet the latter wondered if they were drunk on new wine.

> On peut bien, dit-on, prendre pour un homme ivre celui qui parle sans se faire entendre de personne, mais non celui qui se fait entendre de tout le monde. (Mac. p. 227)

In Acts 2.1-13, he detected the naïveté of a writer who had little experience with foreign languages. When one encounters people speaking one's own language in a foreign country, one tends to exaggerate the lucidity of what they are saying. One is unlikely to assume that they have been drinking, unless they are actually incoherent and that does not happen here. Luke apparently made this mistake because he gave all his attention to enhancing the miracle by his description of its effect on the bystanders, a traditional apologetic device even then. The bystanders according to him have recourse to the idea of drink to explain what astonishes them. The influence of philosophy on Théro reduces his susceptibility to such miraculous edification, hence his embarrassment.

In his debate with the German count in the third letter to R, he devotes an entire page to a discussion of the relationship between Jesus' teaching and the legislation of the Church councils. With the self-assurance of any aspiring minister, he considers the contribution of the councils to Christianity a strength rather than a weakness:

> Ce sont les conciles... qui nous ont enseigné la consubstantialité, les deux natures dans une seule personne, et une seule personne avec deux volontés. Ils nous ont appris que la paternité n'appartient pas au Fils, mais qu'il a la vertu productive, et que l'Esprit ne l'a pas, parce que le Saint-Esprit procède, et n'est pas engendré. (Mac. p. 238)

This docile account of the varying degrees to which the three persons can engender reveals the contradiction Voltaire perceives in the doctrine of Trinitarian equality. How can the Son be equal to the Father if he does not demonstrate the ability to engender as he does? Elsewhere, the count questions the value of speculation on engenderment and procession in the Trinity to begin with: "Ce galimatias théologique est-il bien utile aux hommes" (Mac. p. 241)? He agrees with Théro that the councils established the principal articles of Christian faith, but other councils, as numerous as these, he objects, ratified a contrary doctrine: "Il y a eu autant de conciles en faveur d'Arius et d'Eusèbe qu'en faveur d'Athanase" (Mac. p. 238). While one might quibble over what constitutes a legitimate council and how many decided one way or the other, the statement is generally true. But the count has a more powerful argument based on the futility of the divine intervention on earth. Why would God have let himself be crucified

> pour ne pas annoncer lui-même sa volonté, pour laisser ce soin à des conciles qui ne s'assembleraient qu'après plusieurs siècles, qui se contrediraient, qui s'anathématiseraient les uns les autres, et qui feraient verser le sang par des soldats et par des bourreaux? (Mac. p. 238)

The councils could not have expressed God's will as they claim, because they convened several centuries after his departure, contradicted and even condemned each other, and imposed their decisions by arbitrary and violent means. Behind these charges lies the conviction that the evidence excludes any possibility of divine inspiration in the decisions of the councils and confines their motivation to all the usual political appetites. The Frederickian shadow cast by the count reminds us, moreover, of his competence in detecting such motives:

> Tout se fait, tout s'établit, se détruit, se renouvelle avec le temps à Nicée, à Chalcédoine, à Ephèse, à Antioche, à Constantinople, au milieu des intrigues les plus tumultueuses et des haines les plus implacables. (Mac. p. 238)

Here Voltaire strikes another damaging blow, for, in fact, most of the ingredients in the eventual Trinity cost the Church long periods of vacillating turmoil. He looked upon this vacillation as further proof that God had nothing to do with the dogma.

A few pages later, the count echoes the standard eighteenth-century exaltation of morality over dogma on the grounds of utility. Socrates, Epictetus, and Antonius, he notes, taught moral values contested by no one. What would have happened if they had added:

> "Croyez qu'Epictète procède d'Antonin, ou bien qu'il procède d'Antonin et de Socrate... ou vous périrez sur un échafaud." (Mac. p. 240)

The choice between the single and the dual procession of Epictetus is a satiric model of the quarrel separating the eastern and western churches. It effectively exposes the absurdity of combining personalities, whether mythical or philosophical, in algebraic formulations. Théro admits that one cannot believe such things without Paul's folly of the cross or Augustine's fideism: "Je le crois parce qu'il est absurde" (Mac. p. 240). "Il est aisé," he laments, "de ramener une âme criminelle et tremblante qui ne raisonne pas," but certainly not one who has "des lumières" (Mac. p. 240), such as the count. He finishes his third letter, in fact, by declaring, for the edification of R no doubt,

> Je crois surtout avec vous le miracle éternel de la consubstantialité, non seulement parce qu'il est contraire à ma raison, mais parce que je ne peux m'en former aucune idée. (Mac. p. 243)

The inability of the human mind so much as to conceive of consubstantiality convinced Voltaire that God could never have expected us to believe in it. On the contrary, its mere existence as a dogma convicted its human authors of having tried to fool the rest of us and Voltaire resented the insult to our intelligence. Part of a final declaration in Théro's letter to the professor of theology, the quotation conveys the despair of a young minister torn between the desire to believe and the natural light. Perhaps Voltaire was thinking of Vernes, who must have undergone a similar, internal conflict during the "Genève" affair.

A Voltairian work presenting Genevan characters would not be complete without allusions to Calvin and Servetus. At the thought of certain miracles that seem impossible and fraudulent to him, the old soldier Captain Durôst swears "Ventre-Servet" (Mac. p. 253)! Beaudinet ironically rekindles the green fagots Calvin supposedly ordered for the burning of Servetus, "afin de savourer le doux plaisir de lui voir expier ses péchés plus longtemps" (Mac. p. 294). The contrast between the ferocious idea and the bantering tone is a well-known Voltairian satirical technique. Covelle summarizes the state of the Genevan conscience (which intrigued Voltaire) by taking comfort in lesser guilt than a list of historical adversaries, including "les partisans d'Athanase et ceux d'Arius." He adds,

> Nous n'avons point imité les fureurs de saint Cyrille contre ceux qui appelaient Marie *mère* de Jésus, et non pas *mère* de Dieu. (Mac. p. 271)

The Creator, by definition, can have no mother. The pretext of Cyril's crusade against Nestorius provoked Voltairian common sense as flagrantly as any of the absurdities he discerned in Christian history.

His *Questions sur les miracles* are in sum a defense of the natural light from the encroachments of Christianity. All his Genevan correspondents and even Théro[157] support the commonsense point of view, which he apparently believed indigenous with them, in spite of occasional irony at their expense. The only correspondents who speak for

[157] And despite R and Rousseau, who are not correspondents.

unreasonable Christianity are clergymen, the Protestant Montmolin of Môtiers-Travers and the Catholic intruder Needham. Needham plays the part of the villain in this melodrama, for Voltaire exploits Genevan chauvinism without sacrificing his enduring sympathy for Genevans themselves, except Vernet, Rousseau, and a few others.

The *Dictionnaire*

Among Rousseau's sins against reason was a remark in the *Vicaire savoyard* that still angered Voltaire three years after the publication of *Emile*. "Si la vie et la mort de Socrate sont d'un sage," Rousseau had written, "la vie et la mort de Jésus sont d'un Dieu."[158] In 1767, Voltaire complained to the abbé d'Olivet that a charlatan had dared to say, "Si Socrate mourut en sage, Jésus-Christ *mourut en Dieu*" (Jan. 5). His quotations are notoriously approximate.[159] Not that he objected to the idea of Socrates dying the death of a wise man, but he resented the notion that God can die:

> comme s'il y avait des dieux accoutumés à la mort, comme si on savait comment ils meurent, comme si une sueur de sang était le caractère de la mort de dieu, enfin comme si c'était dieu qui fût mort.

Whatever misgivings the ex-Jesuit d'Olivet may have had about the theological implications of this protest, he must have admired the relentless logic of his former pupil. The death of God in Rousseau's context offended Voltaire on both semantic and theological grounds. An immortal being could not die and God, as he understood him, could have no such human weaknesses. He found Christianity presumptuous in pretending to know how God had submitted to death. The creator of the Savoyard vicar betrayed deism by endorsing the Christian myth of God's death. The gospel accounts of the passion persuaded Voltaire that Jesus was very much a human being and by no means the divine figure Christians had made of him.

Although he had published the *Dictionnaire philosophique portatif* in the same year as Rousseau's *Emile*, the earlier editions of this antichristian juggernaut contain surprisingly little material on our subject. A long and boring article, for instance, "Christianisme" rehashes several standard Voltairian arguments, the conflict between the genealogies in Matthew and Luke, the implausibility and uselessness of Jesus' miracles and his fidelity to Judaism. He begins the article by puzzling with "plusieurs savants" (*Dict*. p. 109)[160] over the scarcity of allusions to Jesus by his non-Christian contemporaries. Like most

[158] *Oeuvres complètes* (Paris, 1969), IV, 626.
[159] Because he relied on his memory.
[160] Raymond Naves, ed., *Dictionnaire philosophique* (Paris, 1961).

modern critics and even many in his day, he condemns the reference to Jesus in Josephus' *Jewish War* as a fraudulent insertion (see p. 33). He considers the silence of this historian, who lived in and wrote about Jewish Palestine shortly after Jesus' death, fatally damaging to Christianity. The impact of Jesus on his contemporaries, Voltaire submits, must have been negligible if a historian as informative as Josephus ignored him, or worse, knew nothing of him. The rarity of references to him by Gentiles reinforces this opinion, which few modern scholars dispute.

Also in "Christianisme," Voltaire breathes a little life into his stricture against the absence of Trinitarian and Christological dogma from the New Testament:

> [Jésus] cacha à ses contemporains qu'il était fils de Dieu, éternellement engendré, consubstantiel à Dieu, et que le Saint-Esprit procédait du Père et du Fils. Il ne dit point que sa personne était composée de deux natures et de deux volontés. (*Dict.* p. 112)

Jesus reserved this information, Voltaire piously explains, for future revelation by the Holy Spirit. He thus insinuates, ironically to be sure, that Jesus foresaw the strategy of Christian apologists and anticipated their needs. In the Holy Spirit, he saw nothing more than a subterfuge designed to overcome the absence and silence of Jesus, whom they integrated into a metaphysical system he had never dreamed of. The decisive role of Nicaea in the elaboration of this system also drew his fire in "Christianisme." First, he describes the positions of the Arian and Athanasian parties with inhabitual thoroughness and equanimity. Then he turns to the council:

> Après bien des disputes, le Saint-Esprit décida ainsi dans le concile, par la bouche de deux cent quatre-vingt-dix-neuf évêques contre dix-huit:... (*Dict.* p. 131)

Following this colon, he quotes from the confession of faith adopted by the council. The responsibility of the Holy Spirit for the decision is an irony accessible only to readers familiar with his attitude. The commentary following the quotation, however, conveys more obvious irony. Affirming (incorrectly) that two thousand priests backed Arius,[161] he concludes, "On voit par cet exemple combien les évêques

[161] Jeanne Monty detects "a serious misreading" by Voltaire (p. 63) of the *Annals of the Coptic Church* (tenth century) by the Alexandrian Patriarch Eutychius. According to John Selden, trans., *Eutychii patriarchae Alexandrini annales* (Oxford, 1656), as many as 1048 priests of various ranks disagreed with each other and formed various opposing factions. Monty, "Voltaire's Rhetoric: The Use of Written Evidence in the Alphabetical Works," *SVEC*, 120 (1974). The Selden translation is undoubtedly Voltaire's source, but see n. 165 below.

l'emportaient sur les simples prêtres" (*Dict.* p. 132). Though erroneous, the box score of 2018 to 299 appeals directly to common sense. Voltaire is insinuating that pride accruing from rank determined the outcome of the council and not divine inspiration, whether from the Spirit or any other source. He finishes this paragraph in "Christianisme" by a few details about Constantine's vacillation between Athanasianism and Arianism. This vacillation by the emperor of Christendom suggests anything but divine influence. Aside from these passages, the editions of the *Dictionnaire* published before 1767 offer only a meager harvest of fresh ideas on Christology and the Trinity.

In the edition printed that year, however, he added several articles of particular interest to us here. "Arius" is far more exciting than the corresponding paragraph in "Christianisme." "Voici une question incompréhensible" (*Dict.* p. 33), begins the first sentence, a long enumeration of all the different kinds of trouble caused by this incomprehensible question.[162] The sentence announces the idea which will unify the article, the idea of much ado about nothing. Next comes a long series of short questions, each of them taking a point in Trinitarian dogma seriously. In accumulating these abstractions, Voltaire creates an impression of fantasy that increasingly undermines the solemnity of so persistent an interrogation:

> Jésus est-il Verbe? S'il est Verbe, est-il émané de Dieu dans le temps ou avant le temps? S'il est émané de Dieu, est-il coéternel et consubstantiel avec lui, ou est-il d'une substance semblable? est-il distinct de lui, ou ne l'est-il pas? est-il fait, ou engendré? Peut-il engendrer à son tour? a-t-il la paternité ou la vertu productive sans paternité? Le Saint-Esprit est-il fait ou engendré, ou produit, ou procédant du Père, ou procédant du Fils, ou procédant de tous les deux? Peut-il engendrer, peut-il produire? son hypostase est-elle consubstantielle avec l'hypostase du Père et du Fils? (*Dict.* pp. 33-34)

This true-false examination illustrates the futility of the quarrels embroiling Christendom in centuries of strife. Having given the examination, he confesses to ignorance of the answers and insists that no one else knows them either, "et c'est la raison pour laquelle on s'est égorgé" (*Dict.* p. 34). This is a variation on a Voltairian theme: the ambition to know the unknowable and impose belief in such speculation on others had produced all the turmoil in Christian history. When Voltaire says no one can understand, however, he implies re-

[162] "[Elle] a exercé depuis plus de seize cents ans la curiosité, la subtilité sophistique, l'aigreur, l'esprit de cabale, la fureur de dominer, la rage de persécuter, le fanatisme aveugle et sanguinaire, la crédulité barbare, et qui a produit plus d'horreurs que l'ambition des princes, qui pourtant en a produit beaucoup" (*Dict.*, p. 33).

striction of the inquiry to empirical method. The study of phenomena inaccessible to the senses lies beyond the reach of common sense, hence the temptation to deny that they exist. Voltaire cultivates this temptation by pretending not to understand and encouraging his readers not to make the effort.

When he revised "Arius" for the *Questions sur l'Encyclopédie* (1770) and re-entitled the article "Arianisme," he replaced this passage by another: "Ces questions, si au-dessus de la raison, avaient certainement besoin d'être décidées par une Eglise infaillible" (*Dict.* p. 453). Substituting one irony for another, he holds the Church specifically responsible for the invention of dogma. The arrogance of pretending to infallibility in the performance of illusory speculation particularly angered him. The conditions under which such speculation acquired the force of law bring him back, once again, to Alexandria at the beginning of the third century. To describe the intellectual activity in this ancient city, he manipulates a trivial saying, so as to reduce the activity to trivia: "Les Grecs égyptiens... coupaient un cheveu en quatre; mais cette fois-ci, ils ne le coupèrent qu'en trois" (*Dict.* p. 34). Reworking the forthright data in "Christianisme," he presents the positions of the opposing parties, less in the interest of informing his readers than making them laugh. He naturally ridicules the leaders of each:

> Alexandros... s'avise de prêcher que Dieu étant nécessairement individuel, simple, une monade dans toute la rigueur du mot, cette monade est trine. (*Dict.* p. 34)

The exotic terms *monade* and *trine* in this approach to the familiar dichotomy between Trinitarian unity and diversity re-enhance the subject. *Trine* is a technical equivalent of "triple" in the vocabulary of theology. *Monade* especially suits the context because, in Alexandrian Neoplatonism, it designates the supreme, original unity from which all things derive and to which all creatures aspire.

Neoplatonism conditioned the thinking of both Alexandros and "Arios ou Arious, que nous nommons Arius" (*Dict.* p. 34). Voltaire does not bother to explain the latter's position, but rather cites his reaction to Alexander's monad and associates him with others condemned as heretics: "Il ergote en partie comme Sabellious, qui avait ergoté comme le Phrygien Praxéas, grand ergoteur" (*Dict.* p. 34). He seems to have chosen these names at random, for the men who bore them had little in common with Arius.[163] He in fact leaves the reader

[163] Sabellius taught an extreme monarchianism (modalism) and Tertullian's opponent Praxeas professed a similar doctrine, both in the second century.

with the impression that Arius' theology amounts to no more than quibbling. With obscure aggression on one hand and the defense of an absurdity on the other, enlightened monarchy intervenes. Voltaire admits Constantine's crimes in a lengthy enumeration, which he leaves unfinished, "*transeat*; mais il avait du bon sens" (*Dict*. p. 34). Constantine's good sense transpires from the letter he entrusted to his envoy Hosius. In addition to previous "quotation" from this letter, one finds Constantine's opinion of the quarrel: "tant de bruit sur un sujet si mince" (*Dict*. p. 35).[164] It was not the divinity, Voltaire hastens to explain, that Constantine thought a meager subject, but rather "la manière incompréhensible dont on s'efforçait d'expliquer la nature de la divinité" (*Dict*. p. 35). Voltaire therefore forgets neither the idea of much ado about nothing nor the theme of the incomprehensible question announced in his introduction.

Except for a brief conclusion, he devotes the rest of "Arius" to a speech allegedly delivered by Hosius. Though probably apocryphal,[165] this speech demonstrates that Hosius' sense is as good as his master's. "Si l'objet de la dispute était essentiel," he lectures the adversaries, "Jésus-Christ... en aurait parlé" (*Dict*. p. 35). Since Jesus did not mention it, however, the dispute is futile. Hosius also challenges their ability to decide specific points: "Personne de vous ne peut savoir si Jésus est fait ou engendré. Et que vous importe sa nature" (*Dict*. p. 35)? Nor does Hosius shrink from sweeping conclusions. God, he argues, would not have sent his Son, unless he intended for him to teach us our catechism: "Tout ce [que Jésus] ne nous dit pas expressément est l'ouvrage des hommes, et l'erreur est leur partage" (*Dict*. p. 35). Christianity itself, therefore, is in large measure, subject to error. Voltaire refrains from interpreting Hosius in the sense we have seen elsewhere, yet he was certainly convinced that, if his Christian readers

[164] The "quotation" is an accurate paraphrase: "C'est pour de petites et même de très minimes choses que vous disputez" (Boularand, II, 187). The idea of *tant de bruit* is amply developed in the preceding text.

[165] Voltaire furnishes a false reference: "Le patriarche arabe qui a écrit l'*Histoire de l'église d'Alexandrie*" (*Dict*., p. 35). He is referring to Eutychius, patriarch of Alexandria from 933 until 940, whose *Annals of the Coptic Church* contain neither this speech nor any allusion to the Council of Nicaea, either in a modern critical edition in the original Arabic (Louis Cheikho, *Eutychii Patriarchae Alexandrini Annales* [Louvain, 1962]) or in a French translation available to Voltaire (J.M. Vansleb [Johann Wansleben], trans. or ed.? *L'Histoire de l'Eglise de l'Alexandrie* [Paris, 1677]). I wish to thank Mr. Toni Naufal for his search of the Arabic text. Monty notes that Hosius' alleged speech is not in John Selden's translation of Eutychius' *Annals*, although she finds that Selden's work furnishes information about the Council of Nicaea used by Voltaire. This discovery raises suspicion of both Voltaire and Selden!

took Hosius' opinion seriously, they would have to abandon everything that distinguished them from the Jews. Without going this far, Hosius dispenses with the incomprehensible questions posed at the beginning of the article, for Jesus raised none of them. Consequently, one must distinguish between Voltaire's commonsense bishop and the historical Hosius, who helped to involve Christianity more deeply in the discussion of these very questions.

Although Voltaire gives his readers little useful information in "Arius," he does much to persuade them that the questions in his first paragraph are not only incomprehensible but also futile. In the *Questions sur l'Encyclopédie* of 1770, his additions to the article, which he re-entitled "Arianisme," furnish the kind of facts perspicuously absent in "Arius." Most of them do not concern the Council of Nicaea itself, but rather the intrigue which persuaded the bishops on neither side in the dispute to join the faction against Arius. Enemies of Arius' most influential supporter, Eusebius of Nicomedia, convinced the emperor that Eusebius had lent his support to Constantine's rival Licinius. Voltaire briefly describes the persecution of the Arians that resulted from this maneuver and concluded, "dès le premier grand concile, l'intrigue, la cabale, la persécution sont établies avec le dogme, sans pouvoir en affaiblir la sainteté" (*Dict.* p. 454). The final phrase, of course, means the opposite of what it says. In Voltaire's opinion, the turpitude instrumental in creating the Trinitarian precedent of Nicaea obviated the holiness ascribed to it. Not only does he disdain the intrigue and persecution implicitly condoned by the Council, but also the variations that buffeted its decision during the rest of the century. He obtained this argument by implicitly turning Bossuet's accusation of variations in Protestantism against the Church itself.

He also stresses the alternation of imperial favor:

> Constantin, qui avait exilé Arius pour ne pas croire le Fils consubstantiel, exila Eustathe pour le croire.[166] (*Dict.* p. 454)

> Arius, et Athanase, son plus grand ennemi, sont condamnés tour à tour par un homme qui n'était pas encore chrétien. (*Dict.* p. 455)

Yet Voltaire is treating Christianity generously, for once. Despite his tardy baptism, Constantine behaved much as the pagans who had preceded him on the throne. In the exercise of power, he used the Christian sects as his predecessors had used the pagan ones. After his death, Voltaire observes,

[166] After Hosius and Alexandros, Eustathius was the most influential opponent of Arianism at Nicaea.

> La flatterie des peuples romains... fut portée à un tel excès que ceux de l'ancienne religion en firent un dieu, et ceux de la nouvelle en firent un saint. (*Dict*. p. 455)

Voltaire evidently relished the irony in this parallel between deification by pagans and canonization by Christians. He believed, with good reason, that the latter had derived from the former. But he must have appreciated the additional irony in the apotheosis of an emperor whose "good sense" had failed to discourage bickering over the degree of divinity in Jesus. This passage, in any event, illuminates the psychology of apotheosis to the detriment of Christ's divinity and insinuates the polytheistic heritage of Christianity. The context motivates the apotheosis of Constantine by his subjects' urge to flatter his filial successors. Thus Voltaire casts doubt on the value of testimony in certification of Godhood. With this purpose in mind, perhaps, he gives more emphasis to Constantine's crimes than his "good sense" in the 1770 additions. If men are capable of deifying such a criminal, whatever their motive, they might bestow this presumptuous honor on anyone. The canonization of Constantine, who was barely a Christian, therefore tends to weaken the credibility of Jesus' deification.

After the further history of Arianism, Voltaire turns to what he describes, in the manner of his Christian sources, as a continuation of the same heresy in the sixteenth century. This time, however, he at least recognizes a lapse of ten centuries between the disappearance of the trend initiated by Arius and the appearance of Reformation antitrinitarianism. More thorough reading appears to have resulted in the correction of old errors and the acceptance of new ones. He credits the legend of the sixteenth-century academy founded at Vicenza by forty noblemen who purged their Christianity of all inessential dogmas (see p. 99):

> Jésus fut reconnu pour verbe, pour sauveur et pour juge; mais on nia sa divinité, sa consubstantialité, et jusqu'à la Trinité. (*Dict*. p. 456)

Although his source, Fleury's *Histoire ecclésiastique* (XXIX, 595), misled him, an Anabaptist council meeting in Venice in 1550 came to a similar conclusion. He follows the *Histoire* in naming Lelio Sozzini and Giovanni Valentino Gentile as members of the academy and adds the name of Servetus who probably never set foot in Italy.[167]

[167] "Dès l'année 1546 quarante personnes des plus distinguées par leurs rangs, leurs emplois et leurs talents avaient établi une espèce d'académie à Vicence... Ils niaient la divinité du fils de Dieu, qu'ils reconnaissaient seulement pour un homme au-dessus des autres, né d'une vierge par l'opération du Saint-Esprit, mort par l'ordre de Dieu, pour

After a routine paragraph on Servetus, he implicates Calvin in the condemnation of Gentile. But Gentile recanted and went free, only to be executed eight years later in Bern. Confusing the Genevan trial with the Bernese, Voltaire states that witnesses accused Gentile of daring to say that the terms *Trinity, essence*, and *hypostasis* were not in Scripture.[168]

> Sur cette déposition, les juges, qui ne savaient pas plus que lui ce que c'est qu'une hypostase, le condamnèrent sans raisonner, à perdre la tête. (*Dict.* p. 456)

Of the three terms, Voltaire emphasizes the one most difficult to understand, for a hypostasis can be conceived only by means of the relations between three of them. Only the existence of these relations distinguishes them from the unifying essence or substance, with which together they form the Trinity. None of the three terms or the concepts they represent appear anywhere in the authentic text of the Bible.[169] The beheading of Gentile for having said that a book does not contain words which in fact it does not contain, especially when these words themselves are incomprehensible, dramatizes the tyranny and barbarity perpetrated in the name of the Trinity. Voltaire completes "Arianisme" with a historical summary of antitrinitarianism in Poland and England. He mentions Newton, Locke, and Clarke who "se déclara hautement arien... Il n'allait jamais à sa paroisse le jour qu'on y récitait le *symbole* de saint Athanase" (*Dict.* p. 456).[170] Conspicuous by their absence from this summary are the Genevan ministers, whose contemporaneous unitarianism no longer inspired hopes of conversion or alliance in 1770.

By 1767, he was placing greater reliance on historical examples, as in "Conciles." He introduces the subject with irony over the unsaintly behavior of prelates attending councils and the frequency with which councils contradict each other. Noting that Nicaea was called to determine "si Jésus était créé ou incréé" (*Dict.* p. 143), he finds the

nous procurer la rémission des péchés, ressuscité par la puissance du père et glorieux dans le ciel." Claude Fleury, *Histoire ecclésiastique* (1720-1738), XXIX, 593.

[168] "Nel giugno del 1558 venne denunciato... per avere sostenuto che il solo Dio è il Padre, che ha trasmesso la sua divinità al figlio. Questa dottrina fondamentale era accompagnata dalle solite considerazioni sui termini 'Trinità,' 'essenza,' 'ipostasi,' estranei alla Scrittura, e sulla impossibilità di fondare scritturalmente la dottrina della Trinità." Delio Cantimori, *Eretici italiani di cinquecento* (Florence, 1967), pp. 225-26.

[169] In other words, excluding the Trinitarian formulations in Mt. 28.19 and 1 Jn. 7.8 (variant in the Vulgate). See pp. 53 and 93.

[170] Voltaire seems to have learned this from Clarke himself when he visited him in England. See n. 118.

question frivolous because it does not impinge on morals. One must be good, he elaborates, whether "Jésus ait été dans le temps, ou avant le temps" (*Dict*. p. 143). After many altercations, the council decided that

> le Fils était aussi ancien que le Père, et *consubstantiel* au Père. Cette décision ne s'entend guère; mais elle n'en est que plus sublime. (*Dict*. p. 143)

The last sentence reformulates the Voltairian contrast between absurdity on the level of common sense (*ne s'entend guère*) and wisdom on that of religious mysticism (*sublime*). The grammar of the final clause (*mais elle n'en est que plus*) triggers suspicion of the word *sublime*, usually sedate in eighteenth-century usage, thus the second sentence contaminates the first. Consubstantiality and coeternity derive from the ideas of space and time freed of their empirical limitations. Consubstantiality especially amused and irritated Voltaire, for he wondered how his fellow men could have fought over the multiple personification of an ethereal substance without the slightest proof that it existed beyond their own imaginations. Yet coeternity annoyed him too. Empirical time depends on the comparison of incidents detected by the senses or remembered from past experience. The study of documents, a special kind of sensual experience, extends empirical time to a very distant past, but no further. Then how could one determine the existence of any person, except the Creator, before this time? Convinced that one cannot, Voltaire rebels against the presumption of assigning coeternity with God (and consubstantiality as well) to a fellow man. In reaction to apologists exaggerating the significance of Nicaea, he remarks that the formula ratified by the council says nothing about the Trinity and includes the Holy Spirit, who "fut traité bien cavalièrement" (*Dict*. p. 143). He delights in the repeal of the most significant decision at Nicaea by the twin councils of Rimini and Seleucia (359):

> Six cents [infaillibles] après quatre mois de querelles, ôtèrent unanimement à Jésus sa *consubstantialité*. Elle lui a été rendue depuis. (*Dict*. p. 144)

That these Arian councils do not qualify as ecumenical because the pope had no part in them mattered little to him. The gap between pretentions and the support of evidence seemed ludicrous to him in all councils, whatever their official status might be in Rome.

He might have exploited the excesses of Ephesus in 431 even more satirically than he did. This council condemned Nestorius, he says, for having taught "qu'à la vérité Jésus était bien Dieu, mais que sa mère n'était pas absolument mère de Dieu, mais mère de Jésus" (*Dict*. p.

144). This doubletalk complicates the issue at Ephesus by mingling it with that of Nicaea. The latter decided that the Father and the Son shared the same divinity, without denying the Son's humanity, while Ephesus considered the relationship between the Son's divinity and his humanity. Cyril of Alexandria exploited this issue by implicating Nestorius in apparent disregard for Mary, whom the common people revered. Cyril relied on their support to impose the title mother of God, thus emphasizing Jesus' Godhood which he believed to predominate. In the *Dictionnaire*, Voltaire merely indicates that the council acted against Cyril as well as Nestorius, "ce qui embarrassa fort le Saint-Esprit" (*Dict.* p. 144). In the *Questions*, on the other hand, he gives enough detail for an understanding of what happened at Ephesus in 431 and demonstrates the good sense behind Nestorius' position on Mary.[171]

The Church designates Ephesus 431 as ecumenical, but not Ephesus 449, the Robber Council. The latter pitted Flavian, who insisted on two natures in Christ, against Eutychius, who admitted only one. Voltaire has satirical affection for Eutychius,

> moine qui avait beaucoup crié contre Nestorius, dont l'hérésie n'allait pas à moins qu'à supposer deux personnes en Jésus: ce qui est épouvantable. (*Dict.* p. 144)

He inflates the alleged evil by many words warning of its magnitude, then punctures it by a concise overstatement (*épouvantable*). Obviously, Nestorius' sin does no practical harm whatsoever. The violence of this council particularly exposes it to Voltaire's strictures. In 1767, he remarked that it "se tint à coups de bâton... La nature de Flavien fut moulue de coups et deux natures furent assignées à Jésus" (*Dict.* p. 144), an error, since he was given only one. What happened to Flavian, however, shows which nature has exclusive commonsense significance. In 1771, Voltaire used the traditional name for this monophysitic council, "*le brigandage*." The Egyptian delegation, he states, shouted, "*il fallait déchirer en deux tous ceux qui diviseraient en deux Jésus-Christ*" (*Dict.* p. 489). Consequently, both articles underline the violence of the Robber Council, the earlier one, physical violence, and the later one, verbal violence. Manifestly, the God who endows us with the natural light had nothing to do with such a council.

"Conciles" in the *Dictionnaire* tells us nothing about the Council of Chalcedon (451), except that "Jésus fut réduit à une nature" (*Dict.* p.

[171] He explains this position as follows: "La sainte vierge Marie, mère de Jésus-Christ, n'était point mère de Dieu, parce que... Jésus-Christ étant le verbe fils de Dieu consubstantiel à son père, Marie ne pouvait pas être à la fois la mère de dieu le père et de dieu le fils" (*Dict.*, p. 489). See p. 87.

144), another error, since this time he was given two. Voltaire therefore confused the decisions of Ephesus 449 and Chalcedon with each other, and he may even have done so deliberately to provoke clerical scholars. The context amplifies his indifference to such distinctions, providing the contradictions between the councils be fully recognized. At the risk of redundance, moreover, he might have reminded us that the Christological councils contradicted each other just as the Trinitarian ones had and for the same reason, politics. The depravity of the councils and the contradictions between them seemed as significant to him as the eventual recourse to a mystery so incomprehensible that it cannot be rationally disputed. In dogma, he saw an arbitrary accumulation of sordid victories, each of which might easily have been a defeat. The councils impressed him as a series of colossal jokes beneath the dignity of God, who in any case brooked no human contamination.

In the brief "Divinité de Jésus," he pretends to argue this point from the Socinian point of view, but he is really speaking for himself. Tongue in cheek, he compares Socinians to ancient philosophers, Jews, Mohammedans, and others who

> osent prétendre... que l'idée d'un Dieu homme est monstrueuse, que la distance d'un Dieu à l'homme est infinie, et qu'il est impossible que l'Etre infini, immense, éternel, ait été contenu dans un corps périssable. (*Dict.* p. 171)

He is confusing spatial and temporal infinity with divine transcendence. Pascal may have misled him by insisting on the disproportion between man and God. Voltaire's objection nevertheless remains valid, insofar as the Christian idea of a man-God combines physics and metaphysics on the pretext of sacred mystery. Nor does he tire of repeating that this gratuitous reconciliation of opposites enjoys no support in Scripture. Again he tells us that Paul never calls Jesus God and often calls him a man. Furthermore,

> Les chrétiens passèrent trois siècles entiers à former peu à peu l'apothéose de Jésus, et... ils n'élevaient cet étonnant édifice qu'à l'exemple des païens. (*Dict.* pp. 171-72)

The last point foreshadows the 1770 addition to "Arius" exposing the canonization-deification of Constantine. Tracing Christian practices to pagan origins entangles Christianity in its own contradictions, because, in its formative period, it had to define itself in terms of its rivalry with paganism.

With this thought in mind, no doubt, Voltaire enumerated the steps he believed Christians had taken in their apotheosis of Jesus:

> un homme inspiré de Dieu...
> une créature plus parfaite que les autres...
> [qui occupe] une place au-dessus des anges...
> une émanation de Dieu produite dans le temps...
> [né] avant le temps même.
> Enfin... Dieu, consubstantiel à Dieu. (*Dict.* p. 172)

Each of these opinions prevailed somewhere and at some time between the baptism of Jesus and the Council of Constantinople in 381, but they did not succeed each other in the orderly progression indicated by Voltaire. As he well knew, several of them in various combinations co-existed at any given time during most of this period. But they did appear or disappear roughly in this order and so his simplification has at least pedagogical value. Having implied in "Divinité" that men alone had deified Jesus, he wanted to show how apotheosis had actually taken place. He knew that most of his readers neither expected nor wished a more rigorous demonstration, which he probably could not have supplied anyway.

Could he have refuted the Trinity on grounds as coldly logical as those in the Encyclopedia article "Unitaires" by Diderot's "petit frère" Naigeon?[172] Perhaps, but he chose rather to borrow several pages from the article, re-entitle them "Antitrinitaires," and acknowledge his source. Except for two minor changes,[173] an unusual statistic for a quotation by Voltaire, the text is identical to the original. He nonetheless appended a final paragraph of his own against the suspect Trinitarian passage in 1 John 5.27 (see p. 93). Calmet himself admits, he says, that the passage does not appear in any ancient manuscript and that John says nothing of the Trinity in his gospel. All of these reasons and others as well, he concludes,

> pourraient excuser les antitrinitaires, si les conciles n'avaient pas décidé. Mais comme les hérétiques ne font nul cas des conciles, on ne sait plus comment s'y prendre pour les confondre. (*Dict.* p. 29)

The futile triumph of the councils and the comic frustration of this coda parody apologists opposed to "Socinianism." We know what Voltaire thought of the councils! If he had adopted the cross-reference technique of the *Encyclopédie* along with Naigeon's article, he would have referred his readers to "Conciles."

[172] Voltaire thought the abbé de Bragelogne had written "Unitaires."

[173] The terms in brackets are in Naigeon's text: "Qu'on ne peut produire aucun [un seul] passage qui l'autorise" (*Dict.*, p. 27); "C'est une certaine distinction incompréhensible, qui fait que l'on [qu'on] distingue dans une nature unique en nombre, un Père, un Fils et un Saint-Esprit" (*Dict.*, p. 28).

A further allusion to antitrinitarians occurs in "Papisme," one of several amusing dialogues apparently inserted in the *Dictionnaire* to enliven it. This article consists of a conversation between a papist or priest and a treasurer, who are subjects of the same prince. The priest objects to the admission of unitarians into the principality where, much to his chagrin, Lutherans, Calvinists, Quakers, Anabaptists, and even Jews already reside. These hard-working unitarians, the treasurer reassures him, will help the economy, so that the regularity of his wages will improve. The priest concedes that he would regret the loss of his wages even more than the admission of such heretics, "mais enfin ils ne croient pas que Jésus-Christ soit fils de Dieu" (*Dict*. p. 333). What difference does that make? the treasurer asks, as long as the priest enjoys religious freedom and material comfort. The Jews do not believe Jesus to be the Son of God either, yet the priest willingly invests his money with them. "Saint Paul lui-même n'a jamais parlé de la divinité de Jésus-Christ; il l'appelle franchement un homme" (*Dict*. p. 333). The treasurer then quotes Romans 5.17, where Paul declares, "les justes régneront par un seul *homme* qui est Jésus" (*Dict*. pp. 333-34). All the earlier fathers agreed with Paul and "pendant trois cents ans Jésus s'est contenté de son humanité" (*Dict*. p. 334). The treasurer's competence in such matters and the kind of tolerance he recommends identify him as a philosophe. But he belongs to the Voltairian school of philosophy, because he bases his plea for tolerance on an economic argument and serves in the prince's government, a role Voltaire thought especially appropriate for philosophes. His banker Jean-Robert Tronchin, whom Louis XV had appointed *fermier général*, may have been in the back of his mind, although neither the treasurer nor the priest seem to represent anybody in particular. Such lectures of priests by treasurers simply figured in his dreams of reforming society.

The *Dictionnaire* figured largely in these dreams, for he looked upon it as an alphabetical catechism of reform. The most numerous readers, those whose opinion carried the greatest weight, would find it convenient. They had neither the patience nor the motivation to plough through learned treatises, but they could discover Voltaire's opinion on the subjects that interested them very quickly in his dictionary. His wit and concision appealed to their mentality, the mentality of common sense.

The Late Sixties

His faith in the natural light sustained an enormous production of antichristian writings in the late sixties. Far from discouraging him, his decreasing life expectancy spurred him on to mightier efforts against the "infamous," which he steadfastly believed to be crumbling. Although most of what he wrote was to some extent repetitious, his ability to renew old themes continued unabated. Nor had his skill in revitalizing satiric genres diminished. In 1767, he published four sermons under the title of *Homélies prononcées à Londres en 1765*. He seems to have imagined an English Socinian church, for his preacher's theology, though Christian, is too radical for any bonafide sect in England at the time. One of these sermons, entitled "Sur la superstition," deplores the Trinitarian and Christological disputes from the fourth to the seventh centuries, because they ignored the absence of any support for these doctrines in Scripture. "Dieu nous a donné l'entendement," he continues,

> il ne peut vouloir que vous le pervertissiez. Comment une proposition dont vous ne pouvez jamais avoir d'idée pourrait-elle vous être nécessaire? (M. XXVI, 334-35)

By necessity, one must understand moral necessity. Voltaire is assuming that God equips humans with sufficient intelligence to meet all moral requirements for life on earth. Exceeding the natural light in a vain attempt to know divine mysteries amounts to perversion of God's gift. Yet Voltaire does not deny the existence of exceptional individuals:

> Que Dieu... ait donné à un homme plus de lumières... cela se voit tous les jours... qu'il en ait fait le modèle de la raison et de la vertu, cela ne révolte pas le bon sens. (M. XXVI, 335)

Thus reason and virtue go hand in hand, whether they exceed common sense or not. Good sense, in fact, willingly recognizes reason and virtue superior to its own, because common experience furnishes it with frequent exceptions to its rule. It can therefore accept Jesus as a man of superior reason and virtue, but no more. The preacher indicates that he has Jesus in mind, but he immediately cautions against exaggerating the value of his exceptional enlightenment: "Craignons qu'en voulant aller trop au delà nous ne renversions tout l'édifice" (M. XXVI, 335). Since the divinity of Jesus escapes human experience, it necessitates belief contradictory to good sense. According to Voltairian hyperbole, such belief constitutes abandonment of reason or fanaticism.

Likewise published in 1767, the *Essai historique et critique sur les dissensions des églises de Pologne* presents an ironical reversal of this theory. In this work, he abstains from examining the dogmas separating

Greek, Roman, evangelical (Lutheran), reform (Calvinist), and other sects:

> Je laisse ce soin à ceux qui sont éclairés d'une lumière divine. Il faut l'être sans doute pour bien savoir si le Saint-Esprit procède par spiration du Père et du Fils, ou du Fils seulement. (M. XXVI, 456)

The question about the spiration (breathing) of the Spirit also figures in the examples given by the London preacher just before he warns against perversion of the natural light. Readers unfamiliar with Voltaire may not realize the irony of his self-disqualification in the *Essai*, an ingenuous work for him. Clearly, the author of the *Homélies* does not believe in any divine light enabling one to determine whether the Father alone (Greek Church) or both the Father and the Son (Roman Church) breathe forth the Spirit. The natural light convinces him that neither the Spirit nor the Son exist to begin with.

Another passage in his preacher's second sermon exposes the chauvinism implied by the apotheosis of Jesus. The preacher professes to be speaking for orthodox Christians:

> Nous savons que Dieu étant venu sur la terre, et étant mort du dernier supplice pour tous les hommes, il ne veut pourtant avoir pitié que de notre petite assemblée. (M. XXVI, 336)

In this formula, Voltaire not only ridicules the presumption of assigning human limitations to God, a familiar idea, but also that of denying the benefit of God's human life and death to other communions, a novel idea for Voltaire. In his fourth sermon, the preacher asks, "Qu'était Jésus aux yeux des hommes, qui ne pouvaient certainement soupçonner sa divinité" (M. XXVI, 353)? A good man, a poor man, a man who preached to the poor against the superstition of the rich, the Pharisees, and the other priests: "C'était le Socrate de la Galilée" (M. XXVI, 353). He died the death of any rebel challenging the predominant superstition of his country. Suddenly, Voltaire felt or pretended to feel sympathy for Jesus, whom he associated with Socrates, a philosophic hero. Was it because Jesus had attacked the "superstition" of the priesthood? It seems more likely that his change of heart resulted from the publication of atheist propaganda by d'Holbach.[174] Perhaps it also dawned on Voltaire that he shared the experience of persecution for his superiority over other men with the Socrates of Galilee, however little they otherwise had in common. Yet his sympathy with Jesus the man does not diminish his hostility to the divine

[174] Jeroom Vercruysse lists five editions of d'Holbach's *Le Christianisme dévoilé* (1766) published in 1767: *Bibliographie descriptive des écrits du baron d'Holbach* (Paris, 1971).

Son of God. On the contrary, his apparent acceptance of Jesus as a sympathetic fellow sufferer implies the rejection of his divinity.

In further support of his manhood, the fourth sermon offers an interesting digression from Voltaire's habitual emphasis on his Judaism. Unaware of the extent to which many ancient Jews had assimilated Greek culture, he denies, by the intermediary of his preacher, that any Jew could have written the fourth gospel. As proof, the preacher seizes upon John 13.34: "I give you a new commandment: love one another." He explodes this claim by quoting Leviticus 19.18: "You must love your neighbor as yourself." The confrontation of these two texts effectively rebuffs apologists who claim that Jesus distinguished himself from Judaism by his message of brotherly love. The preacher attributes the error to faulty translation from Hebrew—we would say Aramaic—to Greek over fifty years after Jesus' death. A copyist, he asserts, probably substituted "Je vous fais un commandement nouveau" for "Je vous fais un commandement qui n'est pas nouveau" (M. XXVI, 350). Although, scientifically speaking, this solution qualifies as no more than a hypothesis, it satisfies common sense and that, Voltaire thought, was good enough.

One finds further reinforcement of Jesus' Judaism in the *Lettres à son altesse monseigneur le prince de* [*Brunswick*], which he published in the same year. In "Sur les Juifs," he paraphrases Matthew tendentiously:

> Till heaven and earth disappear, not one dot, not one little stroke, shall disappear from the Law until its purpose is achieved. (Mt. 5.18)

> Les Juifs nous objectent que, selon Jésus-Christ, aucun point, aucun iota de la loi ne doit être transgressé. (M. XXVI, 515)

The shift in meaning from the durability of the Law to Jesus' recommendation of the strictest obedience to it may be subtle, but it serves Voltaire's purpose too well to have come from a lapse in memory. In the context, he furnishes habitual evidence of Jesus' fidelity to Judaism in order to separate him from Christianity.

He also incorporates this theme in the *Dîner du comte de Boulainvilliers* (1767), although he fails to give it any interesting new twist. He antedated this publication 1728 and attributed it to Saint-Hyacinthe, a dead enemy. During the first two months of 1768, in fact, he insisted on this date and attribution in his correspondence, thus cultivating the scandal raised by the work. In the *Dîner*, he supposes the conversation at a dinner party to which the count and countess de Boulainvilliers have invited Fréret and the abbé Couet, vicar-general to the archbishop of Paris, Cardinal de Noailles. Couet may to some extent represent the archbishop, a notoriously fainthearted Jansenist, for the abbé's defense of Christianity tends to betray it. The author of the

Dîner obviously knew of Boulainvilliers and Fréret's secret, free-thinking activity, even if they had not admitted him to their circle as Pomeau argues.[175] Together with the countess, they torment the Epicurian *abbé*, who has no peace before, during, or after dinner, the periods into which Voltaire divides the dialogue.

The count sets the tone by confronting Couet with several passages from the Bible[176] that "effrayent le sens commun et l'humanité" (*Dial.* p. 183).[177] Later, pressed by the count for an explanation of why Christianity condemns the great pagans, Couet confesses his sympathy for them. If only Scipion, Cicero, Epictetus, and Antonius had known of the Spirit's procession, the Son's engenderment, and his possession of everything belonging to the Father except paternity! "Quels avantages n'auraient-ils procuré aux hommes" (*Dial.* p. 185)! Had these great men investigated consubstantiality and transubstantiation, they could have been vicars-general to the archbishop. Thus Couet' subaltern vanity blinds him to a superiority exceeding that of his own pious, but weak master. The essential step in Voltaire's transformation of the historical Couet into a caricature of the priesthood was probably the amputation of his common sense. The uncritical Couet in the *Dîner* has naturally become the docile tool of the hierarchy. On the other hand, Boulainvilliers, to whom Voltaire assigns his own antichristian preoccupations, plays the role of a commonsense judge.

During the meal, the count subjects the second coming to a destructive analysis, beginning with quotations from Luke 21 concerning the kingdom of God, among them verse 32: "Before this generation has passed away, all will have taken place." Yielding to the Voltairian taste for hyperbole, he declares this passage explicit, detailed, and false. "Il faudrait être fou," he remarks, "pour oser dire... que le fils de l'homme vint dans une nuée avec une grande puissance" (*Dial.* p. 193). Unsatisfied merely to expose the failure of the prophecy to come true, he speculates on its source. It is known, he claims, that

[175] "Voltaire avait eu des relations avec le célèbre comte de Boulainvilliers, animateur... d'une importante 'coterie.' Fut-il initié à ses mystères? Il ne semble pas" (Pomeau, *La Religion*, p. 96). Perhaps not initiated, but certainly aware by 1767!

[176] "Contrains-les d'entrer" (Lk. 14.23). "Je suis venu apporter le glaive et non la paix" (Mt. 10.34). "Que celui qui n'écoute pas l'Eglise soit regardé comme un païen, ou comme un receveur des deniers publics" (Mt. 18.17). "Je leur parle en paraboles, afin qu'en voyant ils ne voient point, et qu'en écoutant ils n'entendent point" (Mt. 13.13). "Je n'ai été envoyé qu'au troupeau d'Israël" (Mt. 15.24). "Les rois ne reçoivent les impôts que des étrangers, et les enfants en sont exempts" (Mt. 17.24-26).

[177] Later, in a summary of the abbé de Saint-Pierre's thought, he describes the Bible as "un gros livre qui est le tombeau du sens commun" (*Dial.*, p. 210).

> le dogme de la fin du monde et de l'établissement d'un monde nouveau était une chimère reçue chez presque tous les peuples. (*Dial.* p. 193)

The half-Jewish, half-Christian evangelists,[178] he says, adopted this doctrine. As Jesus failed to reappear at the end of each period estimated by Christian interpretors of the prophecy, they simply extended their estimate. The count illustrates this maneuver by an anecdote about a charlatan operating at the end of the Pont-Neuf. For eight days, the charlatan announced that he would cut his cock's throat and resuscitate it immediately if people bought his medicine. Although his medicine sold well, he never kept his promise. The story has a moral: "La farce de l'attente de la fin du monde, dans le christianisme, a duré huit siècles" (*Dial.* p. 193). Couet has no reply to this assault on his religion and church. Voltaire realized that, when Jesus, according to the synoptic gospels, prophesied the kingdom of God in the immediate future, he permanently frustrated all attempts to prove his divinity before the tribunal of reason.

In keeping with his newfound respect for the Socrates of Galilee, however, he was anxious to defend Jesus' human dignity against the superstitious encroachments of Christians. In a protest against the ridicule they inflict on him, the count deplores "le pigeon qui... engrosse [la vierge Marie]" (*Dial.* p. 197). An ugly insinuation lurks behind this joke. It not only implies the absurdity of a pregnant virgin, but also the bestiality of impregnation by a bird, accentuated by Voltaire's habitual substitution of a vulgar pigeon for the usual dove.

In the *Dîner*, the scholar Fréret is a more ruthless partisan of the natural light than Boulainvilliers, although Voltaire supplies him with few original arguments. One exception nonetheless deserves attention here. In reviewing the more shameful events in Fleury's *Histoire ecclésiastique*, Fréret cites "les athanasiens et les ariens remplissant l'empire romain de carnage pour une diphtongue" (*Dial.* p. 199). To be sure, the originality of this remark is only verbal. The conflict between proponents of *homoiosios* and *homoousios*, between similarity and identity of the divine substance, had drawn ample comment before Voltaire. A radical Arian faction clung to similarity, while a moderate faction eventually compromised with the Athanasians on the basis of identity, which therefore became orthodox. A minor modification in the morphology of an exotic word hardly conveyed to ordinary readers the importance of the distinction indicated. Again Voltaire neglects the political rivalries behind the doctrinal struggle and emphasizes the resulting bloodshed to illustrate his theme of

[178] This description applies to Matthew and John at best.

much ado about nothing. The Trinity re-emerges as the product of undignified haggling.

Such reasoning by Fréret and Boulainvilliers eventually drives the phlegmatic Couet to something like revolt, but only after dinner:

> Quand même on mépriserait assez la consubstantialité et la procession du Saint-Esprit par le Père et le Fils... vous resteriez encore chrétiens. (*Dial.* p. 206)

These concessions by the exasperated vicar-general expose the superficiality of his adherence to dogmas he and his fellows require others to believe. Realizing that Couet has practically sacrificed orthodox Christianity for social tranquillity, Fréret moderates his tone. He agrees that the word *chrétien* will subsist, but

> on adorera Dieu sans mélange, sans lui donner ni une mère, ni un fils... sans lui dire qu'il est mort par un supplice infâme. (*Dial.* p. 207)

This remark recalls the objection to associates given God in the *Sermon des cinquante* (see p. 146). Fréret is removing anthropomorphic accretions in the form of family relations from the concept of the divinity. His edifying commentary on Couet's grudging conversion to "reasonable" Christianity provides Voltaire with the transition to deism which he needs to conclude the conversation. Although greed, a customary clergical vice,[179] has brought the vicar-general to Boulainvilliers' table, he receives more intellectual nourishment than he bargained for.[180]

Le Pyrrhonisme de l'histoire,[181] which Voltaire probably wrote in 1768, is a very different kind of work. Although he assigned this essay to "un bachelier en théologie" (title page), an obviously satirical ploy, he concentrates on the serious criticism of historical errors. In the second chapter, he exposes the sanction of error through eloquence and authority by Bossuet in his *Discours sur l'Histoire universelle* (1681). He illustrates this abuse by "quoting" the phrase, "*ces hérésies tant prédites par Jésus-Christ.*"[182] The phrase definitely implies that many sayings

[179] During the dinner, Couet punctuates his remarks by the phrase *à boire*.

[180] In his correspondence, Voltaire exploits the pun implicit in the title of the work, as in the following examples: "Il y a [beaucoup] de barbarie à m'attribuer un *dîner*, moi qui ne me mets plus à table" (D 14747); "[Je] suis très affligé d'un bruit qui court dans Paris, que j'ai dîné autrefois avec le comte de Boulainvilliers et l'abbé Couet" (D 14749). He especially intended such denials of what almost everyone knew he had written as publicity.

[181] Not to be confused with a preface to *L'Histoire de Charles XII* with the same title.

[182] A very inaccurate quotation. Bossuet actually wrote, "Jésus-Christ qui les a prévus et prédits [schismes et hérésies]." Jacques Bossuet, *Discours sur l'histoire universelle* in *Oeuvres complètes* (Paris, 1878), XVII, 93.

attributed to Jesus in the gospels foresee future Christian heresies. "Il n'en a parlé en aucun endroit" (M. xxvii, p. 237), Voltaire objects, a fact. Neither the word *heresy*, he adds, nor the word *dogma* appear in any gospel, also a fact, though a less significant one. The primitive notions corresponding to these concepts might be said to exist in Jesus' gospel testimony, but this proposition would require an exegesis surpassing Voltaire's intention of reaching ordinary readers. Having refuted Jesus' prediction of heresies, he attacks the necessary implication that Jesus promulgated Christian dogmas: "Jésus n'ayant annoncé par lui-même aucun dogme, ne pouvait annoncer aucune hérésie" (M. xxvii, 237). To dramatize the absurdity of Bossuet's assumption, he tells us what Jesus never said according to the gospels: "Vous croirez que je suis consubstantiel à Dieu... que le Saint-Esprit procède du Père et du Fils [etc.]" (M. xxvii, 237). Such abstractions obviously do not suit the synoptic Jesus, less obviously, the Jesus of the fourth gospel, and yet sufficiently to persuade anyone familiar with that work too. Putting them in Jesus' mouth makes him appear vain and petty, thus distorting his character insofar as it is known. Voltaire realized that assigning the language of dogma to him would illuminate the contrast between his rudimentary Judaism and the Hellenistic sophistication of Christianity. He concludes this development in his criticism of Bossuet by the remarks that Jesus never said a word, either about dogmas then unknown or "les contestations qu'ils excitèrent longtemps après lui" (M. xxvii, 237). Absolving Jesus of the conflicts from which dogma emerged amounts to impugning Bossuet's conception of Church authority.

Voltaire included further comment on Jesus in *L'Epître aux Romains* (1768), a satiric imitation of the epistles written by Paul, whose title he borrowed. Count Passeran,[183] the author he alleged this time, describes himself as a Roman nobleman in exile. Supposedly translated from an Italian original, his epistle deplores the Christian fate of Rome and his fellow Romans, to whom he addresses it. In "Article v," he imagines what would have happened if Paul, Peter, Matthew, or Luke had appeared before the senate to relate the version of Jesus' life in the (synoptic) gospels. Voltaire as usual designed this testimony, most of which concerns the mythical nativity material, as an invitation to derision. At the end of the story, he inserts a modification of his habitual remark about Jesus' public crucifixion and private resurrection:

[183] Count de Corbera in the 1775 "encadrée" edition of the *Oeuvres complètes*.

> Pontius le fait pendre... Jésus ressuscite secrètement, monte au ciel, et envoie publiquement un autre Dieu, qui tombe en plusieurs langues de feu sur les têtes de ses disciples. (M. xxvii, 92)

The missionary addressing the senate then expresses the hope that these tongues of flame will fall on the heads of his listeners. Passeran surmises that the least of the ushers in the senate could have delivered a scornful refutation of this testimony.[184] The sending of another God who fell in flames on the disciples' heads and the parallel hope that they will likewise fall on the heads of the senate probably impressed Voltaire's readers as ludicrously impertinent. Their classical education suggested an absurd contrast between the dignity and wisdom of the listeners and the enthusiastic presumption of the speaker. Our understanding of the Roman and other senates does not inspire the same respect. Consequently, Voltaire's performance seems dull, despite his masterful control of a dialogue related by a persona.

One comes to expect at least routine mockery of Jesus' miracles in such works, but Passeran does a little better than that when he traces several of them to pagan sources:

> Athalie, Hippolyte, Alceste, Pélops, Hérès étaient ressuscités quand on ne parlait pas encore de la résurrection de Jésus, et Romulus était né d'une vestale plus de sept cents ans avant que Jésus passât pour être né d'une vierge.[185] (M. xxvii, 89)

He belittles the resurrection by the number of pagan precedents and the virgin birth by the antiquity of the precedent. These arguments break the usual standoff between apologists and critics over the priority of Christianity or paganism in such matters. Satisfied with his commonsense proof, Voltaire left to science the far greater difficulty of determining whether these Christian myths actually derived from the pagan sources he cites.

In "Article Premier," he found a way to combine his opposition to the papacy with his criticism of the second coming: "Si Jésus ne vint pas dans les nuées avec une grande puissance, du moins les papes ont eu cette grande puissance" (M. xxvii, 84). The unaccomplished prediction of heavenly power clashes ironically with the unpredicted ac-

[184] Voltaire provides a partial example of such a refutation: "Vous êtes des fourbes... Vous en avez menti... Vous êtes des ignorants" (M. xxvii, 92).

[185] Voltaire apparently meant *Athalides*. For Athalides, Hippolytus, Alcestis, and Romulus, see n. 86 above. Voltaire borrowed these examples from Meslier and that of Pelops as well: "Pélops fils de Tantale, roi de Phrygie, ayant été mis en pièces par son père pour le faire manger aux dieux, eux... ramassèrent tous ses membres, les réunirent et lui rendirent la vie" (Meslier, i, 184).

complishment of earthly power. Passeran is implying the spiritual failure and the temporal success of an ideology dependent upon the supremacy of spiritual over temporal values. This implication serves to remind his fellow Romans that the pope has usurped power over them on the pretext of spiritual sovereignty. Passeran's predictable criticism of dogmatic development includes a lengthy quotation from the *Apostolic Constitutions*, which had come to Voltaire's attention in the early sixties. Apparently written between 380 and 430, this document expresses the opinion either of an Apollinarian or an Arian, for it tends both to deny Jesus a human soul and subordinate him to God. Voltaire, who believed it to date from the second century, accepted it as evidence that Trinitarian and Christological dogma had changed since then. "Vous y trouverez bien trois personnes," Passeran informs the Romans, "mais jamais trois personnes en un seul Dieu" (M. xxvii, 99). The text, he continues, says nothing of consubstantiality. Further on, he compares the apotheosis of Jesus with that of Bacchus, Perseus, Hercules, and Romulus, who are familiar to his Roman correspondents,[186] and then protests against elevating a mortal to the status of the Creator. These stern lamentations by a noble Roman exile conforming to Voltaire's classical nostalgia may well have struck a deep chord in his contemporaries, but his pathos has lesser impact on modern readers who do not share his idealistic illusions. Under these circumstances, the repetitive aspects of his antitrinitarian and antichristological satire do not rekindle for us here. One regrets that his creation of a new subgenre, the satiric epistle,[187] which supplements a genre including the sermon and the catechism, did not yield more captivating results.

A moral flaw rather than an anachronistic flaw mars the *Discours aux confédérés catholiques de Kaminiek en Pologne* (1768), for it condones the military intervention in that country by Catherine the Great of Russia.[188] The Prussian Major Kaiserling, a dead acquaintance of Voltaire, delivers this condescending appeal for tolerance, a variation on the satiric sermon. Yet any consideration of Poland inevitably re-

[186] All of these figures were thought to be the offspring of a god and a woman. Hercules and Romulus underwent an apotheosis.

[187] He was probably thinking of Paul's Epistle to the Romans.

[188] Kaminiec-Litewski is 200 km. east of Warsaw. Roman Dyboski says that the Russians intervened on the pretext of settling religious unrest caused by nonconformist Protestant sects. "The result was a civil war in Poland, which was in reality a war between Russian troops and the Roman Catholic gentry who had formed a confederation in the town of Bar (1768) to oppose Russian intervention" (pp. 129-30). The war led to the partition of Poland between Prussia, Austria, and Russia in 1772. Dyboski, *Outlines of Polish History* (London, 1925).

minded Voltaire of Socinianism, even though the movement had practically disappeared, and we find him true to form in this work. Kaiserling reassures his Catholic audience of "l'utilité des sociniens," "ces impies qui s'en tiennent à l'Evangile et qui n'y ont jamais vu que Jésus s'appelât Dieu, ni qu'il ait parlé de la Trinité" (Mac. p. 393). Although his Protestant background and Frederickian service shift the accent of this humorless irony away from Voltaire, they do not suggest a very interesting point of view. For this reason, his spokesman does not succeed in renovating these threadbare themes, but he does illustrate his point by an amusing example, which comes as welcome relief in the arid *Discours*. A Socinian cook, Kaiserling affirms, will do a better job than any papist cook:

> Si vous ordonnez à un rôtisseur papiste de vous mettre trois pigeons à la broche, il sera tenté d'en manger deux, et de ne vous en donner qu'un, en disant que trois et un font la même chose. (Mac. p. 393)

The pragmatic major reduces theology to the status of cookery, the Trinity to the kind of theft occurring in the kitchens of prelates, and the three persons, instead of the usual third alone, to a common species of bird. This complex reduction conveys the further notion that these persons are merely ornithologic projections, unified by a deliberate contradiction under the guise of sacred mystery to avoid the stigma of polytheism. The wit encapsuled in the joke about papist cooks, however, exceeds Major Kaiserling's usual performance in the *Discours*.

"Compère Mathieu," the ostensible author of Voltaire's *Relation du banissement des Jésuites de la Chine* (1768), inspired a far more lively text. The abbé du Laurens had published a licentious novel entitled *Le Compère Mathieu ou les Bigarrures de l'esprit humain* (1766) which had been attributed to Voltaire. Since this novel enjoyed some popularity, he does not seem to have resented the attribution. In a letter to Bordes, he affectionately describes the *Relation* as

> une plaisanterie infernale de ce Maturin[189] Laurent, réfugié à Amsterdam chez Marc Michel Rey.[190] C'est un drôle qui a quelque esprit, un peu d'érudition et qui rencontre quelquefois. (April 4, 1768)

Du Laurens' pseudonym suited Voltaire for the *Relation*, because the abbé's publication of a violent satire against the Jesuits and the other Catholic orders[191] had forced him to leave France in 1761. The Paris

[189] For Mathieu. Voltaire frequently altered names for satiric effect.
[190] Huguenot publisher in Amsterdam who published many of Rousseau's works and some of Voltaire's.
[191] *Le Balai, poème héroï-comique*.

Parlement, which was proceeding against the Jesuits then, dissolved the Company a year later.

Their downfall in Europe naturally reminded Voltaire of their expulsion from China in 1724 by the emperor Yung-Cheng. The *Relation* presents an interview between this emperor and Brother Rigolet, whom the Company has chosen to represent it rather for his zeal than his intelligence. "Il avait toute la simplicité de l'enthousiasme d'un persuadé" (*Dial.* p. 219), in other words, no common sense at all. Rigolet's naïve account of the nativity astonishes and confuses the emperor:

> Un Dieu charpentier! un Dieu né d'une femme! (*Dial.* p. 221)
>
> Dieu coucha avec sa mère pour naître ensuite d'elle? (*Dial.* p. 222)

Voltaire achieves both effects by a logical interpretation of Trinitarian unity. The identity of God with a carpenter (Jesus) relegates the Creator to making things out of wood. The Creator's birth from his own creature reverses the logical order of their relationship to each other. Rigolet compounds the disproportion between child and mother by the disproportion between the divine and human partners in the act of reproduction. The identity of father and child implies an incestuous absurdity, which the salacious reputation of Mathieu amplifies.

Rigolet's opacity to the natural light continues to contrast with the emperor's transparency. Fascinated by the prospect of baptizing a Chinese emperor, he mistakes his astonisment for inspiration: "Vous y êtes, Sacrée Majesté, la grâce opère déjà" (*Dial.* p. 222). On the simple foundation he believes the emperor to have assimilated, he builds a more complicated edifice, a method familiar to Voltaire, former pupil of the Jesuits: "Dieu se changea en pigeon pour faire un enfant à la femme d'un charpentier, et cet enfant fut Dieu lui-même" (*Dial.* p. 222). This circular series of transformations inflicts the even more demeaning creaturely state of pigeon on the Creator, implicates the mother of God in bestiality as we have seen before, and suggests animal worship, a shocking insult to Christianity. The emperor's difficulty in keeping track of God's metamorphoses relegates the Trinity to the status of a satiric plaything. As His Majesty puzzles over the Christian worship of two Gods, a carpenter and a pigeon, Rigolet hastens to add a third, the father of the other two. According to him, therefore, God begets a bird as well as a human, as if he were supplementing his creative activity by heteroclite sexual reproduction. Unaware of these damaging implications, Rigolet burdens His Majesty's tolerance with an ultimate absurdity: "au fond, ces trois dieux n'en font qu'un" (*Dial.* p. 222).

Complimenting him nonetheless on the clarity of his teaching, the emperor reasons: "Si ton dieu est né, il est sans doute mort" (*Dial.* p. 223)? Imagine the Jesuit's delight! He eagerly supplements the story of Jesus' beginning by that of his end:

> Il déguisa si bien sa divinité qu'il se laissa fouetter et pendre malgré ses miracles; mais aussi il ressuscita deux jours après sans que personne le vît, et s'en retourna au ciel. (*Dial.* p. 223)

Voltaire was exposing none of these ideas for the first time. As usual, the degrading circumstances of Jesus' execution reinforce the evidence of death itself, which convinces common sense of his humanity. As usual, the lack of disinterested witnesses to Jesus' resuscitation and ascension, both of which violate natural laws, excites suspicion of fraud. Later, the emperor returns to Jesus' death when Rigolet, itching for a conversion, offers him sainthood. For the sake of diplomacy, His Majesty makes an enigmatic reply:

> Tout ce que je demande, c'est que je ne sois pas pendu comme ton dieu l'a été: car il me semble que c'est acheter la divinité un peu cher. (*Dial.* p. 227)

The commercial phraseology, which facetiously suits Rigolet's attitude, insinuates that this divinity is a bad bargain. The remark exposes the contradictions between immortality and mortality in the doctrine of the two natures. Elsewhere, we find Rigolet interpreting Jesus' anticipation of the kingdom of God in Luke 21.8-36 as a prophecy of the second coming. "Le malheur est qu'il ne revint point" (*Dial.* p. 223), laments Rigolet, thus revitalizing the argument by infusing it with comic disappointment. His good humor, self-assurance, and innocence in fact save the entire *Relation* from the pitfall of routine. The emperor himself acknowledges his indefatigable charm: "Viens, frère Rigolet, que je t'embrasse" (*Dial.* p. 223). Already informed by someone else, no doubt, His Majesty then asks about the God who preceded the one born, whipped, hung, and buried. The Jesuit recites the Voltairian repertory of absurdities from the Old Testament characterizing Yahweh.[192] When he has finished his testimony, the emperor passes judgment on Roman Christianity. His tribunals, he tells Rigolet, do not take offence over the absurdities of his faith:

[192] "Celui-là ne se laissait pas pendre comme l'autre... Il s'avisa de prendre sous sa protection une horde de voleurs et de meurtriers, en faveur de laquelle il égorgea... tous les bestiaux et tous les fils aînés des familles d'Egypte [etc.]" (*Dial.*, p. 223).

> Ils vous plaignent d'être infatués du plus détestable ramas de fables que la folie humaine ait jamais accumulées; ils plaignent encore plus le malheureux usage que vous faites du peu de raison qui vous reste pour justifier ces fables. (*Dial.* p. 232)

Belief in the dogma necessitates the outright abandonment of reason; defense of the faith requires subversion of the natural light. The *saint* and *sot* Rigolet,[193] who allegedly exemplifies Jesuit Christianity, has in fact demonstrated both kinds of aberration. The emperor, therefore, according to Compère Mathieu, does not expel the Jesuits for their faith, but rather because they blindly serve "l'ambition d'un petit lama italien" (*Dial.* p. 232), who has a reputation for interfering in foreign countries. This is obviously the justice of an enlightened monarch.

Voltaire's Yung-Cheng has little to do with the historical model,[194] whose name and banishment of the Jesuits he adapted to his antichristian project. In the *Relation*, the wit and tolerance of the emperor contrast with the ignorance and zeal of Rigolet, yet both win the readers' affection. A self-defeating spokesman of the cause he defends, the Jesuit unwittingly sharpens Voltaire's blunted weapons. Not only does Voltaire endow this clown with unusual vitality, but also he incarnates in him the Jesuit's well-known flexibility in the interpretation of Christianity for the benefit of prospective converts. The satire of Christology and the Trinity in this work eclipses that of others published in 1768. Though interesting in their own right, the *Conseils raisonnables à M. Bergier*, the *Homélie du pasteur Bourne*, and the *Instruction du gardien des capucins de Raguse* are largely repetitive in this respect.

Dieu et les hommes

This repetition continued in 1769, another year of heavy production. Only one work is of significance here, *Dieu et les hommes par le docteur Obern*, supposedly translated from the English. Plain, as Voltaire's

[193] "On demandait un jour à Oliva, général des jésuites, comme il se pouvait faire qu'il y eût tant de sots dans une société qui passait pour éclairée; il répondit: *Il nous faut des saints*. Ainsi donc saint Rigolet comparut devant l'empereur de la Chine" (*Dial.*, p. 219).

[194] Yung-Cheng was far less decisive than Voltaire implies in the *Relation*. He merely ratified a ban of the Christian cult by the viceroy of Fukien in 1724, then conceded a request by the Jesuits at his court to go to Canton instead of Macao. The missionaries were allowed to return in secret until 1732, when they were ordered to Macao. Yet Jesuits were allowed to remain in Canton and Peking. Once again, the emperor was on the verge of banishing them, but the Jesuits managed to have the decision postponed until the end of Yung-Cheng's reign in 1735. See Arnold Rowbotham, *Missionary and Mandarin* (Berkeley, 1935), pp. 196 ff.

Englishmen go, Obern does not particularly succeed in giving new life to a worn repertory. The work nonetheless differs from the others we have examined, in that Voltaire's polemic against the atheism of d'Holbach and his group alter his antitrinitarian and antichristological propaganda. Otherwise, it resembles the *Examen important*, from which Voltaire simply lifted chapters seven through nine in *Dieu*. It begins as a natural history of religion, but after a survey of ancient cults, Voltaire narrows the scope to the Judeo-Christian tradition and eventually, to the usual shortcomings of Christianity itself. He corrects one error in the *Examen* by admitting that the idea of a messiah characterized the thinking of Jesus' contemporaries and makes another by claiming that the Jewish people had no need for a liberator.

Chapter 31, "De Jésus," begins with a vociferous defense of the right to "examiner l'histoire de Jésus par les lumières de la raison," but Obern cannot resist the Voltairian urge to examine it with someone else's reason, that of a "citoyen de l'ancienne Rome qui lirait les histoires de Jésus pour la première fois" (M. xxviii, 194). In the event that Obern's phlegm does not guarantee equity of judgment, the citizen of ancient Rome, who never heard of Jesus, can have no prejudice against him. The question of whether Jesus ever really existed, gives Voltaire the opportunity to review several ancient contemporaries who do not mention him, Josephus, Justus of Tiberiade, and Philo. The Roman infers that, although Jesus existed, he was obscure. This question decided, he asks another: "Qui était cet homme? Le fils reconnu d'un charpentier de village: les deux partis en conviennent" (M. xxviii, 196). The two factions, as Voltaire saw them, are represented by the gospels in Greek on one hand and, on the other, the *Toldoth Jeschu*, which he continued to date from the early second century. They agree on the identity of the man socially accepted as Jesus' father, but they disagree on that of his natural father. Jews of the *Jeschu* tendency consider him the bastard son of the soldier Panther, while Christians worship him as the Son of God in a genetic sense. The disinterested Roman rejects these extremes and proposes a commonsense solution, one "qui est plus naturel[le]": Mary's husband, "qui lui fit d'autres enfants, lui fit encore celui-là" (M. xxviii, 196). Thus Voltaire abandoned the illegitimacy of Jesus, which he had probably held from the beginning of his antichristian career (see p. 112). This opinion apparently seemed too radical to him in 1769, perhaps because it was advancing the cause of atheism more rapidly than that of deism. The propaganda pouring from d'Holbach's "synagogue" drove him to the defensive tactic of playing extremes against each other. He was beginning to find truth in moderation, a change that had its impact on his conception of the natural light.

This new conservatism does not inhibit his criticism everywhere in *Dieu*. The next chapter gives more serious consideration than ever before to the possibility that Jesus was a violent revolutionary, a surprisingly modern theory. Here Voltaire ponders the account in the *Toldoth Jeschu* of armed resistance by two thousand followers before Jesus' arrest. Though unaware of the work's medieval origin, he might have substantiated his case by the episode in all four gospels telling how one of Jesus' followers struck off the ear of a servant in the arresting party with his sword. But this incident only convinces him, or so he says, of Jesus' pacifism. Espousing the Roman viewpoint, he concludes that, if armed resistance actually occurred, "Jésus aurait été aussi criminel que Barcochébas" (M. XXVIII, 197), or Bar Kokhba. His reverence for Latin antiquity precluded any sympathy with the Jewish remembrance of this national hero.

Curiously, he seems less inclined to believe the Temple cleansing in all four gospels than the armed violence in the *Toldoth*, although the cleansing is undoubtedly the strongest available evidence of violence committed by Jesus:

> Il est bien difficile que des marchands établis par les magistrats se soient laissé battre et chasser par un étranger sans aveu, arrivé de son village dans la capitale, à moins qu'il n'ait eu beaucoup de monde à sa suite. (M. XXVIII, 199)

Apparently, it did not occur to him to explore the possibility that, despite the silence of the gospels, many followers and perhaps armed followers helped him expel the Temple merchants. Obern leaves protest to freethinkers like Woolston[195] and Bolingbroke, who find Jesus' act

> aussi répréhensible que si un fanatique s'ingérait parmi nous de fouetter les libraires qui vendent auprès de Saint-Paul le livre des *Communes prières*. (M. XXVIII, 198-99)

Such an incident would indeed parallel Jesus' act, because *The Book of Common Prayer* is as necessary an accessory in the service of the Church of England as sacrificial animals were in the Temple worship of first-century Israel. Though eclipsed by Canterbury, St. Paul's in

[195] "Woolston dira, tant qu'on voudra, que Simone Barjone coupant l'oreille au sergent Malchus, et Jésus rendant au sergent son oreille, est un des plus impertinents contes que le fanatisme idiot ait pu imaginer... Il prouve du moins que l'auteur, quel qu'il soit, regardait Jésus comme un homme pacifique" (M. XXVIII, 202).

London enjoys somewhat the same kind of prestige as the Temple in Jerusalem did. An assault on booksellers authorized to sell the prayerbook on the cathedral grounds would indeed have caused a scandal in the eighteenth century just as Jesus' disruption of the Temple concessions almost certainly did in the first. Voltaire therefore reconstitutes Jesus' act in a frame of reference familiar to Obern, thus making it accessible to the common sense of his readers. The rest of *Dieu* offers little of interest to us here for, when it does not suffer from repetition of earlier works, it belabors points made more effectively elsewhere.

Questions sur l'Encyclopédie

The same faults detract from the *Questions sur l'Encyclopédie*, an alphabetical work inspired by rivalry with the Encyclopedia. Voltaire had already published most of the best articles in the *Dictionnaire philosophique*. The first edition appeared in 1771 and the second, with substantial additions, in 1772. While none of the new material greatly supplemented or varied what he had previously written on Christology or the Trinity, there are interesting allusions to these subjects in articles on other topics.

He subtitled "Miracles" III (1771)[196] "De ceux qui ont eu la témérité impie de nier absolument la réalité des miracles de Jésus-Christ." He devoted this section to applause for three clergymen who had turned against the clergy, Woolston, Meslier, and Antoine, but only his treatment of the first and the last offer anything of interest to us here. As for Woolston,

> Aucun prêtre ne se déclara plus ouvertement ennemi des prêtres. Il osait même autoriser cette haine de celle de Jésus Christ envers les pharisiens et les scribes. (*Dict.* p. 583)

In attacking the Christian priesthood, Woolston was therefore conscious of imitating Jesus. Evidently, Voltaire is hinting at further evidence of the contradiction between Christianity and its unknowing founder. Woolston's picturesque iconoclasm likewise interested him and he delighted in the names the Englishman had dared to call Jesus:

> un vagabond, un gueux... un frère quêteur... qui, avant de se faire prédicateur de grand chemin, n'avait été qu'un misérable garçon charpentier. (*Dict.* p. 583)

[196] Section IV in M.

Why is there no relic from his workbench in Rome, no wooden stool or nutcracker?[197] It is Woolston's audacity that fascinated him, for even he had never dared to write such insults against Jesus. This scorn for humble, parasitic, and wandering occupations flattered his bourgeois snobbery. Woolston's relegation of Jesus to the very bottom of the social scale served as a blasphemous antidote for apologetic poison, but Voltaire refused to accept responsibility for it: "C'est à regret, c'est en tremblant que je rapporte ces passages" (*Dict.* p. 584). The first remark is a playful lie and the second an ironical truth, since it really denotes fear of retaliation and not fear of sacrilege, as its association with the first one implies. In the spirit of the *Lettres philosophiques*, Voltaire nonetheless emphasizes the Englishman's freedom to publish and even sell such a book at his place of residence. He does not mention that Woolston spent the rest of his life in confinement for it. Woolston's scepticism over the resuscitation of three dead bodies by Jesus, those of Lazarus, Jarius' daughter, and the son of Nain's widow,[198] also figures in "Miracles" III. The Englishman dwells on the enormous publicity these miracles would have generated throughout the Roman Empire, an argument in which Voltaire himself had great confidence:

> Trois morts rendus à la vie auraient été trois témoignages de la divinité de Jésus, qui auraient rendu en un moment le monde entier chrétien. (*Dict.* p. 584)

Although the gospels make much of public enthusiasm over these miracles, it is true that non-Christians do not mention them anywhere. Voltaire draws no conclusions, but Woolston is clearly undermining the proof of Jesus' divinity by his ability to raise the dead.

While Woolston had rebelled against the Anglican hierarchy and Meslier had left a posthumous repudiation of his Catholic priesthood, Nicolas Antoine, a Calvinist minister after conversion from Catholicism, had finally embraced Jewish monotheism. Voltaire wholeheartedly approves the second conversion in his commentary: "Il n'y a qu'un Dieu" (*Dict.* p. 587). In his Genevan trial, Antoine was accused of blasphemy against the Trinity and Christ, of declaring Christ an idol and denying that Christ had been the true messiah,

[197] "During the time of his ministry, he was but a wanderer, like a mendicant friar, or an itinerant preacher; and before that time was no better than a journey-man carpenter (of whose workshop I wonder the Church of Rome has no holy relics, not so much as a three-footed stool or a pair of nutcrackers)." Thomas Woolston, *Third Discourse on the Miracles of our Saviour* (London, 1728), p. 8.

[198] Lazarus: Jn. 11; Jairus' daughter: Mk. 5.22-24, 35-43; Lk. 8.41-42, 49-56; Mt. 9.18-19, 23-26; son of Nain's widow: Lk. 7.11-17.

whom he continued to expect. When he led his congregation in the recitation of words about Christ in the Apostle's Creed, "il marmonnait entre ses dents."[199] In short, an ideal antipriest and antitrinitarian saint! In his review of the trial, Voltaire concedes the presence of moderate ministers in the consistory of seventeenth-century Geneva. They proposed to treat Antoine for madness, he says:

> On l'accoutumerait insensiblement à prononcer le nom de Jésus-Christ, ou du moins à l'entendre prononcer sans grincer des dents. (*Dict*. p. 587)

Since Antoine did suffer from attacks of insanity, gnashing his teeth over Jesus' name seems appropriate. The ministers recognizing that Antoine was no serious threat to Calvinism opposed more numerous colleagues who gnashed their teeth over the word *tolerance*. These gentlemen were "charmés... de [l']occasion de faire brûler un homme, ce qui arrivait très rarement" (*Dict*. p. 588). They condemned him to burn at the stake and the miraculous survival of Sidrak, Meshak, and Abednego did not recur (Da. 3.94). "[Antoine] ne pleura point," remarks Voltaire, who credited the *Toldoth* account of Jesus weeping when arrested.[200] He thought Antoine a more respectable martyr and, since Antoine had died for monotheism, Voltaire probably looked upon him as a kind of deist martyr.

The claim that the prophets in the Old Testament heralded Jesus, Christology, and the Trinity undergoes further strictures in "Prophéties" II (1771).[201] This article opposes the opinion of Jewish rabbis to that of Christian theologians, as the first sentence suggests:

> Il n'appartient qu'à l'Eglise infaillible de fixer le véritable sens des prophéties: car les Juifs ont soutenu avec leur opiniâtreté ordinaire qu'aucune prophétie ne pouvait regarder Jésus-Christ. (M. XX, 288)

He reinforces his ironical objection to their obstinacy by ironical regrets that, of all the Fathers, only Ephraem,[202] Origen, and Jerome knew Hebrew. He sabotages the infallibility proclaimed in the opening sentence by presenting the systematic refutation of the Christian

[199] "Il aurait blasphémé contre la sainte trinité et la personne de notre seigneur Jésus-Christ, soutenant tant de bouche que par écrit que c'était une idole... En récitant les paroles du Symbole des Apôtres où il est parlé de notre seigneur Jésus-Christ... il marmonnait entre ses dents." Trial record in Julien Weill, "Nicolas Antoine," *Revue des études juives*, 37 (1898), 179-80.

[200] "Il fut arrêté, se mit à pleurer, demanda pardon, mais en vain: on le fouetta, on le lapida, et ensuite on le pendit:" thus Voltaire summarizes the *Toldoth* in the *Examen important* (M. XXVI, 223).

[201] III in M.

[202] Who spent most of his life in Edessa and died in 379.

position in Isaac Ben Abraham's *Ramparts of the Faith*.[203] Isaac demonstrates that all of the prophecies applied to Jesus actually refer to someone else and that the Trinity is nowhere to be found in the Old Testament. His erudition therefore wrecks the thesis that the prophets support the divinity of Jesus by their miraculous foreknowledge of what Christians believe about him and the Trinity. Having listed a number of examples drawn from the *Ramparts*, Voltaire assumes a third position, the impossibility of penetrating the sense of the prophecies to begin with:

> Si un Chinois, un Tartare, un Africain, réduit au malheur de n'avoir que du bon sens, lisait toutes ces prophéties, il lui serait impossible d'en faire application, ni à Jésus-Christ, ni aux Juifs, ni à personne. (M. xx, 291)

To good sense guaranteed by ignorance of Christianity as well as indifference to it, the prophecies mean nothing. In Voltaire's opinion, the question of whether they apply to Jesus is therefore vain.

The "Christianisme," which, in 1772, he substituted for the *Dictionnaire* article with the same title, continued the trend of sympathy for the historical Jesus. After elaboration on the multiplicity of enthusiastic sects among the common people of Palestine, he reminds us nonchalantly, "on s'imagina que le monde était près de sa fin." One of the rare sarcasms in the article follows:

> Ce fut dans ces temps préparés par la divine Providence qu'il plut au Père éternel d'envoyer son Fils sur la terre: mystère adorable et incompréhensible auquel nous ne touchons pas. (M. xviii, 162)

Although he does not specifically say so, Providence appears to have prepared the arrival of God's Son by the proliferation of enthusiastic and eschatological sectarianism. The ironical reversal of what he sees as cause and effect constitutes the unquestionable mystery referred to after the colon. The exaggerated respect for this mystery incites the suspicion that, in reality, eschatological enthusiasm inspired the illusion of God's Son arriving on earth.

In "Religion" ii (1771), Voltaire has Jesus himself dissipate such illusions. The unnamed narrator of this section relates his voyage to a Voltairian afterworld somewhere in space. Here he discovers the bones of many millions who have died in religious conflicts, nearly all of them victims of Judeo-Christian conflicts. At the end of each aisle between the piles of bones stands a "hero of humanity" contemplating

[203] Voltaire found this work along with the *Toldoth* in Johann-Christopher Wagenseil, *Tela ignes satanae* (1681), a work in his library at Ferney.

them with compassion. Having questioned several of them, the narrator passes from Socrates to

> un homme d'une figure douce et simple, qui me parut âgé d'environ trente-cinq ans... Je fus étonné de lui trouver les pieds enflés et sanglants, les mains de même, le flanc percé, et les côtes écorchées de coups de fouet. (*Dict*. p. 611)

The victim testifies that he has fallen to priestly hypocrisy. He denies that he ever intended to introduce a new religion, and insists on his fidelity to the ancient law. As for the bones lying before him, he had no part in the slaughter that occasioned them. Nor did he initiate the ritual, the opulence, and the traditions of the cult named after him. "Eh bien," responds his earthly visitor, "s'il en est ainsi, je vous prends pour mon seul maître" (*Dict*. p. 613). Why does Voltaire refuse to name his Jesus in "Religion" II? Probably because the name fatally evokes the Christian image rather than the Jewish original. Voltaire's greatest tribute to the historical Jesus therefore serves as an unconditional rejection of the Christian Jesus. Though fabulous, the testimony of his Jesus appeals directly to reason, for he has sought to render the anecdote as believable and realistic as possible.

In "Hérésies" I (1771), he further exploits the gap between Jesus and Christianity by focusing attention on the intermediary role of his disciples. The so-called Apostles' Creed, he notes, which mentions neither consubstantiality nor the Trinity, appeared only in the time of Augustine and Jerome. He complains:

> Il semble à notre faible entendement que l'on devait attendre des premiers disciples... une profession de foi complète et inaltérable, qui terminât toutes les disputes passées et qui prévînt toutes les querelles futures: Dieu ne le permit pas. (M. XVIII, 335)

From a historical point of view, this requirement seems absurdly unreasonable, and so Voltaire intended it. He is taking the Christian claim to the unique favor of God seriously. Though resigning himself (ironically) to God's decision not to assert his will and all the disastrous consequences, this very resignation dramatizes an alleged violation of reason by the author of reason himself. Voltaire is insinuating that, since God could not contradict himself, he never granted Christianity the unique favor it claims.

This uniqueness seems meaningless in view of the permanent schism between the eastern and western Churches. Dissensions between the Polish branches of each provided Voltaire with another opportunity to rub this painful truth in. "Schisme" (1772) is an extended metaphor describing the antagonism between the two churches as an epidemic:

> Les uns se sont imaginés, dans les convulsions de cette maladie, que le Saint-Esprit procédait du Père et du Fils, et les autres ont crié qu'il ne procédait que du Père. (M. xx, 402)

Voltaire usually follows such statements by facetious remarks igniting their comic potential, but that does not happen here. The passage leaves the reader with the impression that the wit which had always sparked from his pen misfired on this occasion.[204]

Despite the paucity of the antitrinitarian and antichristological material in his radical encyclopedia, it would be premature to speak of his declining creativity. Even though the early seventies were the late seventies for him, his efforts in other directions bore more delectable fruit. In 1773, he sent Frederick some verse telling of a Dantesque descent into hell where he discovers many trinities: the three rivers—Phlegethon, Cocytus, and Acheron; the triple-headed or bodied Hecate, goddess of evil; the three fates; the three-headed Cerberus, the guard dog of Hades; and the three judges—Minos, Rhadamanthys, and Aeacus:

> Que ma surprise était profonde...
> De voir ainsi de tout côté
> Des trinités dans l'autre monde. (April 22)

He then invokes "le héros qui s'est tant moqué des trinités," for Frederick's power reaches even unto hell, and by dint of this appeal the poet survives his visit. This macabre joke referred to his most recent brush with death, a forty-five minute fainting spell. All opportunities being welcome, he took advantage of this one as well to cast aspersions on trinities in general.

The Late Seventies

His energy diminished in the late seventies and Holbachian atheism continued to divert much of it from his polemic against Christianity. Thus Sherlock, the English narrator of the *Histoire de Jenni* (1775), disposes of the Trinitarian faith in Chapter 3 before devoting the rest of the work to an attack on atheism. After the capture of Barcelona by a British army, Freind, an Anglican divine, completes the conquest by victory in a debate with Papalamiendo, a bachelor from the University of Salamanca. Bluntly, Freind distinguishes between his church and Papalamiendo's: "Vous êtes esclaves d'un étranger, et nous ne som-

[204] Except for the ending perhaps: "Il se trouve des facultés de médecine à Salamanque, à Coïmbre, en Italie, à Paris même, qui soutiennent que le schisme, la déchirure, est nécessaire à l'homme... parce que la paix amène les plaisirs et les plaisirs à la longue pourraient adoucir la noble férocité qui forme les héros" (M. xx, 403).

mes soumis qu'à notre raison" (Bénac p. 499). Yet the Church of England was not as tolerant as Freind will have his opponent believe. Pride of victory or Voltairian hyperbole? Probably the latter. Freind nonetheless incarnates the natural light in *Jenni* and therefore wins all his arguments with Papalamiendo.

A caricature of scholasticism, Papalamiendo keeps trying to lure Freind into making statements vulnerable to disputation. Noting Freind's Protestant reflex of entrenching himself in Scripture, he asks him for his opinion on a Voltairian catalogue of gospel miracles, such as the annunication and the exorcism that resulted in the drowning of the two thousand pigs. But Freind limits his reply to respect for the miracles in the gospels and refuses to discuss them further on the grounds "qu'elles sont trop au-dessus de la faible raison humaine" (Bénac p. 501). This is certainly not Voltaire's opinion, but he did not want to make any concessions to d'Holbach. Papalamiendo then inquires about the Anglican refusal to designate the holy virgin as the mother of God. The Council of Ephesus in 431, Freind admits, quarreled over whether Mary was *theotikos* and

> si, Jésus-Christ étant Dieu à la fois et fils de Marie, il se pouvait que Marie fût à la fois mère de Dieu le Père et de Dieu le Fils. (Bénac p. 501)

While Voltaire modifies his presentation of the genetic contradictions between the Trinity and the incarnation, the absurdities remain the same: How can a son be identical to his father? How can a woman give birth to her sexual partner? Voltaire reconditions them nonetheless by Freind's disdain for them: "La Société royale de Londres ne s'en mêle pas" (Bénac p. 501). Voltaire implies what Freind does not express: since science, represented by the Royal Society, refuses to deal with these problems, they exist only in the imagination of theological disputants. The bachelor of theology, however, does not even understand the word *theotikos*, for he knows no Greek, an admission in which Freind promptly entraps him.

Unperturbed, Papalamiendo bombards Freind with speculative alternatives on other points. Does Jesus have one person, one nature, and one will, or two persons, two natures, and two wills, or two wills, two persons, and one nature, etc.? Voltaire is simply juggling combinations, some of which figured in ancient controversies and some of which did not, for the distinction matters little to common sense. Faithful to his profession, as Voltaire saw it, Papalamiendo persists:

> [1.] Pensez-vous qu'il n'y ait que trois personnes en Dieu, ou qu'il y ait trois dieux en une personne? [2.] La seconde personne procède-t-elle de la première personne, et la troisième procède-t-elle des deux autres,

> ou de la seconde *intransecus*, ou de la première seulement? [3.] Le Fils a-t-il tous les attributs du Père, excepté la paternité? [4.] et cette troisième personne vient-elle par infusion, ou par identification, ou par spiration? (Bénac p. 502)

This enumeration is not as comic as Voltaire seems to have thought, because he found no novel device to trigger laughter and the mere accumulation of such absurdities has lost its humorous resilience. Still, their derivation presents us with a series of problems to solve. The first question imposes a choice between three persons in one God or three gods in one person, in other words, between a simple formulation of the orthodox Trinity and its logical opposite, apparently never a serious consideration. The absurdity of three gods in one person nevertheless contaminates the traditional respect for the converse. The second question asks (a) whether the second person proceeds from the first, and the third from the other two, or (b) if the third proceeds from the second *internally*, or (c) from the first alone. Voltaire ignores the dogmatic distinction between the generation of the Son and the procession of the Spirit, a difference in vocabulary designating a mysterious difference in the manner of reproduction. He presumably intended to expose what he considered the subterfuge of an inconceivable distinction. As we have seen, the Roman Church disagrees with the Greek over whether the Spirit proceeds from the first two persons or from the first alone. The untiring Papalamiendo proposes a third solution to complicate the problem, confuse his opponent, and inflate the vanity of solving it. But the third question itself amounts to a restatement of an exception that disproves the rule. The fourth question considers the means by which Christians receive the Holy Spirit. Freind dismisses all of these propositions by the observation that the gospels do not treat the subject and squelches further pursuit of the matter by an abrupt remark: "Jamais saint Paul n'écrit le nom de Trinité" (Bénac p. 502). Voltaire is relying on English etiquette, which does not require response to inquiry about matters thought unworthy of discussion. Since Freind explicitly cites reason and not the pope as the ultimate authority recognized by his church, he is in fact undermining a dogma which the Anglican clergy had by no means abandoned. His criticism of the Trinity recalls Clarke, an occasional saint in Voltaire's heaven and one who may have served as a model for Freind. Unfortunately, the effort expended by the elderly Voltaire to confront a Spanish scholastic with an English unitarian seems to have dulled his wit.

Although he published the *Bible enfin expliquée* a year later (1776), he may well have begun this satirical commentary at Cirey, as Wade argues. But he probably wrote the final section on the New Testament in 1774 and this one contains a passage appropriate to our investigation. Here Voltaire selects Jesus' testimony in John 17.3 for comment: "Eternal life is this: to know you, the only true God, and Jesus Christ whom you have sent." This verse interested him particularly because the Arians and the Socinians had both used it to justify their positions. He again subscribes to the error that Socinianism continued Arianism and describes the Arian interpretation as follows: "Ce passage annonce manifestement l'unité de Dieu, et... il dit clairement que Jésus est un simple homme envoyé de Dieu" (M. xxx, 310). Yet the Arians, unlike the Socinians, believed Christ to have been a divine being ever since God generated the Word, while the original Socinians believed him divine only from the resurrection on. Voltaire's version of John 17.3, in which the idea of the one being sent is resumed in the word *apostle*, misled him. By this word, he naturally understood a human being like the other apostles in the New Testament. Having quoted other passages from John, Matthew, and Paul treating Jesus as a man, he infers facetiously:

> Le voile qui couvrait sa divinité ne fut levé que par degrés aux faibles yeux des hommes, qui auraient pu être éblouis d'un subit éclat de lumière. (M. xxx, 310)

The explanation, as he intended, seems far-fetched. Would such a flash of light not have caused a sensation powerful enough to leave its trace in non-Christian history? The sentence provides an ironical excuse for the failure of Revelation to designate Jesus' divinity in a divine manner. Voltaire is satirizing an apologetic technique to heighten the contrast between Christian obscurantism and philosophical enlightenment.

His war on Christianity continued in the posthumous "Opinion en alphabet," a third alphabetical work appearing for the first time in the Kehl edition of his complete works (1785-1789). Unfortunately, it consists of new articles on subjects already treated in the other alphabetical works, articles more ample in detail, but less endowed with wit. Only two of them contain material worth consideration here, "Baptême" and "Conciles." "Baptême" (II in M.) returns to the inauthenticity of Matthew 28.19. Voltaire objects that the apostles appeared to baptize in the name of Jesus Christ alone: "Jamais les *Actes des apôtres* ne font mention d'aucune personne baptisée au nom du Père, du Fils, et du Saint-Esprit" (M. XVII, 546). For once, the facts justify his use of an unqualified negative, for no other baptismal invocation of the Trinity appears anywhere in the Bible. Scholars agree that the earliest Christians baptized exclusively in the name of Jesus.

The late insertion in Matthew of a Trinitarian saying by Jesus raises suspicions of fraud, not only about the authenticity of the formula, but also, the Trinity itself. The Trinity appears to have come as an afterthought here and afterthoughts seem more human than divine.

The third-generation "Conciles" (I in M.) includes a digression on Luke's account of Jesus preaching in the synagogue of Nazareth. Only this evangelist quotes the text read by Jesus from Isaiah, which begins:

> The spirit of the Lord has been given to me,
> for he has annointed me.
> He has sent me to bring the good news to the poor.[205]

According to Luke, Jesus antagonizes the congregation by implying that, although the prophecy applies to him, he cannot work miracles in Nazareth, because "no prophet is ever accepted in his own country" (Lk. 4.24). Enraged, the townspeople hustle him to the top of the hill on which Nazareth stands with the intention of throwing him over a cliff. Yet he slips through the crowd and walks away unharmed. Voltaire terminates his summary of Luke at the hilltop and adduces Mark 3.21, part of a different episode in Nazareth, to explain Jesus' escape: "Ses proches vinrent pour se saisir de lui: car ils disaient et on leur disait qu'il avait perdu l'esprit" (M.XVIII, 205). In earlier years, he would not have missed the opportunity to elaborate on this allegation of madness, perhaps in connection with the illusions of prophecy. But here he abruptly changes the subject and evokes Jesus' fidelity to Judaism, an overworked theme.

The rest of "Conciles" justifies the title. He added, for instance, a fresh detail to his latest presentation of the quarrel between Arius and Alexander: "Le désordre vint à un tel point que les païens, sur leurs théâtres, tournaient en raillerie le christianisme" (M. XVIII, 207). Voltaire's own drama suggests that he looked upon the theater as, among other things, an instrument for the reform of religion. The irony of pagans exposing a Christian controversy to dramatic satire must have seemed appropriate revenge for Christian abuse of paganism, many aspects of which he thought culturally superior. The "Conciles" in the "Opinion" also offers a full page of tongue-in-cheek mirth over pious speculations on the holy number of bishops present at Nicaea, that number itself being entirely controversial. To his otherwise routine account of the council, he added two anecdotes worthy of note. In the first, the Arian bishops, Eusebius of Nicomedia and Theogonius of Nicaea used a trick to avoid signing the formula approved by the council: "Dans le mot *omoousios* ils insérèrent un *iota* qui faisait

[205] Quotation of Is. 61.1 in Lk. 4.18.

omoiousios" (M. xviii, 210). This subterfuge affords him an opportunity to emphasize the disproportion between the doctrinal dispute and the resulting power struggle. No facetious remark enlivens this anecdote, but one does enliven the other. The Arian bishops Theonas of Marmaric and Secundus of Ptolemaichus, he relates, bribed Constantine's archivist to erase their signatures from the conciliar decree.

> Heureusement, pour remplacer leurs signatures et conserver le nombre mystérieux de trois cent dix-huit, on imagina de mettre [le manuscrit] sur le tombeau de Chrysante et de Misonius, qui étaient morts pendant la tenue du concile. (M. xviii, 210-11)

After a night of prayer, their signatures appeared on the manuscript. The adverb *heureusement* upsets the sobriety of the account, rather by anticipation than in retrospect as usual. Thus Voltaire accentuates the convenience of a miracle supporting a trivially superstitious conception of the divinity. Would God, the origin of the natural light, have recourse to a miracle merely in order to maintain a number without any perceptible significance? No.

Voltaire's treatment of the controversy raised by Eutychius in a later century likewise deserves attention. After the condemnation of Nestorius at Ephesus in 431 for recognizing two persons in Christ, Voltaire wrote, Flavian recognized two natures in him. In composing the next sentence, he cannibalized two sentences from the 1767 "Conciles":

> [*Dictionnaire*] Eutichès était un moine qui avait beaucoup crié contre Nestorius... Le moine, pour mieux contredire son adversaire, assure que Jésus n'avait qu'une nature. (*Dict.* p. 144)
>
> ["Opinion"] Un moine nommé Euthichès, qui avait déjà beaucoup crié contre Nestorius, assura, pour mieux les contredire l'un et l'autre [Nestorius et Flavien], que Jésus n'avait aussi qu'une nature. (M. xviii, 212)

Voltaire shifts the focus of his irony from Eutychius' revulsion over two persons in Jesus, "ce qui est épouvantable" (*Dict.* p. 144), in the *Dictionnaire* to the condemnation of his error in the "Opinion": "Le moine se trompa" (M. xviii, 212). Consequently, the more laughable version in the *Dictionnaire* ridicules the presumption of a fanatic, while the "Opinion" text derides the presumption of a vainglorious assembly. In either case, however, the target is the claim to know what the natural light does not tell. Since Ephesus approved Eutychius in 449 and Chalcedon condemned him only two years later, who can distinguish between truth and error in such matters? In this context, "le moine se trompa" is an ironical simplification. Further passages on Christological councils likewise demonstrate that the author of the

"Conciles" in the "Opinion" could occasionally summon the powers at his disposal earlier in his career. The basic technique of appeal to common sense remained the same, but he continued to find variations capable of freshening the material he had treated so many times before. Since the harvest of passages inviting analysis is meager, however, more than the usual regrets that he did not have the time to finish the work seem unnecessary.

Another posthumous work, the "Histoire de l'établissement du christianisme," appeared in the Kehl edition too. As in the *Examen important* and *Dieu et les hommes*, Voltaire assigns the "Histoire" to an English freethinker, although he does not name him this time. It resembles those works closely enough to justify the question of whether it deserves more than routine space here. A few passages nonetheless escape the inevitable monotony of repetition. Voltaire has a new comment, for instance, on the Holy Spirit's descent in the form of a dove on the head of Jesus after his baptism. He points out that Matthew does not state whether the dove proclaimed God's satisfaction with his Son. Nevertheless,

> c'était un beau spectacle; et on ne sait pas comment les Juifs osèrent pendre un homme que Dieu avait déclaré son fils si solennellement devant eux. (M. xxxi, 64)

The question of whether the dove spoke draws attention to the fabulous nature of the episode, so that the reader will interpret the beauty of the spectacle in an illusory sense. Voltaire seeks immediately to substantiate the impression of illusion by the argument that the Jews would not have condemned a man whom God had publicly designated as his Son. He does not mention that the Jews who turned Jesus over to Pilate for crucifixion lived far from the scene of his baptism and in a very different environment. Even the gospels distinguish between the scepticism of the priests and the enthusiasm of the humble. Knowledge of this distinction, which could scarcely have been rare, would have enabled any critic to demolish his argument. The younger fox had been wilier.

In the "Histoire," he modified his presentation of the miracle involving the signature of the Nicene decree by the two bishops who had died during the council. Rather than celebrate in advance the result of leaving the document on their tomb, he stresses the brevity of their return to life. After signing, "ils n'eurent rien de plus pressé que de remourir" (M. xxxi, 94). Voltaire had already used the verb *remourir* in his account of the same miracle in the "Conciles" (1771) of the *Questions*, but the context there fails to underline the futility of momentary resurrection.[206] Here the folly of returning to life only long enough to add two signatures to an overwhelming majority of 316 others flies in the face of reason. Death impresses itself on common sense as a definitive disappearance.

Elsewhere in the "Histoire," Voltaire paraphrases Deuteronomy 13.2-4, 6:

> S'il s'élève parmi vous un prophète; s'il vous prédit des prodiges et que ces prodiges arrivent, et qu'il vous dise (en vertu de ces prodiges): Suivons un culte étranger etc.; qu'il soit massacré incontinent. (M. XXXI, 112)

In this text, Voltaire had obviously found a decisive answer to the Christian interpretation of Old Testament prophecy. "Les docteurs chrétiens," he observes, "ne se sont pas aperçus que ce passage est la condamnation formelle de leur Jésus-Christ" (M. XXXI, 112). He thus insinuates that they deliberately ignored it. His use of Deuteronomy reminds us that prophecy from a remote past lends itself to purposes unforeseen by the prophet. But the language of Deuteronomy, which Voltaire has accurately paraphrased, actually exceeds the intentions of its author. By themselves, the words condemn the Christian interpretation of Jesus. Except for the foregoing examples, Voltaire's final work on our subjects added little new to all that he had written before.

Synthesis

When he died in 1778, he left a copious accumulation of writings critical of the historical Jesus, Christology, and the Trinity. The passages analyzed above are merely a portion of the whole seeming significantly to illustrate his polemical technique. His production actually accelerated at a time in life when most writers ride the crest of their momentum. Frequent repetition was therefore inevitable, yet one dare not dismiss the repetitive material without analysis on the assumption that it will reveal nothing, for here Voltaire harbors further surprises for critics who assume they know him by heart. The preceding sections of this chapter therefore present the results of a comprehensive investigation. It is time to survey them for evidence of the relations between them and synthesis. A number of frequently recurring themes concern the historical Jesus.

The contradictions between the nativity stories in Luke and Matthew, the discrepancies in each, and the predominance of

[206] Voltaire connoisseurs will recall Candide's protest when the baron refuses to allow him to marry Cunégonde: "Je te retuerais si j'en croyais ma colère" (Bénac, p. 217).

miraculous material raised Voltaire's suspicions, some of which modern scholars implicitly confirm. According to the consensus among them, he had good reason to reject the conflicting genealogies in Luke and Matthew, the impregnation of Mary by the Holy Spirit, and the virgin birth. He was probably right when he assumed that Joseph and Mary engendered Jesus in the natural manner and probably wrong when he credited the accusation of illegitimacy in the *Toldoth*. The Jewish horror of illegitimacy, which motivated this medieval slander to begin with, would have condemned Jesus to infamy in his Galilean society if he had been born out of wedlock, and most of us would now be practicing some other religion. Yet one can understand why this hypothesis appealed to Voltaire, for the gratuitous mythology enhancing the conception of Jesus in Luke and Matthew suggests the attempt to camouflage a shameful rather than a merely humble origin. One must appreciate Voltaire's reluctance to accept this solution as definitive, however, and his inclination at other times, even before the menace of Holbachian atheism, to restore Joseph to a status less vulnerable to masculine satire. The natural paternity of Joseph was enough to support the ruin of the miraculous conception when Boulainvilliers deplores the impregnation of the virgin by a pigeon and the destruction of the Trinity when Rigolet tells the emperor that God slept with his own mother in order to engender himself. To be sure, Voltaire achieves this ruin and destruction only within the limits of common sense, but only within these limits could most of his readers rationalize Christian belief on the subject anyway. His own motivation as usual far exceeds mere protest against violation of the natural light. There is no more flagrant injustice than discrimination against illegitimate children. While this prejudice characterized Voltaire's society less than others—d'Alembert's career proves the point[207]—the stigma remained. Either he was an illegitimate child or believed himself to be one (see p. 112), practically the same thing for our purposes here. His lifelong revolt against injustice in general may in fact have sprung from this initial injustice. His letters[208] and works display an exaggerated nonchalance about illegitimacy, a likely symptom of preoccupation in the mind of a writer disinclined to confession. Take *Candide*, whose hero he created, to some extent, in his own self-image.[209] Having ascribed the revelation of Candide's illegitimacy to

[207] D'Alembert was the illegitimate child of Mme de Tencin.

[208] His disclosure that Rochebrune was his natural father is an excellent example. See n. 14.

[209] "It is remarkable to what extent *Candide* is a protrayal and an expression of Voltaire. In a superficial way, we see this portrayal at every turn, but we see it, in truth,

the servants, the narrator elegantly diverts our attention to his father's extraordinary and yet inadequate credentials for marriage to his mother.[210] His attitude towards Jesus' birth is less equivocal. Perhaps the comic reputation of adultery on a social and intellectual level he disdained aggravated a secret shame. Perhaps the shame drove him to suspicion of a privileged birth in, as he saw it, a social and intellectual inferior, whose name was frequently used to inhibit his freedom of expression.

Nor did he ever really forgive Jesus for being a Jew, despite his sympathy for him in later years, dictated at least in part by d'Holbach's atheism. How often did he remind Christians that Jesus was Jewish? More often than recorded here and frequently in the campaign against the infamous during the sixties. He stresses Jesus' fidelity to Judaism and the absence of any desire on his part to found a new religion, to the point of imagining testimony by Jesus himself to this effect. He defends Antoine for having taken the logical step of converting to Judaism in order to follow Jesus. He even protests against the very idea that God could have been a Jew, and not only because if God had been a Jew he would have been a man, but also because if God had been a man he would not have been a Jew. Whether historical or literary, on the other hand, the criticism of Christianity by Jews is welcome to him. Isaac convinces him that not a single prophecy in the Old Testament applies to Jesus, and Akib that the Jews never crucified anybody. How could they have recognized in a devout Jew the God of an as yet inexistent religion? How could they have anticipated the spiritual interpretation of the messiah when they expected a military liberator? On this score, Voltaire's sympathy with them seems almost sincere. Constantly, he acknowledged the cultural, religious, and racial differences between them and most of his readers, but his own attitude towards them varied.[211] Having lost heavily in the London bankruptcies of Medina and Acosta, he held no real grudge against them[212] and continued to frequent the Acostas. While

ambiguously since we have trouble distinguishing between the *Candide* that is Voltaire, and the *Candide* that is *Candide*." Ira Wade, *Voltaire and Candide* (Princeton, 1959), p. 306.

[210] "Les anciens domestiques de la maison soupçonnaient qu'il était fils de la soeur de monsieur le baron, et d'un bon et honnête gentilhomme du voisinage, que cette demoiselle ne voulut jamais épouser parce qu'il n'avait pu prouver que soixante et onze quartiers, et que le reste de son arbre généalogique avait été perdu par l'injure du temps" (Bénac, p. 137).

[211] Pierre Aubéry offers the best treatment of this delicate question I have seen in "Voltaire et les juifs: ironie et démystification," *SVEC*, 24 (1963), 67-79, but he seems too lenient on Voltaire.

[212] He apparently limited his resentment to calling Medina a "damned Jew" in his letter to Thiériot on May 2, 1728.

his quarrel with Hirschel in Berlin cost him proportionately less, the recriminations were mutual and bitter. When the Portuguese Isaac Pinto protested against "Des Juifs" (1756), he answered with esteem for Jews like Pinto and a promise to eliminate the derogatory material, a promise he nonetheless failed to keep. His fondness for the definite article in this essay was particularly offensive: "Ils sont le dernier de tous les peuples parmi les musulmans et les Chrétiens, et ils se croient le premier." The context does not allow us to dismiss "cet orgueil dans leur abaissement" (M. XIX, 512) as mere polemic against Christian origins. Evidently, he succumbed in some measure to the anti-Semitism rooted in Christianity. Through personal contact and study, he knew the Jews better than most of his contemporaries and yet, like most Gentiles, he took their aloofness for pride. Whether authentic or imaginary, feelings of superiority on both sides widened the chasm between Jews and Gentiles. Since Jesus was for Voltaire one of "them" not one of "us," the hypocrisy of appropriating part of Judaism to endow Christianity with an ancient pedigree revolted him.

But he also thought that the historical Jesus, whom he suspected of ignorance, enthusiasm, and demagogy, little deserved worship. Since Jesus had left no written works and the New Testament, written by apologists anxious to reveal his every merit, gives no indication of his literacy, Voltaire assumed that he could not read and write, a reasonable assumption, because few inhabitants of rural areas were literate in those days. Although information about rural Galilee was not as reliable then as now, he fully perceived the enthusiasm thriving in that province and permeating the gospels. There can be little doubt that the ignorance contributed to the enthusiasm, as he constantly insinuates, but they do not seem to have resulted in demagogy, an accusation he also makes. Given Polichinelle's education, Jesus probably would have learned a lot more than how to sign his name. He did not appeal to a charlatan's public and, so far as we know, he never indulged in the kind of enthusiasm that Voltaire compares to drunkenness. The charges of self-seeking equalitarianism, chauvinism, and prophecy carry little weight, for none of the evidence suggests that Jesus entertained the kind of ambition Voltaire had in mind, the desire to rise from a humble origin to a position of power in the existing world. Despite the testimony of the synoptists, Voltaire could not accept Jesus' sincerity, hence his scorn for a social inferior, who would have made much trouble for him had he preached at Ferney. Yet d'Holbach's propaganda forced him to rehabilitate the Socrates of Galilee, the adversary of priestly superstition and wealth. The coexistence of the sympathetic and the antipathetic Jesus in the *Questions* of 1771 reveals the predicament of a polemicist facing both atheist and

Christian propaganda at the same time. The Jesus with whom he sympathized, however, belonged neither to Christianity, nor to the New Testament, nor to Judaism. In 1762, he wrote Mme de Fontaine that the statue of Jesus he had procured for his church at Ferney "a l'air d'un empereur romain" (March 19), a metamorphosis which obviously flattered his admiration of Roman antiquity. His attitude towards the historical Jesus, on the other hand, seems never really to have changed. Probably the great cult devoted to a man he believed unworthy of such attention offended his pride, because he had never received the recognition he felt he deserved. Aware of his talent and encouraged by his success as a writer, he aspired to the highest social rank. His bourgeois ambition not only moved him to flatter the nobility, but also to scorn the common people, from whom Jesus, as he saw it, had sprung. Furthermore, the synchronized complexity of his Newtonian mind generated a self-confidence intolerant of reliance on external inspiration. The two most important manifestations of eighteenth-century Jansenism, the faith-healing convulsions near the tomb of Deacon Pâris, in which his brother had participated, and the political ambitions resulting in the suppression of the Jesuits, aggravated his natural fear of enthusiasm. And the historical Jesus had many symptoms of what he considered a contagious disease. The motivation for his attacks on Jesus also contained an irrational element, the inability to forgive Jesus' unintentional foundation of an intellectual tyranny hostile to him.

He may not have realized that Christ's failure to return was the greatest weakness in Christianity, but he at least recognized it as a weakness and persistently exploited it. Although he did not fully understand the kingdom of God, he exposed Jesus' prophecy that it would come very soon as explicit, specific, and false. He implied that the Jews and the Christians had borrowed their belief in a forthcoming end of the world from other nations. Every time it failed to materialize as predicted, Christians simply postponed their deadline. In the *Dîner*, Boulainvilliers tells of a charlatan on the Pont Neuf promising day after day to kill and resuscitate his cock without ever keeping his promise. While the son of man never returned with power, Passeran complains, the pope himself usurped great power. One might add a score of other allusions, in Voltaire's works, to the failure of this prophecy to come true, but they present no interesting variation on the theme. He knew that he had caught Christianity in an empirical trap from which it could not retreat to the spiritual sanctuary where it habitually denied the rights of reason. The synoptic gospels lend no support to a spiritual understanding of the kingdom of God by Jesus and confirm that he persistently prophesied a specific empirical event which never took place. Voltaire perceived that varying and conflicting interpretations of this fatal prophecy had plagued Christianity ever since the followers of Jesus had begun to exploit the Jewish belief in prophecy as a means by which God communicates with men. Exposed to the natural light coming from God, the failure of such a prophecy to materialize eliminates any possibility of divine inspiration. Since Jesus therefore lacked divine inspiration, he does not qualify as the Son of God in the Christian sense. An ordinary man, who like many others believed himself to be inspired, he merely amplified the enthusiastic expectations of his fellow Galileans.

Arbitrary, violent, and rebellious acts, Voltaire thought, also disqualify him as the Son of God. Though entirely justified from the Jewish point of view, Jesus' disapproval of Roman taxes struck Voltaire as unforgivably subversive. Protests against the drowning of two thousand swine, which proliferate in his works, range from the impossibility of the crime to the injustice perpetrated and the improbability of the herdsmen's docility. Jesus' assault on the Temple merchants and the disruption of their officially authorized business also angered him. Obern imagines the comparable scandal of a fanatic whipping the merchants authorized to sell the *Book of Common Prayer* on the grounds of Saint Paul's in London. Voltaire was probably right to assume that Jesus could not have acted alone and he understandably wondered about the rumor of two thousand armed retainers in the *Toldoth*. The criminal execution of Jesus by the Romans, whom he respected, reinforced his suspicions that he had fomented rebellion, anathema to the lord of Ferney! The evangelists conceal Jesus' relations with the Zealots and falsify his relations with the Pharisees, but his teaching largely parallels both of theirs. Brandon, in fact, partially confirms Voltaire's suspicions (see n. 47). The fear of indocility among the common people became chronic at Ferney, where Voltaire conducted his entire campaign against the infamous. There especially he sought to encourage the subservience of the lower classes by promoting a God who rewards and punishes in the afterlife, which he privately denied. Having yearned for acceptance by the aristocracy, he attained aristocratic power and responsibility at Ferney, but this very success may have aggravated a feeling of insecurity inspired by privileges depending on the acquiescence of the humble. Historical bias may well have accompanied this social prejudice. How could the Romans have been wrong to occupy Palestine and the Jews right to resist their hegemony? Voltaire's Latin culture and empirical creed allied him with enlightened, central government against the revolt of provincial ignorance, superstition, and fanaticism. The Jews of first-century Palestine, he felt, had much to learn from the Romans. The thought that Jesus might have opposed the Romans accounts, at least in part, for Voltaire's assurance that he deserved crucifixion.

Voltaire's investigation of Jesus' death and the events said to have followed it enabled him to formulate a sharp contrast between the historical Jesus and the Christ of the Church. He was convinced that the rabble-rousing upstart from Galilee deserved the cruel and humiliating punishment inflicted on him. Jesus' dejection and fear of death in Gethsemane and on the cross persuaded Voltaire that he was a man. The alleged departure of his soul showed that his followers believed him to be a man. If he resuscitated others, why did he die himself? And how could God die anyway, to say nothing of a disreputable death like crucifixion? Voltaire frequently referred to Jesus' public execution and private resurrection, a combination rich in ironical innuendo, and ascribed belief in his resurrection to borrowing from pagan mythology. The activity of the risen Christ and the ascension invited his scepticism, which likewise inspired his explanation of how apologists had converted a dead man into a resurrected God. In any case, he argues, if God had submitted to death, he would not have left the accomplishment of his will to councils meeting hundreds of years later. His treatment of Jesus' death and resurrection stems from the commonsense conviction that all men die and that none ever return to life. The gospels persuaded him that, while Jesus died the disgraceful death he deserved, his followers tried to compensate for this disgrace by the myth of his resurrection. Their refusal to accept the finality of his death defied reason, and their success in propagating a fraudulent miracle offended Voltaire's sense of justice. He had faced death often enough to appreciate what it meant, not only in the loss of cherished friends, but also in his own scrapes with it.[213] His playful and yet apparently sincere anticipation of death began early in his life and continued until the very end. He even used the proximity of death as a tactic intended to dampen the anger of enemies and reassure irritated authorities. His nonchalance could only have come from spontaneous and inexhaustible courage in facing the inevitable. This courage seems all the more admirable in that he did not believe in an afterlife. He seems to have suspected the clergy of promising salvation to create a need for their services. They promoted the myth

[213] In 1723, he nearly died of smallpox and his friend de Maisons did die of this disease. He was also present when the actress Adrienne Lecouvreur (1730), his friends Mme de Fontaine-Martel (1733) and Mme du Châtelet (1747) died.

of Jesus' resurrection, he thought, so that Christians might found an illusory hope on it. Since this hope attracted the masses, the resurrection was essential to the clerical authority he so resented. If he could destroy faith in that myth, he calculated, the authority would crumble. Consequently, he amplified all arguments tending to establish that Jesus had died the natural and definitive death awaiting any man caught in his predicament.

In contrast with the resurrection, the miracles involving the Holy Spirit seemed gratuitous to him. Three interventions by the Holy Spirit particularly amused him: (1) The "pigeon" alighting on Jesus' head after his baptism inspires a dry comment: "C'était un beau spectacle" (M. XXXI, 64): (2) The risen Christ resorted to a magician's trick when he breathed the Spirit into his disciples; (3) Voltaire took the beating wings and babbling tongues at Pentecost no more seriously than Bienfait's wheelbarrow grinding across the floor upstairs and his incomprehensible jargon. Unaware of the more primitive probabilities (see p. 34), he interpreted the descent of the dove as an attempt to establish Jesus' divinity. It made little difference to him that the breathing of the Spirit and the Pentecost miracle were intended to assure the continuation of divine inspiration on earth after the departure of Christ. They attracted his attention rather because of their picturesque obscurity, for he found no profound significance in them, and they do not figure very often in his works. Although he did not bother to speculate on their origin, he probably attributed them, as usual, to pious fraud by cynical priests.

Unlike the miraculous interventions of the Spirit, the divinity of Jesus was a critical issue for Voltaire, who accumulated a variety of arguments against it. In addition to those already cited, he stressed the improbability that God would live a human life and especially the life of a Galilean miracle worker, a Jew and not a Roman; the delay of three hundred years (a gross exaggeration) before Jesus was declared divine; the lack of Scriptural support and particularly in Paul; Origen's subordinationism; the opposition of Jesus' fellow Jews and modern antitrinitarians. His stubborn efforts to enlist the Genevan ministers under the banner of deism went beyond the usual polemic to a militant proselytism, including private persuasion and public disclosure. Energetic but psychologically misconceived, this campaign produced results contrary to his intentions, yet the experience prepared him for more fruitful projects devoted to the reform of judicial errors.[214]

[214] Those involving Calas, Sirven, de La Barre, etc.

Why did he try so hard to convince his public that men alone had deified Jesus? He seems to have had two reasons in particular: On one hand, he resented the apotheosis of a man he thought beneath such an honor and especially in comparison with the great men of antiquity he admired. On the other, he persuaded himself that the divinity of Jesus was the only obstacle to the inevitable evolution of Christianity towards deism. He had almost certainly derived this theory from Bossuet who condemned Protestantism as a stage in the decline of Christianity leading to Socinianism.[215] It is ironical that the champion of rigid orthodoxy should have inspired such confidence in the certainty of this evolution, but Voltaire was no less confident in his own ability to pry an admission of Socinianism, deism to him, out of the Genevan ministers. Infatuated with his grand design, he apparently never bothered to examine the difference between deism and Genevan unitarianism and he steadfastly failed to realize that, by challenging the ministers' pride, he was only hardening their will to resist him. When he finally admitted defeat, though only to himself, he may have understood this psychological error, but certainly not his basic misconception. Both Genevan unitarianism and true Socinianism differ from deism in that the redemptive role of Christ remains intact. Voltaire neglects redemption in his criticism of dogma[216] and fails to account for the powerful appeal of salvation in a civilization conditioned by the hope of an afterlife. Unfearful of death, he did not yearn to escape the annihilation it suggests to common sense. Apparently unaware that belief in the divinity of Christ depends, at least in part, on the desire for salvation and not vice versa, he concentrated most of his fire on the wrong target.

But this target also obsessed him because the deification of a man he took for an ignorant fanatic eclipsed the reputation of the great intellectuals he fervently admired. Though, under the threat of atheism, he condescended to compare Jesus with Socrates, he nicknamed Jesus the Socrates of Galilee and not Socrates the Jesus of Athens. He was apparently trying to appease Christians by the association of Jesus with a great philosopher who, like him, had failed to leave any written

[215] Florida observes, "Bossuet... demonstrated that the logical end of Protestantism was Socinianism" (p. 55). In his *Avertissements aux Protestants sur les lettres du ministre Jurieu* (1688-1691), Bossuet wrote in effect: "On peut donc étendre... la tolérance jusqu'à ceux qui nient la divinité de Jésus-Christ; ce dogme est devenu indifférent... C'est tout ce que demandent les Sociniens, qui gagneront bientôt tout le reste [des Protestants], si on leur accorde ce point." *Oeuvres complètes de Bossuet* (Paris, 1872), xv, 235.

[216] Preliminary work on a project entitled "Voltaire and the Redemption" convinced me of Voltaire's indifference to this subject.

works. Yet he did not hold this deficiency against Socrates and did against Jesus. A comparison of references to Socrates and Jesus in his works reveals more esteem for the Greek than the Jew.[217] The contrast between his admiration for the great men of Roman Antiquity and his usual contempt for Jesus is evident. He welcomed Meslier's anger over the apotheosis of a man unworthy of those deified by the pagans[218] and profited from every opportunity to defend pagans like Julian from Christian polemic. He even took this issue personally. The only afterlife to which he seems to have aspired was the prosperity of his posthumous reputation. The care with which he corrected and revised each successive edition of his works right up to the last year of his life illustrates his desire for this kind of "immortality." His determination to ensure a decent burial of his body despite the Church's thirst for revenge proves his concern for dignity beyond the grave. The idea that the envious and the mediocre might denigrate him in the name of Christ when he could no longer defend himself incited him no doubt to greater aggression against the divinity of Christ.

Less passion and more calculation characterized his satire of the Trinity. In the New Testament, he found few passages supporting the dogma and many contradicting it. He gave special emphasis to sayings of Jesus stating his subordination to the Father and leaving the Holy Spirit unmentioned. Modern exegesis tends to confirm his attacks on the authenticity of the few Trinitarian formulations appearing in the Bible. Subordinationism and the limitation of the deity to two persons among the early Fathers convinced him that the orthodox Trinity had evolved only later. The Hellenistic syncretism of the councils which had legislated the consubstantiality of the Son and the procession of the Spirit proved vulnerable to his satire. Nor did he spare the sordid politics of the councils and the variations between them. As effective a critical tool as history, logic exposed the contradictory and inconceivable absurdities of the Trinity to his irony. He fondly regretted the

[217] Raymond Trousson qualifies this esteem, nonetheless: "Voltaire... ne s'est soucié de Socrate que comme d'un thème commode, d'une machine de guerre propre à écraser l'ennemi." *Socrate devant Voltaire, Diderot et Rousseau* (Paris, 1967), p. 44.

[218] "Les païens n'ont ordinairement attribué la divinité qu'à des grands hommes... ou des personnes qui ont excellé en quelques vertus, ou en quelques belles et rares perfections, qui ont, par exemple, inventé les sciences et les arts, qui ont rendu quelques signalés services au public, ou qui ont fait quelques grandes et généreuses actions... mais nos déichristicoles, à qui attribuent-ils la divinité? A un homme de néant, qui n'avait ni talents, ni esprit, ni science, ni adresse, et qui était tout à fait méprisé dans le monde... à un fou, à un insensé, à un misérable fanatique et... pendard." Jean Meslier, *Oeuvres de Meslier* (Paris, 1970), I, 391.

Son's incapacity for Fatherhood and delighted in the conception of God by God himself in his relations with Mary, an imbroglio mingling the immaterial with the material. The procession of the Spirit by spiration also invited his irony and he approved the Turks in their contempt for the polytheism and idolatry implied by the Trinity.

This plethora of satire indicates the extent of Voltaire's preoccupation with the subject. To him, however, the Trinity seemed less an insidious temptation than an expedient sophism imposed by authority. He found it so vulnerable to common sense that it beckoned to him even when he was after other game, such as atheism in the *Histoire de Jenni*. Convinced that the Church had enshrined an absurdity, he never tired of hammering away at it, for he knew the whole structure of Christianity would suffer. He believed the dogma to have been contrived to remove the problem of reconciling monotheism with the divinity of Christ, which had divided Christianity against itself, from the possibility of rational solution. The blasphemy of justifying a deliberate mystification by ascribing it to the author of the natural light excited his contempt. On this theme, his true opinion seems to have coincided more nearly with that of the common sense to which he was appealing than on any of the others concerning Christology and the Trinity.

The Arian controversy, which he exploited late in life, afforded him a different kind of opportunity for antichristian satire. The failure of his campaign to convert the Genevan ministers seems to have persuaded him to broaden his appeal and enrich his propaganda with fresh arguments. Several times, he contrasted Constantine's "good sense" with the quibbling that separated the two parties. No one can possibly establish the pedigree of the divine family, he admonished, or determine whether the Word was created or engendered. He doubted that, after appearing on earth, God would have left decisions about his nature to mortals assembling hundreds of years later. At the Council of Nicaea, he erroneously objected, prelates imposed their opinion on a less powerful majority of priests. Furthermore, the profession of faith adopted neglects the Holy Spirit. The following councils contradicted Nicaea and each other, as Constantine vacillated between Arianism and Athanasianism. Voltaire ironically deplored all the carnage over a dipthong and the satire of the controversy on the pagan stage.

In his haste to gather propaganda, however, he seized upon the more obvious and neglected some of the more powerful. He interpreted the dispute as a collision between major factions within Christendom over a trivial and yet inconceivable problem in theology. He does not seem to have suspected the ominous motives behind the struggle, motives far more dangerous for apologetic assurances of divine control. How odd that the historian of Louis XIV and Peter the Great, the friend and victim of Frederick the Great, and the dupe of Catherine the Great should have misunderstood Constantine! His admiration for Roman antiquity inspired approval of the emperor's good sense, leniency for his crimes, and neglect of his ruthless ambition. He admitted Constantine's vacillation between Athanasians and Arians because it served his satirical purpose, but, to a surprising extent, the sordid politics of the controversy escaped him. He described the chief adversaries as petty quibblers who somehow managed to embroil great numbers of fanatic supporters in a pointless and disastrous dispute. He failed to recognize in nearly all the antagonists the coexistence of the desire for eternal life and the worst of temporal passions. Thus he neglected the causes of the controversy and capitalized on the effects. The conduct of the adversaries, the presumption and futility of the conciliar decisions, and the haphazard vacillation of doctrine nonetheless provided him with formidable propaganda. Such evidence was adequate for common sense and, in this case, for an old man in a hurry.

He studied the controversy from which the two natures emerged during the same period as the Arian dispute, but he began to ridicule the dogma itself much earlier. In treating this controversy, he as usual underlined the triviality and absurdity of the issues as well as the arrogance and violence of the adversaries. He neglects neither the contradictions between the councils nor the conflict between the two natures implied by certain functions, such as the human praying to the divine and the divine involving itself in human necessities. According to the gospels, Jesus never said anything about his two natures, which Voltaire, in any case, thought incompatible. Even with the addition of repetitive passages, however, the material on this subject in Voltaire's works does not reveal a major effort by him. His polemic against the divinity of Christ implicitly refutes the two natures as well and his study of the Arian controversy taught him much the same lessons as the Nestorian controversy. Less complicated than the Trinity, the two natures nevertheless resulted from the same desire to curtail discussion by eliminating the possibility of dispute. Like other absurdities masquerading as divine mysteries, the dogma was vulnerable to Voltairian satire.

He himself designated a final theme to be considered here as Socinianism, under which he subsumed both Trinitarian and antitrinitarian heresy from the Reformation on. The brunt of his assault on Calvin for the judicial murder of Servetus was a part of his clumsy campaign to extract an admission of Socinianism from the Genevan ministers. Mistaking Servetus for an antitrinitarian, he reveled in the illusion of Calvinist ministers professing the doctrine of Calvin's victim and deploring his crime. While their heresy actually surpassed Servetus', their sincerity left much to be desired, and the burning of Servetus embarrassed them more than it revolted them. Servetus himself evolved in his thinking from a fanatic to a victim innocent even of the heresy for which Calvin condemned him, an exaggeration; but Calvin remained a fanatic. Voltaire also sympathized with the Italian antitrinitarians, several of whom he followed, in his studies, to Switzerland. Although he wrongly considered Lelio the founder of Socinianism, he otherwise understood the importance of Fausto's work in Poland. Of the English unitarians, he knew Clarke best and admired Newton for his religious thought as well as his scientific achievement. His attempt to portray the English Socinians as a coherent group early in his career may have been wishful thinking. He later abandoned the error of continuing opposition to the Trinity ever since its inception, though regretfully. His enduring sympathy with Trinitarian and antitrinitarian heresy stemmed from the enticing proximity of such heresy to deism. He may well have counted on the inevitable decline of Catholicism to Protestantism to unitarianism to deism.[219] The campaign to convert the Genevan ministers differed from the war on the infamous by scope and method rather than intention. The naïve hope of precipitating a fatal process drove him to feverish activity at Les Délices and Ferney where, several times, he managed to convince himself that a radical transformation in the religion of his society was imminent. He bears surprising resemblance to Jesus announcing the kingdom of God, for at the height of the scandal over "Genève," he wrote Théodore Tronchin, "On touche à une grande révolution dans l'esprit humain" (D 7584). Even his rhetoric approaches that of Jesus on June 17, 1764, several weeks before the publication of the *Dictionnaire philosophique*: "Le règne de la vérité est proche." For a commonsense critic, he had a surprising capacity for self-delusion.

[219] The idea vaguely suggests Hegel and the nineteenth century.

BIBLIOGRAPHY

Aldridge, A. Owen. Review of Ira Wade: *The Intellectual Development of Voltaire*. *Comparative Literature*, 23 (1971), 189.

Anchor Bible. New York, 1964-.

Astruc, Jean. *Conjectures sur les mémoires originaux dont il paraît que Moïse s'est servi pour composer le livre de la Genèse*. Bruxelles, 1753.

Athanasius. *Contra Gentes and De Incarnatione*. Trans. Robert W. Thomson. Oxford, 1971.

________. *Select Treatises*. Trans. John Newman. London, 1895.

Aubéry, Pierre. "Voltaire et les juifs: ironie et démystification." *Studies on Voltaire and the Eighteenth Century*, 24 (1963), 67-79.

Augustine. *Letters 131-164*. Trans. Wilfrid Parsons. *The Fathers of the Church*, Vol. 16. New York, 1953.

________. *On the Trinity*. Trans. Stephen McKenna. *The Fathers of the Church*, Vol. 18. Washington, 1963.

________. *A Work of the Predestination of Saints*. London, 1550.

Baltzer, Klaus. *The Covenant Formulary in Old Testament, Jewish and Early Christian Writings*. Philadelphia, 1971.

Barbier, Edmond. *Chronique de la Régence et du règne de Louis XV (1718-1763)*. 8 vols. Paris, 1857.

Barrett, C.K. *The Holy Spirit and the Gospel Tradition*. London, 1966.

Barnard, L.W. *Justin Martyr, His Life and Thought*. Cambridge, 1967.

Basil of Caesarea. *The Treatise de Spiritu sancto*. Trans. Blomfield Jackson. *A Select Library of Nicene and Post-Nicene Fathers*. 2nd series, Vol. 8. Oxford and New York, 1894.

Bayle, Pierre. *Dictionnaire historique et critique*. Paris, 1820-1824.

Becker, Carl L. *The Heavenly City of the Eighteenth-Century Philosophers*. New York, 1960.

Bender, Wolfgang von. *Die Lehre über den Heiligen Geist bei Tertullian*. Munich, 1961.

Black, Matthew. "The Maranatha Invocation and Jude 14, 15 (I Enoch 1:9)." *Christ and Spirit in the New Testament*. Cambridge, 1973, pp. 189-96.

Boobyer, G.H. *Jesus and the Politics of His Time*. Salisbury, 1968.

Bornkamm, Günther. *Jesus of Nazareth*. New York, 1960.

Bossuet, Jacques-Bénigne. *Oeuvres complètes*. 31 vols. Paris, 1872.

Boularand, Ephrem. *L'Hérésie d'Arius et la "foi" de Nicée*. 2 vols. Paris, 1972.

Brandon, Samuel. *Jesus and the Zealots*. Manchester, 1967.

Brown, Harcourt. "The Composition of the *Letters Concerning the English Nation*." *The Age of Enlightenment*. Ed. W.H. Barber *et al*. Edinburgh and London, 1967, pp. 15-34.

Brown, Raymond. *The Virginal Conception and Bodily Resurrection of Jesus*. London, 1973.

Bull, George. *The Works of the Right Reverend George Bull*. 2 vols. London, 1725.

Bultmann, R. *Theology of the New Testament*. 2 vols. London, 1952.

Calmet, Augustin. *Commentaire littéral sur tous les livres de l'Ancien et du Nouveau Testament*. 24 vols. 1707-1716.

Calvin, Jean. *Déclaration pour maintenir la vraie foi touchant la Trinité*. Genève, 1554.

———. *Johannis Calvini Epistolae et responsa*. Genève, 1617.

———. *Lettres de Calvin*. Ed. Jules Bonnet. Paris, 1854.

———. *Johannis Calvini Opera quae supersunt omnia*. 59 vols. Brunswick, 1863-1900.

Campenhausen, Hans von. *Les Pères latins*. Paris, 1967.

Cantimori, Delio. *Eretici italiani de cinquecento*. Florence, 1967.

Chaponnière, Paul. *Voltaire chez les calvinistes*. Genève, 1932.

Châtelet, Emilie du. "Examen de la Genèse." Bibliothèque de Troyes, Ms. 2376-2377.

Clarke, Samuel. *The Scripture Doctrine of the Trinity*. London, 1712.

Clement of Alexandria. *Writings of Clement of Alexandria*. Trans. William Wilson. Edinburgh, 1867-1869. Rpt. *The Ante-Nicene Christian Library*, Vols. 4 and 12. Buffalo, 1885.

Clement of Rome and Ignatius of Antioch. *Epistles*. Ed. James Kleist. London, 1961.

Cohn, Haim. *The Trial and Death of Jesus*. New York, 1971.

Collini, Côme-Alexandre. *Mon Séjour auprès de Voltaire*. Paris, 1807.

Cullmann, Oscar. *The Christology of the New Testament*. London, 1963.

Cyril of Alexandria. *S. Cyril, Archbishop of Alexandria*. Oxford, 1881.

Davies, William D. *Invitation to the New Testament: A Guide to Its Main Witnesses*. London, 1967.

Denzinger, Heinrich. *The Sources of Catholic Dogma*. Trans. Roy DeFerrari. Saint Louis-London, 1957.

Derrett, J. Duncan. *Jesus's Audience: The Social and Psychological Environment in Which He Worked*. London, 1973.

Descartes, René. *Oeuvres philosophiques de Descartes*. Ed. Ferdinand Alquié. 3 vols. Paris, 1963-1973.

Desné, Roland. "The Role of England in Voltaire's Polemic against Pascal." *Eighteenth-Century Studies*. Ed. Peter Gay. Hannover, 1972.

Devresse, Robert. "Essai sur Théodore de Mopsueste." *Studi e testi*. Biblioteca Apostolica Vaticana, Vol. 141. Rome, 1948.

Diderot, Denis. *Correspondance*. Ed. Georges Roth. Paris, 1955-1970.

________. *Encyclopédie ou Dictionnaire raisonné des sciences, des arts et des métiers*. 17 vols. Paris, 1751-1766.

Dodd, C.H. *The Founder of Christianity*. London, 1971.

Duvernet, Théophile. *La Vie de Voltaire*. Genève, 1786.

Dyboski, Roman. *Outlines of Polish History*. London, 1925.

Elcock, W.D. *The Romance Languages*. London, 1960.

Erasmus. *Desiderii Erasmi Operum Omnium*. Vol. 7. London, 1707.

________. *Paraphrasis in epistolas Joannes*. Basel, 1540.

Eutychius. *Eutychii Patriarchae Alexandrini Annales*. Ed. Louis Cheikho. Louvain, 1962.

________. *Eutychius Patriarcha Alexandrinus*. Trans. John Selden. Oxford, 1661.

________. *L'Histoire de l'Eglise d'Alexandrie*. Trans. Johann Wansleben. Paris, 1677.

Evans, C.F. *Resurrection and the New Testament*. London, 1940.

Extrait des Registres de la Vénérable Compagnie de l'Eglise et de l'Académie de Genève, du 10 février 1758. Genève, Ms. Gf 315/319. Archives Coll. Gerod 156/11.

Fleury, Claude. *Histoire ecclésiastique*. 36 vols. Paris, 1740-1751.

Florida, R.E. *Voltaire and the Socinians: Studies on Voltaire and the Eigheenth Century*, 122 (1974).

Frend, W.H.C. *Martyrdom and Persecution in the Early Church*. Oxford, 1965.

Fuller, Reginald. *The Formation of the Resurrection Narratives*. London, 1972.

Gregory Nazianzen. *Select Orations*. Trans. Charles Browne and James Swallow. Oxford, 1893. Rpt. *Select Library of Nicene and Post-Nicene Fathers*, 2nd series, Vol. 7. Grand Rapids, n.d.

Grillmeier, Aloys. *Christ in Christian Tradition*. New York, 1965.

Grimm, Melchior. *Correspondance littéraire, philosophique et critique*. 16 vols. Paris, 1877-1882.

Harrison, R.K. *Introduction to the Old Testament*. London, 1970.

Hiers, Richard. *The Historical Jesus and the Kingdom of God: Present and Future in the Message and Ministry of Jesus*. Gainesville, 1973.

Horatius, Flaccus Quintus. *Odes and Epodes*. Ed. Clement Smith. Boston, 1896.

Hulme, Edward M. "Lelio Sozzini's Confession of Faith." *Persecution and Liberty: Essays in Honor of George Lincoln Burr*. New York, 1931, pp. 211-25.

Hunt, John. *Religious Thought in England*. 3 vols. London, 1873.

Irenaeus of Lyon. *Five Books of Irenaeus, Bishop of Lyons, against Heresies*. London, 1872.

Jerusalem Bible. New York, 1966.

Josephus, Flavius. *The Works of Flavius Josephus*. Philadelphia, n.d.

Justin. *Oeuvres de saint Justin philosophe et martyr*. Paris, 1554.

________. *Writings of Justin Martyr*. New York, 1948.

Kelly, John. *Early Christian Creeds*. London, 1963.

Kenyon, Kathleen. *Archeology of the Holy Land*. London, 1970.

Klausner, Joseph. *Jesus von Nazareth: seine Zeit, sein Leben und seine Lehre*. Jerusalem, 1952.

Köhler, Ludwig. *Old Testament Theology*. London, 1957.

Lamenski, Adolf. *Der Heilige Geist als Geist Christi und Geist der Gläubigen… Athanasios von Alexandrien. Erfuhrter Theologische Studien*, Bd. 23. Leipzig, 1969.

Langton, Edward. *Essentials of Demonology: A Study of Jewish and Christian Doctrines*. London, 1949.

Larousse du XXe Siècle. Paris, 1931.

La Sor, William. *The Dead Sea Scrolls and the New Testament*. Grand Rapids, 1972.

Leo I. *The Tome of Pope Leo the Great*. Trans. E.H. Blakeney. London, 1923.

Lettre à Diognète. Trans. Henri Marrou. Paris, 1965.

Longchamp, Sébastien, and Wagnière, Jean-Louis. *Mémoires sur Voltaire et sur ses ouvrages*. 2 vols. Paris, 1826.

Lundin, Robert. *Principles of Psychopathology*. Columbus, 1965.

Manuel, Frank E. *The Religion of Isaac Newton*. Oxford, 1974.

Marxsen, Willi. *The Resurrection of Jesus of Nazareth*. Philadelphia, 1970.

Meslier, Jean. *Oeuvres complètes*. Ed. Roland Desné, Jean Deprun, and Albert Soboul. 3 vols. Paris, 1970-1972.

Metzger, Bruce. "The Punctuation of Rom. 9:5." *Christ and Spirit in the New Testament: In Honour of Charles Moule*. Cambridge, 1973, pp. 95-112.

Monty, Jeanne. "Voltaire's Rhetoric: The Use of Written Evidence in the Alphabetical Works." *Studies on Voltaire and the Eighteenth Century*, 120 (1974), 41-77.

Mury, Paulo. *Historia de Gabriel Malagrida*. Lisbon, 1875.

Naves, Raymond. *Voltaire et l'Encyclopédie*. Paris, 1938.

Nestorius. *Le Livre d'Héraclide de Damas*. Paris, 1910.

New Catholic Encyclopedia. Washington, 1967.

Newton, Isaac. *Sir Isaac Newton, Theological Manuscripts*. Ed. Herbert McLachlan. Liverpool, 1950.

Norris, Richard A. *Manhood and Christ: A Study in the Christology of Theodore of Mopsuestia*. Oxford, 1963.

O'Collins, Gerald. *The Easter Jesus*. London, 1973.

Origen. *Commentaire sur Saint Jean*. Trans. Cécile Blanc. *Sources chrétiennes*, Vol. 120. Paris, 1966.

———. *Contra Celsum*. Trans. Henry Chadwick. Cambridge, 1953.

———. *Entretien d'Origène avec Héraclide*. Trans. Jean Scherer. *Sources chrétiennes*, Vol. 67. Paris, 1960.

———. *Origen on First Principles*. Trans. G.W. Butterworth. London, 1936.

Pascal, Blaise. *Pensées*. Ed. Louis Lafuma. Paris, 1962.

Philips, Edith, and Perkins, Jean A. "Some Voltaire Marginalia." *Studies on Voltaire and the Eighteenth Century*, 114 (1973), 7-78.

Plato. *The Timaeus and the Critias or Atlanticus*. Trans. Thomas Taylor. Washington, 1944.

Pollard, T.E. "The Exegesis of John X.30 in the Early Trinitarian Controversies." *New Testament Studies* (Cambridge), 3 (1956-1957), 334-49.

Pomeau, René. *La Religion de Voltaire*. Paris, 1956.

Quasten, Johannes. *Patrology*. 3 vols. Utrecht and Brussels, 1951-1960.

Reimarus, Hermann. *The God of Jesus and His Disciples*. Leiden, 1970.

Robinson, H. Wheeler. *Corporate Personality in Ancient Israel*. Philadelphia, 1964.

Robinson, John A.T. "The Use of the Fourth Gospel for Christology Today." *Christ and Spirit in the New Testament*. Cambridge, 1973, pp. 61-78.

Rousseau, A.-M. *L'Angleterre et Voltaire: Studies on Voltaire and the Eighteenth Century*, 145-147 (1976).

Rousseau, Jean-Jacques. *Oeuvres complètes*. 4 vols. Paris, 1959-1969.

Rowbotham, Arnold H. *Missionary and Mandarin*. Berkeley, 1935.

Schmaus, Michael. *God and His Christ*. New York, 1971.

————. *Die psychologische Trinitätslehre des heiligen Augustinus*. Münster, 1967.

Schwarzbach, Bertram. *Voltaire's Old Testament Criticism*. Genève, 1971.

Schweitzer, Albert. *The Quest of the Historical Jesus*. London, 1931.

Servetus, Michael. *Christianismi restitutio*. N.p., 1553.

————. *The Two Treatises of Servetus on the Trinity*. Trans. Earl Wilbur. *Harvard Theological Studies*, 16. Cambridge, 1932.

Sewel, William. *The History of the Rise, Increases and Progress of the Christian People Called Quakers*. New York, 1844.

Solana, Marcial. *Historia de la filosofía española*. Madrid, 1941.

Sozomen. *The Ecclesiastical History of Sozomen*. Ed. Edward Walford. London, 1855.

Sozzini, Fausto. *Fausti Socini Senensis opera omnia*. 2 vols. Irenopolis, 1656.

Spinoza, Baruch. *Traité théologico-politique* in *Oeuvres*, Vol. II. Paris, 1965.

Strauss, David. *The Life of Jesus Critically Examined*. London, 1892.

Tertullian, Quintus Septimii Florentis. *Tertullian's Treatise against Praxeas*. Trans. Ernest Evans. London, 1948.

————. *The Writings of Tertullian*. Edinburgh, 1869-1870. Rpt. *Ante-Nicene Christian Library*, Vols. 3 and 4. Buffalo, 1885.

Theodore of Mopsuestia. *Les Homélies catéchétiques de Théodore de Mopsueste*. Trans. Raymond Tonneau. *Studi e testi*, 145. Vatican, 1949.

Theodoret and Evagrius. *History of the Church*. London, 1854.

Torrey, Norman. *Voltaire and the English Deists*. New Haven, 1967.

————, and Wade, Ira. "Voltaire and Polier de Bottens." *Romanic Review*, 31 (1930), 147-55.

Trapnell, William. "Survey and Analysis of Voltaire's Collective Editions." *Studies on Voltaire and the Eighteenth Century*, 67 (1970), 105-99.

————. *Voltaire and the Eucharist: Studies on Voltaire and the Eighteenth Century*, 198 (1981).

Trechsel, F. *Die protestantischen Antitrinitarier vor Faustus Socin*. 2 vols. Heidelberg, 1839.

Trousson, Raymond. *Socrate devant Voltaire, Diderot et Rousseau*. Paris, 1967.

Turmel, Joseph. *Histoire des dogmes*. 6 vols. Paris, 1931-1936.

Vaux, Roland de. *Histoire ancienne d'Israël*. Paris, 1971.

————. "The Revelation of the Divine Name YHWH." *Proclamation and Presence. Old Testament Essays in Honor of Gwynne Henton Davies*. London, 1970, pp. 48-75.

Vercruysse, Jeroom. *Bibliographie descriptive des écrits du Baron d'Holbach*. Paris, 1971.

Vermes, Geza. *Jesus the Jew*. London, 1973.

Vernes, Jacob. *Catéchisme à l'usage des jeunes gens qui s'instruisent pour participer à la sainte-cène*. N.p., 1778.

Vernet, Jacob. *Instruction chrétienne ou catéchisme familier pour les enfants*. 2nd ed. 2 vols. Genève, 1756.

________. "Lettre à Mr. de Voltaire à Lausanne." *Journal helvétique* (Neuchâtel), juin 1757, pp. 611-27.

________. *Lettres critiques d'un voyageur anglais sur l'article Genève du Dictionnaire encyclopédique et sur la Lettre de Mr. d'Alembert à Mr. Rousseau touchant les spectacles*. 2 vols. Utrecht, 1761.

________. *Traité de la vérité de la religion chrétienne*. 2nd ed. 9 vols. Genève, 1748-1788.

Voltaire. *L'Affaire Calas*. Ed. Jacques Van den Heuvel. Paris, 1965.

________. *The Complete Works of Voltaire*. Ed. Theodore Besterman. Banbury, 1968-.

________. *Dialogues et anecdotes philosophiques*. Ed. Raymond Naves. Paris, 1966.

________. *Dictionnaire philosopique*. Ed. Raymond Naves. Paris, 1961.

________. *Essai sur les moeurs*. Ed. René Pomeau. 2 vols. Paris, 1963.

________. *Letters Concerning the English Nation*. Rpt. New York, 1974.

________. *Lettres philosophiques*. Ed. Gustave Lanson. Paris, 1964.

________. *Mémoires pour servir à la vie de M. de Voltaire*. Paris, 1965.

________. *Oeuvres complètes*. Ed. Louis Moland. 52 vols. Paris, 1877-1882.

________. *Romans et contes*. Ed. Henri Bénac. Paris, 1960.

________. Voltaire: *Facéties.* Ed. Jean Macary. Paris, 1973.

Wade, Ira. "The 'Epïtre à Uranie.'" *Publications of the Modern Language Association*, 47 (1932), 1066-112.

________. *The Intellectual Development of Voltaire*. Princeton, 1969.

________. *Voltaire and Candide*. Princeton, 1959.

________. *Voltaire and Mme du Châtelet: An Essay on the Intellectual Activity at Cirey*. Princeton, 1941.

Weill, Julien. "Nicolas Antoine." *Revue des études juives*, 37 (1898), 161-96.

Weippert, Manfred. *The Settlement of the Israelite Tribes in Palestine*. London, 1971.

Weiss, Johannes. *Jesus' Proclamation of the Kingdom of God*. Norwich, 1971.

Wells, George. *The Jesus of the Early Christians*. London, 1971.

Werner, Martin. *The Formation of Christian Dogma*. New York, 1957.

Wilbur, Earl. *A History of Unitarianism*. Cambridge, 1947.

Williams, George. *The Radical Reformation*. Philadelphia, 1962.

Wolfson, Henry. *The Philosophy of the Church Fathers*. 3rd ed. Cambridge, Mass., 1970.

Woolston, Thomas. *Discourses on the Miracles of Our Saviour*. 6 vols. London, 1727-1728.

Yeivin, Samuel. *The Israelite Conquest of Canaan*. Istanbul, 1971.

INDEX